RECORDS OF EARLY ENGLISH DRAMA

Records of Early English Drama

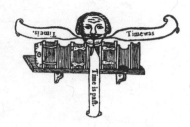

LINCOLNSHIRE

EDITED BY JAMES STOKES

1
The Records

THE BRITISH LIBRARY

and

UNIVERSITY OF TORONTO PRESS

© University of Toronto Press Incorporated 2009
Toronto Buffalo
Printed in Canada

First published in North America in 2009 by University of Toronto Press Incorporated
ISBN 978-1-4426-4000-9
and in the European Union in 2009 by
The British Library
96 Euston Road
London NW1 2DB

British Library Cataloguing in Publication Data
A catalogue record for this title is available from The British Library
ISBN 978-0-7123-0948-6

Printed on acid-free, 100% post-consumer recycled paper
with vegetable-based inks

Library and Archives Canada Cataloguing in Publication

Lincolnshire / edited by James Stokes.

(Records of early English drama)
Includes bibliographical references and index.
Contents: 1. The records – 2. Editorial apparatus.
ISBN 978-1-4426-4000-9 (set of 2 volumes)

1. Performing arts – England – Lincolnshire – History – Sources.
2. Theater – England – Lincolnshire – History – Sources.
I. Stokes, James (James David) II. British Library

PN2595.5.L46L46 2009   792.09425'3   C2009-901213-8

The research and typesetting costs of
Records of Early English Drama
have been underwritten by the
National Endowment for the Humanities and the
Social Sciences and Humanities Research Council of Canada

Contents

Records of Early English Drama

The aim of Records of Early English Drama (REED) is to find, transcribe, and publish external evidence of dramatic, ceremonial, and minstrel activity in Great Britain before 1642. The executive editor would be grateful for comments on and corrections to the present volume and for having any relevant additional material drawn to her attention at REED, 150 Charles St West, Toronto, Ontario, Canada M5S 1K9 or s.maclean@utoronto.ca. Detailed information about the REED series can be found on the internet at <http://www.reed.utoronto.ca/publist.html>.

Acknowledgments

For an editor the best part of a REED volume (apart from it's being finished) is the opportunity to acknowledge those who have contributed to its making. On the formal level REED is a pre-eminent scholarly team; it is also a seemingly endless informal network of generous experts on several continents, ready to help in ways great and small. I am honoured and delighted to be able to thank one and all for their invaluable contributions to the making of this collection, but with a special thanks to REED's Executive Editor and Associate Director, Sally-Beth MacLean. She has been a guiding friend to this collection from first day to last.

On the formal level, during production the book becomes a sustained collaborative effort of the most intellectually rewarding kind. During that process the contributions of the REED editorial team are substantive and too various to fairly represent, but I will try: Sally-Beth MacLean (oversight of all aspects of production, the contribution of bibliographical backup research, original research for venues featured on the *Patrons and Performances Web Site*); Abigail Ann Young (managing editor of production, paleographical checking, Latin translations, Latin Glossary checking and compiling, Old French checking and translation, proofing); Arleane Ralph (managing editor of production during the first phase, paleographical checking, Index); Carolyn Black (editorial checking, copy editing, proofing); Patrick Gregory (Latin translations checking and glossary checking and compiling); Jason Boyd (editorial checking, original patrons research and troupes/events data on the *Patrons and Performances Web Site*); Tanya Hagen (bibliographical checking); Toby Malone (bibliographical backup research); Gord Oxley (computer corrections, typesetting); William Cooke (English Glossary); Subhash Shanbhag (cartography); Sylvia Thomas (checking in Lincolnshire); Jessica Freeman and Stephanie Hovland (checking in London); Kirstie Jackson (checking in Oxford and Cambridge); William Edwards (Old French checking and translation); and John Craig, REED Senior Advisor (identification of a new entry in the Leverton churchwardens' accounts). I would also like to thank Robert Tittler, member of the REED Executive, and two anonymous external readers, all three of whom provided extremely helpful comments and suggestions on the Introduction to the collection; and REED's Director, Alexandra Johnston, for checking the English Glossary and helping complete the check of the Index for Volume 2. My thanks as well to former REED bibliographers Ian Lancashire and Theodore DeWelles, for their invaluable bibliographical research on Lincolnshire early in the project.

A number of fellow REED editors most generously provided assistance: Anne Brannen

(Cambridgeshire and Huntingdonshire), for on-going dialogue concerning cross-border identity and connections among musicians and players; John Coldewey (formerly for Essex), for references to Lincolnshire waits in the Nottingham civic records; James Gibson (Kent), for transcriptions and other assistance with Tattershall College records; David Klausner (Wales), for Lincolnshire records at the Huntington Library; John McKinnell (Durham), for information concerning Stamford Priory accounts at Durham; Barbara Palmer and John Wasson (Derbyshire, Yorkshire West Riding), for references to Stamford waits in the Clifford and Slingsby family papers, and the records of Bolton Abbey; and Diana Wyatt (Beverley), for access to her research on civic drama in Beverley. I hope that I might return in kind these very considerable favours.

I would like to offer special thanks to several additional individuals: Andrew Ashbee, Chairman of Snodland Historical Society and Honorary Curator of Snodland Millennium Museum; Roger Bowers, Jesus College, Cambridge University; Bruce Barker-Benfield, the Bodleian Library; Michael Carter and Allison Cresswell, Centre for Kentish Studies; Caroline Dalton, Archivist, New College, Oxford; Fiona Kisby; Suzanne Paul and Gill Cannell (Sub-librarians, Corpus Christi College, Cambridge University); Mary Robertson, the Huntington Library; the late Graham Runnells, Professor Emeritus, School of European Languages and Culture, University of Edinburgh, for providing transcriptions, translations, and descriptions from the household accounts of King John of France; Jim Turner, NEH Fellowships Program Analyst (for his assistance in navigating the process of applying for an NEH fellowship); Robin Harcourt Williams, Librarian and Archivist, Hatfield House; Magnus Williamson, University of Newcastle; and Frances Willmoth, Cambridge University Library.

A great many people in Lincolnshire provided access to the records and offered generous assistance of other kinds during my twelve years of research on the collection. I owe particular thanks to the entire staff of Lincolnshire Archives for their unfailingly helpful responses to my many requests for documents, microfilm, and other assistance, notably G.A. Knight, Principal Archivist, and his successor, Susan Payne, Principal Keeper; Adrian Wilkinson, Collections Officer; Nigel Colley, former Search Room Supervisor; and Joanne Finch, former Search Room Assistant (the latter three for answering innumerable questions and for their friendship through the years); Claire Mitchell, Librarian; Amanda Goode, former Keeper, Collections Management; Kevin Best, Collections Officer, and Christine Smith, Clerical Officer. I am privileged to offer special thanks as well to Dr Nicholas Bennett, Vice-Chancellor and Librarian, Lincoln Cathedral; Eleanor Nannestad, Community Librarian, and Gill Major, Library Assistant, Lincoln Central Library; John Wilson, Archivist, Mrs Carol Moss, Archives Assistant, and the late Edward Gillett, Honorary Archivist, North East Lincolnshire Archives, Grimsby; J.W. Belsham, Honorary Curator, and his successor Tom Grimes, Spalding Gentlemen's Society; Denis Seward, Mayor's Officer (retired), and Bob Williams, Honorary Archivist of the library at Stamford Town Hall, Stamford; Jean Barber, Stamford Library, for assistance with early sources related to the Stamford bull-running; Mrs Jean Howard, Honorary Curator, The Museum, Louth, for information about early Louth, including streets and dwellings; Mr I. Farmer, Committee Services Manager and his assistant, Mr Twiddy, Boston Town Hall, for access to the Boston civic records before the transfer of those records to Lincolnshire Archives; Rev. Duncan Barnes, Vicar of Donington and Bicker; Chris Williams, Senior Deputy Headteacher, Christ's Hospital

School, Lincoln, for his answers to queries concerning the early records of Lincoln School; and to Ruth Kennedy, Royal Holloway, University of London, for sharing her ground-breaking work on a guild poem to St Katherine in its connection with the town of Stamford.

The University of Wisconsin has provided sustained and absolutely essential support in various ways that reflect its traditional commitment to research. From the University of Wisconsin-Stevens Point, my gratitude to Michael Williams, Chair of English; successive deans of the College of Letters and Science, Justus Paul, Lance Grahn, and Charles Clark; the University Personnel Development Committee; and successive vice-chancellors and provosts, William Meyers, Virginia Helm, and Mark Nook. My gratitude, as well, to the University of Wisconsin System for two sabbaticals; to the Institute for Research in the Humanities, UW-Madison, for System Fellowships in 1997–8 and 2002–3, and honorary fellowships there in 2005–6 and 2006–7; and to the Friends of the UW-Madison Libraries for a grant-in-aid to conduct bibliographical research in 2003.

Several institutions and individuals provided absolutely essential financial support. I would like to express my appreciation to the National Endowment for the Humanities for its ongoing support of the REED project, and for an NEH Fellowship in 2006–7 that made both the completion of this book and substantial progress on the REED collection for Suffolk possible; the American Philosophical Society for research grants in 1996 and 1998 to complete the primary research for the book, on site, in England; Father Edward Jackman and The Jackman Foundation; the Social Sciences and Humanities Research Council of Canada; the British Academy; and the F.K. Morrow Foundation.

The following libraries, repositories, and individuals gave permission to publish extracts from manuscripts in their collections: Bibliothèque nationale de France; Bodleian Library, University of Oxford; The British Library; Dean and Chapter of Lincoln and Lincolnshire Archives; Diocese of Lincoln and Lincolnshire Archives; Grimsthorpe and Drummond Castle Trust and Lincolnshire Archives; Huntington Library, San Marino, California; Lumley MSS, Earl of Scarborough's Children's Trust, Sandbeck Park, Yorkshire; Marquess of Bath, Longleat House, Warminster, Wiltshire; Marquess of Salisbury, Hatfield House, Hatfield, Hertfordshire; North East Lincolnshire Archives, Grimsby, Lincolnshire; Donington Parish Church Council; The National Archives, Kew, Richmond; Somerset Record Office (who sought to contact the depositor of the Letters of Thomas Tuke to Sir William Armine); Spalding Gentlemen's Society; Stamford Corporation; Trustees of the Grimsthorpe and Drummond Castle Trust and Lincolnshire Archives; Trustees of the 10th Lord Monson and Lincolnshire Archives; and Viscount De L'Isle, Penshurst, Kent.

My special thanks to my mentor and friend, John Wasson, for opening the doors to a life of scholarship; to Tamara Stasik, doctoral candidate, Indiana University, for her valuable work as my research assistant during two summers in Lincoln; and to my dearest wife Bobbie, for just about everything.

RECORDS OF EARLY ENGLISH DRAMA

Symbols

BL	British Library
BN	Bibliothèque nationale de France
Bodl.	Bodleian Library
CKS	Centre for Kentish Studies
LA	Lincolnshire Archives
NELA	North East Lincolnshire Archives
SRO	Somerset Record Office
STH	Stamford Town Hall
TNA: PRO	The National Archives: Public Record Office
A	Antiquarian Compilation
AC	Antiquarian Collection
ESTC	*Eighteenth-Century Short-Title Catalogue*
ODNB	*Oxford Dictionary of National Biography* online edition (2004–9) <http://www.oxforddnb.com/>
REED	Records of Early English Drama
STC	A.W. Pollard and G.R. Redgrave (comps), *Short-Title Catalogue ... 1475–1640*
VCH	*The Victoria History of the Counties of England*
Wing	D.G. Wing (comp), *Short-Title Catalogue ... 1641–1700*
*	(after folio, membrane, page, or sheet number) see endnote
⟨...⟩	lost or illegible letters in the original
[ ]	cancellation in the original
(blank)	a blank in the original where writing would be expected
° °	matter in the original added in another hand
⌜ ⌝	text written above the line
⌞ ⌟	text written below the line
ʌ	caret mark in the original
...	ellipsis of original matter
|	change of folio, membrane, page, or sheet in continuous text
®	right-hand marginale
†	marginale too long for the left-hand margin

Diocese of Lincoln

c **1235–53**
Bishop Robert Grosseteste's Letters and Mandates
Letter 107*

contra scotales Robertus Dei gracia Lincolniensis episcopus dilecto in Christo filio archidiacono 5
N. salutem graciam & benediccionem. Ex relatu fidedigno audiuimus quod
plurimi sacerdotes archidiaconatus vestri, Deum non timentes nec homines
reuerentes, horas canonicas aut non dicunt aut corrupte dicunt et id quod
dicunt sine omni deuocione aut deuocionis signo, imo magis cum euidenti
ostensione animi indeuoti dicunt. Nec horam obseruant in dicendo que 10
comodior sit parochianis ad audiendum diuina, sed que eorum plus consonat
libidinose desidie. Habent insuper suas focarias quod, & si nos & nostros
lateat cum inquisicionem super huiusmodi fieri facimus hijs per quos fiunt
inquisiciones periuria non timentibus, non debet tamen vos sic latere qui
presencialiter super eos tam per vos quam per decanos & bedellos vestros 15
continue vigilare tenemini. Faciunt eciam vt audiuimus clerici ludos quos
vocant miracula, & alios ludos quos vocant inductionem Maij siue Autumpni,
& laici scotales, quod nullo modo vos latere posset si vestra prouidencia
super hijs diligenter inquireret. Sunt autem quidam rectores & vicarij &
sacerdotes qui non solum audire fastidiunt predicacionem fratrum vtriusque 20
ordinis sed sicut possunt, ne audiat eos populus predicantes aut eis confiteatur,
maliciose prepediunt. Admittunt eciam, vt dicitur, predicatores questuarios ad
predicandum qui solum talia predicant qualia nummum melius extrahunt,
cum tamen nos nullum questuarium licenciemus ad predicandum sed solum
concedimus vt per sacerdotes parochiales eorum negocium simpliciter 25

Letter 107 collation: 5m contra scotales] *CD omit* 5–21. Robertus ... confiteatur]
missing in A due to loss of leaf 5 Robertus] *B omits* 6 N.] tali *CD* 10 indeuoti]
deuoti *C, corrected to* ⌈in⌉deuoti *by C or C¹* 11 sit] *B omits* 17 miracula] *BC*
omit 17 siue] festum *D* 18 posset] possit *D* 18 prouidencia] prudencia *CD*
20 qui non] no*n* no*n C* 20 predicacionem] praedicatores *D* 24 licenciemus]
licentiamus *B, corrected to* licentiemus *by B or B¹* 25 vt] quod vt *B*

exponatur. Quia igitur vos estis Iudas Machabeus debentes templum Domini
ab omni inquinacione purgare, non eneruiter sed viriliter & fortiter, ad eius
imitacionem in hijs & huiusmodi agentes, nos autem vicem tenemus senis
Mathatie filio precipientis de zelo obseruationis legum paternarum & de
fortiter pugnando contra legum diuinarum aduersarios. Vos in Domino   5
monemus, exhortamur, & firmiter iniungimus quatinus ad predicta & hijs
similia purganda vos sicut vir accingatis, prelia Domini fortiter preliantes &
inordinata predicta & similia ad ordinem reducentes, compellendo sacerdotes
ad debite peragendum diuina obsequia, ad focarias expellendum, ad
inducendum efficaciter populum vt fratrum vtriusque ordinis predicaciones   10
deuote & attente audiat eisque humiliter confiteatur, ad non admittendum
questuarios ad predicandum. Miracula eciam & ludos supranominatos
& scotales, quod est in vestra potestate facili, omnino exterminetis &
cohabitacionem Christianorum cum Iudeis, quantum vobis possible est,
impedire curetis. Valeat, &c.   15

1236
Bishop Robert Grosseteste's Letters and Mandates
Letter 22*

20

Robertus Dei gracia Lincolniensis episcopus dilectis in Christo filijs vniuersis
archidiaconis per episcopatum Lincolniensem constitutis salutem graciam
& benediccionem.
    Quia ad pastoris spectat officium hijs qui ignorant & errant condolere
& gregem sibi commissum peruigilare quasi racionem pro gregis animabus   25
redditurum ipsumque gregem pascere, sicut in Ieremia scriptum est, sciencia
& doctrina, nos hec attendentes & hijs qui in grege nobis licet indignis,
Domino disponente, commisso ignorant & errant pro posse nostro cupientes
mederi, quosdam eorum perniciosos errores per deuium tenebrosum &
lubricum ad inferos deducentes presenti pagine duximus inserendos quosdam 30
vestro ministerio per archidiaconatus vestros populo ignoranti & erranti
declarandos & dissuadendos quosdam vero prohibendos & censura canonica
compescendos.

Letter 107 collation continued: 3 agentes] agetes *B*   6 iniungimus] *iniungimur C*
7 sicut] *B adds* [s]   8 similia] *C adds* et   9 peragendum] *B adds* ob   10 fratrum]
fraternum A   11 deuote] *B adds* [audiant]   11 &] *C omits*   12 questuarios]
quostuarios *B*   13 est] *D omits*   14 vobis] *B omits*   15 Valeat] *A adds sancta
paternitas*
    Letter 22 collation: 21 Robertus] *(blank) A*   26 ipsumque] ip*s*um que *C, C¹
corrects to* ip*s*umque   29 perniciosos] per uiciosos *A;* per viciosos *C*

26/ Ieremia: *Jer 3.15*

Et quia frustra contendit alia vicia subiugare qui gulam & ebrietatem non suppeditauerit, in primis firmiter iniungendo precipimus vt compotaciones que vulgo dicuntur scotales tam in sinodis quam in capitulis vestris prohibeatis & per singulas ecclesias archidiaconatuum vestrorum per singulos annos plures prohiberi faciatis & contra prohibiciones canonice premissas venire 5 presumentes ecclesiastica censura compescatis animaduersione canonica eosdem percellentes. Sicut enim scriptum est vinum – id est omne quod inebriat – multum potatum, irritacionem, & iram, & ruinas multas facit, amaritudinem anime & impudentem offensionem, minorans virtutem & faciens vulnera. Deformat insuper in homine Dei imaginem vsum rationis 10 auferendo, ligat actus naturales, morbos inducit pessimos, vitam abreuiat, principium est apostasie, aliaque mala procreat innumera. Ad extirpandam igitur tantorum malorum radicem remissi esse non debemus qui ad huiusmodi euellendum & destruendum & disperdendum & dissipandum constituti sumus.

Ad hec adicientes precipimus vt secundum formam suprascriptam 15 prohibeatis & prohiberi faciatis contemptores prohibicionis compescendo & puniendo arietum supra ligna & rotas eleuaciones ceterosque ludos consimiles in quibus decertatur pro brauio, cum huiusmodi ludorum tam actores quam spectatores, sicut euidenter demonstrat Isidorus, immolent demonibus talium ludorum inuentoribus & auctoribus & cum eciam 20 huiusmodi ludi frequenter dent occasiones ire odij pugne & homicidij.

Alios autem ludos diebus festiuis actos qui non consueuerunt dare fomitem discordie predicacione salubri faciatis dissuaderi quia, teste beato Augustino, cum multo minori peccato diebus solempnibus nerent & texerent mulieres & ararent homines aliaque opera huic vite sustentande neccessaria & vtilia 25 facerent quam huiusmodi ociosis & voluptuosis indulgerent. Dies namque sancti toti debiti sunt obsequiis diuinis & operibus sanctis que immediate proficiunt in salutem animarum a quibus incomparabiliter longius distant ea que sunt otiositatis & voluptatis quam que sunt neccessitatis & vtilitatis.

Letter 22 collation continued: 2 firmiter] [firmiter] firmiter B   2 vt] A originally omits but inserts in left margin   5 pluries] plures C   7 percellentes] procellentes C   7 est[1]] C omits   7 id est] D omits   9 impudentem] impudentis D   9 minorans] [minorans] minorans B   14 & destruendum & disperdendum &] B omits   14 disperdendum] dispergendum D   15 adicientes] sitientes D   16 prohibeatis & prohiberi] perhibeatis & perhiberi A   17 supra] super B   20 demonibus] demonijs B   20 cum eciam] B originally omits but inserts cum in right margin   22 festiuis] festis D   25 huic] B omits   25 sustentande] sustentenda AC   26 ociosis] [ocijs ociosis indulgerent] · B   27 que immediate] [que immediate] que immediate C   29 sunt[1]] B adds [ocij]

7–10/ vinum … vulnera: cp Ecclus 31.38–40
19/ Isidorus: cp Isidore of Seville, Etymologiae 18.27 and 51
23/ teste beato Augustino: cp Augustine, Sermon 9.3

Faciatis quoque per frequentem commoneri predicacionem vt qui conueniunt ad vigilias noctis in vigilijs sanctorum ad eorum ecclesias vel memorias vel ad exequias defunctorum ibidem solis vacent diuinis obsequijs & oracionibus ne, scurilitatibus vel ludis vel forte peioribus vt fieri consueuit intendentes, sanctorum iras in se prouocent quorum venerunt impetraturi 5 suffragia & ne in defunctorum exequiis de domo luctus & recordacionis nouissimorum in precaucionem peccaminum faciant domum risus & iocacionis in multiplicacionem peccaminum, quorum extrema luctus occupabit eternus & tenebrosa obliuio quam illustrabit sapientia vel sciencia vel racio. 10

Ab ecclesijs autem & cimiterijs omnes huiusmodi ludos commonicione premissa arceri faciatis ecclesiastica censura quia loca sancta ab vsibus humanis nedum ab humanis iocis abstracta sunt & in vsus diuinos conuersa & qui econtra presumunt de domo & loco oracionis speluncam latronum faciunt. 15

Faciatis quoque in singulis ecclesiis frequenti predicacione commoneri ne matres vel nutrices paruulos suos in lectis suis iuxta se collocent, ne forte eosdem vt frequenter contigit incaute suffocent & inde fiant eisdem mortis occasio vnde putatur vite tenere patrari confocio.

Clanidestina quoque matrimonia frequenti predicacione districte prohiberi 20 faciatis & pericula que inde sequuntur euidenter & diligenter exponi vt precognito mali sequentis periculo fortius & causius deuitetur ipsius origo.

Ad hec in singulis ecclesijs districtam faciatis fieri inhibicionem ne ad processiones in annua visitacione & veneracione matris ecclesie aliqua parochia decertet cum vexillis suis alij parochie antecedere, cum inde soleant 25 non solum lites sed crudeles sanguinis effusiones prouenire. Econtra vero de cetero presumentes canonica feriatis animaduersione quia huiusmodi decertatores inde matrem ecclesiam violant & inhonorant vnde eam sanctificare & honorare debuerant. Nec debent aliquatenus a pena dimitti immunes qui matrem spiritalem inhonorant cum hij qui matres carnales 30 inhonorant per legem diuinam maledicuntur & morte puniuntur.

Preterea in quibusdam ecclesiis inuenimus hanc pro consuetudine inoleuisse corruptelam quod in die Pasche non recipiuntur oblaciones parochianorum

---

Letter 22 collation continued: 1 Faciatis] *B adds* [que]   6 exequiis] obsequiis *B* 7 faciant] *B adds* [do]   9 quam] q*uonia*m *AB*   9 vel sciencia] *C omits*   12 arceri] [acereri] arceri *C*   13 humanis[1]] *B omits*   13 conuersa] *omnino* sit *C, C[1] deletes* omnino *and adds con*uersa *in right margin*   14 econtra] con*tra B*   18 incaute] *B omits*   19 patrari] *prestari B*   24 annua] a*nima C, C[1] cancels and adds* annua *in left margin with carets*   27 de cetero presumentes] presumentes de cetero *B, later marked for inversion*   28 decertatores] desertatores *A*   30 inhonorant] i*n*horant *C, C[1] adds* no *in right margin with matching sigla*   30–1 cum … inhonorant] *C omits, C[1] adds in left margin*

nisi celebrata missa cum ad sacratissimum dominici corporis & sanguinis
sacramentum veniunt. Quam corruptelam de cetero sub graui pena faciatis
arcius prohiberi, cum graue scandalum turpisque nota cupiditatis inde
oriatur ecclesie prelatis plurimumque prepediatur deuocio populi ad tantum
sacramentum accedentis. Ad hec quia alicubi inuenimus contra statutum 5
tam generalis quam prouincialis concilij pro pecunia non soluta denegari
sacramenta ecclesiastica & eciam in die pasche sacramentum Eucaristie,
ne quis in hac parte quasi per ignorantiam speciem aliquam excusacionis
pretendere valeat quod in hac parte in concilijs statutum est faciatis non
solum in synodis sed eciam in capitulis frequenter recitari, eos qui contra 10
presumpserint canonica punientes districcione.

c 1239
Bishop Robert Grosseteste's Diocesan Statutes
Chapter 23*   15

Hortamur eciam precipientes ne mimis, ioculatoribus, aut histrionibus
intendant, neque ad aleas seu taxillos ludant aut ludentibus assideant quia,
licet hec quibusdam videantur leuia, tamen secundum sanctorum patrum
doctrinas, qui talia faciunt demonibus prestant sacrificia.   20

Chapter 35*

Execrabilem eciam consuetudinem, que consueuit in quibusdam ecclesijs
obseruari, de faciendo festo stultorum speciali auctoritate rescripti apostolici 25

Letter 22 collation continued: 1 ad] *AC omit*   1 dominici] *domini C, C¹ adds* ci
above the line   2 de cetero] *D adds* recepturi   6 concilij] *consilij AC*   6 pecunia]
peccata B   6 denegari] *degari C, C¹ adds* ne *above the line*   9 valeat] *ABC omit*
9 concilijs] *consilijs A;* consilijs *B;* consilijs *C*   11 districcione] *B adds* Hec est
ep*istola* lincoln*ensis* 22. & sequit*ur* ep*istola* 24.
   Chapter 23 collation: 17 eciam] *igitur F*   17 mimis] nimis *ACFH*
17 ioculatoribus, aut histrionibus] hystrioni*bus* ioculatorib*us J*   17 histrionibus] *D*
adds sacerdotes seu ben*eficiati*   18 intendant] *B omits*   18 neque] n*i*h*i*l *E;* ne *H*
18 aleas] alias *G*   18 seu] u*e*l *A;* neq*ue* ad *CG*   18 aut] seu *E*   18 assideant]
assistant *BE*   19 licet hec] hec li*cet C*   19 hec] *B omits;* talia a q*ui*b*us*dam *I*
19 quibusdam videantur] uideantur quibusdam *D*   19 tamen] no*n* t*a*men su*n*t
sed *D*   19 secundum] *G omits*   19 sanctorum] *DE omit*   20 faciunt] faciant *E*
20 prestant] faci*u*nt *A; H adds* obsequ*i*a
   Chapter 35 collation: 24–5 consueuit in quibusdam ecclesijs obseruari] *in*
quib*us*dam ec*c*lesijs *con*sueuit *A*   24 quibusdam] quib*us F*   25 obseruari] *con*seruari
GJ   25 festo] festu*m DE;* festa *G*   25 speciali] de sp*eci*ali *C*   25 rescripti] *F*
omits   25 apostolici] apostolica *F;* apostoli *H*

penitus inhibemus ne de domo oracionis fiat domus ludibrij & acerbitas circumcisionis Domini Iesu Christi iocis & voluptatibus subsannetur.

Chapters 39–40

Precipimus eciam vt in singulis ecclesijs denuncietur solempniter ne quisquam leuet arietes super rotas vel alios ludos statuat in quibus decertatur pro brauio, nec huiusmodi ludis quisquam intersit. Prohibeantur similiter compotaciones que vulgo dicuntur scotales. Omnes quoque ludi & placita secularia a locis sacris omnino arceantur.

1552
Bishop John Taylor's Visitation Articles   *stc*: 10228
sig A v verso

…

ℂ Whether any doth in Enterludes, Playes, songes, Rymes or by open wordes declaryng, or speke any thynge in depravynge or, despysinge the sayde boke or any thynge therin contained.

…

1580
Bishop Thomas Cooper's Visitation Articles   *stc*: 10230.5
sig B ij

…

   22 Whether your own Parson, Vicar, or Curate, be any common resorter to open Games, Playes, or Assemblies whatsoeuer (in ciuil causes:) or doe keepe or suffer to be kept in his Parsonage, Vicarage, or other his dwelling house, any Alehouse, Tipling house or Tauerne: or that he doe or haue kepte any suspected woman in his house: or that he being vnmaried doth kéepe any woman in his house vnder the age of .lx. yeres, except their Daughter,

Chapter 35 collation continued: 1 penitus] *G omits*   1 de domo] dom*us DGI*; demo *J*   1 fiat domus ludibrij] dom*us* ludi fiat *D*   1 &] *I omits*   2 circumcisionis] circusic*ionis F*; *G omits*   2 Domini] *ADEHI add* n*o*stri*; G adds* n*o*stri   2 subsannetur] subsannentur *H*

   Chapters 39–40 collation: 6 Precipimus … ecclesijs] It*em in* qualibet eccl*e*sia *D*   6 eciam] *H omits*   6 ecclesijs] *H adds* dec[a]nt[e]   6 quisquam] quis *DG*   7 leuet] *DG omit;* levat *E*   7 decertatur] dece⌈r⌉tet*ur J*   8 huiusmodi ludis quisquam] quisq*u*is ludis huiusmodi *D*   8 ludis] locis *B*   8 similiter] *eciam DI*   9 que] qui *F*   9 vulgo] a vulgo *I*   9 scotales] scothales *HJ*   9 ludi] *B adds* scotales; *E omits*   10 secularia] *D adds* ut

17/ declaryng: yng *cancelled by hand in Bodleian copy*
17/ boke: *Book of Common Prayer*

Mother, Aunte, Sister, or Néece, and those of good and honest name: or
whether he himselfe be any haunter of Alehouses, Tauernes, or suspected
places, an hunter, hawker, dicer, carder, swearer, or any otherwise do giue
euill example of life, whereby the worde of God and the forme of Religion
nowe vsed by the lawes of Englande, is or may be any way euill spoken of: 5
And generallye, whether he behaue not himselfe, soberly, godly, and honest,
as becommeth a Minister of Gods moste holy worde.

…

sig B iiij   10

…

   33 Whether your Minister & Church-wardens haue suffred any Lords of
Mis-rule, or sommer Lords or Ladies, or any disguised persons in Christmasse,
or at May-games, or Morice Dauncers, or at any other times, to come
vnreuerently into the Church or Church-yarde, and there to daunce or play   15
anye vnseemly parts, with scoffes, iests, wanton gestures, or ribalde talke,
namely, in the time of common Prayer: & what they be that commit such
disorder, or accompany or maintaine them.

…
                                                                               20

1585
Bishop William Wickham's Visitation Articles   STC: 10231
sig B j

…

   21 Whether your owne Parson, Vicar, or Curate be any common resorter   25
to open games, plaies or assemblies what soeuer (in ciuill causes) or doe keepe,
or suffer to be kept in his Parsonage, Vicarage other his dwelling house any
Alehouse Tipling house or Tauerne: or that he do, or haue kept any suspitious
woman in his house: or that he being vnmarried doth kéepe any woman in his
house vnder the age of lx yeares, except his daughter, mother, aunt, sister or 30
néece, & those of good & honest name: or whether he himselfe be any haunter
of Alehouses, tauernes, or suspected places, an hunter, hawker, dicer carder, a
swearer, or otherwise doo giue euill example of life whereby the word of God,
& the forme of religion now vsed by the lawes of England is, or may any way
be euill spoken of: And generally whether he behaue not himselfe soberly,   35
godly and honestly, as becommeth a Minister of Gods most holy word.

…

sig B ij verso

…
                                                                               40
   27 Whether your Minister and Church-wardens haue suffred any Lords

27/ other: *for* or other

of misrule, or sommer Lords, or Ladies or any disguised person in Christmas, or at maigames, or morris dancers or at any other time, to come vnreuerently into the Churchyard, and there to daunce or play any vnsemely part with scoffs, iestes, wanton gestures, or ribald talk, namely in the time of common praier: and what they be that commit such disorder, or accompany or maintaine them.   5

…

1588

Bishop William Wickham's Visitation Articles   STC: 10232   10
sigs A4v–B1

…

25 Whether your owne Parson, Vicar, or Curate bee any common resorter to open games, playes or assemblies whatsoeuer (in ciuill causes) or do kéepe, or suffer to be kept in his Parsonage, Vicarage, or other his dwelling   15 house, any Alehouse Tipling house or Tauerne: or that hee doe, or haue kept any | suspicious woman in his house: or that he being vnmarried doth keepe any woman in his house vnder the age of 60 yeeres, except his daughter, mother, aunt, sister or neece, and those of good and honest name: or whether he himselfe bee any haunter of Alehouses, Tauernes, or suspected   20 places, an Hunter, Hawker, Dicer, Carder, a Swearer, or otherwise doe giue euill example of life, whereby the worde of God, and the forme of Religion now vsed by the lawes of England is, or may any way be euill spoken of: And generally whether he behaue not himselfe soberly, godly and honestly, as becommeth a Minister of Gods most holy word?   25

…

sig B2v

…

Vnseemely
parts in
Church or
Churchyard

44 Whether any Lordes of misrule, Dauncers, Players, or any other   30 disguised persons do daunce or play any vnseemly partes in the Church or Churchyarde, or whether are there any playes, or common drinking kept in Church or Churchyarde, who maintaine and accompany such.

…

35

1591

Bishop William Wickham's Visitation Articles   STC: 10233
sigs A4v–B1

…

25 Whether your owne Parson, Vicar or Curate, be any common resorter   40 to open games, playes or assemblies whatsoeuer (in ciuil causes) or do keepe, or suffer to be kept in his Parsonage, Vicarage, or other his dwelling house, any Alehouse, | Tiplinghouse or Tauerne: or that he do, or haue kept any

suspicious woman in his house: or that he being vnmarried, doth kéepe any woman in his house vnder the age of 60 yeeres, except his Daughter, Mother, Aunt, Sister or Neece, and those of good and honest name: or whether he himselfe be any haunter of Alehouses, Tauernes, or suspected places, an Hunter, Hawker, Dicer, Carder, a Swearer, or otherwise do giue euill example   5
of life, whereby the word of God, and the forme of Religion now vsed by the lawes of England is, or may any way be euill spoken of: And generally whether he behaue not himselfe soberly, godly and honestly, as becommeth a Minister of Gods most holy word?

...   10

sig B2v

...

Vnseemely
partes in
Church or
Churchyard

   44 Whether any Lords of Misrule, Dauncers, Players, or any other disguised persons do daunce or play any vnseemly partes in the Church or   15
Churchyard, or whether there are any Playes, or common drinking kept in Church or Churchyarde, who maintaine and accompany such.

...

1594   20
Bishop William Wickham's Visitation Articles   STC: 10234
sigs B2–2v

...

®Unseemly
partes in

Church or
churchyard

   44 Whether any Lords of Misrule, Dauncers, Players, or any other disguised persons, doo daunce or play anie vseemelie | parts in the Church   25
or Churchyard, or whether there are anie Playes, or common drinking kept in Church or Churchyarde, who maintaine and accompany such.

...

1598   30
Bishop William Chaderton's Visitation Articles   STC: 10235
sig A3

...

®Church and
churchyard.

   1 First, whether your Church, Chappell, or Chancell, be well and sufficiently repaired, and cleanly kept, and the mansion house of your   35
Parson, or Vicar, with the buildings thereunto belonging, be likewise well and sufficiently repaired, and your Churchyard well fenced, and cleanly kept? And if any default be made in the premisses: or your said Church, Chappell, or Churchyard, be abused or prophaned by any vnlawful or vnseemely act, game, or exercise, as by lords of misrule, sommer lords, or   40
ladies, pipers, rush-bearers, morice-dancers, pedlers, bowlers, bearewards,

34/ First: *elaborate decorated* F

and such like. Then thorough whose default, and what be the names of
the offenders in that behalfe.

…

1601

Bishop William Chaderton's Visitation Articles   *STC*: 10235.5
sig A3

…

® Church and churchyard.

First, whether your Church, Chappel, or Chancell, be well and sufficiently
repaired, and cleanely kept, & the mansion house of your Parson, or Vicar,
with the buildings thereunto belonging bee likewise well and sufficiently
repaired, and your churchyard well fenced, and cleanly kept? And if any
default be made in the premisses: or your said Church, chappell, or
churchyard, be abused or prophaned by any vnlawefull, or vnseemely act,
game, or exercise; as by lords of misrule, sommer lords, or ladies, pipers, rush-
bearers, morice-dancers, pedlers, bowlers, beare-wards, and such like. Then
thorough whose default, and what be the names of the offenders in that behalfe.

…

1604

Bishop William Chaderton's Visitation Articles   *STC*: 10236
sig A3

…

® Church and Churchyard.

First, whether your Church, Chappell, or Chancell, be well and sufficiently
repaired, & cleanely kept, and the mansion house of your Parson, or Vicar,
with the buildings thereunto belonging, be likewise well & sufficiently
repaired, and your Churchyard well fenced, and cleanly kept? And if
any default be made in the premisses: or your said Church, Chappel, or
Churchyard, be abused or prophaned by any vnlawful, or vnseemely act, game,
or exercise; as by lords of misrule, sommer lords, or ladies, pipers, rush
bearers, morice-dancers, pedlers, bowlers, beare-wards, and such like. Then
through whose default, and what be the names of the offenders in that behalfe.

…

1607

Bishop William Chaderton's Visitation Articles   *STC*: 10236.5
sig A3

…

2. Whether hath your Church or churchyard bin abused and prophaned
by any fighting, chiding, brawling or quarrelling, any playes, lords of misrules,
sommer Lords, Morrisse dauncers, pedlers, bowlers, berewards, butchers,

9, 24/ First: *elaborate decorated* F

feastes, scooles, temporall courts, or Leetes, lay Iuries, musters, or other
prophane vsage in your Church or Churchyard, any bells superstitiously
rong, on holy daies, or their Eues, or at any other time without good cause,
allowed by the minister, and churchwardens; haue any trees been felled in
your churchyard, and by whome?   5
...

1613
Archbishop George Abbot's Metropolitical Visitation Articles   STC: 10237
sig B3   (Concerning churchwardens and sidesmen)   10
...
1 VVhether you and the Church-wardens, Quest-men or Side-men, from
time to time, doe, and haue done their diligences, in not suffering any idle
person to abide eyther in the Church-yard Or Church-porch, in Seruice or
Sermon time, but causing them either to come into the Church to heare   15
Diuine Seruice, or to depart, and not disturbe such as be hearers there? And
whether haue they, and do not diligently see the Parishioners duelie resort to
the Church euerie Sunday and Holidaie, and there to remaine during Diuine
seruice or Sermon? And whether you, or your predecessours, Churchwardens
there, suffer any Plaies, Feasts, Drinkings, or any other prophane vsages, to 20
bée kept in your Church, Chappell, or Church-yards, or haue suffered to
your and their vttermost power and endeuour, any Person or Persons to be
tipling or drinking in any Inne or Victuling House in your Parish, during
the time of Diuine Seruice or Sermon, on Sundaies And Holidaies?
...   25

1614
Bishop Richard Neile's Visitation Articles   STC: 10238
sig C1
                                                                                  30
   12 Whether haue you, or your successors the Church-wardens, suffered
any Playes, Feasts, Bankets, Suppers, Church-ales, Drinkings, temporall
Courts, or Léets, Lay-iuries, Musters, or any other prophane vsage, to be
kept in your Church, Chappell, or Church-yard, or the Bels to be rung
superstitiously vpon Holy-dayes, or éeues, abrogated by the booke of Common 35
prayer, or at any other time, without good cause.
...

1618
Bishop George Mountain's Visitation Articles   STC: 10239   40
sig A2   (Concerning the church, churchyard, parsonage, and vicarage)
...
   2 Whether hath your Church, or Church-yard béen abused & prophaned

by any fighting, chiding, brawling or quarrelling, any plaies, Lords of
misrule, Summer Lords, Morris dancers, Pedlers, Bowlers, Bearewardes,
Butchers Feasts, Scholes, temporall Courtes or Léetes, Lay Iuries, Musters,
or other prophane vsage in your Church, or Church-yard, any Bels
supersticiously rung on Holy-daies or their Eeues, or at any other times,   5
without good cause allowed by the Minister and Churchwardens; and
haue any trées béen felled in ye Church-yard, & by whom?

...

sig B1   10

...

   41 Whether doth your Minister resort to any Tauernes, or Ale-houses,
except for his honest necessities, or doth he boord or lodge in any such
place. Doth he vse any base or seruile labour, drinking, riot, Dice, Cards,
Tables, or any other vnlawfull games. Is he contentious, a Hunter,   15
Hawker, swearer, dauncer, suspected of incontinencie, or giue euill example
of life.

...

1622   20
Bishop John Williams' Visitation Articles   STC: 10240
sig A2   *(Concerning the church, churchyard, parsonage, and vicarage)*
...

   2 Whether hath your Church or Church-yard béen abused & prophaned
by any fighting, chiding, brawling, or quarrelling, any plaies, Lords of   25
misrule, Summer Lords, Morris dancers, Pedlers, Bowlers, Bearewardes,
Butchers, Feasts, Schooles, temporall Courts or Léets, Lay Iuries, Musters,
or other prophane vsage in your Church, or Church-yard, any Bels
superstitiously rung on Holydaies or their Eeues, or at any other times,
without good cause allowed by the Minister & Church-wardens; & haue   30
any trées béene felled in the Church-yard, & by whom?

...

sig B1

...   35

41 whether doth your Minister resort to any Tauernes, or Ale-houses,
except for his honest necessities: or doth he boord or lodge in any such
place: doth he use any base or seruile labour, drinking, riot, Dice, Cards,
Tables, or any other vnlawfull games: is he contentious, a Hunter,
Hawker, swearer, dauncer, suspected of incontinencie, or giue euill example   40
of life?

...

1625
Bishop John Williams' Visitation Articles   STC: 10241
sig A2v

...

Prophaners.   4. Whether haue your Church or Church-yard beene prophaned or   5
abused with plaies, quarrels, fighting, scoulding, or ill words, or with
feasts, Pedlars buying and selling, Courts, or any such like, and by
whome? And whether have any Trees been cut downe in the Churchyard, and by whom?

...   10

1627
Archdeacon Morgan Wynne's Visitation Articles   STC: 10245.3
sig A3

...   15

   18 Whether haue you in your Church, Chappell, or Churchyard, any
Playes, gaming at Bowles, Tennis, or Football, or any other playing; Either
any Feasts, Church-Ales, Temporall Courts, Leetes, Musters, or any other
prophane vsage there? and by whom?

...   20

Bishop John Williams' Visitation Articles   STC: 10242
sig A2v

...

Prophaners.   4 Whether hath your Church or Church-yard beene prophaned or abused   25
with plaies, quarrels, fighting⟨.⟩ scoulding, or ill words, or with feasts,
Pedlars buying ⟨...⟩ selling, lay-Courtes, or any such like, and by whom?
⟨...⟩ whether have any Trees been cut downe in the Church-yard, and by
whome, and how imployed?

...   30

1630
Bishop John Williams' Visitation Articles   STC: 10243
sig B1*

...   35

®Gaming and   11 Whether have there been in your Church, Chapell, or Churchyard, any
playing, and   plaies, gaming at bowls, tennis, or football, or any other playing? Either
feasts in   any feasts, Churchales, temporall courts, leets, or any other profane usage
Churchyards.   there, and by whom?

...   40

sig B4*   *(Concerning parishioners only)*

…

®Observing of
the Sabbath.
Profaners of the
Sabbath. Rude
behaviour in
the Church.

2 Whether have your people observed the Sabbath day duly in all sobernes
and godly conversation? or there be any which have profaned the same, by
playing at cards, tables, foot-ball, dauncing, bowling, excessive ringing,   5
immoderate drinking, or other foolish delight, or vain pleasure?

…

1635

Bishop John Williams' Visitation Articles   STC: 10244   10

sig C3v   *(Concerning churchwardens and sidesmen)*

…

1. Whether you, and the churchwardens, questmen, or sidesmen, from time
to time, do and have done their diligence, in not suffering any idle person
to abide either in the churchyard or churchporch in service or sermon-time,   15
but causing them either to come into the church to heare divine service, or
to depart, and not disturb such as be hearers there. And whether they have,
and you do diligently see the parishioners duely resort to the church every
sunday and holiday, and there to remain during divine service and sermon.
And whether you, or your predecessours, churchwardens there, suffer any   20
playes, feasts, drinkings, or any other profane usages, to be kept in your
church, chappell; or churchyards; or have suffered to your and their uttermost
power and endeavour, any person or persons to be tipling or drinking in
any inne or victualling house in your parish, during the time of divine Service
or sermon on sundayes and holidayes.   25

…

1637

Archdeacon Morgan Wynne's Visitation Articles   STC: 10245.8
sigs A3–3v*   30

…

85.

88.

2 Whether your Church, or Chappell, Chancell and Churchyard be
kéept in good reparations, as well within as without? whe⟨.⟩her any
profanation be vsed-in them, or any man hath incroached vpon them, or
pulled downe any part of the Church or Chancell without licence first   35
obtained from the ordinary? Whether hath there bin in your parish Church
or Church-yard any | Playes, Feasts, Faires, Temporall Courts or Léets, lay
Iuiryes, Musters, or other profane vsage and méetings in either of them,
and by what persons, and whether your Parsonage or Vicarage house and
all the housing thereunto belonging, bée likewise maintained in sufficient   40
reparations? if not, through whose default is it? and what is the defect?

…

1638
Archbishop William Laud's Visitation Articles STC: 10245
sig B3   *(Concerning churchwardens and sidesmen)*
...

1. Whether you and the Church-wardens, Quest-men, or Side-men, from   5
time to time, do, and have done their diligence, in not suffering any idle
person to abide either in the Church-yard or Church-porch, in Service or
Sermon time, but causing them either to come into the Church to heare
divine Service, or to depart, and not disturbe such as be hearers there? And
whether they have, and you do diligently see the Parishioners duly resort to   10
the Church every Sunday and Holiday, and there to remaine during divine
Service and Sermon? And whether you or your predecessors, Churchwardens
there, suffer any Playes, Feasts, Drinkings, or any other prophane usages, to
be kept in your Church, Chappell, or Church-yards, or have suffered to
your and their uttermost power and endevour, any person or persons to be   15
tipling or drinking in any Inne or Victualling house in your Parish, during
the time of divine Service or Sermon, on Sundayes and Holidayes?
...

1641   20
Bishop John Williams' Visitation Articles   Wing: C4053
sigs B3–3v*   *(Concerning churchwardens and sidesmen)*
...

VVHether you, and the Churchwardens, Questmen, or Sidemen, from time
to time, do and have done your diligence, in not suffering any idle person   25
to abide either in the churchyard or churchporch in service or sermon-time,
but causing them either to come into the church to hear diuine service, or
to depart, and not disturb such as be hearers there. And whether they have,
and you do diligently see the parishioners duly resort to the church every
Sunday and Holiday, and | there remain during Divine Service and Sermon.   30
And whether you, or your predecessours, Churchwardens there, suffer any
playes, feasts, drinkings, or any other profane usages, to be kept in your
Church, Chappell; or Churchyards; or have suffered to your and their
uttermost power and endeavour, any person or persons to be tipling or
drinking in any Inne or victualling-house in your parish, during the time   35
of Divine Service or Sermon on Sundayes and Holidayes.
...

Boroughs and Parishes

ADDLETHORPE

1543–4
St Nicholas' Churchwardens' Accounts
  LA: ADDLETHORPE PAR/10/1
f [10v]* *(January–January)*
...

Item payde to the player*es*   iiij d.
...

1545–6
St Nicholas' Churchwardens' Accounts
  LA: ADDLETHORPE PAR/10/1
f [21]* *(January–January)*
...

Item payd to certayne plaers & ffor shottyng of a bolte   ij d.
...

1546–7
St Nicholas' Churchwardens' Accounts
  LA: ADDLETHORPE PAR/10/1
f [6]* *(January–January)*
...

Item payde vntyll ye players at chrystmes   iij d.
...

f [6v]
...
Item payde for ye syghte of ye bane of wytthern   ij s.
...

ALLINGTON

1611
Inventory of Edward Russell   LA: INV 111/151
single sheet   *(28 October)* *(In the house)*   5

…

Item three paire of pipes a sackbutt and a recorder   vj. s. viij d.

…

ASHBY DE LA LAUNDE   10

1520–1
AC *Thomas de la Launde's Complaint against John Babyngton*
    BL: Additional MS 4937
    ff 85–5v*   15

…

The Compleynte of Thomas de la Laund of Assheby, against Frere John
Babynton of the Order of S. John of Jersusalem, Fermer of the Commaundry
of Temple [Bruer] for certeyn grete Injurys done to hym by the said
Babyngton: Put yn afore my Lord Cardynall [Wolsey.]   20
1. Petuosly compleyneth & shewith unto your Grace your daly Orator &
Bedeman, Thomas de la Launde of Assheby next Bloxham in the Countie
of Lincoln, Gentleman, that
2. whereas your said Orator beyng seased in his demeane, as of Fe, of a Parcel
& a Pece of Ground & Pasture callyd Asheby Heith, in the Parishe of   25
Assheby in the Countie of Lincoln aforesaid.
3. the which Pasture & Heith your said Orator & all other his Tenauntes,
& all thay whos Estate he hath in the said Manor, & their Tenauntes, at
all Tymes, without Tyme of Mynd of Man, hath occupyed, & taken the
Profittes of the said Heythe wyth their Shepe & other Cataell necessry for 30
the Compastryng, Gaynyng & Tyllyng of the said Lond & Lyfyng within
the seyd maner, without Impedyment or Lett of any Person,
4. unto now of late that one Frere Babyngton of the Order of Relegion of
S. John of Jerusalem & Fermer of the Commaundry of Temple Bruer in
the Countie aforesaid, causid his Chapleyn and xvi. of his servauntes (whos 35
Names your said Orator knoweth not) in the Rogation days, in the xi. Yere
of the Kyng that now is, to go in a riotos Manor (that is to say, with Bylles,
Bowys, Arrowes, Swerdes, & Bucklers, & oder wepynes) under the Color of
a Procession, aboute the said Heithe of Asheby;
5. And also causid and commaundyd them to marke and cleyme the said   40

19/ [Bruer]: *square brackets in* MS   36–7/ the Rogation days … now is: *30 May –*
20/ [Wolsey.]: *square brackets in* MS   *1 June 1519*

Heithe to be Parcell of the *said* Commandry of Tempull, and to put out
the Catell of yo*ur said* Orator and other hys | Tenaunts without any Right
or Title, (the whiche Commaundment they did observe and kepe), but
only intending by his Myght of Power to vex and troble yo*ur said* Orator
and his Tenaunts for occupying and takyng the profitts of the *said* Heithe,   5
and to cause them to avoyde from theyr Fermes of Ashby afores*aid*.

…

7. And also the *said* Frere John Babyngton, in the Wynter Season, in the
said xi^th. yere, caused his Servaunts to bayt with Dogs the Shepe & Catall
of yo*ur said* Orator & other his Tenaunts, when they wer dryven by Tempest   10
of Wether, in the Night-Tyme, unto the Felds of Temple Bruer.

…

f 86v*

…   15

13. Wherefore, the Premisses tenderly considered, yt may please yo*ur*
Grace, to graunt a speciall Comyssyon to be directed to certeyn Personnes,
comaundyng them by the same to call a fore them the sayd Syr John, to
aunswere to the Premisses, & all other Varyances bytwene the *said* Partyes
to here; & to determyne all Things concernyng the same. Or ells to certefy,   20
afore the Kyngs most hon*o*rable Councell, at a certeyn day, what they have
done concernyng the same.

1521–2
AC   *John Babyngton's Answers to the Complaint of Thomas de la Launde*   25
      BL: Additional MS 4937
      f 87*

*Made at Sleaford before Sir John Hussey, Robert Hussey, John Wymbyssh, Mr
Dysney, and Richard Clark, recorder of Lincoln*   30

…

1.   The s*ai*d Syr John saith, the said Bylle ys untrue, & the more Parte
of the Mater of the same fayned by the said Thomas, for the Vexation of
the said Syr John without gode Grounde or Cause. But, for Aunswer &
Declaration of the Trewthe in the Premisses, the s*ai*d Syr John sayth,   35
2. as to any Ryot, Rout, or unlawfull Assemble, or other Mysdemeanor in
the s*ai*d Bylle agaynst the Kyng*es* Pease supposeid to be done, he is nothing
gylty; &, as to the Residue of the said Mater conteyned in the said Byll, the
said Syr John, as Fermor of the sayd Com*m*aundre saith,
3.   That the said Heathe, which the s*ai*d Thomas surmysyth and claymeth   40
to be Assheby Heithe, is, and out of Tyme of Minde hath bene, Parcell of
Temple Heyth.

4.   And at such tyme as the said Syr John entred as Fermor of the said
Temple the same Parcell of Heyth amongst other was shewn to be parcell
of the said Temple Hethe by certeyn olde Boundes and Markes now knowen
in the said Cuntrie, by Reason whereof the said Syr John at dyvers Tymes
hath had both Shepe and oder Bests kept uppon the seyd Heyth in lyke   5
Manner and Forme, as Master Newport late Comaunder of the same and
other ther Predecessors have kept on the same.

...

f 87v*   10

...

7. And sayth, that the sayd xj^th Yere, the Begynnyng thereof, was verray dry.
8. And the sayd Syr John beyng at London, his Preste, and v. oder Men
Persons & three Wormen Persones, went in Procession, in peaseable &
devout Maner, about all the Temple Heythe, to pray for seasonable Wedder.   15
9.   And as he understode at hys Comyng fro London they went upon ye
said Heyth claymd by ye said de la Laundes; and by the old Marks and
Bounds of the same.
10.   And if any of the said Marks were renewyd, it was the same Compas
that the olde Marks was, as may appere at this Day.   20
11.   And further that the said Thomas takyth upon hym as Chief Lord in
Ashby, wher the said Syr John supposith he is but a Tenaunt, and that the
Lordship belongith to the said Comaundrie.

...

                                                                             25

BARDNEY

1576
Will of Alexander Burton, Piper   LA: LCC WILLS 1576
ff 146–6v   (22 September; proved 17 November)   30

In the name of god amen the xxij^ti of september Anno domini 1576 I
Alexander Burton of bardney within the countye of Lincoln pyper do ordeyne
constitute & make this my last will & testament in manner & forme folowinge
ffirst I bequethe my sowle vnto Allmightye god my Creator & Reademer &   35
my bodye to be buryed within the churche yarde of bardney/ Item I geue
vnto the churche of bardney xij d. Item I bequethe vnto margaret Burton my
dowghter one ij yeare old kine & one browne steare being a yeare olde & two
Ewes Item I geue vnto Henry beston of burton one payre of gallygaskyngs
so called and to his sonn Edmond Beston one browne kine calfe whyte blacke   40
and to Agnes Beston the dowghter of the said Henry Beeston one lambe at
clipping tyme next Cominge Item I geue to my other three children to euery

one of them one hogg sheepe Item I geue vnto Thomas wright of Handbye my
whole Case of pypes Item I geue vnto my father Abram Burtoun my horse
Item I geue vnto my mother Burtoun one Ewe ffarther more I will that my
coople of oxen shalbe solde & three kyne bought with them for three of my
wifs children which was geuen vnto them by my predecessor in his last will &   5
testament being ther father The rest and residew of all my goodes moveable
& vnmoveable my dettes legacyes & funerall expenses | Deducted & paid &
I honestly brought vnto the earthe I geue vnto my wife whome I do make
my hole executrix of this my last will and testament Item I will that Edmond
Mellors my neyghbour shalbe the superviser of thys my will and testament   10
to se all thinges herin truly performed & he to have for his paynes taking
herin ij s. These being wittnesses Thomas Collingwood clarke Richard
Knowelles Hughe Sunsonn Robert Kendall with others.

...
                                                                              15
Inventory of Alexander Burton, Piper   LA: INV 59/275
single sheet   *(30 October) (In the parlour)*
...
Item hys cais of pyips   x s.
...   20

1638
Archdeaconry of Lincoln Visitation Book   LA: Diocesan Vij/21
f 4v*   *(September)*
                                                                              25
*Presentments made during the visitation of Lincoln, Longoboby, and Graffoe
deaneries by Morgan Wynnterly and others*
...
Timberland   °stet°
predicta
               Willelmus Boulton & Ralfe Collidge of Bardney presented for fidlinge in   30
Bardney   the Alehouse in tyme of divine service & sermon.
In wraggoe./   °vide postea apud Bardney stet in hoc loco./°
...

BARNETBY LE WOLD   35

1629/30
Archdeaconry of Lincoln Visitation Book   LA: Diocesan Vij/19
f 46a*   *(9 January)*
                                                                              40
George Collyer of Barnetbie was heretofore presented for committing

1/ Handbye: *probably Hanby, Lenton parish*

fornication with one Susanna Plummer; and he now vseth her companie to
entise her to the like wickednes againe, as shee her selfe complaineth.
He is oftentimes absent from the Church on the Sabbath day, as now of late,
on Sunday beeing the xxij^th of Nouember; on sunday beeing the xx^th of
December. on sunday beeing the xiij^th of December (in the time of Euening   5
prayer he was setting cocks togither to fight; as is reported by some of them
who did owe the cocks:) on sunday beeing the xxvij^th of December.

…

BARROW UPON HUMBER   10

1533
Letter of John Coke to Thomas Cromwell   BL: Cotton Galba B.x.17
f 44*   *(22 May)*

15

1533. Barowe
22 Maij. Io*hn*
Coke./

Right honorable sir and my right syngulier and especiall good maister after
moost humble recomendacions precedyng as to y⟨…⟩ right honorable
maistership apperteyneth/ It shall please the same to vnderstonde howe that
a naughty person of Andwar⟨…⟩ resorted to this towne of Barowe this
Pasche marte wi*th* lm⟨…⟩ and pictures in cloth to sell amongyst the which   20
clothes he had the picture of o*ur* soueraigne lord the kyng (whom o*ur* lord
preserue) And this day settyng vp the same picture vpon th⟨.⟩ burse to sell/
he pynned vpon the body of the said picture/ a wenche made in cloth
holdyng a paier of balance in her hand*es*/ in thone balance was fygured too
hand*es* togeder/ An⟨.⟩ in thother balance a fether/ wi*th* a scriptiue ou*er* her   25
hed. sayn⟨.⟩ that love was lighter than a fether/ wherat the Spanyard and other
of the Duche Nacion had greate pleasure/ in deridy⟨..⟩ Iestyng and laughyng
therat/ And spekyng sondry obprobrio⟨…⟩ word*es* ayenst his moost noble
grace & moost gracious quene his bedfelowe/ wherupon Inmediatly and
wi*th* all diligen⟨..⟩ and haast possible (after I had knowleige therof) I resorted   30
the Scowte, borowmaisters and Skepyns of the said towne of Barowe,
declaryng vnto them the maner of this naughty p*er*son, and facion of the
Spanyard*es* and other. who inco*n*tyne sent for the said p*er*son, and examyned
hym streightly ⌃⌜therof⌝ which excused hymself, allegyng that he meaned
therby no hur⟨.⟩ Neu*er*theles he said that a certeyn spanyard (to hym vnknow⟨.⟩   35
desired hym to lette it stande, & he shuld be borne out/ wherup⟨..⟩ they
co*m*maunded hym to co*m*mytte no suche like thyng eft sone⟨.⟩ vpon payne
of forfaiture of all hys m*er*chandises/ and furthe⟨.⟩ to be punyshed in exemple
of other/ And thus after my humble servys presented vnto yo*ur* moost
honorable maistership wi*th* my daily praier. I Lowly beseche the holy goost   40

19/ Andwar⟨…⟩: *perhaps the town of Anderby (?)*

to sende the same thaccomplisshyng of your noble desires/ written at
Bar⟨...⟩ the xxijth Day of May/ Anno xv^C xxxiij^{ti}/

> by the handes of your moost humble seruant Iohn ⟨...⟩
> Secretary vnworthy to the merchant A⟨...⟩   5

BARTON UPON HUMBER

1641

AC ***St Mary's Churchwardens' Accounts***   Ball: *Social History and Antiquities*   10
  of Barton
p 8*

...'to Winterton singers, in aile, 1s.'...
...   15

BASTON

1388/9
Certificate of the Guild of St John Baptist   TNA: PRO C 47/39/76   20
single sheet*

> Certificacio ffraternitatis Gilde *sancti* Iohannis Baptiste in ecclesia
> eiusdem *sancti* de Baston in com*itatu* Lincoln*ie*
> Iohannes Cranemere & alij de vicinis suis ville de Baston circa annum   25
> quadragesimum domini Edwardj nuper Regis Anglie aui Regis nunc In honore
> domini nostri iesu christi beate Marie sancti Iohannis Baptiste & Omnium
> Sanctorum & in augmentacionem cultus diuini & deuocionis humane
> concordiam inierunt quod de bonis & catallis suis quoddam lumen xxvj
> cereorum coram altari sancti Iohannis Baptiste in ecclesia predicta annuatim   30
> ordinarent. quod quidem lumen tunc temporis perfecerunt & hucusque
> continuatum est ibidem per adiutorium vicinorum dicte fraternitatis &
> vlterius in maioris deuocionis & sanctitatis augmentacionem concordati
> fuerunt quod si facultates dicte fraternitatis ad dictum cultum diuinum
> faciendum collate intantum augmentarentur quod Capellanum exhibere   35
> potuissent tunc Capellanum ibidem inuenirent & sic Capellanum quendam
> anno vltimo preterito ibidem exhibebant Et pro regimine dicte gilde
> constitutum est inter fratres & sorores dicte Gilde vt omnes veniant in vigilia
> sancti Iohannis Baptiste ad portandum lumen ad ecclesiam ad primam
> campanam ∧⌈vesperarum⌉ & quod nullus sit absens sine licencia dicte   40

4/ ⟨...⟩: *20mm missing*   5/ A⟨...⟩: *60mm missing*

fraternitatis nisi habeat licitam causam excusacionis sub pena vnius libre
cere & quod omnes fratres & Sorores dicte fraternitatis veniant ad ecclesiam
in die sancti Iohannis Baptiste insimul ad oblacionem & quod nullus deficiat
nisi habeat licenciam dicte fraternitatis vel licitam causam excusacionis
sub pena vnius libre cere Et si aliquis illorum fuerit rebellis fraternitati erit   5
premunitus semel secundo & tercio & si non velit emendari vel si talis sit
latro vel si soror dicte fraternitatis sit mala de corpore suo expelletur de
fraternitate. Item. si aliquis illorum habeat aliquam porcionem catallorum
dicte Gilde in manibus suis & ⟨…⟩ emere & vendere in augmentacionem
dictorum catallorum set permittit illa casse iacere? adiuuamen inde erit ad   10
voluntatem dicte fraternitatis Item si aliquis illorum habeat officium per
ordinacionem fraternitatis & noluerit illud facere soluat vnam libram cere
ad dictam Gildam Item quod omnes sorores dicte fraternitatis vel alique
nomine suo venient in die sancti Iohannis Baptiste tripidiare cum sororibus
suis sub pena vnius modij ordei. Item si contingat quod si aliquis illorum   15
moriatur tunc omnes fratres & Sorores venient cum lumine & hercia ad
dirige circa corpus & in die sepulture ad oblacionem & nullus eorum erit
absens nisi habeat licenciam dicte fraternitatis nisi licitam causam habeat
se excusandi sub pena vnius libre cere Item quod quilibet eorum distribuat
pauperibus pro elimosina pro animabus eorum ₍∧₎⌜vnum obolum⌝ Item quod   20
omnes sorores predicte Gilde intersint vesperis & ad matutinas in vigilia
sancti Iohannis Baptiste lumen in manibus portantes aceciam in die
tripidiantes nisi sint ad talem senectutem redacte vel in infirmitate vel
peregrinacione aut negocio aliquali fuerint per fraternitatem excusate sub
pena vnius chori ordei Et dicta fraternitas habere solebat quendam Custodem   25
dicte Gilde qui vocabatur aldermannus set anno vltimo preterito taliter
ordinauerunt quod vlterius talem non haberent set omnia dictam fraternitatem
contingencia per eandem insimul gubernarentur honeste & deuote Et nullam
habent communem pixidem nec faciunt sacramenta aliqua nec congregaciones
assembleas vel conuiuia aliter quam supra ordinatum est nisi quod dicto   30
die sancti Iohannis conueniunt in honore sancti & manducant & bibunt
& ordinant pro salario dicti Capellani & luminis & aliorum in honorem
sancti sine liberata confederacione manutenencia vel riota in legis retardacionem
Et nulla habent priuilegia statuta ordinaciones vsus vel consuetudines
aliter quam supradictum est Et nulla habent terras tenementa redditus vel   35
possessiones mortificatas vel non mortificatas in manibus suis nec aliorum
nec aliqua bona catalla vel monetam ad opus dicte fraternitis. nisi xxviij
quarteria brasij precij sex marcarum Et nullas habent cartas vel litteras patentes
de concessione Domini Regis vel progenitorum suorum dictam Gildam
aliqualiter tangentes vel concernentes   40

9/ ⟨…⟩: *40mm missing due to hole in parchment*

BENINGTON

1577–8
All Saints' Churchwardens' Accounts
 LA: BENINGTON IN HOLLAND PAR/13/1   5
f 19*   *(Rendered 2 November 1578)* *(Receipts)*

...

It*e*m receyved for the collection on ploughm*o*nday xxvj s. viij d.

...

                                                                      10
(Payments)
It*e*m payed for naýles viij d. to Chard towne vj d. to the
players of Boston vij d.   .   xxj d.

...

                                                                      15

1609
Archdeaconry of Lincoln Visitation Book   LA: Diocesan Vij/12
p 465*   *(28 July)*

d*imittitur*   Tho*mas* Statherne gard*ianus* for beeinge absent from prayer vppon sunday   20
after St Peeter*e*s day last & then was at a morrice dance & after com*m*inge in
vnto the s*er*mon was warned to fetche the rest of the companie vnto s*er*mon
but he sette still in the churche & did not. °28 Iulij apud Lincoln*iam* cit*atus*
&c comp*aru*it et obiecto ar*ticu*lo fass*us* est vnde habet ad agnoscend*um*
crimen et ad cer*tifica*ndum in pr*oximum* [⟨.⟩c]° 20 Sept*em*bris 1609. cer*tifica*vit 25
& d*imittitu*r/

...

BIGBY

                                                                      30
1567
Archdeaconry of Lincoln Visitation Book   LA: Diocesan Vij/3
f 143*   *(11 April)*

Presentments made during the visitation of Yarburgh deanery held in the parish 35
church at Market Rasen by John Twidall, MA, official
...

d*imitittur*   Com*mun*e conviuiu*m* fecer*un*t in ecc*l*esia vocat*um* le plaie feast et [l]
biblia sunt lacerata xx° die novembr*is* 1567 ap*ud* linc*ol*n*iam* citati vnus

---

8/ ploughmonday: *13 January 1577/8*   20–1/ sunday after St Peeter*e*s day last: *either 7*
12/ Chard towne: *possibly Chard, Somerset*   *August 1608 or 2 July 1609*

comp*ar*uit et fatetur h*ab*et ad reformand*um* imposterum p*r*o conviuio/ et
quoad biblia h*ab*et ad emendand*um* et certificand*um* ante festum natalis domini
p*r*oximum xxj^mo Ianuarij 1567 ap*u*d linc*olniam* apparitor certific*auit*
et sic

BOSTON

1514–15
Guild of the Blessed Virgin Mary Accounts   BL: Egerton MS 2886
f 5v*   *(8 June–31 May) (Bailiff's account)*
…

C*ust*us Nauicul*i*
Noe

Et in diu*ersis* custub*us* rep*a*racion*is* Nauicul*i* Noe vocat*i* Noeschip hoc anno
vt in p*r*ec*i*o vn*ius* pec*ie* ⌜iiij d.⌝ cordul*i* in a*nno* p*r*oxim*o* empt*e*/ iij pe*ci*arum
⌜viij d.⌝ h*uius*mod*i* cordul*i* hoc Anno empt*arum*/ facture ⌜vj d.⌝ vn*ius* rote
ad man*us* Iohann*is* Hond Carpen*ar*t*ij* iux*t*a conuenc*io*nem in grosso/ ij   15
homin*ibus* ⌜viij d.⌝ operant*ibus* in le riging dict*i* Nauicul*i* p*er* ij dies/ mercede
⌜v s. iiij d.⌝ viij homin*um* laboranc*ium* in cariagio dict*i* Nauicul*i* vi*delicet* in
fest*is* pent*e*cost*is* & Corporis chr*ist*i cuiuslib*et* capient*is* viij d. p*er* dictos ij dies/
in p*r*ec*i*o ⌜xx d.⌝ pulu*er*is saxi noui empt*i* ad dict*as* vices/ & in ⌜viij d.⌝
dissoluc*ione* Ieiunior*um* eor*undem* viij p*er*son*arum* ix s. x d.   20
…

f 16   *(Chamberlains' account) (Wax and wax-working expenses)*
…

Et in pane ceruis*ia* carn*e* & al*ijs* victual*ibus*   25
quibuscumq*ue* cum focal*ibus* cariagio cere & al*ijs*
n*e*c*cessar*ijs empt*is* temp*ore* op*er*is dict*e* cere hoc
Anno op*er*at*e* vna cum h*uius*mod*i* expens*is* fact*is*
d*om*inica in Carnipr*i*uio in communi aula p*r*o
recreac*i*one Aldermann*i* & alior*um* confr*atru*m   30
infra villam ∧⌜de⌝ Boston p*er* manus dictor*um*
Cam*er*ariorum Computanc*ium* cum cirotec*is* dat*is*
portitor*ibus* Cruc*ium* ac regard*is* dat*is* portitor*ibus*
luminu*m*/ histrionib*us* Mimis & al*ijs* p*er* p*ar*cellas
quat*er*nis Computanc*ium* insimul computat*is* &   35
hoc Anno restit*utis*   iiij li. xvj s. x d. q*ua*.

18/ fest*is* pent*e*cost*is* & Corpor*is* chr*ist*i: *4 and 15 June 1514*
29/ d*om*inica in Carnipr*i*uio: *18 February 1514/15*

(Corpus Christi expenses)

...

· Et in expens*is* fact*is* ad *f*estu*m* Corporis chri*s*ti in
co*mmun*i Aula vocat*a* Saint Mary hous temp*ore*
conuocacionis Alderma*nn*i Camerar*i*orum Capell*a*noru*m*   5
Cleric*orum* & alior*um* mini*s*trorum hu*ius* gilde
necno*n* f*ratrum* & soror*um* confluenciu*m* tam temp*ore*
dissoluc*ionis* ieiuniorum quam ad iantacul*um* & cena*m*
vt in pane vino ceruis*i*a biro carne bouina multon*ina*
vitul*ina* auc*ina* pulcin*aria* & h*uius*modi victual*ibus*   10
vna cum xxvj s. viij d. de feod*o* Coci & regard*is* dat*is*
al*ijs* seruient*ibus* portitor*ibus* vexill*orum* cruciu*m*
torchiar*um* turibil' histrionib*us* Mimis & al*ijs* p*er*
man*us* Camerariorum Compu*tantium* hoc A*nn*o per
parcell*as* qu*a*ternis s*uis* lucid*ius* app*arentibus*   xxj li. xiiij s. v d. ob. 15

...

f 24   *(Alderman's account) (Rewards)*

...

Et in Cons*imilibus* den*a*rijs regardat*is* ... Mimis ⌈iij s.⌉ in ffesto Corporis   20
chri*s*ti...

...

1515–16
Guild of the Blessed Virgin Mary Accounts   BL: Egerton MS 2886   25
f 32v   *(31 May–15 May) (Bailiff's account)*

...

Custus Nauic*u*li   Et in den*a*rijs p*er* d*i*ctu*m* Computantem Solut*is* ⌈iij s. iiij d.⌉ x^{cem} hom*inibus*
Noe   laboranc*ibus* in Cariag*i*o cuiusd*am* Nauicul*i* vocat*i* Noeshipp circa villam
                      de Boston hoc anno singul*o* capien*te* p*ro* labore s*uo* iiij d. & p*ro* precio ⌈viij   30
                      d.⌉ ij l*i*brarum Sulphur*is* empt*arum* ad eandem vicem vt patet p*er* quodd*am*
                      quaternu*m* coram Auditor*e* ostensu*m* examin*atum* & probatu*m* & int*er*
                      Memora*nda* hui*us* Anni remane*ns* iiij s.

...

35

f 42v   *(Chamberlains' account) (Wax and wax-working expenses)*

...

...Et in pane Ceruis*i*a. Carn*e* & al*ijs* victual*ibus* quibuscumqu*e*. cu*m* ffocal*ibus*
& al*ijs* nec*cessarijs* empt*is* temp*ore* op*er*is dict*e* Cere. hoc anno op*er*ate vna

---

3/ *f*estu*m* Corporis chri*s*ti: *15 June 1514*   20–1/ ffesto Corporis chri*s*ti: *15 June 1514*
15/ lucid*ius*: *2 minims for second* i *in* MS   29/ laboranc*ibus*: *for* laborantibus

cum huiusmodi Expensis. factis. Dominica in Carnipriuio in Communi Aula.
pro recreacione Aldermanni & Aliorum Confratrum intra villam de Boston.
per manus dictorum. Camerariorum Computancium cum Cirotecis. datis
portitoribus Crucium Ac Regardis datis portatoribus luminum histrionibus
Mimis & alijs ∧⌜per⌝ parcellas. quaternis Computancium Insimul Computatis   5
& hoc Anno restitutis. lxx s. ix d.

...

f 43   (Corpus Christi expenses)

                                                                                           10
Et in Expensis factis. ad festum. Corporis christi in
Comuni Aula vocata Saynt Mary Hous tempore.
Conuocacionis. Aldermanni. Camerariorum Capellanorum
Clericorum & aliorum Ministrorum. huius Gilde
Necnon fratrum & Sororum. confluentium tam tempore   15
dissolucionis Ieiuniorum. quam ad Iantaculum & Cenam
vt in pane vino seruisia. biro. carne bouina. Multonina.
vitulina. Aucina. pulcinaria & huiusmodi victualibus
vna cum xxvj s. viij d. de feodo Coci. & Regardis datis alijs
seruientibus portatoribus vexillorum Crucium torchiarum.   20
turibil' histrionibus mimis & alijs per manus Camerariorum
Computantium hoc anno per parcellas quaternis suis
lucidius. apparentibus   xxiiij li. vj s. ix d.

...

                                                                                           25
f 51   (Alderman's account)
...
Et in concimilibus Regardis datis Mimis ⌜v s.⌝ ...
...

                                                                                           30
1516–17
Guild of the Blessed Virgin Mary Accounts   BL: Egerton MS 2886
f 61   (15 May 1516–4 June 1517) (Bailiff's account)

Custus nauiculi   Et in denarijs solutis super Nauiculum Noie vna cum stipendiis viij   35
Noe   hominum laborancium in cariagio eiusdem per quaternum reparacionum
                 Computantis vij s. ij d.
                 ...

1/ Dominica in Carnipriuio: 3 February 1515/16
11/ festum. Corporis christi: 7 June 1515
28/ concimilibus: for consimilibus

f 72v   *(Chamberlains' account)   (Wax and wax-working expenses)*
...
Et in pane ceruic*ia* Carn*e* & al*ijs* victual*ibus*
quibuscum*que* cum focal*ibus* & al*ijs* necess*arijs* empt*is*
temp*ore* op*eris* dict*e* Cere hoc Anno op*erate* vna c*um*   5
Expens*is* fact*is* dom*in*ica in Carnipr*iu*io in Communi
Aula p*ro* recreac*ione* Aldermann*i* & al*iorum* confratr*um*
infra villa*m* de Boston p*er* man*us* dict*orum* Camerari*orum*
Computanc*ium* cum Cirotec*is* dat*is* portato*ribus* Cruci*um*
Ac regard*is* dat*is* portato*ribus* luminu*m* hist*r*ion*ibus*   10
Mimis & al*ijs* p*er* p*ar*cell*as* quat*er*n*is* Computanc*ium*
insimull computat*is* & hoc a*n*no restitut*is* cu*m* lij s.
vij d. q*u*a. p*er* Th*omam* ffade & xxxix s. iiij d. q*u*a. p*er*
Athelard hoberd   iiij li. xj s. x d. ob.
...   15

(Corpus Christi expenses)
Et in expens*is* fact*is* ad f*estu*m Corporis chr*isti* in
Commun*i* Aula vocat*a* Sanct Mary house temp*ore*
con*uo*cac*ion*is Aldermann*i* Camerari*orum* Capella*norum*   20
Cleric*orum* & al*iorum* Ministr*orum* hui*us* gilde Necnon
f⌜r⌝atr*um* & Soror*um* confluenc*ium* tam temp*ore*
dissoluc*ion*is Ieiunior*um* q*ua*m ad Iantacul*um* & cena*m*
vt in pane vino ceruis*ia* biro carn*e* bouin*a* Multon*ina*
vitul*ina* Aucin*a* pulcin*aria* & hui*us*mod*i* victual*ibus*   25
vna c*um* xxvj s. viij d. de feodo Coci & Regard*is* dat*is* al*ijs*
s*er*uient*ibus* portato*ribus* vexil*lorum* Crucium torchiar*um*.
turibil' hist*r*ion*ibus* Mimis & al*ijs* p*er* man*us* Camerari*orum*
Comput*antium* hoc Anno p*er* p*ar*cell*as* quat*er*nis suis
lucidius. app*ar*ent*ibus*   xxiiij li. xj s. j d. ob. 30
...

f 82v   *(Alderman's account)   (Rewards)*
...
...Mimis ⌜iiij s. iiij d.⌝ gilde s*anct*e kat*er*ine/ al*ijs* Mimis ⌜vij s.⌝ in festo   35
Corp*oris* chr*isti*/...
...

6/ dom*in*ica in Carnipr*iu*io: *22 February 1516/17*
13, 14/ Th*omam* ffade, Athelard hoberd: *guild chamberlains in 1516–17*
18, 35–6/ f*estu*m Corporis chr*isti*, festo Corp*oris* chr*isti*:   *22 May 1516*
30/ lucidius: *4 minims for* iu̇ *in* MS

1517–18
Guild of the Blessed Virgin Mary Accounts   BL: Egerton MS 2886
f 88v   *(4 June–27 May) (Bailiff's account)*
...

Custus nauiculi
Noe

Et in denarijs solutis ix^uem hominum ⌈v s. ij d.⌉ Cariancium Nauiculum   5
Noie iuxta vij d. ad vices./ emendacione ⌈ij s.⌉ dicti Nauiculi/ emendacione
⌈iij d.⌉ de le Banershafte/ & in precio vnius ⌈v s. iij d.⌉ paribus nouarum
rotarum pro eodem vt in quaterno Reparacionum plenius Apparet inter se
xij s. x d.
...   10

f 97   *(Chamberlain's account) (Corpus Christi expenses)*
...

Et in expensis factis ad festum Corporis christi in Communi Aula vocata
Sanct Mary House tempore Conuocacionis Aldermanni Camerariorum   15
Capellanorum Clericorum & aliorum Ministrorum huius gilde/ Necnon
fratrum sororum & aliorum extraniorum confluencium tam tempore
dissolucionis Ieiuniorum quam ad Iantaculum & cenam vt in panc vino
ceruisia biro/ carne bouina/ multonina/ vitulina/ aucina pulcinaria &
huiusmodi victuarijs cum alijs regardis datis alijs seruientibus/ portatatoribus   20
vexillorum/ crucium/ torchiarum/ turibil'/ & xiij s. iiij d. de medietate feodi
Coci vna cum alijs regardis histrionibus Mimis & alijs per manus Computantis/
vltra residuum per alium Camerarium socium eiusdem/ per quaternum suum
plenius liquet & alijs computis precedentibus xij li. liij s. vj d.
...   25

f 99v
...

Et in expensis factis ad festum Corporis christi in Communi Aula vocata
sanct Mary House tempore Conuocacionis Aldermanni Camerariorum   30
Capellanorum Clericorum & Aliorum Ministrorum Huius gilde/ Nec non
fratrum Sororum & Aliorum extraniorum confluencium/ tam tempore
dissolucione Ieiuniorum quam ad Iantaculum & cenam vt in pane vino
ceruisia biro/ carne bouino/ multonina vitulina/ Aucina pulcinaria/ volatili/
Cegnetina/ gruina/ & huiusmodi cum alijs diuersis expensis & regardis Mimis   35
& seruientibus ac portatoribus ∧⌈vexillorum⌉ & Histrionibus & alijs per

---

5/ hominum … Cariancium: *for* hominibus … Cariantibus
14, 29/ festum Corporis christi: *11 June 1517*
20/ portatatoribus: *for* portatoribus
33/ dissolucione: *for* dissolucionis
34/ bouino: *for* bouina

manus Computantis pro parte sua vltra residuum per alterum Camerarium
Socium eiusdem Computantis per quaternum suum particulariter Luculencius
Apparet xij li. iiij s. vj d. ob.

...

1518–19

Guild of the Blessed Virgin Mary Accounts   LA: Misc. Don. 169
f 7v   *(27 May–16 June) (Bailiff's account)*

...

Custus Nauiculi Noe

Et in denarijs solutis viij ⌈v s. ix d.⌉. hominibus Nauiculum Noie diebus
sancti spiritus Paracliti & Corporis christi cariantibus ingrossum conductis
I libre gonnepouuder ⌈xij d.⌉ Empcione Carteclowtes & ⌈iij d.⌉ stubbys cum
⌈j d.⌉ alijs prouisis pro eodem Nauiculo per predictum quaternum plenius
patet etc. vij s. j d.

...

Guild of the Blessed Virgin Mary Accounts   BL: Egerton MS 2886
f 117   *(27 May–16 June) (Chamberlain's account) (Corpus Christi expenses)*

...

Et in expensis factis ad festum Corporis christi in Communi Aula vocata
Saint Mary house tempore Conuocacionis Aldermanni Camerariorum
Capellanorum Clericorum & aliorum Ministrorum huius gilde Necnon
ffratrum sororum & aliorum extraniorum confluencium tam tempore
dissolucionis Ieiuniorum quam ad Iantaculum & Cenam vt in pane vino
ceruicia birra Carne bouina multonina vitulina Aucina pulcinaria &
huiusmodi victuarijs cum alijs Regardis datis alijs seruientibus portatoribus
vexillorum Crucium torchiarum turibil' & xiij s. iiij d. de medietate feodi Coci
vnacum alijs Regardis histrionibus Mimis & alijs per manus Computantis
vltra residuum per alium Camerarium socium eiusdem per quaternum suum
plenius liquet & alijs Computis precedentibus xij li. v s. x d.

...

f 119

...

Et in expensis factis ad festum Corporis christi in Communi Aula vocata
saynt Mary house tempore Conuocacionis Aldermanni Camerariorum
Capellanorum Clericorum & aliorum Ministrorum huius gilde Necnon
fratrum sororum & aliorum extraniorum confluencium tam tempore
dissolucionis Ieiuniorum quam ad Iantaculum & Cenam vt in pane vino
Ceruisia Birra Carne bouina multonina vitulina Aucina pulcinaria volatili

10–11/ diebus ... christi: *23 May and 3 June 1518*
20, 35/ festum Corporis christi: *3 June 1518*

cignet*ina* gru*ina* & huiusmod*i* cum al*ijs* diuersis expen*sis* & regard*is* Mimis & seruien*tibus* ac portator*ibus* ve˄⌈x⌉illor*um* & histrionib*us* & alijs p*er* man*us* Comput*antis* p*ro* p*ar*te s*ua* vltra residuu*m* p*er* alt*er*u*m* Cam*er*arium socium eiusd*em* Comput*antis* vt in iiij.ᵒʳ folijs papir*i* sup*er* Comp*utum* restitut*is* pleni*us* Apparet &c xij li. v s. x d.

…   5

1519–20
Guild of the Blessed Virgin Mary Accounts   BL: Egerton MS 2886
f 135   *(16 June–31 May) (Bailiff's account)*   10

Cust*us* Nauic*ule*
Noic

Et in denar*ijs* solut*is* vij^{tem} hom*i*nib*us* ⌈iiij s. j d.⌉ Nauic*ula*m Noie dieb*us* s*an*cti sp*irit*us* paracliti & Corporis chr*is*ti cariantibus sing*ulo* cap*iente* p*ro* labor*e* s*uo* vij d./ ij libr*is* le gonnpowder ⌈ij s.⌉ empt*is* xiiij vln*is* ⌈v s. iij d.⌉ le Canues empt*is* iux*t*a iiij d. ob. p*ro* qualibet vlna &c Necnon Al*ijs* diuersis   15 ⌈xxiij d.⌉ necc*essar*ijs empt*is* p*ro* eadem Nauic*u*la p*er* quaternum Comput*antis* restit*utum* & examin*atum* & int*er* memor*anda* remanen*s* xiij s. iij d.

…

f 142   *(Chamberlains' account) (Corpus Christi expenses)*   20
…

Et in expen*sis* fact*is* ad festu*m* Corporis chr*is*ti in Commun*i* Aula voc*ata* saint Mary house temp*ore* Conuocac*ionis* Aldermanni. Cam*er*arior*um* Cap*ell*anor*um* Clericor*um* & alior*um* Ministror*um* hui*us* gilde. Necnon fr*atru*m sororu*m* & alior*um* extranior*um* confluencium tam temp*ore*   25 dissoluc*ionis* Ieiunior*um* quam ad Iantac*u*lum & Cenam vt in pane vino seruicia birra Carne bouin*a* Multon*ina*. vitulin*a*. Aucina pulcin*aria* & huiusmod*i* victuar*ijs* cum al*ijs* Regard*is* dat*is* al*ijs* seruien*tibus* portator*ibus* vexillor*um* Crucium torchiar*um* & turibil' & xiij s. iiij d. de Med*ieta*te feod*i* Coci vnacum al*ijs* Regard*is* histrionib*us* Mimis. & alijs p*er* man*us* Comput*antis*   30 vltra resid*uum* p*er* aliu*m* Camerar*ium* socium eiusd*em* p*er* quaternu*m* suu*m* plenius liquet & al*ijs* Comp*utis*. preceden*tibus* xj li. xv s. iiij d.

…

f 152v   *(Alderman's account) (Rewards)*   35
…

…Et in cons*im*ilibus regard*is* ministrator*ibus* quibusdem Mimis al*ias* Trumpputers ad festu*m* Corporis chr*is*ti. ib*idem* facien*tibus* melodiam cu*m* instrument*is* suis &c. iij s. iiij d.…

…   40

12–13/ dieb*us* … chr*is*ti: *12 and 23 June 1519*
22, 38/ festu*m* Corporis chr*is*ti, festu*m* Corporis chr*is*ti: *23 June 1519*

1520-1

Guild of the Blessed Virgin Mary Accounts   BL: Egerton MS 2886

f 162v   *(31 May–23 May)   (Final adjustments to bailiff's account)*

…

…ix s. *pro* vection*e* Nouic*ule* Noie in dieb*us* Pentecostes & Corp*or*is chri*sti*   5
circa villam ib*idem* & Smigmate *cum* al*ijs* empt*is* *pro* eadem. Nauic*ula*
si*militer* post Clausu*m* eiusdem &c

f 169   *(Chamberlain's account)   (Corpus Christi expenses)*

…   10

Et in expen*sis* fact*is* ad f*estum* Corp*or*is chri*sti* in C*om*mun*i* Aula voc*ata*
saynt Mary House temp*ore* Conuocac*ionis* Aldermann*i* Ca*m*erari*orum*
Cap*ellanorum* Clericor*um*. & alior*um* Ministror*um* huius gilde Necnon
fra*trum* Soror*um* & alior*um* extranior*um* confluenciu*m*. tam temp*ore*
dissoluc*ionis* Ieiunior*um* quam ad Iantac*ulum* & Cenam vt in pane vino   15
Ceruis*ia* birro Carn*e* bouin*a* Multon*ina*. vitulin*a* aucin*a* pulcin*aria* volatil*i*.
Cignet*ina* gruin*a* & h*uius*mod*i* *cum* alijs diu*er*sis expen*sis* & Regard*is*
Mimis & s*er*uient*ibus* ac portatoribus vexill*orum* & histrionibus ac al*ijs* p*er*
man*us* Comp*utantis* p*ro* p*ar*te s*ua* vltra residu*um* p*er* alteru*m* Cam*er*arium.
socium eiusdem Comp*utantis* p*er* quaternu*m* s*uum* plenius & p*ar*ticulariter   20
pate*t* xj li. x s. ij d. ob.

…

f 179   *(Alderman's account)   (Livery and clothing)*

…   25

…Et in h*uius*mo*di* denar*ijs* solut*is* sup*er* empc*ione* pann*i* lan*ei* *pro* le
Mynstrell*es* *cum* ij s. *pro* faitu*ra* earu*n*d*em* togar*um* suar*um* p*er* p*ar*uum
qu*a*ternum Comp*utantis* penes seips*um* remanen*tem* xxvij s. Et solut*is* *pro*
⌈xviij d.⌉ di*midio* quart*erij* vellewet p*ro* le badges dict*e* toge &c I vnce ⌈ij s.
viij d.⌉ de venysgold & le broderyng ⌈ij s.⌉ & factu*ra* dict*orum* le badges vt   30
in dorso eiusdem qu*a*terni penes Comp*utantem* remanen*tem* &c vj s. ij d.

…

1521-2

Guild of the Blessed Virgin Mary Accounts   BL: Egerton MS 2886   35

f 186v   *(23 May 1521–12 June 1522)   (Bailiff's account)*

…

Custus Nauic*ule*
Noie

Et solut*um* p*er* Comp*utantem* in Anno p*ro*ximo preced*enti* post clausu*m*

5/ Pentecostes: *final es corrected over erasure*
5/ dieb*us* … chri*sti*: *27 May and 7 June 1520*
11/ f*estum* Corp*or*is chri*sti*: *7 June 1520*
29/ dict*e* toge: *for* dictarum togarum *(?)*

Comp*uti* *scilicet* in vectione Nauic*ule* noie in dieb*us* Pentecostes & Corp*oris*
chr*isti* circa villam de Boston c*um* emp*cione* Smigmat*is* & Al*iorum* empt*orum*
p*ro* eadem Nauic*ula* simi*liter* post Cl*ausu*m eiusd*em* cont*inentis* tam*en* Adtunc
notic*iam* Comp*utantis* &c ix s.

...   5

f 204v   *(Alderman's accounts)*

...

liberatu*ra* vestur*a* de le waytes Et solut*um* p*ro* panno laneo empt*o* p*ro* Mimis al*ias* waytes hoc anno vid*elicet*
p*ro* liberatu*ra* *sua* vt in sepedi*ct*o quaterno plenius cont*inetur* *pro* ij Ann*is*   10
fi*nitis* in Cl*ausu*m huius Comp*uti* &c xlviij s. viij d.

...

1522–3
Guild of the Blessed Virgin Mary Accounts   BL: Egerton MS 2886   15
f 234   *(12 June–28 May)* *(Alderman's account)* *(Rewards)*

...

...Regard*o* Mimis al*ias* Mynstrell*is* dom*i*ni Reg*is* xx s....

f 238   *(Necessary expenses)*   20

...

...Nicho*lao* Alyn broderer p*ro* fa*c*tura coronar*um* imponend*arum* super
tunicas Mimor*um* voc*atorum* le waytes & p*ro* le sewingsylk xij d. p*ro* di*midio*
qu*a*rterij de velvet p*ro* eisd*em* xviij d. p*ro* di*midio* vnc*ie* de le vennys gold
p*ro* eijsd*em* xvj d....   25

...

f 238v*

...expen*sis* le playing*e* de le ent*er*lute die p*ara*ceues & pasche v s. ij d....   30

...

(Necessary purchases and payments)
...Ric*ardo* hick*es* in precio ij vl*narum* le canvas empt*arum* p*ro* lc Golyes ad
proc*c*ssionem die Corp*oris* chr*isti* xvj d....   35

1–2/ dieb*us* ... chr*isti*: *19 and 30 May 1521* ·
22/ imponend*arum*: *5 minims for* im *in* MS
25/ eijsd*em*: *for* eisdem
30/ die ... pasche: *3 and 5 April 1523*
35/ die Corp*oris* chr*isti*: *19 June 1522*

f 239

...pro alio le Corde pro le noye Shipp iiij d.... pro le grese pro le noye ship I d....

...

1523–4
Guild of the Blessed Virgin Mary Accounts   BL: Egerton MS 2886
f 263   *(28 May–19 May) (Alderman's account) (Rewards)*

...to the kynges Mynystrelles vj s. viij d....

...

...Regardo le waytes de london cum vino super esdem expendito xiij s. iiij d....

...

1524–5
Guild of the Blessed Virgin Mary Accounts   BL: Egerton MS 2886
f 296*   *(19 May 1524–8 June 1525) (Alderman's account) (Rewards)*

...

...in in Regardo subvicecomitis in aduentu suo vsque boston cum regis processu pro auro regine ij s. cuidam The∧⌈the⌉riste domini Regis in festo Corporis christi iiij s. iiij d. lez Kinges mynstrelles in octaua eiusdem festi x s. lez Trumpytours Comitis Arundel. ij s. iiij d....

...

f 296v

...lez Myŋystrelles domini Regis x s....

...

(Guild officers' expenses in entertaining visitors)
...expensis lez Mynystrelles domini Regis xx s....

f 297v   *(Necessary payments)*

...xjᶜᵉᵐ hominibus pro Cariagio de le Noyeship ad ij vices cum iiij d. pro

---

13/ esdem: *for* eisdem
21 in in: *dittography*
22–3/ festo Corporis christi: *26 May 1524*
23/ octaua eiusdem festi: *26 May–2 June 1524*

dissolu*cione* Ieiun*iorum* su*orum* vij s. viij d.... Ric*ard*o Aleyn p*ro* fac*t*ura Corone & le Stuff p*ro* eisdem p*ro* le Mynstrel*les* de Boston iiij s....

f 298*

...M*agistro* Thomlynson p*ro* tot denar*iis* p*er* ip*s*um sol*utis* Mimis in festo Corp*or*is chr*ist*i & non sibi alloc*atis* in Comp*ut*o *suo* existen*ti* Cam*er*ario xiij s. iiij d....

1525–6
Guild of the Blessed Virgin Mary Accounts ʟᴀ: BB 4/C/1/1
f 14v   *(8 June–24 May) (Chamberlains' account) (Corpus Christi expenses)*
...

Et in expen*sis* fac*t*is ad f*estu*m Corp*or*is chr*ist*i in Communi aula voc*ata* Saynt Mary howse temp*ore* Conuocac*ionis* aldermann*i* Cam*er*ari*orum* Capel*l*anor*um* Clericor*um* & al*iorum* Ministror*um* hui*us* gilde Necnon Confr*atru*m Sororum et al*iorum* extranior*um* confluenc*ium* tam temp*ore* dissoluc*ionis* Ieiun*iorum* quam ad Iantac*u*lum & Cen*am* vt in pane vino seruic*ia* birra C᭄⌐a⌐rnib*us* bouin*a* Multon*ina* vitulin*a* auc*ina* pulc*ina*ria & hui*us*mod*i* victuar*ijs* c*um* regard*is* dat*is* al*ijs* seruient*ibus* portator*ibus* vexil*lorum* Crucium torchiar*um* Turibil' c*um* xiij s. iiij d. de M*edietat*e feodi will*e*lmi pynell Coci vna c*um* al*ijs* al*ijs* Regard*is* Histrionib*us* Mimis & al*ijs* p*er* man*us* Computan*tis* vltra resid*uum* p*er* Alium Cam*er*arium p*er* quatern*um* su*um* plen*ius* liquet ac in Comp*ut*is prece*entibus* &c viij li. viij s. j d. ob. q*u*a.
...

f 24v*   *(Alderman's account) (Rewards given)*
...

...le Trumpytours seruient*ibus* Comit*is* de Arundell ad v*t*as Corp*or*is chr*ist*i iij s. iiij d. fratr*ibus* limitator*ibus* de boston eadem vice viij d. Cuidam Sether*i*ste eadem vice iij s. iiij d.... le wayt*es* de Notyngh*am* iij s. iiij d. le Baynerd*es* de Swyneshed play x s....

2/ Corone: *for* Coronarum *(?)*
6–7/ festo Corp*or*is chr*ist*i: *4 June 1523*
14/ fest*u*m Corp*or*is chr*ist*i: *15 June 1525*
14/ Communi: *9 minims in* ᴍꜱ
19/ bouin*a*: *4 minims in* ᴍꜱ
22/ al*ijs* al*ijs*: *dittography*
30/ v*t*as Corp*or*is chr*ist*i: *15–22 June 1525*

f 25*

...Iohanni Englishe & socijs suis lusoribus domini Regis xl s....

...

f 26   (Necessary expenses)

...

...Ricardo Aleyn pro le Broderyng Coronarum pro le waytes cum ve∧⌈l⌉vet
& le vennys sylke iiij s....

f 28v*

...

...Nicholao feild ⌈ij s. viij d.⌉ pro vino expendito tempore filie sue existentis
Regine apud Boston...

...

1538–9
Guild of the Blessed Virgin Mary Accounts   LA: BB 4/C/1/2
f 11*   *(13 June–29 May)* *(Purchases)*

...

...in Custibus emendacionis de Noe chippe et le pety Iudas xiiij d....

...

1552–3
Inventory of St Botolph's Church Goods   TNA: PRO E 117/3/57
single sheet*   *(17 August)*

...

In primis v olde copis for childrene   vj s. viij d.

...

1553–4
Sale of St Botolph's Church Goods   TNA: PRO E 117/3/60
f [1]*   *(26 May)*

...

Item to Iohn Dobe v old Copes for Children   vj s. viij d.

...

1554–5
Inventory of John Wendon, Burgess   LA: INV 21/167
single mb*   *(20 December)* *(In the hall)*

...

Item A pare of Clavicordes   xx s.

...

1567–8
Council Minute Book   LA: BB 2/A/1/1
f 68v   *(9 May)*
…

Also yt is agreide yat the xiiij s. payde to the Scholemaster towardes the   5
charges of his play shalbe allowed. and also ye x s. that is gyven to the
wates of Cambridge
…

1572–3
Will of William Neudike, Musician   LA: LCC WILLS 1573i
f 129   *(16 March 1572/3; proved 7 April 1573)*

In the name of god Amen the xvith daye of march 1572 and in the xvth
yere oure sufferaine lady Elizabethe by the grace of god queene of   15
in⌐g⌐lande france and irland defendor of the faithe &c I william ncudike
of boston in the county of lincolne singinge man sicke in bodye but hole
in mind and of perfectt remembrauns do make this my last will and
testamente/ … Item I geue to Thomas my younger sonne x l. to be paiede
to him when he shall cume to the age xxiiijth years Item I geue more to   20
the saide Thomas all my apparell my virginalls clavigoulds and bookes
of musicke….
…

1573–4
Council Minute Book   LA: BB 2/A/1/1
f 128v*   *(27 March)*

1573 Tempore Ricardi Brigges maioris
Also where as Edward Astell of Boston musicion with his seruauntes and   30
apprentizes be appoynte to be the waytes of this Borough and to play euery
mornyng throwe out the Borough from Michaelmas vntill Cristynmas and
⌐from⌐ the xijth day untill Ester (Sondayes holydayes and ffridayes except)
vnlesse som cause reasonable may be to the contrarie/ ytt is therfore agred
att this assemble that for and toward their paynes and travell in this behalf/   35
euery Alderrman to pay vnto the said Edward yerely so long as he shall
contynue and be wayte of this Borough iiij s. at Cristynmas & Ester by
evyn porcions and euery one of the xviij Burgesses to pay yerely ii s. at
like dayes and tymes by evyn porcions and euery other Inhabitaunte and
dweller within this Borough to pay yerly to the same Edward at like dayes   40
by evyn porcions all such somme and sommes of money as shall from tyme
to tyme be rated taxed and sessed seuerally upon euery of them by the maior
Recorder and Alderman of the same Borough.

Inventory of William Neudike, Musician   LA: INV 55/137
single mb   *(6 April)*

…

Item A payre of olde virginalls Clavigold*es* &
musicke bookes   xvj s.   5

…

Inventory of John Skynner   LA: INV 55/150
single sheet*

…   10

I*tem* one luyt   xij s.

…

I*tem* songes & ballet*es*   xij d.

…

                                                                                            15

1576–7
Council Minute Book   LA: BB 2/A/1/1
f 179v   *(20 March 1576/7)*

…

Allso it is agreed that there shalbe no mo playes nor interludes [nor] in the   20
churche nor in the Chancell nor in the hall nor Scolle howse/

1578–9
Council Minute Book   LA: BB 2/A/1/1
f 185v*   *(17 February 1578/9)*   25

…

At this assemble it is agred that at the requeste of diuers of this Boroughe
that the play of the passion &c shalbe suffred to be plaiede in the hall
garthe at Ester or Whitsontide when they shalbe moste mete and prepared
for the same/   30

…

1605–6
Inventory of John Coppley, Gentleman   LA: INV 100/223
f [2v]*   *(8 October) (In the chamber over the buttery)*   35

…

Inp*ri*mis one trendlebed w⟨.⟩th a fetherbed with thing*es*
app*er*teninge/ A pare of virgynall*es*   xxvj s. viij d.

…

1606–7
Episcopal Court Book   LA: Diocesan Cj/16
p 154   *(19 February 1606/7)*

…

Iidem *contra* Iacobum Leeman Clericum *Curatum* de wrangle for [goei]   5
mumeing in Boston in disguised apparell.

⌐xixº ffebr*uarij* 1606 coram m*agist*ro Edw*ard*o Clark Surr*ogat*o &c⌐ [Quo
2 s. 6 d.   die] comp*aruit* p*er*sonal*ite*r d*ic*tus Leeman et se submisit et fassus est ar*ticulu*m
12 d. scrutin*io*   et d*om*i*n*us ex caus*i*s dimisit cum cum monic*ione*

…   10

1607–8
Will of Arthur Oudum, Musician   LA: LCC WILLS 1608ii
f 37*   *(3 March 1607/8; proved 21 April 1608)*

…   15

In the name of god Amen the third daie of March 1607 I Arthure Oudum
of Boston in the countie of Lincoln Muzirian heinge sicke in bodie but of
good & p*er*fect memorie the lord bee praised doe make & ordaine this my
laste will & testam*ent*…

                                                                                                       20

f 37v*

…I will & [bequeath] desire my brother Willi*a*m ffox sup*er*uisor of this my will
to see all thinges p*er*formed accordingly as my truste is in him And I giue him
for his paines takinge therin my best Iersey stockinges a little still shawme & two   25
shillinges in money … Item I giue vnto Barnard Lynam my greate bagge…

…

Inventory of Arthur Oudum, Musician   LA: INV 105/101
single sheet   *(21 March 1607/8) (In the great parlour)*   30

…

It*em* one dobble Curtal Instrument the ffowrthe p*ar*te of a noyse of
recorders the one halfe of a noyse of old violens w*it*h theire cases   iiij li.

…
                                                                                                       35

1609–10
Will of William Fox, Musician   LA: LCC WILLS 1609i
f 244   *(6 November; proved 22 December 1609)*

In the Name of god Amen the sixt daye of Nouember, 1609 I William ffox   40

5/ Iidem: *for* Idem

of Boston in the Countie of Lincoln Muzitian, sick in bodye but of good
and perfect memorye, the Lord be praised doe make & ordeyne this my
last will and testament in manner & fforme ffollowing ... Item I gyve vnto
Richard Knott my sonne in Lawe All my Instrumentes whatsoever, with
certaine tooles for mending of Instrumentes ... Item I gyve vnto Richard   5
Oudum All my skrowes & songe books in a lyttle Coffer And a ffyfe which
was his vnckle Raffe Oudum...

Bailiff's Account   LA: BB 4/B/1/1A
mb 3d   *(29 September–29 September)* *(Officers' livery)*   10
...

...Et de iiij li. xviij s. iij d. solutis Iohanni Ampleford pro sex liuerijs
musicorum anglice the wates panni lanei vocati broade blew sicut apparet
per billam particulorum...

...   15

Inventory of William Fox, Musician   LA: INV 106/302
single mb   *(12 December)* *(In the yard)*
...

Item one single Curtle ffor Musick & other
Instrumentes, violens & recorders   iij li. xj s. viij d.   20
...

1613–14
Council Minute Book   LA: BB 2/A/1/2   25
f 77   *(26 May)*
...

ffortie shillinges   At this Assemblie there is paide into the Treasurye ffortye shillings dew to this
is brought in   house by one Stevenson upon Bonde and the Bonde is deliuered to be Cancelled
by Stevenson   which ffortye Shillinges ys deliuered to Mr Hickes for ffortye Shillinges paide   30
                    by Mr Hickes with the Consent of this house to the Queenes Players
...

1620–1
Council Minute Book   LA: BB 2/A/1/2   35
f 146*   *(20 October)*
...

viij l. vj s. payd   Item at this Assembly there is payd out of the treasury to Master Maior money
to Master Maior   which he hath giuen out vnto the Captaines men the Earle of Ruttland
for money by   Secretary & for bringinge of [bukes] buckes & money giuen to players to ridd   40
him layd out for   them out of the towne & other waies layd out by him the some of viij l. vj. s.
this howse.
....

1621–2
Council Minute Book   LA: BB 2/A/1/2
f 155v*   *(4 June)*

…

xv. s. p*ai*d to doctor Baron for soe much giuen by him to the children of the   5
Reuells for their forbearinge to play in the towne†
Item at this Assembly there is taken out of the treasury the some of xv s. &
deliu*er*ed to m*aste*r doctor Baron for money w*hi*ch he gaue to the children
of the Reuells for their forbearinge to play in this towne this yeare./

…   10

1624–5
Council Minute Book   LA: BB 2/A/1/2
f 191*   *(21 May)*

…   15

xxj s. 6 d. p*ai*d
to m*aste*r Maior   Allsoe att this Assembly there is taken out of the treasury and paid to M*aste*r
Maior xxj s. vj d. for moneyes by him giuen to players for pr*e*venting their
playing in this Towne

…

  20

f 194v⁺   *(23 August)*

…

ij l. v s. v d.
p*ai*d to m*aste*r
Maior   Att this Assemblie there is ij l. v s. v d. taken out of the treasury & paid to
m*aste*r Maior in full dischardge of money giuen to S*i*r Willyam Armins man,
to players & to a messinger for bringeing pr*o*clamac*i*ons   25

…

f 197v*   *(28 January 1624/5)*

…

xxx s. paid
Mr Cammock   Att this Assembly there is xxx s. taken out of the Treasurie and paid to mr   30
Iohn Cammock for soe much by him expended giuen to the princes players

…

1633–4
Council Minute Book   LA: BB 2/A/1/2   35
f 279*   *(8 November)*

…

xliiij li. viij s. j d. paid to m*aste*r Maior†
At this Assembly there was taken out of the Treasury xliiij li. viij s.
wibberton
rents iiij li. vij s.   j d. & paid to m*aste*r Maior for soe much laid out by him as followeth   40
Sessions Dynn*er*s
iij li. xj s.   vizt. to Robert Ingram for the reminde*r*s of the arrerages of Wibberton
outrents iiij li. vij s. for the last Sessions Dynners of the Iusticies &

to poore
souldiers &c.
iiij li. iiij s. xj d.

the Iuryes iij li. xj s. to poore souldiers marryn*ers* & Players iij li. iiij s.
xj d....

...

1634–5
Council Minute Book   LA: BB 2/A/1/2
f 284v*   *(4 August)*

[vj li. xiij s. iiij d.
per annu*m*
graunted to the
wates./.]

               Tempore Thoma Haughton./.
At this assembly it is agreed that the waytes shall haue yearly paid them by
this house towar*des* theire maintenance the sume of sixe pound*es* thirteene
shillings & four pence ouer & aboue theire liueries & such ordinary
allowances as they usually haue from priuate men the said wates finding
from time to time such sufficient musicke as this house shall appointe or

[xiij s. iiij d.
giuen to the
wates./.]

approve of & there is xiij s. iiij d. paied out of the treasury towar*des* the
chardges of the two new wates comeinge./.

...

1635–6
Council Minute Book   LA: BB 2/A/1/2
f 289*   *(21 April)*

...

*Maste*r Maior
his accompte./.

At this assembly *Maste*r Maior hath accompted to this howse ... for four
pound*es* paid to the waytes at Lady day last...

...

f 293v*   *(24 December)*

...

vj li. v s. ix d.
paid to Iames
Neaue./.

At this assembly there is vj li. v s. ix d. taken out of the treasury & paid to
Iames Neaue for soe much oweing to him for cloth for the coats for the
waits & for Tointon & the Pauyer in the time of mr Haughtons Maioraltie./.

...

1638–9
Council Minute Book   LA: BB 2/A/1/3
f 308   *(9 July)*

...

xx s. p*ai*d to
m*aste*r maior

Att this Assembly there is xx s. taken out of the Treasurye and paid to m*aste*r
maior for soe much by him given for the avoideinge of a company of players
from playinge in the towne:

...

3m/ iiij li.: *for* iij li.   9/ Thoma: *for* Thome

BRANSTON

1618
Episcopal Visitation Book   LA: Diocesan Vj/24
f 69v*   5

Presentments made during the visitation of Lincoln, Longoboby, and Graffoe
deaneries held in Lincoln Cathedral

...

Potter hanworth   d*imittitu*r   10
Branston   Francis Bett of Braunston *presented* for open ill behavior vpon [B] the
                  saboath day: x⁰ oct*obris* 1618 cit*atus* &c comp*aruit* et obiect*o* ar*ticu*lo
*soluitu*r pro   f*atetu*r that he beinge a piper did play vpon his instrum*ent* after eveninge
feodo suo p*er*   prayers vpon the saboath day et se subm*ittit* &c vnde cu*m* monic*ione*
ap*paritorem*   d*imittitur* mon*icione*   15
eod*em* die
                  ...

BRANT BROUGHTON

1618   20
Episcopal Visitation Book   LA: Diocesan Vj/24
f 55v*   *(24 or 29 July)*

Presentments made during the visitations of Loveden deanery, held in the parish
church of Sleaford, and Grantham deanery, held in the parish church of Grantham,   25
by Christopher Wyvell, LLD, vicar general and official principal of the bishop of
Lincoln, and Thomas Raymond, STB, commissary, in the presence of John Pregion,
registrar, and John Buffeild, notary public and deputy registrar

...

d*imittitu*r   30
Hen*ricus* Sills miln*er* *presented* ffor playinge vpon a fiddle or instrum*ent*
in th*e* str*ee*t*es* of Brantbroughton vpon the Saboath day before morning
prayer being the xix^th of Iuly 1618 and for not cominge to morninge and
eveninge prayer./ °8⁰ oct*obris* 1618. ques*itus* &c vijs in *proximum* p*ostea*
comp*aru*it Rob*ertus* Needham ex p*arte* d*icti* Sills ad cuius petic*ionem*   35
d*omi*nus reser*uauit* d*ictum* Sills in *proximum* fiat interim sced*ula* ad
agnoscend*um* &c et cert*ificandu*m in *proximum* postea d*omi*nus ad petic*ionem*
d*icti* Rob*er*ti d*ictu*m Sills dimis*it*°

...

12/ x⁰: *corrected over erasure*
14–15/ mon*icione* ... mon*icione*: *second occurrence redundant*

1636
Will of Henry Sills, Musician   LA: LCC WILLS 1636
f 367v   *(Proved on or after 2 September)*

In the name of god Amen I Henry Sills sicke body but god be praysed   5
perfect and hole in memory I Comitt my soule to god that gaue it & my
body to be buried in the Churchyard of Brandbrougton and also I giue
vnto Thomas Sills my eldest Sonne Ten pounds my Cloake and all my
Instrument*es* And the house where I now dwell after my wiffe decease to
him & his heires for ever...   10

...

Inventory of Henry Sills, Musician   LA: INV 144/141
single mb   *(August)*
...   15
Item three fiddles   xxvj s. viij d.
...

BURNHAM
          20
1638
Archdeaconry of Lincoln Visitation Book   LA: Diocesan Vij/21
f 57v*   *(12 November)*

Presentments made during the visitation of Yarburgh deanery held in the parish   25
church at Grimsby before Thomas Hirst, cleric, surrogate judge, in the presence
of John Milward, notary public
...

Horkstow   Bridgit ux*or* Thome Tripp p*resent*ed for miscallinge and raileinge on [he]
d*imittitu*r   the Churchward⟨...⟩ and sidsmen for doeinge theire dueties & saying they   30
paup*er*   were busie sliueinge fellowes & came for a fee./ 11 *decem*bris 1638 q*uesita*
                 vijs in p*roximum*. 18 Ianuarij 1638 p*er* vijs p*reconizata* non co*m*paruit
                 ex*communicata* °vlt*imo* ffebru*arij* 1638. vt con*tra* virum infra &c &
                 cert*ificandum* 2 non cert*ificauit* vnde ex*communicata*° °22 Ianuarij 1639
                 r*espond*e*atu*r cert*ificariu*m in proximam vis*itacionem*° °ex*communica*ta   35
                 cert*ificauit* &c d*imittitu*r°

d*imittitu*r   Thomas Tripp. p*resent*ed for y*a*t hee being a victualler & tipler att Burneholme
paup*er*   faire did suffer people to stay play & dance in his boothe in time of comon
                 prayer the 30th of sept*ember* last in ye after noone./   40

5/ body: *for* in *or of* body   34/ cert*ificandum*: *for* ad certificandum
30/ Churchward⟨...⟩: *obscured by tight binding*

Simili*te*r q*uesitus* vijs in *proximum*. 18 Ianuarij 1638. *Citato per* vijs *preconizato* non com*paruit* ex*communicatus* °vltim*o* ffebruarij 1638 comp*aruit* App*aritor* &c & petijt ⟨…⟩nem &c vnde f*acta* fide f*acta* absq*ue* &c h*abe*t ad agnoscend*um* & cert*ificandum* in 2 non cert*ificauit* vnde ex*communicatus*° °22. Ianuarij 1639 re*spondeatur* cert*ificarium* &c in prox*imam* visi*tacionem*.° °Ex*communica*to cert*ificauit* &c d*imittitu*r°

George Ellis *presented* for the like/ 11. decem*bris* 1638 comp*aruit* App*aritor* fatetur vnde h*abe*t ad agnoscend*um* & cert*ificandum* in 2. °29 Maij 1639: p*er* vijs in prox*imum*./° 22 Iunij 1639. *Citato per* vijs & *preconizato* non comp*aruit* ex*communicatus*. °19 Iulij 1639. comp*aruit* App*aritor*°

Barton (margin)

CAISTOR

AC

c 1631

Orders and Ordinances of Caistor School
  Carlisle: *Concise Description of the Endowed Grammar Schools* p 794*
  …

5. Item, the said Schoolmaster or Usher are not to refrain the School upon the Eves of Holidays, or any other days, before Three of the Clock in the Afternoon,—nor then neither but rarely, and that at the Shoolmaster's discretion, except it be in case where some Gentleman Stranger, or other, desire or request of the said Schoolmaster a Play-day for the Scholars, which is rarely to be granted at any one's request for more time than one afternoon;—And upon such Play-days - - - - - School Exercise, as Verses, Epistles, or Latins, - - - - - - master appointed to the Scholars fit for such exercises - - - - - make against the next day.
…

CONINGSBY

1601

Archdeaconry of Lincoln Visitation Book   LA: Diocesan Vij/10
f 64v*   *(1 April)*

Presentments made during the visitation of Horncastle, Hill, and Gartree deaneries, held in the church at Horncastle by Thomas Randes, MA, the archdeacon of Lincoln's official
…

3/ facta … facta: *second occurrence redundant*
26, 27/ - - - - -: *dashes by Carlisle presumably to indicate lost or illegible text*
26/ - - - - - -: *dashes by Carlisle presumably to indicate lost or illegible text*

d*imittitu*r

Alex*ander* Butterworth for a drunckard and for v⟨...⟩ god*es* name in vaine
in rymes ixᵒ Maij 1601 citat*us* d*ic*tus Butterworth no*n* comp*aruit* &
pena Reservata in *quinde*nam prox*imam* 22ᵈᵒ Maij 1601 comp*aruit* [dc]
Barth*olomae*us Salmon ad cuius petic*ionem* d*ominu*s ips*um* Butterworth   5
dimisit

...

Bill of Complaint in Lincoln v. Dymoke, Lovill, et al

   TNA: PRO STAC 5/L13/33   10
sheet 2*   *(23 November)*
...

...⟨...⟩ge sondaie (by the then previtie knowledge and incurredgment of
the said Edward dimocke) One Talbois dimocke of Kime in the Countie of
Lincoln, gent*leman* brother to the said Edward dimocke beinge of a verie   15
careless disposition and [a common knowne drunkard and] an ale house
haunter Richard M⟨...⟩ iiij daies before assalted hurte and wounded a pore
laboringe man that he was in daunger of his lyfe, and beinge sought for by
the Iustices warrant ∧⌜°for ⟨...⟩ of a manslaughter ⟨...⟩ by his arrest°⌝ fledd
therevppon, and henrie fawcett whom he knewe to be disorderid p*er*sons   20
Iohn Cradocke thelder and Iohn Cradock the younger Iohn Pargett Iohn
Corke ⟨...⟩ ∧⌜°⟨...⟩ ffrancys Harvey°⌝ Richerd dixon, Rob*er*te kirkeby Edward
wiles of Conisbie aforesaid yeome*n* and xlᵗⁱᵉ dissolute and vagarant p*er*sons
more a⟨...⟩ least, did vnlawfullie Riotusly & Routously assemble them selves
togeather in the forenoone of the same daie at kyme aforesaid and there soe   25
assembled in warlike manner with ⟨...⟩ Conysbie in the said Countie of
Lincoln, being the next towne adioyninge to Tattershall ⟨...⟩ ∧⌜°which Tow⟨..⟩
of Tattershall°⌝ your subiecte then did and yet doth dwell (in w*h*ich towne
of Conisbye the said Edward dimocke hath a mannor and the command of
diverse tenants. ∧⌜°there°⌝ The said Riotous and disorderid p*er*sons havinge   30
⟨...⟩ted thither ⟨...⟩ente but of his ⟨...⟩ therafter ⟨...⟩ the same day march in
disordered manner in the streetes of Conisbie aforesaid drawinge to there
Companie diuers other dissolute and lude p*er*sons dwellinge thereaboute*s*,
and theire in like disorderid sorte, enterid into all or moste of the Tiplinge
howses in Conisbie aforesaid, whereof theire were diuers to the number of   35

13/ ⟨...⟩ge: *item 1 reads* the xxvjᵗʰ day of the said
  monethe of Iulye beinge
17/ M⟨...⟩: *item 1 reads* Morrice of kyme affores⟨...⟩
  gent*leman* who was termed theire Capteyne, Richard
  Hunte who not three or
26/ with ⟨...⟩: *item 1 reads* flagges and drummes
  dep*ar*ted thense toward

28–30/ (in ... ⌜°there°⌝: *closing parenthesis omitted*
30–1/ havinge ... ⟨...⟩ente: *item 1 reads* having so
  resorted thither did aboute ⟨...⟩
31/ ⟨...⟩ente: *50mm illegible*
31/ ⟨...⟩¹: *10mm illegible, apparently 1 word*
31/ ⟨...⟩²: *15mm illegible*

viij or tenne ⟨…⟩ ther*e* did spend the ⟨…⟩ day in drinking and in beastlie
disorder wastinge and consuminge all all the drincke in the said ˄⌜°ale°⌝
howses somme of them gevinge out that they had druncke the towne drie,
and then comminge forth some of them being drunken and other greatlie
distempered thereby, the said malefactors and Riotus the same Saboth daie   5
in riotus & vnlawfull ⟨…⟩ being armed and ar⌜r⌝ied with swordes, rapiers
daggers, and other weapons, aswell invasive as defensive, Marched in the
streetes w*h*ich ledd into the meadowes over againste the Castle of Tattershall
wherein your subiecte then dwelled w*i*th his howsehould and familie,
intendinge (as it seemed) to shoe them selues in ⟨…⟩nne in there braveinge   10
⟨…⟩ against the said Castle in w*h*ich there marchinge in the said streete, your
subiecte not thinckinge of anie such disorderid assemblie or persons beinge
˄⌜°Ryding on horseback &°⌝ accompanied with ij servaunt*es* only on horsse,
and fyve or six his servaunt*es* on foote, vppon occasion of busines beinge
to passe that waie, p*er*ceavinge sutch Companie soe there assembled sente   15
often vnto them requiringe them ⌐°⟨…⟩°⌐ they would ⟨…⟩ staie the noyse of
there drummes, and displayinge there flagg*es* that he might quietlie passe
by them which neuerthelesse they did not forbeare but rather incresed there
disorder and Cryed stricke vpp drummes, stricke vpp drumes, wherevppon
one Thomas Pigott gent*leman* your subiectes servaunte, beinge on horssebacke,   20
Rydinge toward*es* them to haue p*er*swaded them to haue staide, they came
vppon him with theire drummes and flagges in sutch violent manner, as
the said Pigott was thereby with the sturringe of his horsse, by reason of
the noyse of the drumme, and the seight of the flagge or banner, caste of
his horsse downe to the grounde and beinge an adged man and corpulent,   25
receaved thereby a sore and daungerous fale, and lay there in good space
for deade, being greevously brused by the favle vntill somme of there owne
Companie, more Compassionat then [then] the reste, lifted him vpp and sett
him on his foote, which theire insolencie riottes and vnlawfull misdemeanors
beinge observed by your Subiecte, in prevention of daunger and hurte to   30
his person, your said subiecte was inforsed to retorne ˄⌜°back°⌝ with greate
speede towardes his said howse at Tattershall Castle for that the said riottous
p*er*sons followed him with intencion likewise as yt plainly appeared, to have
offerid violence to your said subiecte, yf they had ouertaken him, whoe as
speedelie as he coulde in his retorninge to his said howse, sent forthwith the   35
same daie one of his servaunt*es* to Ioseph Mellers the Cunstable of Conisbie
aforesaid, to resorte to those disorderid p*er*sons, and to p*er*swade and
Commaund them in your highnes name to deseste theire said actions and

1/ ⟨…⟩²: *item 1 reads* Saboth   6/ ar⌜r⌝ried: *for* arraied
2/ all all: *dittography*   11/ ⟨…⟩: *item 1 reads* armour
6/ ⟨…⟩: *item 1 reads* disorder

to disperse themselves and keepe your heighnes peace, whoe then and theire
resortinge to them accordinglie, with purpose to staie them and requiringe
them in your heighnes name to disperse them selves and to keepe your
heignes peace) diuers of the said dissolute persons as namelie the said Talbois
dimocke, Richard Morrice, ∧⌈°Iohn Cradock theldre Iohn Cradock the yonger   5
Richard kersshawe ffrancys harvey°⌉ and Richard Hunte with others of the
sayd Companie, then and theire riotously routously and vnlawfullie did drawe
theire swordes, and assulted the said Constable, both in the streetes and in
the Curtch yarde of Conisbie aforesaid and other places there with theire said
swordes drawne, and somme of them did strike him with theire weapons in   10
the said Churtch yarde, And they soe continewed there Companie togeather
till nighte, delayinge the said time, vntill the said Earle was gone to his bedd
to take his reste, and then they beinge Commaunded by the said Cunstable
to goe to there reste and to be forth comminge the next morninge, to the
intent that he mighte haue them before your said subiecte, or somme other   15
of your heighnes Iustices of peace, there to answere to theire disorders
according to the lawe, they answerid that they were goinge to kime, and yf
your said subiecte or the said Cunstable would haue any thinge to doe with
them they should come aftere them to kime to the said ∧⌈°Sir°⌉ Edward
dimockes howse theire, which vnlawfull assemblie riott, and route, so beganne   20
at kime aforesaid the said xxvj^th daie of Iulie (beinge sondaie) in the forenoone,
and continewed at Conisbie in the afternoone of the same daie as well in
the time of divine sevice as otherwise without intermission…

1602   25
Interrogatories for Defendants in Lincoln v. Dymoke, Lovill, et al
TNA: PRO STAC 5/L13/33
sheet 6   *(before 7 April)*
…

1   Imp*ri*mis whither were you at South Kyme in the countye of Lincoln on   30
theq xxvj^th day of Iuly last past being sonday if you wert who by name were
in yo*u*r company & did not you & others in yo*u*r company come from
Kyme to conesbye in the afternoone of the same day or not whith*e*r in
yo*u*r goying thither had you or any of yo*u*r company any flagg*es* drummes
or oth*e*r warlike munic*i*on or not?   35

2   It*e*m when you and yo*u*r company ∧⌈so⌉ came to Conesby as aforesaid,
whith*e*r did you or any of yo*u*r company & which of them by name, march
in Conesby stretes, what weapons had you or they, how many in number
were they, and to what entent came you or they thith*e*r/?   40
…

2/ accordinglie,: *comma used for opening parenthesis*   31/ the xxvj^th … sonday: *26 July 1601*

Depositions of Defendants in Lincoln v. Dymoke, Lovill, et al
TNA: PRO STAC 5/L13/33

sheet 26   (7 April) (Examination of Richard Morrys, 28, yeoman, of
    South Kyme)

...   5

1   To the first Interrogatory he saieth that he was in Southkime the same day
    yat the may game went to Cunsbye/ being on a sabboth day butt whether
    it were the day mencioned in the interrogatory he knoweth nott and that
    there was in Companye Mr Taylboyes Dymocke Iohn Cradocke Roger
    Byarde Iohn Patchett ∧⌜&⌝ Iohn Cocke and yat he this examinate and   10
    these persons before named with some others went in the after noone of
    the same day from kyme to Cunsbye and somme of the companye had
    reedes tyde together lyke speares with a paynted paper of the toppes of
    them and one of them had a drumme and an other a flagge as he thinketh
    butt no other warlyke municion had they   15

2   To the second Interrogatory he saieth that when he with his companye
    came to Cunsbie as aforesaid they did march throughe the streetes to an
    alehouse and their lighting sett vppe their horses and saieth yat he this
    examinate had his sword about him that he did vsuallie weare when he did
    Ryde butt doth nott know of any that had weapons in his companye and   20
    saieth (that they were) when they came in to Cunsbye about xiij or xiiijteene
    persons and that there commyng to Cunsbye aforesaid was to be merrie and
    nott to harme any man

sheet 28   (Examination of John Patchett, 34, yeoman, of South Kyme)   25

1   To the first Interrogatory saieth yat he was at Southkyme on the day
    mencioned in the Interrogatory being Sunday and there was in his companye
    mr Taylboyes Dymocke Iohn Cradocke the yonger Richard Morys ∧⌜and⌝
    Iohn Cocke, and this examinate and ye persons before named with some   30
    others to the number of xij or xiij in all went from kyme to Cunisbye in
    the afternoone of the same day and there was a drumme and sixe of the
    companye had warlyke weapons made of Reedes lyke to speares with paynted
    papers of there endes and the Reedes themselves lykewise paynted butt they
    had no flagges or other warlyke Municion   35

2   To the second Interrogatory he saieth that this examinate being so accompanied
    did march on horseback two and two together throughe the streetes in
    Cunisbye aforesaid with the foresaid weapons in their handes to one wyles
    his house who kept an alehouse and their did leave their horses and sayeth   40
    yat there intent was butt onelie to be Merrie with Cunisbye men and yat
    there were nott aboue two swordes amongest them

    ...

1603

Interrogatories for Witnesses on Behalf of the Earl of Lincoln

TNA: PRO STAC 5/L13/33

sheet 49   *(before 1 September)*

...   5

2   Item wheather doe you knowe or haue you harde That one Taylboies
Dymocke Richard Morris Richard Hunte Iohn Cradocke the yonger Henry
Fawcett Iohn Easton Iohn Cocke Iohn Patchett Richard Dixon or what
Number & what be their names who by the sounde of a dru*m*me did gather
& assemble them selues togeather in a Riotous tumulteous & disordered   10
manner At Cunsbye in the Countie of Lincolne vppon or aboute the xxvj^th
daye of Iulye in the *(blank)* yere of her M*aies*ties Reigne or aboute what
time as you knowe or haue hard, and was it not vppon the Sabothe daye
declare the whole trueth & what be their seu*er*all names.

                                                                        15

3   Item wheather had the said disordered p*er*sons drumes, fflagg*es* or Streamers
And a Captaine or leader in warlike mann*er* & wheather did they not marche
aboute in Bravinge manner against the Castell of Tattershall beinge the
pl*aintiffes* and wheare he then Remayned, & in what sorte did they behaue
them selues to y*our* knowledge or remembrance   20

4   Item wheather did not the compl*ainant* beinge in a narrowe lane w*hich*
forced him to passe by them send worde to the said companye to intreate
them to hould still their noyse & drumes and also their flagg*es* or streymers
that he might quietlie passe by them withoute danger of scarringe his horse   25
& whoe did he so send vnto them for that or the like purpose and what
answere did they or any of them make when they weare required therunto,
And wheather did not they or some of them crie or call w*ith* a lowde voice
dyvers times (strike vp drume) and some of them Rune vppon one Thomas
Piggott gent*leman* the said Earles s*er*uante and then messenger (beinge sent   30
vnto them to p*er*swade them) w*ith* their flagg*es* streamers or auncient*es* in
such violent manner, that they caused his horse to cast him to the grounde,
And is not the said Piggotte a heavie aged & corpulent man and had he not
greate hurte & damage therbie & what be their names that did soe mysbehaue
them selves in that assembly to y*our* knowledge or as many of them as you   35
knowe, and was not the companie then so gathered togeather by the direction
appointm*ent* pro*c*urement comaundm*ent* or privitie of the said S*ir* Edward
dymocke as you knowe or verelie thincke in y*our* conscience.

5   Item wheather was not the said Earle the nowe compl*ainant* enforced w*ith*   40
their outragious behaviour to flie homeward*es* from them & wheather did

12/ the *(blank)* yere: *for* the xliij^th yere *(?)*

they not pursue & hastelie followe the said Earle and wheather did they
staie or hould their attempt*es* vntill the Cunstable of the towne at the said
Earles intreatie cam forthe & comaunded them in the Quenes ∧|maiestics|
name to hould still their noyses & disorderes, And did they not drawe their
swordes or bend their weapons against the castell & refuce to obey the said   5
Cunstable and what other resistance violence or threatining*es* ∧⌈or⌉ insolent
wordes did they offer vnto the said Cunstable, And did they not the same
day (beinge the sabothe day) goe frome Alehouse to Alehouse swearinge or
sayinge that they had druncke ∧⌈all⌉ the towne drie or woold doe it before
they went, and what other word*es* of Ribaldry or disorder did they vse   10

…

Depositions of Witnesses on Behalf of the Earl of Lincoln

TNA: PRO STAC 5/L13/33

sheet 42   (1 September)   (Deposition of Charles Grisley, 40, mercer,   15
  of Tattershall)

…

To the ffowerth interrogatorie he sayth that Coming to the Crosse at Conysbie
he found mr Pigott servant to the Compl*ainan*t there seeming to him to
be yll at ease & went vnto him & asked him howe he did to whome he   20
sayd that the sayd Compl*ainan*t had sent him to certayne persons in a Maye
game to pray them that they would hould still theyr drommes that he &
his Company might passe by them on horse backe who continewing still
theyr drumming the sayd Piggott*es* horse Cast him & hurt him being
afrayd of the drumme & ffurther sayth that the sayd mr Piggott seemed to   25
him not to be able to go by reason of the sayd hurte being an old & heavie
man & further to this interrogatorie he Cannot depose

…

(Deposition of Richard Baylye, 36, yeoman, of Aslackby Park)   30

…

To the second interrogatorie he sayth that before or about Lammas in the
xliij^th yeare of the raigne of the late Queenes M*aies*tie Talboys Dymocke Iohn
Cradocke Richard Morrys & divers other whose names he knoweth not to
the number of thirtie or thereaboutes on horsebacke & divers on foote were   35
assembled together having a Drumme amongst them w*hi*ch was playd on

To the third interrogatorie he sayth they had amongst them a drumme & a
flagg & the sayd Cradocke was Called the lord amongst them & further to
this Interrogatorie he Cannot depose   40

To the fowerth interrogatorie he sayth that the nowe Compl*ainan*t ryding
to Consbye to meete one mr Irbie hard the noyse of people showting & of

a drumme & demanding what yt should be yt was answered that yt was a
Maygame wherevppon the Complainant sent his footeman to desyre them
to forbeare theyr drumming till he were past them bycause he ridd of a wylde
mare & that footeman not readely retorning he sent one of his gentlemen
Called mr Piggott to make the lyke request, following after himselfe a softe   5
pace this deponent & others attending vppon him & Comming to the lane
end where the Company was this deponent did see mr Piggott on foote &
ryding to him asked him how he did who told him that the sayd Company
Came about him & he that Caryed the flagg florished the same before his
horse whereby his horse Cast him, of which fall he receyved such harme as   10
he was not perfectly well by the space of a fortnight & divers of the persons
willed at divers tymes to stryke vpp the drumme but who they were that sayd
so he knoweth not. And further to this interrogatorie he Cannot depose
saving that he doth thinke of his Conscience that Sir Edward Dymmocke
did not procure Command nor was privie therevnto   15

To the fifte interrogatorie he sayth that the sayd Richard Morrys being on
horsebacke & having a Cudgell in his hand pressed so nere the Complainant
& the rest of the Company following fast after him as this deponent did
thinke that the sayd Morrys would have stroken him & therefore thrust   20
betwixt them with his horse wherevppon the sayd Complainant retorned
another waye into Conisbie & Calling for a Constable Could fynd none the
sayd Cradocke & the rest still following of the Complainant to the lanes
end hard behynd him with theyr drumme sometymes playing & sometymes
ceasing & the Company showting till at length the sayd Earle having found   25
a constable Commanded him to raise the towne & to staye them by whose
commandment most of them departed & some fower or thereaboutes of
them did staye still but the Earle & his attendantes retorned presently toward
Tattershall And he further sayth that he did he‸⌈a⌉re that after his departure
the said Morrys did drawe his sword vppon the Constable & refused to be   30
at his Commandment And he doth allso saye that he heard that they before
these misdemeanors were drinking at one Alehouse & he thinketh that some
of them were drunke bycause of theyr disordred behaviour & further to this
interrogatorie he Cannot depose
...   35

c 1603

Interrogatories for Defendants' Witnesses in Lincoln v. Dymoke, Lovill, et al   TNA: PRO STAC 5/L13/33
sheet 48*   40
...
3   Item wheather doe you knowe or haue credyblie heard, that the said Sir

Edward Dymocke did forbidd and giue warninge to the said Talboyes Dymock, and others in the bill named, that they should not goe with theire said maygame, to the said towne of Conisbye, and that he afterward*es* mislyked and was displeased therew*i*th yea or noe: ./

...   5

CUMBERWORTH

1566
St Helen's Inventory of Church Furniture　　LA: Dean and Chapter Ciij/36　10
f 197*　*(26 April)*

The invy*nt*ore of all suche papiste ornam*entes* as Remayned in the p*a*rishe churche of Cvmberworth at anie tyme sence the death of the late Quene Marie made by Iohn donyngton & Rychurd page churche wardens ye xxvj^th　15
of April 1566

...

　It*em* one vestement &　　sollde to Iohn herdman and Rychard page
　decon & subd*e*cvn　　　*an*no septymo Elezabeth who hathe sollde
　　　　　　　　　　　　the same agayne to make players cot*es* and　　20
　wh*i*ch Iohn herdma*n* co*n*fesseth y*at* they were cut in pec*es* since the
　last visitac*i*on

...

DONINGTON IN HOLLAND   25

c 1563
List of Names and Parts Played　　LA: DONINGTON IN HOLLAND
　PAR/23/7
single sheet*   30

　　　　　　　　buttffendyke ffor ffyndyng of ⟨...⟩
　　　　　　　　　　　　⟨...⟩
　　　　　　　　　　　　⟨...⟩

                                                                                         35

[yt ys agey]

yt ys Agreyd by ye consent of y*at* hole p*a*ryshe y*at* ev*er*e man y*at* ⟨...⟩ hys tymes here aft*er* specyfyed to forfeyt for every tyme y*at* h⟨.⟩ do xij d. Apece for ev*er*e playr y*at* ys to say   40

34/ ⟨...⟩:　*10–30mm of damage*　　　　　38/ ⟨...⟩:　*10–15mm of damage*

rex		ye
George atkynson		[cowper]
[Iohn wryght] rex	[thomas]	Sawdene [thom*a*s dycconson] ⌊wryght⌋
Iohn Sinear ye steward		ye duke [Iohn page] ⌊Robert [hesis] heris⌋ 5
Iohn Iak*es* holefern*es*		*willia*m str*a*yker messyng*er*
Edward danyell		Iohn law ye harrowlld
Iohn Rayn*er* ⎫		[Iohn I] knyght*es*
Iohn Love ⎬ iij yong me*n*		thom*a*s playn 10
*willia*m browne ⎭		Robert lawranson

ye messyng*eres* ⎫
Iohn toplydge ⎬   *(signed)* Iohn IT Toplyche
thom*a*s watson ⎭   *(signed)* Iohn [Reg] Rener
Robert browne   15
  ye knyght*es*

Iohn Elward	*(signed)* be me george Atkynson	+⟨.⟩
Iohn Stennyt	*(signed)* be me Iohn Swgar	
(signed) Iohn Wryght		
X	*(signed)* Robert Sh	20
(signed) Ihon Newton		

1600
Archdeaconry of Lincoln Visitation Book   LA: Ḍiocesan Vij/9
f 46   *(3 June)*   25

Presentments made during the visitation of North Holland deanery held in the
church at Donington by Thomas Randes, the archdeacon of Lincoln's official
...

d*imittitur*   Eliz*abeth* Lecke   30
d*imittitur*   Agnes Harrington
for making Rymes of Rybauldrie to the grete offence of the p*a*rishioners
xvj° die Ian*uarij* 1600 citate [no] comp*a*ruer*un*t et ar*ticu*lo objecto se
submiser*un*t vnde d*omi*n*us* ip*s*as dimisit

4/ ⌊wryght⌋: *written below line successively replacing* dycconson *and* cowper
5–6/ ⌊Robert ... heris⌋: *written below the line to replace* Iohn page
13/ IT: *Toplydge also makes his personal mark of the initials* I *and* T *interlaced*
17/ +⟨.⟩: *unidentified personal mark*
20/ X: *unidentified personal mark in the form of a circle with four short strokes radiating from it*

EAGLE

1638
Will of Eustace Watson, Musician   LA: LCC WILLS 1638–40
single sheet   *(28 November; proved 1 February 1638/9)*   5

In the name of God. Amen: I Eustace ˄⌐watson⌐ of Eagle in the Countie
of Lincol⟨...⟩ b⟨..⟩nge weake in bodie, but of good and perfect Remembrance
I praise and ⌐thanke⌐ God thearefore doe ⟨...⟩ ⟨.⟩his my Last will and
Testament, in manner & forme followinge ... Inprimis I giue vnto my   10
Sonne ⟨...⟩ one flecked Quee, one Ewe hogg. One Swarme of Beese. Two
Instrumentes: a Trible & a Scitter⟨...⟩ my Bible: two Gunnes. One puter
Dish and one Cheare...
...
                                                                         15

1638/9
Inventory of Eustace Watson, Musician   LA: INV 147/137
f [1]   *(28 January)* *(In the garden)*
...
Item Two Instrewments of Musick   0 10 0   20
...

EPWORTH

1623   25
Archdeaconry of Stow Visitation Book   LA: Diocesan Viij/1
pp 30–1*   *(27 September)*

Detections during the archdeacon of Stow's visitation held at Gainsborough before
John Farmery, LLD, in the presence of Thomas Harrys, notary public   30

cs'
Mr Thomas Lawton for [s] gocinge about with a droome and loude beatinge
the same all or the most of eveninge prayer vppon the Saboth daye beinge
the 4th of Ianuarie to the disturbance of the congregacion [t] that were   35
then in the Church to heare divine service and for beinge absent from all
or the most parte of prayer vltimo Ianuarij Anno domini 1623 in Ecclesia
Cathedralis beate marie Lincolnie loco Consistoriali ibidem Coram
doctore ffarmerie &c [Cv] Citatus fuit dictus Lawton et preconizato non

11, 12/ ⟨...⟩: *35mm missing*

*com*par*uit* s*uspensus* °pub*l*icata fuit suspenc*io* p*redicta* 8ᵘᵒ die ffebruarij
Anno d*omi*ni 1623. p*er* david wierdale.°

d*imittitu*r
Iohn whitacres for the like vlt*imo* Ianuar*ij* 1623 Cit*ato* et p*reconizato* non   5
*com*par*uit* s*uspensus* 2ᵒ Octobris 1624 *com*par*uit* et iurat*us* absol*uitur* [⟨.⟩] et
obiect*o* ar*ticul*o fatet*ur* et se submisit vnde h*abe*t ad agnoscend*um* &c et
cert*ificandum* in p*roximum* postea d*omin*us eu*m* eu*m* cum monic*ione*
dimisit [d⟨..⟩]

                                                                                      10
abijt [in]/.   es'
                  Thomas Birdd for the like vlt*imo* Ianuar*ij* 1623 Cit*ato* et p*reconizato* non
                  *com*par*uit* s*uspensus*

exped*itur*   es'   15
                  Iohn Kelley for the like vlt*imo* Ianuar*ij* 1623 Cit*ato* et p*reconizato* non
                  *com*par*uit* s*uspensus* |

                  es'
                  d*imittitu*r   20
feod*a* solut*a* Iohn Starkie for the like 14ᵗᵒ ffebruar*ij* 1623 quesit*o* et p*reconizato* non
sunt   *com*par*uit* vijs &c in p*roximum* 24ᵗᵒ ffebruar*ij* 1623 ap*u*d Lincoln*iam*
                  citat*o* et p*reconizato* non *com*par*uit* s*uspensus* °20 Ianuarij 1624 cora*m*
                  m*agist*ro Thom*a* Holden cl*er*ico Artiu*m* m*agist*ro Surro*gato* &c p*resent*e me
                  Io*hanne* Buffeild Notario pub*l*ico &c *com*par*uit* personalit*er* d*ict*us Starkie 25
                  et petijt benefic*ium* absoluc*ionis* sibi impendi, tunc d*omin*us ad petic*ionem*
                  d*ict*i Starkie (eodem Starkie p*rius* iurat*o* &c de parendo iuri et stando mandatis
                  Ecclesie) eunde*m* absoluit et restituit &c tunc obiecto ar*ticul*o fatet*ur* eunde*m*
                  *ess*e veru*m* et se submis*it* &c vnde d*omin*us acceptans huiusmod*i* suam
                  confessione*m* iniunxit ei ad agnoscend*um* prout &c et cert*ificandum* in   30
                  p*roximum* postea d*omin*us ad humilem petic*ionem* d*ict*i [certificante] Starkie
                  dimis*it* eu*m* cum monic*ione* q*uod* posthac se diligentius gerat &c/°

                  es'
                  Rober*tus* Hawkin for the like 14ᵗᵒ ffebruar*ij* 1623 quesit*o* et p*reconizato* non 35
                  *com*par*uit* vijs &c in p*roximum* 24ᵗᵒ ffebruar*ij* 1623 citat*o* et p*reconizato* non
                  *com*par*uit* s*uspensus* 9ᵒ Novembris 1624 Cora*m* M*agist*ro Georgio Parker
                  Clerico surro*gato* &c *com*par*uit* et iurat*us* absol*uitur* et obiect*o* ar*ticul*o
                  fatet*ur* that he did see them goe in the streete beatinge a drum but was not
                  w*ith* them vnde d*omin*us cum monic*ione* eu*m* dimisit   40

3/ d*imittitu*r: *corrected over* es'   21/ quesit*o*: q *corrected over* C
8/ eu*m* eu*m*: *dittography*

habitat apud
Londoniam

es'

Edward ffarr for the like 14to ffebruarij Citato et preconizato non comparuit
pena &c in proximum 24to ffebruarij 1623 preconizato non comparuit suspensus

es'

Edward Coggan for the like 14to ffebruarij Citato et preconizato non
comparuit pena &c in proximum 24to ffebruarij 1623 preconizato non
comparuit suspensus

in Hibernia

es'

Iohn Hallifax iunior for the like 14to ffebruarij Citato et preconizato non
comparuit pena &c in proximum 24to ffebruarij 1623 preconizato non
comparuit suspensus

EWERBY

1615

Archdeaconry of Lincoln Visitation Book   LA: Diocesan Vij/15
f 73*

...

dimittitur

Laurence Kighley for keeping diuers fidlers playeng and singing & drincking
in his howse in praier time on the Sabaoth daie after Bartholomew day last
°8o Novembris 1615 citatus extenditur in proximum° °22o Novembris 1615
allegauit Ricardus Kighley eius filius that his father was at church & there
was not anie such disorder vnde facta per eum fide de veritate premissorum
dimittitur°

...

FOSDYKE

1569

Archdeaconry of Lincoln Visitation Book   LA: Diocesan Vij/4
f 62   *(26 May)*

*Presentments made during the visitation of North Holland deanery held in the
parish church of Boston by Robert King, official*

ffosdicke
wigtofte

excommunicatus

dictus Willelmus Loppingtoune est communi(.)er ebrius et diffamato⟨...⟩
religionis suscepte et est histrio et vtitur vocabulis intollerabilibus xvijo die

22/ the Sabaoth ... last: *27 August 1615*   40/ suscepte: *for* suspecte

Septembr*is* 1569. ap*ud* linc*olniam* quesit*us* no*n* ideo vijs et modis vj die
Apr*ilis* 1570/ ap*ud* bostonne citatus no*n* ideo

…

FULSTOW

5

1607/8
Inventory of Thomas Storr, Piper   LA: INV 105/34
single sheet   *(22 January)*

… 10

It*em*: in the chamber two chist*es* & his pipes w*i*th
all other implement*es* their   vj s. viij d.

…

GAINSBOROUGH

15

1587
Exchequer, Special Commission of Inquiry Articles   TNA: PRO E 178/1315
single sheet

20

   Articles to be executed and enquired vpon on the behalf of o*ur* soveraigne
       Ladye the quenes Maiestie by the Comissioners vnder written

Lincoln   1 ffirste wheth*er* do you knowe a pece of grounde com*m*onlye called by the
name of Chappell garthe lyinge and beinge in Gainsburghe in the Countye   25
of Lincoln. And howe longe have you known the same./

2 Item what building*es* are thereon in and vpon the same. or any p*ar*cell
thereof And what are the vttermost boundere and circuyt thereof on eu*er*y
p*ar*te to yo*ur* knowledge. And howe do you know the same/   30

3 Item wheth*er* from the tyme of yo*ur* remembraunce. And by what tyme
before as you have hard was there or hath there bene certen Guyldes ffraternyties
or brotherhod*es* there kepte vsed or mayntayned. And in what sorte were the
same. And what was the manner of theire meeting*es* or vsage of the same./   35

4 Item by what names weere the Cheef p*er*sons of the said ffraternytie or
Brotherhood or the said Guilde called, whether had the Bretheren and
Sisters or those cheef p*er*sons of suche Guilde ffraternitie or Brotherhood
or any of them toward*es* the mayntayning of the same the interest vse   40
proffitt*es* and com*m*odities of the said Chappell garthe./

…

6. Item in what sorte was Masse or other service vsed in thesaid Chappell,
And for what tyme to your knowledge or as you have hard. And whether was
the same onlie at the Assemblyes or meetinges for and concerninge the said
Guilde, or at other tymes./

7. Item whether did the vsinge of the saide Guilde fraternitie or Brotherhood
Chappell and service therein cease to suche purpose and altogether presentlie
at suche tyme as other Chappelles and Chauntries Guildes and ffraternities
&c erected founded and mainteigned for the vse or exercyse of supersticious
service or vse aforesaid did cease and determyn And whether since that tyme
was there ever any other service in the same vse yea or no./
...

Exchequer, Special Commission of Inquiry Depositions
TNA: PRO E 1/8/1313
mb [1]*   (8 October)   (Deposition of Edward Develing of Gainsborough,
   57, sadler)

*Taken at Gainsborough before Peter Evers, Charles Fitzwilliam, and Richard
Smythe, commissioners of the court of the Exchequer*
...
To the first article saith and deposeth that he doth knowe a peece of grownd
in Gainesbrugh in the countie of Lincoln called chappell garth and hath
knowne the same aboute L. yeares

To the second he saith & deposeth that there ys one mansion or dwellinge
howse vppon the same peece of grownd called chappell garth wherein Robert
Dirkson now dwelleth and also one barne late in the occupacion of Thomas
Dobson and the same peece of grownd ys bounded vppon the waie called
Puknall ffee gate towardes the easte and of the river of trente towardes the
west and butteth towardes the north partelie vppon a howse vsed for a fish
howse & partelie vppon a common lane and towardes the south on the hie
waie goinge towardes trente, and this he knoweth to be true for that he was
borne & vpbrought in the towne and that the bownderes were so taken &
reputed when the chappell stoode.

To the third he saith and deposeth that he did knowe L. yeares ago one
guilde called the trinitie guilde mentained by the younge people of the same
towne of Gainesbrough who vsuallie on trinitie sondaie after dinner assembled
them selues together & did ryde or go to Lea a mile distant from Gainesbrough
and there were chosen a Lorde and a Ladie of the same guilde who by the
space of a yeare after were called by that name, and after they were so chosen

they returned to a Chappell then standinge on the said grownde called chappell
garth and there continued vntill toward*es* nighte havinge there breade and
drinck and vsing pastyme & gathering money for the same bread & drincke
whereof the overplus aboue the charge of the said bread and drinck was
imploied towardes the mentenance of the same guilde and of a light called   5
trinitie light mentained in the church of Gainesbrough and of an other
light sometymes sett vpp before the Image of our Ladie called the Ladie of
the chappell in the same chappell. Also he did knowe that at the same tyme
there was a brotherhood or fraternitie of the auncient people of the same towne
called brothers and sisters who mett at the same chappell yearlie vppon corpus   10
cristie daie in the afternoone and there had meat & drinck and gaue money
toward*es* the vses aforesaid w*hich* money was deliuered to certaine p*er*sons
called guild m*aste*rs who were m*aste*rs of both the foresaid companies and he
doth remember that the same guild and brotherhood did continew in mann*er*
aforesaid vntill the beginning of the raigne of kinge Edward the vj^th and   15
after renewed in queene Maries tyme, And he hath hard his father saie that
yt was so vsed in his ffathers tyme.

4   To the fourth he saith and deposeth that the cheif p*er*sons of the said guild
and brotherhood [was] were called the Lord & Ladie and guild m*aste*rs as   20
before he hath deposed in the third art*icl*e. And the same guild m*aste*rs did
yearlie take the proffet*es* of a garden then p*ar*cell of the grownd called chappell
garth toward*es* the vses aforesaid, and oth*er* proffett*es* of the said chappell
garth he never knewe anie.
...   25
To the vj^th he saith and deposeth that he did never knowe masse vsed in the
same chappell, but he doth remember that on trinitie sondaie corpus christi
daie and other festiuall daies there came a processsion from gainesbrough church
to the same chappell and there before the Image called o*ur* Ladie of the chappell
was sunge an himne and so departed and oth*er* service he knoweth none   30

To the vij^th he saith and deposeth that the same guild fraternitie and procession
did cease in the beginning of kinge Edward raigne since w*hich* time saving
in the raigne of quene Marie no service hath beene vsed in the same.
...   35

1606
Bill of Complaint in Hickman v. Willoughby, Tournay, et al
TNA: PRO STAC 8/168/31
sheet 22*   *(30 June)*   40

To the Kinges most excellent Ma*i*estie

Most humbly complayninge s⟨…⟩ vnto your most excellente maiestie your
faithfull loyall and obedient subiect william Hickman of Gainsburgh in the
Countie of Lincoln knight that whereas a most lewde infamous and scandalous
libell was by some lewde persons yet vnknowen to your said subiect of late
synce your Maiesties ^⌐last⌐ free & generall pardon maliciouslie & contemptuosly   5
deuised, contriued, framed, & made in ryme & put in writing tendinge most
vntrulie and vniustlie to rayse & stirre vpp a generall reproch & infamie not
onlie against your said subiect but alsoe against manie other knightes gentlemen
ladies & gentlewomen of good reputacion & credit. And to that wicked ende
& purpose manie copies of the same libell were by the contriuers thereof   10
made, written, cast & scattered abroade & diuulged in diuerse & sundrie
places aswell within the said County of Lincoln as alsoe within the cytie of
London & elsewhere Soe it is most gratious soueraigne that some of these
Copies comminge into the handes of Sir Thomas willughby knight vncle vnto
dame Elizabeth the wife of your said subiect (who in respect of his aliance   15
to your said subiect had receiued many gratuities & freindships at his hands)
he the said Sir Thomas willughbie did not withstandinge such gratuities &
freindshipps so kindely bestowed on him euill requite your said subiect by
scandalizing backbytinge & detracting from him & his good name of sett
purpose to bringe him in hatred with all good men. And albeit your said   20
subiect did in most gentle & freindlie manner admonishe the said Sir Thomas
Willughby thereof, louingly advising him not to degenerate from the noble
house & parentage from whence he is linealie descended puttinge him in
minde what sharpe punishment were like to be inflicted vpon him if he
should be drawen in question for the same by complaint in your highnes   25
honorable court of starre chamber, yet he the said Sir Thomas willughby
nothing regardinge such gentle admonition & friendly advice did about
the moneth of March nowe last past & since your Maiesties ^⌐last⌐ free &
generall pardon most vnlawfullie confederate & combine himself withone
Tristram Turney gentleman & diuerse other euill disposed persons yet vnknowne   30
to your said subiect (whose names togeather with the names of the other lewd
persons before specified when your said subiect can certeinly learne he humble
prayeth to haue leave to insert into this bill) against your said subiect most
wickedly plottinge & deuising howe & in what manner he & they might most
impeche & blemishe aswell the Reputacion & credit of your said subiect &   35
his said ladie ^⌐as⌐ alsoe the reputacion of manie magistrates & persons of
good account. And to that euill ende & purpose he & they did not onely more
& more publish & divulge the libell aforesaid (which they did well knowe
to be most scandalously & falsly contriued raysed & framed) in diuerse &
sundrie publick places but alsoe most vnlawfullie thervnto did adde & insert   40
certaine other most scandalous rimes by them most scandalously & vniustlie
made & written tendinge to rayse greater imputacion aswell vpon your said

subiect ∧⌐and his said wiefe⌐ as also vpon the said other persons of good
account the tenor of so much of the said libell & additions aforesaid as doe
onely concerne your said subiect & his said wife being [⟨..⟩reby] such as
appeareth by a scedule heervnto annexed. But for somuch as the tenor of the
said additions inserted into the said libell is soe vile & scandalous as your said   5
subiect thinketh not fitt to remaine of record hee therefore humblie prayeth
that without preiudice of his cause the reuealinge of such part of the said
libell & additions as are hereunto annexed may be deferred vntill the time
of examinacion of the said offenders vpon interrogatories. The which most
reprochefull addition beinge so as aforesaid inserted & added in & to the said   10
libell formerley made, the said former libell with those addicions were by
the said Sir Thomas willughby & Tristram Turney and other lewde & euill
disposed persons aforesaid to such wicked intent & purpose as is afore said
most lewdly & vnlawfullie published & diuulged in writinge & the same with
a great number of copies by them made & procured to be made were by them   15
caused & procured to be geuen forth to diuerse & sundrie persons scattered
& cast about manie & sundrie publick places within the said citie of london,
counties of Lincoln & Notingam & elsewhere of sett purpose to blemish the
reputacon good name & fame of your said subiect then & yet being one of
your Maiesties Iustices of the peace within the said countie of Lincoln & alsoe   20
to blemish the reputacion good name & fame of diuerse other knights &
gentlemen serving your Maiestie in the like place besides the said ladies and
gentlewomen of good reckoninge & account. And the more to effect such
their wicked drifte & purpose therin the said Sir Thomas willughbye about
the moneth of March aforesaid & since the said generall pardon procured   25
one Leonard Roebuck his horsekeeper or footeboy (a fitt instrument for that
purpose) publickly to singe the said libell & rimes aforesaid or at the least
soe much thereof as tended to the scandalizinge of your said subiect & his said
wife at diuerse & sundrie places within the said Counties of Lincoln Notingam
& else where in the presence of him the said Sir Thomas willughbie and   30
diuerse others And the said Leonard Roebuck being proane to such lewd
exercise did accordinglye not onelie in the open markett of the towne of
Kirton in the said Countie of Lincoln singe the same about the time aforesaid
but alsoe diuulge publish & singe the same to such wicked ende as is aforesaid
in all the seuerall & sundrie places aforesaid & else where all which libell &   35
rimes were made written & copied oute published diuulged & song in forme
aforesaid and the said combinacions & confedracies with all other the
misdeamenors aforesaid comitted & done sithence your Maiesties last generall
pardon. In tender consideracion of all which premisses & for that misdeamenors
of such nature doe tend not onely to rayse sedition among your Maiesties   40

19/ reputacon: *for* reputacion; *abbreviation mark omitted*

subiects to the disturbance of the common peace of this kingdome, but
also to rayse ∧⌜a⌝ great slaunder of persons authorised by your Maiestie to
administer Iustice & are contrarie to your Maiesties lawes & for that the euill
example of the said offendors would tend to the greate encouragement of
manie other lewde persons to comitt offences of the like nature if the said   5
offendors should escape without punishment according to theire deserts in
that behalfe. May it please your most excellent Maiestie to graunt vnto your
said subiect your highnes most gratious writtes of subpena, to be directed
vnto the said Sir Thomas willughby Knight & Trustram Turney ∧⌜Leonard
Roebuck⌝ & the residue of the said lewd persons yet vnknowen commaunding   10
& enioyning euerie one of them therby at a certaine day & vnder a certaine
paine therein prefixed personally to appeare before your highnes honorable
counsell in the starre chamber then & there to stand to & abyde such order
Censure & Iudgment as ∧⌜to⌝ your hyghnes said Counsell of of the same
court shall seeme meete to be therein had & taken. And your said subiect   15
according to his bounden dutie shall daylie praye vnto ∧⌜the⌝ allmightie for
the preseruacion & longe continewance of your Maiesties most prosperous
& hapie raigne

Libellous Ballad in Hickman v. Willoughby, Tournay, et al   20
TNA: PRO STAC 8/168/31
sheet 26*

Sir Hickman of Trent walkes like Iack a lent
He weares a velvet shroud   25
He thought in his vision yat for his religion
He should be taken vp in a Cloud

Sir Hickman of Trent yat hight Iack of Lent
Iettes vp and downe in a velvett shroud   30
A bable is the best toole to bequeath to a foole
He was caught in the Canapie Cloud

A dwarf is no mate for such a cukle headed pate
The knighte would weepe and sweare   35
That the little pretty ape his lady did iape
His house he bad him forbeare

These rimes were shewed to the seuerall deponentes which were examined

14/ of of: *dittography*

on the behalf of *Sir* Willi*a*m Hickman knighte pl*aintiff* against *Sir* Thomas
Willughby Knight and others deff*endantes* at thexecu*cion* aswell of the
ₐ⌜former⌝ Comyssion awarded out of his ma*iesties* moste ho*nora*ble Co*urt*
of starre Chamber betwixt the said p*a*rties (being executed at Gainsburgh in
the weeke after Easter last) as also of this latter Comission being executed at   5
Gainsburgh this *p*resent day 31º Maij 1608
    (signed) George Gylbye

             (signed) Edward North

Answer of Tristram Tourney in Hickman v. Willoughby, Tournay, et al   10
  TNA: PRO STAC 8/168/31
sheet 20   *(July)*
…

…And as to the publishinge and divulginge more and more of the saide libell
annexed vnto the saide Bill To that this defendant saythe That the same longe   15
before this defend*a*nt did ever knowe or heare thereof, having vpon occasion
been longe before in or about the Cittye of London ₐ⌜the same⌝ was verie
famouslie and notoriouslie spredd abroade throughe most p*a*rte of the Countie
of Lincoln In somuche that this defendant com*m*inge into the Countre, and
being att Lincoln assizes, he did theire heare yt publiquelie talked one att   20
most menns tables, and in most mens Companies, wherevpon this defendant
havinge soe often and soe publiquelie hearde the same talked one, and repeated
thinketh that he haith att some tymes vppon occasion of speeches mynistred
in Companyes where hee haith beene thereabout*es*, recyted or repeated either
all or p*a*rte of the saide ₐ⌜libell⌝ not thinkinge that thereby theire Could either   25
more or any slander or discreditt ₐ⌜⟨…⟩⌝ come or growe to the Complaynant
the same beinge before soe Com*m*on and publique in all or most menns
mouthes, especyallie of any noate or place…
…

                                            30

Interrogatories for Tristram Tourney in Hickman v. Willoughby, Tournay,
  et al   TNA: PRO STAC 8/168/31
sheet 17   *(before 10 July)*
…

5.   Item to whome & to how many p*er*sons & at what times & plac*es* & in what   35
    co*m*panyes have you shewed read or rehersed ye said libell & rimes or any
    of them

6.   Item whereas you say in yo*u*r awnswer y*a*t you have somtimes vppon occ*a*sion
    of speches ministred in companies about Lincoln recyted or repeated either   40
    all or p*a*rte of the said libell; whether have you so repeated or recyted all
    thereof or no? And if not all then w*h*ich p*a*rte thereof have you so repeated

or recyted And how much thereof have you or had you in your memory And
how & by what meanes came you to have the same so perfect

...

Examination of Tristram Tournay in Hickman v. Willoughby, Tournay,   5
    et al   TNA: PRO STAC 8/168/31
sheet 13v   *(10 July)*

...

To the vth Interrogatory he sayeth that he hath not att anye tyme shewed or
read the said libell & Rymes or anye of them to anye person or persons But   10
sayeth that he this defendant & [⟨...⟩] Sir Thomas Willoughbye knight beinge
ₐ⌈abowt Easter last past⌉ in Companye together at the howse of the said Sir
Thomas Willoughby & no other Company or persons ₐ⌈being then⌉ present
he the defendant dyd by worde of mouthe as his memorye would serve him
recyte ₐ⌈onlye⌉ vnto the said Sir Thomas the said Libell and Rymes or [ₐ]   15
[⌈or some of the wordes or⌉ the specte therof/.[⟨..⟩].

To the 6 . Interrogatory he sayeth that he ₐ⌈hath⌉ [doth] not so sayed in his
answere as in this Interrogatory ys mencioned. And he sayeth that he hath in
sondry [⟨..⟩] places at sondrye tymes ₐ⌈about & synce Easter last past⌉ recyted   20
vnto sondry persons ₐ⌈to whome or howe many [whome] he remembreth nott)⌉
[some of of] the said libell & Rymes ₐ⌈or the specte thereof as neere⌉ as he
could remembreth, the same libell & Rymes beinge ₐ⌈before oft ₐ⌈tyme⌉ recited⌉
by many others as well as by the defendant by meanes whereof this defendant
came to haue [so ⟨...⟩] ₐ⌈some perfecte⌉ vnderstanding what the said libell &   25
Rymes were. and further to this Interrogatory hee saythe hee Cannott depose.

1608
Interrogatories for Witnesses ex parte Hickman in Hickman v. Willoughby,
    Tournay, et al   TNA: PRO STAC 8/168/31
sheet 6*   *(before 4 April)*   30

...

2. Item whether have yow knowen ₐ⌈heard⌉ or seene the rimes (which are now
    shewed vnto yow) or any of them at any time heretofore said sung rehearsed
    repeated or in any sorte published declared or shewed forth by any person   35
    or persons and by whome & of what and how many persons & how often
    & at what time & places and to whome, & in what & whose presence or
    company have yow so knowen heard or seene the said rimes or any of them
    said sung rehearsed repeated published declared or shewed forth declare the
    whole trueth herein according to your conscyence   40

...

12/ Easter last past: *20 April 1606*   21/ to whome ... nott): *opening parenthesis omitted*

4   Item what skoffing vnseemely disgracefull reprochefull or discontented wordes
doe yow remember yat the said defendantes or eyther of them have spoken
vttered or vsed against the said complainant & the lady his wife or eyther of
them concerning the said rimes or otherwise declare when where how & how
often & in whose presence or company & vppon what occasion ∧⌈& by whome⌉   5
such skoffing vnseemely disgracefull reprochefull or discontented wordes have
been so spoken vttered or vsed

...

7   Item whether did not the said Sir Thomas about ye moneth of March last past
was two yeares at the Complainantes house at Gainsburgh in disgracefull   10
reviling or discontented maner vpbraid the said Complainant with theffect
of some matter or thing which is touched in the said rymes, & how & in
what maner did he the same

8   Item whether have yow knowen or credibly heard that before the said moneth   15
of March last past was 2 yeares the former parte of the said rime was in the
generall libell which was composed against the Complainant and diuers other
knightes & gentlemen in Lincolnshire And whether before the same time
have yow not seene the same generall libell without the latter & more
scandalous parte of the said rymes, & whether doe yow not believe yat the   20
same latter parte was afterwardes inserted or added therevnto And which of
the said rimes was in the said generall libell when yow first sawe the same &
which not Declare the trueth herein

...

14.   Item whether have yow knowen or heard yat the footboy or horsboy of the   25
said Sir Thomas Willughby did at any time heretofore sing say or repeat the
said rimes or any of them in the markett of Kirton or in any other place or
places and whether ∧⌈have you not knowen or heard that the same⌉ was [the
same] so done by the Consent allowance or good lyking of the said Sir Thomas
his master Declare your conscyence herein & when where & how yow have   30
knowen or heard ∧⌈yat⌉ the same ∧⌈was⌉ so sung said or repeated by the said
footboy or horsboy

15.   Item what have yow heard the said defendantes or either of them say or
confesse concerning the partie of whome they or either of them first heard   35
or received, or at any time heard or received the said rimes or any of them
And what vnwillingnes have yow at any time perceived in either of the said
defendantes to reveale or make knowen the same partie And whether have
yow not heard the said defendantes or one of them say & confesse yat they
both iointly together did heare the said rimes of a straunger or another person,   40
or wordes to the like effect? Declare when, where, to whome, & by whome
& in what maner & vppon what occasion such wordes or confession hath
been spoken or vttered

Depositions by Witnesses ex parte Hickman in Hickman v. Willoughby, Tournay, et al   TNA: PRO STAC 8/168/31

sheet 3   *(4 April) (Examination of Edward Southworth, about 40, yeoman, of Fenton, Nottinghamshire)*

5

Taken at Gainsborough before George St Poll, Nicholas Saunderson, George Gilby, and Edward North, commissioners of Star Chamber

...

2   To the Second Inter*rogatory* he saieth he hath seene and hard p*a*rte of the firste twoe menc*i*oned Rymes nowe shewed him, but for the last he saieth he   10 never sawe it written, nor hard it in theise words to his remembrance, neither Can he remember any person by name that hath published or rehearsed the same wholly, but somme one or twoe verses of the two former, by one mr Christopher ffeildinge Clarke and Thomas Dickons in priuate speeche.

...   15

(Examination of Thomas Browneley, 30, of Knaith)

8   To the Eight he saieth that he doth knowe, and hath hard that before the said moneth of march last paste was Tweluemonth the former parte or effect of the two first staves of the said Ryme[s] was in A larger libell *which* he hath   20 seene Composed against the Compl*ainant* and diuers other knightes and gentlemen of Lincolneshire, and for the latter p*a*rte he doth not know it to be inserted at any tyme for that he did never se the same before this *present*.

...

15   To the ffifteenth he saieth that he hath hard S*i*r Thomas willughbye one of   25 the defendantes saie, that Tristram Turner was the first that gaue or shewed the said Rimes vnto him, and that he let him se them at A place called sweete hill, as he taketh it or betwixt it and his house as the said Tristram Turnaie Came vnto him to his said house, And further he saieth he hath seene noe vnwillingnes in neither of the said defend*antes* at any tyme to reveale the   30 Author of the said Rymes, neither doth he know who the Author was, but saieth about whitsontide last meetinge w*i*th Tristram Turnaie at London, and speakeinge w*i*th him about his troubles for the said Rimes he tould him that he firste hard theise Rimes at Lincolne at an Assize time, but of whome he named not vnto me   35

sheet 4*   *(Examination of William Booth, esquire, 26, of Bishop Norton)*
...

2   To the second he saieth that he hath hard all the Rimes now shewed vnto him only repeated by word of mouth, and for the first p*a*rte of them he   40

32/ whitsontide last: *24–30 May 1607*

was tould them by his wiefe aboute so*m*me twoe yeares agon. and for the
second and third he hard them so*m*me twoe monthes after or thereaboutes
repeated by mr Tristram Turnaie in the p*re*sence of Robert wayneman, and
noe other at his house, and that likewise he hard the two latter repeated by
S*ir* Thomas willughby at ffenton in the house of Iohn Thornhaghe Esqu*ie*r   5
in the presence of the said Iohn Thornhagh and the Ladie Thornhagh
his daughter:

...

To the 14. and 15. he saieth that he hard by mr Eustace Bouth (whoe as he
saieth hard the same of mr will*ia*m Gardiner, that one Leonard the horse   10
boy of S*ir* Thomas Willughbies menc*io*ned in the intergatorye did singe or
openly published the said Rimes in the markett of Kirton, and further to
theise intergatories he Cannot depose.

Depositions by Witnesses ex parte Hickman in Hickman v. Willoughby,   15
   Tournay, et al   TNA: PRO STAC 8/168/31
sheet 27*   *(31 May) (Examination of Edward Willoughby, esquire, about
   44, of Barcroft)*

Taken at Gainsborough before George Gilby and Edward North, commissioners   20
of Star Chamber

...

2   To the second Inter*rogatory* he saieth he did once heare theise Rimes read
    by S*ir* Thomas willughbye Knighte defend*ant* w*hi*ch are now shewed vnto
    him as they were A huntinge in Haepam toftes, betweixt them two, and   25
    neu*er* heard them sunge said or otherwise published by any sithence that
    time or before

...

4   To the 4ᵗʰ inter*rogatory* he saieth that he doth not certainely remember
    what scoffinge vnsemely disgracefull reprochfull, or discontented words the   30
    said defend*antes* or either of them haue spoken vttered or vsed against the
    said Compl*ainant*, or the Ladie his wiefe, or either of them saueinge onely
    such repeatinge of the Rimes by the said S*ir* Thomas willughby to this
    examinate as is aforesaid, w*hi*ch rimes seemed vnsemely disgracefull, ∧⌈and⌉
    reprochfull to the Compl*ainant* and the Ladie his wiefe, especially to be   35
    spoken of or vttered by him the said S*ir* Thomas beinge his vncle, ffor this
    examinate vnderstoode the originall and ground of the same reproch to
    be onely vppon the said Compl*ainantes* needefull and fitt mislike of some
    foolishe and Childishe behauiour of A Certaine Dwarfe w*hi*ch behauiour
    was also misliked by the ffather and other ffrends of the said Ladie Hickman   40
    the Compl*ainantes* wiefe

...

sheet 28*   *(Examination of Joseph Godfrey, gentleman, about 30, of Thonock)*

...

2.   To the second Interrogatory he saith he neuer saw theise rimes now shewed
vnto him altogeather before this time, but he hath heard them at seuerall
times rehearsed but neuer svnge or written, but for the first eight lines he   5
doth not remember of whome when or what time he hard them, but for
the latter as he remembreth it was first repeated vnto him by mr Edward
Willughby, but not in such formall manner as in the libell is set downe, And
he saith he had them from Sir Thomas Willvughby who mett him huntinge
in the feilds about Heapom where he repeated them vnto him, And sithence   10
as he remembreth the said Sir Thomas did repeat the same more fullie
then formerly mr Edward Willughby did in his deponentes owne house
none beinge then present but his deponent & his wife & further to this
Interrogatory he cannot depose.

...   15

7.   To the 7. Interrogatory he saith that he well remembreth there was a bitter
fallinge out betwene the Complainant & Sir Thomas Willughby in the
house of the said Complainant some tow or three years past as he taketh
it but in what month he dothe not perfitly remember, wherin after
many reprochfull [speches] and vnfrendly repetitions the said Sir Thomas   20
did seme to affirme yat Sir William Hickmans ill behauior was a cause
of the vntimely death of mr William Willughby the father of the
Complainantes Lady.

...

                                                                                                        25

sheet 29*   *(Examination of Walter Carey, gentleman, 26, of Staple Inn,
   Middlesex)*

...

15.   To the 15th Interrogatory he saith that at the Spittle Sessions in Ianuary
last past the said Tristram Torney tould this examinat & one Luke Martin   30
standinge togeather that he had the said libell & rimes of a gentlewoman
but her name he would not reuaile for he said that by reuaylinge her name
he should but bringe her into trouble & do the Complainant noe good for
she would bringe forth the partie of whome she had it, & that party could
bringe forth another party & so an endles trouble would be occasioned,   35
And this Examinat further sayth that he knoweth that the said Tristram
Turney [wold disclose] haueinge often by his lettres mediacion of friends
& by himselfe in person sewed to the Complainant for his fauor touchinge
his sute, the Complainant hath offered him kindnes so as the said Tristram
Torney wold disclose of whome he had the said libell & rimes which to   40
doe the said Turney hath often in this Examinates hereinge refused to doe,

Affirminge that he would rather abide the extremity of the said suite, And
more he sayeth not to this Interro*gatory*.

...

GRAINTHORPE

1609
Archdeaconry of Lincoln Visitation Book   LA: Diocesan Vij/12
pp 237–8   *(5 May)*

*Presentments made during the visitation of Louthesk and Ludborough deaneries
held in the parish church at Louth, by Otwell Hill, LLD*

...

di*mittitur*   Roberte Hagge our minister for not spendinge his time in the weeke dayes
at his studdie 7 houres of the daie accordinge to the 5th article °7. Maij.
1609. cora*m* m*agis*tro Roberto houghton ∧⌈et⌉ comp*aruit* & obiecto ar*ticu*lo
fatet*ur* & *cum* monici*one* di*mittitu*r° |

di*mittitur*   Mr hagge for singinge ribauld songes vpon the Sabathe daie before prayer and
other times and for vsinge vnreverend and vnseemlie speeches not befittinge
anie man, mutche lesse a minister °7 Maij 1609. vt sup*ra*.°

...

GRANTHAM

1608
Constables' Presentment   LA: Grantham Borough QS 7/2/3/15
f [1]   *(17 December)*

...

17.º die Decembris 1608./
com*paruit* exoneratur.

Thomas Mills   Manucep*er*unt *pro* Edwardo Chapman de Harson Com*itatu* Leic*estrie* Piper
⌈v li.⌉   et p*redic*tu*s* Edwa*rd*us manucep*er*it *pro* seipso in xi li. vi*delicet* qu*od* p*redic*tus
Arthur*us* Tilson   Edw*ard*us Comp*ar*abit Cor*am* Iusticiarijs d*ic*ti dom*i*ni Regis ap*u*d Granth*am*
⌈v li.⌉   p*redic*tam ad p*ro*ximas gene*r*ales sessio*n*es pacis, ac Inter*i*m geret pacem d*ic*ti
                dom*i*ni Regis u*er*sus Cunct*um* populu*m* suu*m* sed p*re*cipue arga Constabular*ios*
Vacat   et al*ios* officiar*ios* ville De granth*am* Quod si in premiss*is* p*redic*tus Edw*ard*us
                defe*cerit*, qu*od* tunnc &c. Capt*a* die &c. An*n*o sup*r*ad*ic*tis Cor*am* Ioha*n*ne
                Hasberd gen*eroso* Alderm*ano* ville et soc*ijs* predictis./

...

32/ Harson: *Harston, Leicestershire*

1618
Episcopal Visitation Book   LA: Diocesan Vj/24
f 57v*   *(24 or 29 July)*

Presentments made during the visitations of Loveden deanery, held in the parish   5
of Sleaford, and Grantham deanery, held in the parish church of Grantham,
by Christopher Wyvell, LLD, vicar general and official principal of the bishop of
Lincoln, and Thomas Raymond, STB, commissary, in the presence of John Pregion,
registrar, and John Buffeild, notary public and deputy registrar

...   10

vide Sidebrook.   Anthonius Wetherill de Sidebrooke *presented* ffor that he vpon the xixth
day of Iulye last being the Saboath day did come from his owne parish to
the parish of Grantham, and their did prophaine the Saboath by pipeinge,
and therbie drew diuerse people together to daunceinge, and others to looke
on them betwixte morninge and eveninge prayer. °8o oct*obris* 1618 cit*ato*   15
&c no*n* comparui*t* reser*uatu*r in proximum° °22o oct*obris* preconiz*ato* &c
no*n* co*mparui*t suspendatu*r* e'°

...

1633   20
Corporation Minute Book   LA: Grantham Borough 5/1
f 2   *(October)*

...

®The Townes   At this Courte, Richard Sentons, Thomas Seemly, [and] Peter Leacock and
Musitians   William Stubes, desiered [desiered] to bee admitted and continued for one   25
Retained   wholl yeare from the daye of the date of this Court to bee the Common
musitians of this Borough, wherevppon their tender of service is generally
by this Court accepted, and, they the said Musitians haue now in open
Court Ioyntly & seuerally bound them selues, for their auncyent and
accustomed Sallary, and by the receipt of twelue pence now given vnto them   30
by M*aste*r Alderman, to performe their wonted & accustomed service for
the terme aforesaid

...

1634   35
Corporation Minute Book   LA: Grantham Borough 5/1
f 13v   *(31 October)*

...

At this Court Came in, Richard Sentons, Thomas Seemely and William
Stubbes, the Townes waytes, and desiered to be Continued in their places   40
vppon their auncyent and wonted sallary for [th] one wholle yeare next
ensuinge, which service, they did Ioyntly and seuerally faithfully ˄⌈promisse⌉
to performe & according to accustomed Manner, Wherevppon they were

retayned, by M*aste*r Ald*er*man in open Court, by givinge vnto them xij d. a
peece, &

1635

Corporation Minute Book   LA: Grantham Borough 5/1   '5
f 27   *(30 October)*

…

The Townes
waites hired
for a yeare

At this Court came in Richard Sentons, Thomas Seemely, William Knewstubbs
and Peter Leacock, the Townes waytes and desiered to bee Continued in their
said places, vppon their usuall and accustomed Reward*es* for one wholl yeare 10
next ensuinge, W*hi*ch service they did Ioyntly and seuerally p*ro*misse to
perfourme accordinge to the accustomed manner of the Townes waytes
Wherevppon they are now retayned by M*aste*r Alderman for one wholl yeare
next ensuinge, by givinge them xij d. a peece in open Court./

…   15

1636

Corporation Minute Book   LA: Grantham Borough 5/1
f 43v   *(27 October)*

…   20

The Townes
waites hired
for a yeare/

At this Court came in Richard Sentons Willi*a*m Knewstubs and Peter Leacock
and desiered to bee Continued the Townes Waytes for this yeare to come
wherevnto this Court doth assent, and M*aste*r Alderman did give vnto them
xij d. a peece vppon receipt whereof they haue seuerally bound them selues
to serve the Towne as their waytes for this yeare to come   25

Will of Thomas Seemly, Musician   LA: LCC WILLS 1636
f 118   *(25 May; proved 7 July)*

In the name of God Amen the fyue and twentie day of May Anno d*om*ni   30
1636 I Thomas Seemly of Grantham w*i*thin the Diocesse of Lincoln Musition
being sick in body but whoole in mynde and in good and p*er*fect remembraunc*e*
praise and thanks be to Almightie God, doe make constitute & ordaine this
my last will & Testament in manner and forme following: … It*e*m I giue
and bequeath unto my sonne Thomas Seemely all & everie my instruments 35
of Musique w*i*th all the song bookes belonging to them and for that use:…

…

Inventory of Thomas Seemly, Musician   LA: INV 144/85
single mb*   *(22 June) (In the hall)*   40

…

It*e*m certaine Instruments of Musique and Musicall Books   xxiiij s.

…

1637

Corporation Minute Book   LA: Grantham Borough 5/1
f 53v   *(27 October)*

…

At this Court came in Richard Sentons, William Knewstubs & Peter Leacock   5
& brought with the servant of the said Knewstubs a Musitian & & desiered
to bee Continued the Townes Waytes for this yeare to come Wherevnto
M*aste*r Alderman & this Court doth assent, And M*aste*r Alderman did give
vnto them, xij d. a peece, whereby they haue seuerally bound themselues to
serve the Towne as their waytes for this yeare to Come./   10

1638

Corporation Minute Book   LA: Grantham Borough 5/1
f 68   *(2 November)*

…   15

The townes   At this Court came in Richard Sentons William Knewstubs, Peter Leacock
waytes hyred   and *(blank)* late servant to the said William Knewstubs and desiered to be
· continued the Townes waytes for this yeare to come wherevnto this Court
assented and ⌐they⌐ are retayned and hired now in open Court by xij d. a
peece p*ai*d and deliuered vnto them by the Chamberlins   20

1639

Corporation Minute Book   LA: Grantham Borough 5/1
f 80v   *(31 October)*

…   25

Att this Courte came in Richard Sentance Willia*m* Knewstubbs & Peeter
Laicocke & desired to be continued the townes Waytes for this yeare to come
wherevnto this |⟨.⟩| Courte doth assente & m*aste*r Alderman did give vnto
them xij d. a peece vppon receipt whereof they haue seuerallie bounde
themselues to serve the towne for theire waites for this yeare to come./   30
Willia*m* Knewstubbs did likewise deliuer in this Court a liverie Coate and
Cullisence w*hi*ch was deliuered to the Chamberline to be kept tell ytt was
other wayes ordered.

…

35

1641

Corporation Minute Book   LA: Grantham Borough 5/1
f 96v   *(21 October)*

…

The townes   Att this Courte Came in Richard Sentance & three other straungers w*i*th   40
Waytes hired   him (viz.) Michaell Walker, Iohn Allett & Edward Allitte and desired they

6/ & &c: *dittography*

mighte bee admitted to be the townes Waytes for this yeare to Come which this Courte considering of, they were in this Courte openlie retained & hired by xij d. a peece payed & delivered vnto them by *master* Alderman./

...

f 99   *(18 November)*

...

⟨..⟩e musi*c*ions formerlie ⟨..⟩red now again discharged

The musi*c*ions formerlie hired refussing to receaue the liveries as the chamberlines doe affirme [as] ∧⌈are⌉ this Courte againe dismised and to haue theire ij quarters wages for this Winter half yeare

...

1642
Corporation Minute Book   LA: Grantham Borough 5/1
f 102v   *(22 July)*

...

Willia*m* Knewstubbs & Georg Reade made free

Att this Courte Came Willia*m* Knewstubs a mussicione & George Reade a Couper both being Strangers & brought in ten poundes a peece which they tendred for theire freedomes according to order and Auntiente Custome of this Borough And in regard they were poore men & like to p*r*ove good townes men, nor like to hurte anie freemen being [*w*ithin this] of theire trades *w*ithin this borough This Courte was willing & did agree that they should paye butt five poundes a peece and the rest to be given them back againe of theire tenn poundes a peece w*h*ich was then paid to the Chamberlines And therevppon they being desirous to be in corporated & made ffree, this Courte Assente wherevppon they tooke theire severall oathes of allegiance, were sworne free Burgesses And paid theire due fees to the Clerke & Sergeants./

...

f 107v*   *(28 October)*

...

The townes waits hired./

Att this Courte Came in Richard Sentance & William Knewstubbs *w*ith twoe of the servants of the said Knewstubbs musicians & desired to be the townes waites for this yeare to Come wherevnto *master* Alderman & this Courte doth assente And *master* Alderman by the Chamberlins did give vnto them xij d. a peece And soe the said Sentance & Knowstubbs haue severallie bounde them selves to serve the towne as theire waytes for this yeare to come./

...

9/ ⌈are⌉: *for* ⌈are by⌉ *(?)*
26/ Assente: *for* Assented *(?)*

5

10

15

20

25

30

35

GREAT HALE

1608
Archdeaconry of Lincoln Visitation Book   LA: Diocesan Vij/11
f 28v*   *(17 February 1607/8 or 22 April 1608)*   5

Presentments made during the visitations of Aveland deanery held in the parish
church of Ancaster by George Eland, cleric, BA, canon residentiary of Lincoln
Cathedral and surrogate judge of Thomas Randes, MA, commissary and official of
the archdeacon of Lincoln, and of Lafford deanery held in the parish church of   10
Sleaford by William Dalby, MA, cleric and surrogate judge of Thomas Randes

...

Georgius Allen
Georg*ius* Tebbatt
for suffering the churchyard to be prophaned by diu*ers* p*er*sons y*at* baited   15
a bull therin & for omitting to p*re*sente the said p*ar*ties. °22. Mar*cij* 1607.
comp*ar*uerunt et obic*c*to a*rticu*lo Tebbat negat that hee sawe the batinge of
the sayd Bull but heard that [the w] there was such p*ro*phanac*i*on vnde h*abet*
ad p*re*sentand*um* delinquen*tes* &c et sic d*imittitu*r Allen s*i*m*ili*t*er* comp*ar*uit
et fass*us* est that he was p*re*sente at the sayd bullbaytinge & did not goe about   20
to hinder the same vnde d*ominus* monuit eu*m* ad p*re*sentand*um* h*uius*mod*i*
delinquen*tes* &c et ad agnoscend*um* crimen cora*m* mi*n*istro et sex vel
plurib*us* inh*a*bitan*tib*us ibide*m* et cer*tificandum* in p*ro*ximum monit*us* &c°
°29 Oc*tob*ris 1608 cit*atus* Allen comp*ar*u*i*t sed non cer*tificavi*t vnde d*omin*us
continuav*i*t cer*tifi*ca*rium* in p*ro*xim*um* [man]/.°   25

f 29
...

chr*is*toferius Lawson of Sleaford for bringing a bull into ye churchyard of Hale
to be baited w*ith* dogg*es* [ye] & braught dogg*es* w*ith* him for y*at* purpose.   30

1634
Abstract of Sir Nathanael Brent's Metropolitical Visitation
  TNA: PRO SP 16/274
ff [1v–2]* *(20 August)*   35
...

The warden and his brethren very kind. In Halle, al*ias* | Hole there is no
chancel, nor hath been these 60 years plus minus. ˄⌜See the petition⌝ The
imp*ro*priation is ye inheritance of one mr R*o*bert Cawdron esq*uier* and is
worth 200 li. p*er* an*num* The businesse of ye May ladie, & of ye clandestine   40
mariage of mr Fitzwilli*a*ms and m*is*tris Creswel, who were maried by a
fire side, being licensed to be maried in facie ecclesiæ, is referred to m*aste*r

Doctor Farmerie, because there was no time to cal ye parties, and examine al circumstances.

...

GRIMSBY

1396–7
Chamberlains' Accounts   NELA: 1/600/5/1
mb 1*

...

...Et in panno pro vestura walteri wayte. iiij s. x d. Et in Ocreis eiusdem walteri. ij s....

...

1424–5
Chamberlains' Accounts   NELA: 1/600/12
single mb dorse   *(9 October–9 October)*

...

Item solutum pro toga walteri waite histrionis ville   vj s. iiij d.

...

1430–1
Borough Court Roll   NELA: 1/101/5/10
single sheet*   *(3 September)*

...

℃ Curia tenta ibidem die [sabbati primo] ⌜lune tercio⌝ die Septembris anno [vt supra] regni regis Henrici sexti xmo

℃ Iohannes de Rasyn queritur de Hans Speryng de placito transgressionis plegium de prosequendo walterus whayte ⌜quesiuit & vterque pars parat⌝ de eo quod vbi concordatum fuit inter eosdem quod ei deliberaret certa instrumenta ⌄⌜joci⌝ vocati Ioly walte and Malkyng die vltimo elapso, & dictus defendens se elongauit dicto die & die sequenti ad diminucionem viij d. et defendens dedicit quod nihil ei fecit transgressionis prout &c. & hoc petit quod inquiratur

...

1441–2
Chamberlains' Accounts   NELA: 1/600/13
mb 1*   *(9 October–9 October)*   *(Wages and fees)*

...

Item solutis pro vestura eiusdem Henrici & walteri wayte per concensum comunitatis xj s. v d....

...

1468–9
Chamberlains' Accounts   NELA: 1/600/16
mb 1d*   *(25 October–15 September)* *(Payments and expenses)*

...

...Et de viij d. solut*is* Maiori p*ro* M*i*nistrall*is* do*mi*ni de Stanley Et de xx d.   5
solut*is* Maiori p*ro* diu*er*sis alijs ministrallis...

...

1499–1500
Chamberlains' Accounts   NELA: 1/600/19   10
mb 1d*   *(8 October–8 October)*

...

De xl d. dat*is* Ministrall*is* princip*is* duc*is* lee bukkyngam et Comit*is*
Northhumbrelandie It*em* diu*er*sis Ministall*is* in die s*an*cti Bartholo*m*ei
ap*os*t*o*li iiij d.... De viij d. dat*is* cuidam lee berward De v d. ob. dat*is*   15
ho*m*i*n*ib*us* de ⟨..⟩itney qui equita*n*t ludum suu*m*...

...

1507–8
Mayor's Court Book   NELA: 1/102/2   20
f 3v*   *(13 January)*

...

Ordinac*io*   ⟨ Ordinat*um* es*t* ad eand*em* Curi*am* p*er* Maiore*m* et tota Co*m*munitat*em*
burgens*ium* i*n* co*mmun*i aula ib*i*d*em* q*u*od le Maryners de Grymesby faci*ant*
unu*m* naue*m* stant*em* in ecclesia b*eat*e marie pertinent*em* lumi*n*e aratri et   25
q*u*od om*ne*s Burgenses eiusd*em* ville soluant p*re*fat*is* le Maryners ad faciend*um*
p*re*di*c*t*um* naue*m* infra spaciu*m* vn*ius* anni xx s.

...

1514–15   30
Chamberlains' Accounts   NELA: 1/600/21
single mb*   *(10 October–10 October)*

...

...Et D*e* xij d. solut*is* le Mynst*er*yls d*e* hull p*er* prec*e*pt*um* Maior*is* Et D*e*
iij s. solut*is* le Mynst*er*yls do*m*ini Darcy ... Et D*e* xvj d. solut*is* Edwar*d*o   35
lytster bereward in reward*o* p*er* precept*um* Maior*is* ... Et D*e* xx d. solut*is*
le Grymelby play p*er* precept*um* Maior*is* Et D*e* ⟨...⟩ solut*is* p*er* precept*um*
di*c*ti Maior*is* ad le Stalingburgh play

...

16/ ludu*m* suu*m*: *for* ludo suo (?)   25/ lumi*n*e: *for* lumini
23/ tota: *for* totam

1515–16
Chamberlains' Accounts   NELA: 1/600/22
mb 1*   *(9 October–9 October) (Payments and expenses)*
…

…De xl d. soluti*s* le Mynst*eryls* do*mini* Darcy *per* precept*um* Maior*is* … Et   5
De ij s. soluti*s* le players de M*a*rschappell *per* precept*um* Maior*is*…
…

1526–7
Mayor's Court Book   NELA: 1/102/2   10
f 6*   *(18 June)*
…

M*e*moran*dum* hordenyt for to prepare for the play of holy Iohn of bowre

     Imp*r*imis   Mr peter Mason   15
                  Mighell Mason
                  Ric*hard* Emp*e*ryngham
                  Thomas chalonner
                  Willi*a*m bedforth
                  Ric*hard* Mudy   20

1546–7
Court Leet Books   NELA: 1/108
f 3   *(14 October)*

                                                                    25

bulls to be   Allso it is panyd that no bowcher schall not kyll no bowlls except thay be
batyd   oppenly batyd Afor Master Mayre & his brethern in payn of vj s. viij d. if
ony bovcher sell his bowll flesh wi*th*in this lib*er*ties vnbattyd And that
theyr be no licens gyven contrary the Co*mm*own ordynans in payne of vj s.
viij d. for eu*er*y offens to be levyd of hym y*at* gyvys lycens contrary the   30
Co*mm*own ordynans &c
…

Court Leet Books   NELA: 1/108
f 2   *(19 April)*   35
…

°bochers°   Allso it is panyd that no bowcher schalnot kyl no buls except thay be
openly batyd afor M*aste*r Mayre & his bretherne in payn of vj s. viij d. for
eu*er*y fawllt acordyng to the co*mm*own ordynans & that theyr be no licens
gyffen contrary the co*mm*own ordinans in the payn of hym that gyff*es*   40
lycens to pay oy*er* vj s. viij d. the on half to the balyeis & the other half to
the town chamber
…

1547–8
Court Leet Books   NELA: 1/108
f 2   *(October)*

…

bovchers   Allso it is panyd that no bovcher schalnot kyll no bovylls except thay be   5
oppenly battyd afor Master Mayre in payn of vj s. viij d. Acordyng to the
comovn ordynans the same payne to be lefyd & whosoeuer gyffes licens
contrarye the commovn ordynans to occure in lyk payn vj s. viij d.

…
                                                                                                    10
f 3

…

Allso it is panyd that no boucher schallnot kyll no bulls except thay be batyd
oppenly afor Master Maire & his brethern in payn of vj s. viij d. for euery
favllt the on half to the balyeis & the oyer half to the town chamber And   15
that Master Mayre schalnot licens contrary this comown ordynans

…

1550–1
Chamberlains' Accounts   NELA: 1/600/27   20
single sheet*   *(28 January–27 January)*

…

…Item v s. payd to the kynges maiestie players…

…
                                                                                                    25
1555–6
Court Leet Books   NELA: 1/108
f 2   *(April)*

…

bulls to be   Allso it is panyd that no bovcher schallnot kyll no bowlls except thay be   30
battyd   openly battyd afor Master Mayre & his brether in payn of vj s. viij d. &
that theyr be no licens gyven contrary the commovn ordinans payn of other
vj s. viij d. to hym yat offendes

…
                                                                                                    35
1556–7
Court Leet Books   NELA: 1/108
f 2B   *(13 October)*

…

buls to be   Allso it is panyd that no bovcher schalnot kyll no bovlls except thay be   40
batyd   oppenly batyd afor Master Mayre & his brether in payne of vj s. viij d. &
he that gyveth lycens contrary to forfeit oyer vj s. viij d.

…

Court Leet Books   NELA: 1/108
f 2C   *(27 April)*

...

Allso it is panyd that no bowcher schall kyll no bulls except thay be openly
batyd Afor Master Mayre and his brether in payn of vj s. viij d. And that   5
theyr be no lycens gyven to the contrary in payn of vj s. viij d.

...

1558–9
Chamberlains' Accounts   NELA: 1/600/31   10
single mb   *(29 September–29 September)*

...

...v s. to a barwarde ... ij s. vj d. p*ai*d at a beyr battyng...

...

                                                                                15
1559–60
Chamberlains' Accounts   NELA: 1/600/33/2
single mb   *(29 September–29 September)*

...

...iij s. iiij d. paid to a berwarde/ ... iiij s. vj d. to the quenes plaer*es*/ vj s.   20
viij d. to a berwod/...

...

1560–1
Chamberlains' Accounts   NELA: 1/600/33/1   25
single sheet   *(29 September–29 September)*

...

...de iiij s. sol*utis* vrsario voc*ato* a berword ... de iiij s. iiij d. *solutis*
ludit*oribus* Regi*ne* voc*atis* ye quenes plaer*es*/...

...   30

1562–3
Chamberlains' Accounts   NELA: 1/600/34
mb 3*   *(29 September–29 September)*

...   35
...*De* x s. solut*is* [vr] custod' vrsoru*m* ... *De* vij s. iiij d. solut*is* lusorib*us*/ ...
De xij s. solut*is* ludit*ori*b*us* do*mi*ni ffit⟨...⟩ *De* vij s. iiij d. solut*is* ludit*oribus*
in marisco ... *De* vj s. viij d. solut*is* ludit*or*⟨...⟩ do*mi*ni de warwike *De* vj s.
viij d. solut*is* custod' vrsoru*m* in die s*an*cti bertholimei/ *De* iij s. iiij d. solut*is*
duob*us* custod*ibus* [vr] vrsorum p⟨.⟩st p*re*dic*tam* diem ... *De* iij s. iiij d. solut*is* 40
custod' vrsoru*m* in marisco...

...

1563–4
Chamberlains' Accounts   NELA: 1/600/34
mb 2   *(29 September–29 September)*

…

…Item solut*is* lusoribus ij s. ij d…. It*em* solut*is* lusoribus iiij s. iij d. It*em*   5
solut*is* aliis lusoribus iiij s. ij d. It*em* solut*is* Alijs lusoribus viij d…. Item p*ro*
expens*is* circa ludum viij d…. It*em* solut*is* lusoribus Regine iiij s. iiij d.

…

1565–6   10
Chamberlains' Accounts   NELA: 1/600/35
single mb dorse   *(29 September–29 September)*

…

…⟨…⟩ vj s. solut*is* custod' vrsor*um* … de iiij d. solut*is* m*a*rtino fotherbie
p*ro* denar*iis* p*er* ips*um* solut*is* Lusorib*us* in absencia maioris…   15

…

Court Leet Books   NELA: 1/108
f 3   *(9 October)*

…   20

for batyng of
bulles

Also that no man*er* of buccher shall kell anye bull ether
in this Towne or in the Contre to sell the beyfe of the
same in this ∧⌐towne⌐ or Markett before he haith ∧⌐bene⌐
betted in this said brough accordyng to the Custome
before m*aste*r Maior and his bretharne [or li] In payne of   25
ev*er*y Defaulte   vj s. viij d.

…

1566–7
Chamberlains' Accounts   NELA: 1/600/37   30
single sheet   *(29 September–29 September)*

…

…de xxv s. x d. solut*is* Lusoribus…

1568–9   35
Chamberlains' Accounts   NELA: 1/600/38
single mb dorse   *(29 September–29 September)*

…

…⟨…⟩ custod' vrsor*um*/…

…   40

25/ and: *corrected from* or *(?)*   39/ ⟨…⟩: *20mm illegible text*

1569–70
Chamberlains' Accounts   NELA: 1/600/39
single sheet verso   *(29 September–29 September)*
...
...De xiij s. solut*is* lusoribus...   5
...

1570–1
Chamberlains' Accounts   NELA: 1/600/30/3
single mb dorse   *(29 September–29 September)*   10
...
...⟨.⟩s. iiij d. solut*is* Lusoribus prout patet ⟨...⟩...
...

1571–2   15
Chamberlains' Accounts   NELA: 1/601/1
f 1*   *(29 September–29 September)* *(Receipts)*
...
Item rec*eived* of m*aste*r maior when the lord of Lecester
plaiers were here   v d.   20
...

f 2v*   *(Expenses)*
...
[It*em* paid to plaiers of Kirton in Lyndesey on   25
childermas daie   xxij d.]
...
[It*em* paid to plaiers the fridaie next after fastens to
my Lord mountioye men   v s.]
...   30
It*em* paid to the Bullward the xxvj of Marche at
m*aste*r maiors comaundem*en*t   xij d.
...

f 3*   35
...
[It*em* to the queenes plaiers the x of Iune   x s. iij ⟨.⟩]
...

28/ the fridaie ... fastens: *21 February 1571/2*

f 3v*

…

[Item to the bearwardes of Louthe the iij of August   viij d.
Item to the plaiers of my lord of Lecester the vj
of august   x s.]   5

…

1572
Mariners' Guild Book   NELA: 261/1
f xlv   10

…

which orders nowe made ⌈is⌉ that no maryner or other persone that hathe any
parte or porcion of the stock belonging to this company and dwelling within
this towne shall absent them selves from the Sommons or comaundement
of the aldermen [or hu] by the husbondes to be gyven [to] before them to or   15
for any cause or matter touching this [or] company or from the meting and
attendance of the same Aldermen and husbondes at the audite and supper on
plowghe night euery yere to forfeit xij d.

1572–3   20
Chamberlains' Accounts   NELA: 1/600/41
f 1v   *(29 September–29 September)*

…De xvij s. viij d. solutis custod' vrsorum de vij s. iiij d. solutis Lusoribus…
…   25

1573–4
Chamberlains' Accounts   NELA: 1/600/42
single sheet   *(29 September–29 September)*
…   30
…De xv s. ij d. solutis costod' vrsorum et lusoribus…
…

1574–5
Chamberlains' Accounts   NELA: 1/600/44   35
single mb dorse   *(29 September–29 September)*
…
…De ix s. solutis lusoribus De ⟨…⟩ lusorib⟨…⟩
…

31/ lusoribus: *4 minims for second* u

1575–6
Chamberlains' Accounts   NELA: 1/600/36
single mb dorse*   *(29 September–29 September)*

...

...De v s. solut*is* Lusorib*us* d*omi*ni Stafford De iij s. solut*is* lusorib*us* Ioh*ann*is   5
Constab*u*li Militar*is* ... De iij s. viij d. solut*is* lusorib*us* Comit*is* Worcest⟨...⟩...

...

1576–7
Chamberlains' Accounts   NELA: 1/600/43   10
single sheet dorse*   *(29 September–29 September)*

...

...De iij s. iiij d. solut*is* wath et socijs lusorib*us* ... De xij d. solut*is* lusorib*us*
xxvij° Maij ... De vj s. viij d. solut*is* Lusorib*us* de Boston....

...   15

1577–8
Chamberlains' Accounts   NELA: 1/600/32
single mb*

                                                                       20
Et solut*is* lusorib*us* iiij d.... solut*is* lusorib*us* vj s. viij d.... solut*is* lusorib*us*
magistro saintpoole xx d....

...

Mariners' Guild Book   NELA: 261/1   25
f C10v*   *(Reckoned 7 January 1578/9)   (Receipts)*

...

It*em* rec*eived* that was gethered by the yonge men   viij s.

...

                                                                       30

1579–80
Chamberlains' Accounts   NELA: 1/600/45
single mb   *(29 September–29 September)*

...

...De xvj s. ix d. solut*is* diu*ersis* lusoribus et custodit*oribus* vrsor*um*...   35

...

Mariners' Guild Book   NELA: 261/1
f C15*   *(Audited 11 January 1580/1)   (Receipts)*

...   40

It*em* rec*eived* of ploughe daye   xxij s. ob.

...

41/ ploughe daye: *11 January 1579/80*

all charges deducted about pales, and reparinge
the ploughe shippe with other ordinarie charges
there remaineth   [xxij s. xviij s.] xx s.

...
                                                                                          5

f C15v*

...

Item what master that is absent at the settinge for of the ploughe ship vppon
ploughe daye shall forfeite ij s. vj d. everie Avner iij s. iiij d. everie marriner
xij d. and everie master that shalbe absent from supper or that payth not for   10
his supper at the Audit shall paie ij s. euery Avner ij s. vj d. euery marriner
xij d. Item euery one that belongith to this [⟨...⟩] ⌈companie⌉ for his absence
shall paye for the like offence xij d.

                    money to receive dewe at this Audit

Inprimis of mr Richard Cooke for beinge absent   15
of ploughe daie   xij d.

...

1580–1
Chamberlains' Accounts   NELA: 1/600/46   20
single mb   *(29 September–29 September)*

...

De xv s. solutis Diuersis lusoribus et custoditoribus vrsorum...

...
                                                                                          25

Mariners' Guild Book   NELA: 261/1
f C18*   *(Reckoned 10 January 1581/2)* *(Receipts)*

...

Item for ⌈money⌉ [⟨...⟩] receyved of ploughe monday   xvj s. xj d.
...
                                                                                          30

f C18v*

...

All chardges allowed for pailes & wheles to the
plowghe shippe & other ordinarye chardges   35
their remayneth   xxv s.

...

16/ ploughe daie: *11 January 1579/80*
29/ ploughe monday: *9 January 1580/1*

1581–2
Mariners' Guild Book   NELA: 261/1
f B2*   *(Audited 7 January 1582/3) (Receipts)*
…

viij s. xj d.   It*em* for money gathered on plowghe daye   viij. s. xj d.   5
…

(Payments)
to the porters   vj d.
to the Dromm*er* & pyper   xiiij d.   10
…

1582–3
Chamberlains' Accounts   NELA: 1/600/47
single mb   *(29 September–29 September)*   15
…
…De xxxij s. iiij d. solut*is* diu*er*sis lusoribus…
…

1583–4   20
Mariners' Guild Book   NELA: 261/1
f B10*   *(Reckoned 7 January 1584/5)*
…

The fynes assessed of them who were absent att supp*er* on plowe munday
accordynge to the auncyent Custome att this Audytte   25

Abraham bearte   xij d.
Mathewe browne   xij d.

1584–5   30
Chamberlains' Accounts   NELA: 1/600/48
single mb*   *(29 September–29 September)*
…
…De iij s. iiij d. solut*is* lusor*ibus* dom*i*ni willughbie p*er* mandat*um* maioris…
…   35

Mariners' Guild Book   NELA: 261/1
f B14v*   *(Audited 10 January 1585/6) (Receipts)*
…
It*em* money gathered on plowe day   x s. xj d.   40
…

5/ plowghe daye: *8 January 1581/2*   40/ plowe day: *11 January 1584/5*
24/ plowe munday: *13 January 1583/4*

(Disbursements)
to the pyp*er* & Drumm*er*   xiiij d.
to ye porters   viij d.
...

5

f B15

Item of Richard Cowp*er* for beinge absent att the settinge
furthe of the ploweshipe & att Supp*er*   iiij s. vj d.
[Item of Chr*is*tofer Roggers for beinge absent att]   10
[Item of Thomas beneworth for beinge [⟨.⟩] absent frome
supp*er* on ploweday att   xij d.
Item of Iohn scarlbie for the like   xij d.]

1585–6   15
Mariners' Guild Book   NELA: 261/1
f B19v*   *(Reckoned 9 January 1586/7)* *(Receipts)*
...
Item receyved & gathered of plowe day   x s.
...   20

1601–2
Letter of James VI of Scotland to James Hudson   TNA: PRO SP 52/68
f [1]*   *(7 July)*

25

Trusty S*er*uitor we greit you hertlie wele/ It being meanit to ws on the behalff
of one Iohnne Henslay englische merchant in grumsbie in lincolmschyre
that about witsonday last he resorting to the sicht of a play/ efter sum wordis
past betwixt him and Nicolas blinstoun his compane3wun he being struckin
be him to the ground/ and hurt in the heid to the great effusioun of his   30
bluid and vponn the morne thairefter lykeuise Iniurit and struckin be the
same nicolas In the tyme of his marcatt/ It fell out accidentlie in his awne
defence that he struck this nicolas in the thie/ and that he happy*n*nit to die
of ye same strok q*ui*lk be his awne vnhappynes he procurit/ At q*ui*lk tyme
this henslay is fader in law chanceing onlie to be pr*es*ent/ he is trubld aswele   35
as him selff for the deid/ Sua that gif this report be trew thair cais is to be
lamented/ And seing we are movit be thair frend*es* heir to be a suittar for
yair lyffes/ We haue tho*ught* guid to desire 3*o*u to try thair report/ and gif
3e find it of treuth To Interceid at ye handis of sic of ye counsall as 3e think
meit for spairing of y*air* lyves and a remissioun to be grantit thame for that   40

12/ ploweday: *11 January 1584/5*   28/ witsonday last: *23 May 1602*
19/ plowe day: *10 January 1585/6*

accidentale slauchter as 3e will do ws guid pleasur and seruice Sua we commit
3ou to god from Falkland this vij of Iuly 1602

(signed) Iames Rex

Letter of George Nicolson to Sir Robert Cecil   TNA: PRO SP/52/68   5
f [1]   (14 August)

…

I acquainted the King with your Honours opening of the lettres he wrote to
mr Aston and mr hudson in their absence at his request, and of her Maiesties
carefull course taken for the mans safety if he had ben in handes: for which   10
he rendred her Maiesty many thankes, and was exceding glad to vnderstand
her Maiesty so kyndely to regard his request. the mans name is Aynesley a
glouer by his trade. and here at Kirkawdy, and the Kings lettres written at
the suite of one of the Kings servantes onely./

…   15

Letter of Roger Dallison, Sheriff of Lincolnshire, to Sir Robert Cecil
Hatfield House: Cecil Papers Vol. 95/66
f [1]*   (10 September)

20

May it please your Honnour vppon the Receipt of your Letter Dated the
second of August last. I Examined the matter Concerninge Iohn Henchelawe
of Grimsbye, and Nicholis Blunston. And wheras her Maiestie hath beene
moued by the Kinge of Scottes ∧⌐his meanes⌐ in the behalf of the said
Henchelawe and his ffather in Lawe, supposinge that Blunston was slayne   25
in Scottland by Henchelawe accidentally in his owne defence, at which tyme
it Chaunced the ffather in Lawe of the said Henchelawe to bee present, who
is therefore troubled for the deed as well as himself. The truth is thereof is
that Henchelawe and Blunston at Whittsontide last, sittinge together at a
Playe at Grimsbye in the County of Lincoln, fell forth there in which place   30
there passed some wordes of Offence betwixt them, and two dayes after
at Caster which is some eight miles from Grimsbye, Blunston meetinge
Henchelawe in the markett place there did first Strike Henchelawe with a
Bastinadoe, wherevppon Henchelawe did drawe his Rapier, and thrust
Blunston into the thigh, vppon which hurt hee died, Henchelawes ffather   35
in lawe being present at the affraye at Caster without weapon, but as I am
enfourmed did encourage his sonne in Lawe by his wordes in the same
affraye, for which he is in her Maiesties Goale at Lincoln, and standeth
indicted of willfull murder for the same fact, untryed at the last Assises
because the witnesses were not then present, and therefore his tryall deferred   40

2/ 1602: _underlined_   29/ Whittsontide last: _23–9 May 1602_
28/ is thereof is: _first is redundant_

till the next Assyses followinge. I Cannot enfourme your Honnour of any other Circumstances Concerninge his offence, for that the Coroners before ∧⌈whome⌉ the verdict was taken [hath] ∧⌈haue⌉ forgotten the Euidence that was then Geuen, [and hath] ∧⌈hauinge⌉ deliuered the Clarke of the Assyses the Examinacion [all Euidences] Concerninge the same, by the which the   5 matter doth more at Large appeare: Henchelawe presently after the fact fledd into Scottland, and there remaineth as is thought, which is all wherof at this tyme I Can enforme your Honour. And so humbly I take my Leaue ffom Laughton this xth of September.

Yours Honoures to bee Commaunded 10
(signed) Roger Dalyson vicecomes

HAGWORTHINGHAM

1525–6   15

A *Holy Trinity Church Book* Grange (ed): 'Hagworthingham Church Book'
p 7*

…

A sheet received by Mr John Littlebury which was will to the Church, By
one Margery to the entente to make a Banner   20
Item a sheet that was borne over the Sacrament
Item an old Kyrchuffe that our Lady's coat is lapped in
Item an old Kyrchuffe for the cross in Lentyn
Item Three Rotchetts and two Surplisses
Item to Peter Babbe for gilding the Trinity   iiii xvi o 25
Item to him for Painting the dancing geere   o o ix
Item for Cloeth for the same   o o ix
Item to George Bullock for Shaping the same   o o I

…

                                                                                                                                    30

1537–8

A *Holy Trinity Church Book* Grange (ed): 'Hagworthingham Church Book'
p 8

…

Paid to Minstrells & Players   o o xi 35

…

1546–7

A *Holy Trinity Church Book* Grange (ed): 'Hagworthingham Church Book'
p 9   40

…

Received of the dancers gathering   o vi o

…

1555–6

A   ***Holy Trinity Church Book***   Grange (ed): 'Hagworthingham Church Book'
p 9*

…

Received of the young men called the Wessell   o v iiii   5

…

HALTHAM

1605/6   10
Bill of Complaint in Dymoke v. Cholmeley   TNA: PRO STAC 8/124/20
sheet 16*   *(21 March)*

To the king*es* moste Excellent Maiestye
In moste humble Manner sheweth and informeth yo*ur* most Excellent   15
Maiestye yo*ur* highnesse faithfull and obedient Subiect Thomas Dymocke
Esquier late Escheator of yo*ur* highnesse Countye of Lincolne for the ye
⟨…⟩ as yo*ur* said Subiect hathe allwaies lyved in Credite good name fame
and reputac*i*on w*i*thall your Maiesties Subiect*es* w*i*thout anie Note tainte
or touche of infamye scandall or slaunder laid or imposed vppon him, Yet   20
soe yt ys if y⟨…⟩ moste Excellent Maiestie That one Nicholas Cholmeley
Esquier then and yet feodarye of yo*ur* highnesse said Countye of Lyncolne
Conceavinge mallice and displeasure against yo*ur* highnes said Subiect for
that he beinge Esceator and there by havinge meanes to observe and see the
Corrupte and extortiue dealings of the said Cholmeley wherew*i*th he the   25
said Cholmeley then did and still dothe greevouslye oppresse and wronge
yo*ur* Maiesties Subiect*es* in the said County of Lincolne and the fraude and
deceipt w*h*ich he then did and still dothe daielie most vnconscionable vse
w*i*thout feare of god or of yo*ur* Maiesties lawes and w*i*thout regarde of
his oathe taken for yo*ur* Ma*iesties* service in his said office did since yo*ur*   30
Maiesties last gen*er*all p*ar*don to the end to bringe yo*ur* subiect into Contempt
slaunder and discreditt amongest yo*ur* Maiesties Subiect*es* combyne practise
and confederate himselfe to and w*i*th *(blank)* and diu*er*se other p*er*souns
vnknowne howe and by what meanes the said Cholmeley and the reast of
the said Confederators yet vnknowne might vniustlie ympeache slaunder   35
and drawe into question the good name creditt and vnspotted reputac*i*on of
yo*ur* said Subiect And for that purpose they the said Nicholas Cholmeley
and the said other lewde p*er*sonns as yet vnknowne not havinge the feare of
god before theire eyes nor anie dutifull regard of yo*ur* Maiesties good and
godlie lawes statut*es* and ordinaunc*es* haue for the space of one yeere last past   40

18/ ⟨…⟩: *80mm missing*   24/ Esceator: *for* Escheator
21/ y⟨…⟩: *50mm missing*   28/ vnconscionable: *for* vnconscionablie

dailye of his and theire mallice [⟨…⟩], sediciouslye contrived made & written
published cast and spreadd abroad a most false sedicious mallicious infamous
and slanderous libell of and against your Maiesties said Subiect thereby to
defame & discreditt your said subiect with and amongest all others your
Maiesties good subiectes And allsoe to make him seeme odious and infamous   5
to all people the tenor of parte of which false slaunderous and sedicious
libell or Ryme soe made and published by the said Cholmeley and the reast
and in reioycinge manner by them songe and said in diuerse places and before
diuerse persons malliciouslye to thintent aforesaid followeth in theise wordes
viz: Thomas my freind and Dymocke reputed, your seate in the Churche ys   10
often disputed; you did them wronge to pester theire presence, that lent you
theire seate in the time of theire absence; you pester the Pew my Ladye
and her traine &c Thoughe Esquier you be for a yeere by escheate, &c. the
residewe whereof your subiect ys not able to sett downe but yet beinge full
of infamous and slaunderous writinges and ymputacions against your subiect   15
beinge your Maiesties Escheator of the said Countye And the said Nicholas
Cholmeley taking offence thereat for that your Subiect did not there in fitt
his bribinge humor did therefore in his said libell raile vppon your said
Subiect aswell in respect of his said office as otherwise to thintent to bringe
your subiect into Disgrace and infamy bothe with your subiectes freindes and 20
straingers And the same libell and seuerall Coppies thereof [did] ⌐the said⌐
Cholmeley and the rest did since the ninetenth daie of Marche in the yeare
of your Maiesties raigne ouer England ffrance & Ireland the first & of Scotland
the Seauen & thirtithe⌐ devuldge disperse and scatter abroad in diuerse places
in the said Countye of Lincolne And further informeth your excellent Maiestye 25
your said Subiect that the said Nicholas Cholmeley beinge your Maiesties
feodarye of the said Countye of Lincolne and by vertue thereof hathe and did
take the vsuall oathe of feodarye and was sworne vppon the holye Evangelistes
before the Master and Councell of your Maiesties Courte of wardes and
liueryes as in like Cases ys vsuall Neverthelesse the said Cholmeley hathe   30
since the firste Daie of Aprill in the ffirst yeare of your Maiesties raigne over
England ffraunce and Ireland And Dailye dothe by Coullor of his said office
of feodarye vse most extreame extorcion briberye and oppression vppon your
Maiesties Subiectes within the said Countye of Lincolne And namelye the
said Cholmeley since your Maiesties last generall pardoun hathe most   35
wickedlye and vngodlie falselie and Corruptlie putt in practise Committed
and donne theise extorcions briberies and oppressions hereafter followinge
… All which periuries false oathes libelling publishinge of libells extorcions
briberies deceiptes abuses and misdemeanors afore said were donne and
Comitted since the first daie of Aprell in the said first year of your Maiesties 40
raigne over England ffraunce and Ireland And were all soe comitted perpetrated
and donne by him the said Nicholas Cholmeley and the reast of the said
persons vnknowne since your Maiesties last generall and free pardoune and

are in Contempt and derogation of your highnes Crowne and Dignitye
and in most dangerous example to suche other evell disposed persons to be
encourraged thereby to perpetrate Comitte and execute the like offences
briberies extorcions and heynous misdemeanors if due punishment be not
inflicted vppon the said offendors In tender Consideracion whereof forasmuche   5
as all and singuler the said libellinge and publishinge of Libells misdemeanors
corrupcions briberies extortions and offences afore said were Comitted and
donne since your Maiesties last generall pardoune and are contrarye to your
Maiesties lawes and statutes and greevous and scandalous to your Maiesties
Subiectes May yt therefore please your moste Excellent Maiestye to graunt   10
vnto your said Subiect your highnesse moste gracious writtes of Subpena to
be directed to the said Nicholas Cholmeley *(blank)* Comaundinge him and
them and euerye of them thereby at a Certaine daie and vnder a Certaine
paine therein to be directed and appointed personallye to be and appeare
before the lordes and others of your Maiesties most honorable previe Councell   15
in your highnesse highe Courte of Starrchamber at westmynster then and
there to make aunswere to the saide premisses and to stand to and abide
suche order and Iudgement therein as to your highnesse said Councell of
the same Courte shalbe thought meete And your said Subiect shall not cease
accordinge to his bounden duetye to pray for the most Longe and happie   20
Raigne of your moste Royall Maiestye over vs.///

HAYDOR

1638/9   25
Court of High Commission Sentence   TNA: PRO SP 16/410
ff [1–3v]   *(24 January)*

...

Proceedings in an ecclesiastical cause against Richard Northen, curate of Haydor,
heard before commissioners of the king at Lambeth, in the presence of Stephen   30
Knyght and John Crampton, deputies, and John Greenhill, notary public

...

The cause is to be informed in and finally sentenced this day, and the said
Richard Northen is to appeare this day and place to heare and receaue the
finall order and Iudgment of the Court. At which day and place the said   35
Richard Northen being publiquely called for appeared personally, in whose
presence the proofes made ex parte officij against him and after that the
breife of his defence were there publiquely read, and the Counsell on bothe[⟨.⟩]
part heard [what] at large what they could enforce out of the proofes made
in this | Cause and vppon mature examinacion thereof it appeared to the   40
Court that the said Richard Northen [that the said Mr Northen] having
beene for these 8 yeares last a Preist in holy orders and Curate of the parish
Church of Hayther together with the Chappells of Caluerthorpe & Kelbye

and hauing a Curate to assist him in the said Cures did within the tyme
articulate, and namely about 7 yeares since baptize the child of one Henry
Nixe in the Church of Haydo[⟨.⟩] articulate without vsing the signe of the
Crosse at the upenning of the said child, or did omite to vse the words vizt
(we doe signe him, or her with the signe of the Crosse) ∧⌈but⌉ at the upening   5
of the said child he vsed these words instead of those aforegoinge, I doe signe
him, or her meaning the said child with the signe of a Token, and that
within the tyme articulate the said Mr Northen [had] hath administred and
deliuered the holy Communion in both kynds to divers of his parishioneres
which did sitt and not kneel at the | tyme of receauing thereof, especially   10
to Sara the wife of Henry Nixe of that parish, And it was further obiected
against the said Mr Northan that his sacred Maiestie that now is hauing by
some booke or bookes, comaunded in all parishe Churches to be published
declared his intentions for the [m] honest & Modest recreacions of his liege
subiectes good protestantes [of] such as frequented their parish Churches   15
duely, after Euening prayers on the Lords day & said Mr Northen did within
the tyme articulate take occasion to preach, and say in his sermon[⟨.⟩] in the
Church of Hayder that he was a theife that did take any Recreacions on
[the] the Saboath day [⟨...⟩], and he was worse then a theife for he was a
villaine and a sacrilegious theife that did take any Recreacions vppon the   20
Saboath day or did allow of them, and about a yeare after the preaching of
this sermon and some two yeares after the publishing of the said ∧⌈book for⌉
Recreacions on a sunday being a ffeast day at Haither [⟨.⟩] some younge
people ∧⌈after Euening prayer⌉ gatt a Piper | or Musitian ∧⌈named William
Keale⌉ and went to dance, which whilst they were at the said Mr Northan   25
and the Constable came & putt the said Piper in the stockes, where he lay
about two houres, and then the said Northan and the Constable ∧⌈coming⌉
to putt [on] one Coxe in the stockes alsoe whilst they were opening the stockes
the said Piper [call named william] slipt out his foote & ranne away which
Mr Northan perceaving he tooke a Pitchfork out of the said hands of one   30
Andrew a watchman and followed the said Piper & in a lane ouertook him
& beat him with the said Pitchfork, and brought him back to the stockes
where the said [lay] Piper lay t⟨.⟩ll the next Morning [Prayer]. And it was
further charged on the said Mr Northen that within the tyme articulate, and
especially [at] ⌈on⌉ an afternoone Catechising in the Church of Hayder in   35
Anno 1635o vppon the 8th Comandement ∧⌈he⌉ deliuered this doctrine,
that there was theft in Kinges and princes, in laying more burdens on their
subiectes then they were able to beare [as it was or fell out nowe a dayes] or
to the like effect, and ∧⌈in⌉ like words and Manner he said | there was theft
in Iudges, Magistrates, and Land lords or to that effect, and lastly that within 40
the tyme articulate the said Mr Northen hath often omitted to weare the

19/ [⟨...⟩]: *50mm crossed out and illegible*

surplice, at the reading of divine service and administrac*i*on of the sacrament*es*, and neglected on seuerall sundayes and holydayes to [div] read divine service in the [s*ai*d] Chappells of Caluerthorpe, and Kelby vnder his Cure as afores*ai*d. All w*hi*ch the suermisses the Court had fully proued against the s*ai*d Mr Northen and him worthy of a seuere censure for the same [especially for those   5 factious and vndutifull ⌃⌜& f⟨...⟩⌝ speeches of his in ⌃⌜delyuering that there was theft in kinges and Princes in⌝ laying ⟨...⟩ burdens on their subiects then they were able to beare as yt fall out now a dayes, or to the like effect.], and therefore in the first place they fined him in one thousand pounds to his Ma*ie*sties vse, and ordered ⌃⌜him⌝ to be comitted prisoner to the Gatehouse   10 there to remaine during the pleasure of the Co*ur*t and they did order him to be [digrased] ⌜wholy suspended⌝ from his | Ministeriall function and required the proctor for the office to prepare a sentence in scriptis against the next Co*ur*t day for that purpose, and lastly the s*ai*d Richard Northen was condemned in expenses or cost*es* of suite w*hi*ch are to be taxed the next Co*ur*t day   15

HECKINGTON

1569–70
St Andrew's Churchwardens' Accounts   LA: HECKINGTON PAR/7/1   20
f [7]*   *(January–January)*
...
payd to the plaheres   viij d.
...

25

1596–7
St Andrew's Churchwardens' Accounts   LA: HECKINGTON PAR/7/1
f [56]*   *(January–January)*
...
It*em* for the Maye poll   vj s. 30
...

HOLBEACH

1539–40   35
All Saints' Churchwardens' Accounts   Bodl.: MS. Eng. misc. b .72
f 88v*   *(13 April–4 April) (Payments)*
...
It*em* payd to Thomas pye wyffe for aylle   j d.

8/ able: *followed by a full line heavily cancelled and illegible*
8/ effect: *followed by two lines heavily cancelled and illegible*

Item payd to Cubbert wattssone & Iohn Lenssay
for a day warke & mendyng of ye Clowd met &
dryke & wages   xij d.

Item payd to iiij mene yat bare ye Marye Cartt   iiij d.

Item payd to merycok for harpyng be foyr ye   5
[sa] sacrement   ij d.

Item payd to ye offeryng of Corpus christi day   iij d.

Item payd [for] Thomas blessed wylliam borned
& wylliam Lyncone for ther denner for beryng
of ye marycart   iiij d. ob. 10

Item payd for [pyns] pynnes   j d.

Item payd for sope to ye clowd   j d.

Item payd for wypp Cord & papar   ij d. ob.

Item payd for a lyne to ye clowd   iij d.

Item payd for ij [lyns] lyndes to ye clowd   iij d. 15

Item payd to Cubbert wattssone & hys ffellows for
kepyng of ye clowd   xviij d.

Item payd for bred & aylle vpon Corpus christi daye   xiiij d. ob.

...

     20

1547

AC **Inventory of All Saints' Church Goods**   Stukeley: *Itinerarium Curiosum*
p 19*

     s.   d.

...   25

Item to William Calow the younger the tabernacle
of Thomas Bekete   iiii.   viii.

Item to William Davy the sygne whereon the plowghe
did stond   xvi.

...   30

Item to John Thorpe for harod's coate   xviii.

Item to William Calow the younger all thapostyls coats
and other raggs   viii.   iiii.

...

Item to Antony Heydon on blewe clothe   ix. 35

...

Item to Antony Heydon for the coats of the iij kyngs
of Coloyne   v   iiii.

Item to Humphry Hornesey the canypye that was born
over the sacrament   xx. 40

3/ dryke: *for* drynke   18/ Corpus christi daye: *5 June 1539*
7/ Corpus christi day: *5 June 1539*

Item to William Calow thelder and John Thorpe iiij
owlde pantyd clothes   vi   viii.

…

Item of John Mays wyffe for the Dracon   iii.
Item of Alys Boyds debt to christus corpys gilde   ii.   5

…

Item for seyten vestments and trashe in the chest in
trinete quere sold to Davy   xxxiii.   iiii.

…

                                                                                10

p 20*

More superstitious ornaments of the church were sold in queen Elizabeth's
time, 1560.

…   15

1560
All Saints' Churchwardens' Accounts   Bodl.: MS. Eng. misc. b .72
f 90*

…   20
Item payd to Mr callowe for the playeres   v s.

…

1601
Archdeaconry of Lincoln Visitation Book   LA: Diocesan Vij/10   25
f 116v*   *(2 April)*

Presentments made during the visitation of South Holland deanery held in the
church at Boston by Thomas Randes, the archdeacon of Lincoln's official

…   30
〈.〉imittitur
Edward ffreman for suffring dauncing play & drincking in his house &
other abuses vppon the sabboth and holly daies in time of devyne service
having [being] bene admonished to the contrarie/ 26. ffebruarij 1601
apud Lincolniam dictus ffreman citatus comparuit. et objecto articulo se   35
submissit et promisit posthac seipsum reformare in premissis vnde dominus
eum cum monicione dimisit

…

5/ christus corpys: *for* christi corpys *(?)*

· HORBLING

1564/5
Inventory of Heathenish Church Goods   LA: Diocesan FUR 2
f 17*   *(18 March)*   5
...

Thinventarie of all suche copes vestementes and other monumentes of
superstition as remayned at any tyme with in the parishe church of horblinge
sens the deathe of the lat quene marie made by Thomas Buckmynster
and Iohnne Burgies churchwardens the xviij^th daie of marche anno   10
domini 1565

...

   Item two vestmentes   the one haith Thomas wrighte of horblinge
and haithe cut yt in peces and made bedd
hanginges therof And thother was geven to   15
Richard Colsonne a scoller and he haith made
a players cote thereof in anno primo Elizabeth

f 17v*

...   20
   Item three banner clothes   which were geven awaie to childerne to make
plaiers cotes of anno primo Elizabeth

...

HOUGHAM   25

1638
Archdeaconry of Lincoln Visitation Book   LA: Diocesan Vij/21
p 194

                                                                 30
Presentments made during the visitation of Grantham and Loveden deaneries
...
dimittitur   Thomas Barson of ye same for playeinge and runeinge at Cockes in the
Churchyard vppon ye sabboth day °1o Martij 1638 Citato preconizatus non
°comparuit°   comparuit excommunicatur,° °[2] 4o die Iulij 1639 comparuit et facta fide   35
absoluitur vnde dominus eum cum monicione dimisit coram magistro
Iohannem Crispe Clerico surrogato &c Ita testatur Samuel Hoxcroft
notarius publicus°

dimittitur   William swetterall pro consimili °1o Martij 1638 Citato preconizatus non   40
°comparuit°   comparuit excommunicatur° °4to die Iulij 1639 Similiter vt contra [Paul]
Barson dimittitur°

*dimittitu*r
°*comparuit*°

Iaruase Orson *pro* consi*m*ili °*Citato* 1o Martij 1638 *Citato preconizatus* non co*m*paruit ex*communicatur*° °4to die Iulij anno d*o*mini 1639 dimitt*itu*r vt supra° d*imittitu*r

*dimittitu*r

Edward Light *pro* consi*m*ili °1o Martij 1638 *Citato preconizatus* non co*m*paruit ex*communicatur*° °19 Iulij 1639 com*paruit Magiste*r Nelson ad *p*eticio*nem* cuius d*omin*us dimisit d*ictum* Light quia puer est° 5

*dimittitu*r
°*comparuit*°

Edward Ellis *pro* consi*m*ili °1o Martij 1638 *Citato preconizatus* non co*m*paruit excommunicatur° °4to die Iulij anno d*o*mini 1639 com*paruit* et facta fide absolut*u*r vnde d*omin*us eum dimisit cum monicione° d*imittitu*r 10

KIRKBY ON BAIN

1638 15
Archiepiscopal Visitation Book   LA: Diocesan Vj/30
ff 118–18v

Presentments made during the visitation of Horncastle deanery
… 20

Horncastle

Radulphus Collin *p*resented for fidlinge & singinge of songs in the houçe of Tho*mas* Gibson the houce standinge neare Tumbye moore in tyme of diuine seruice/ °2o Maij 1638o q*uesitus* vijs in *p*roximum.° °vltimo maij 1638: Cit*ato* vijs *p*reconizatus non co*m*paruit ex*communicatur*°

25

d*imittitu*r

Kirkbye

Tho*mas* Gibson and his Wife *p*resented for keepinge of companye with the sayd fidler the tyme of deuine seruice °2 Maij 1638. com*p*ar*u*it & fass*u*s est vnde h*ab*et ad agnoscend*um* & cert*ificandum* in 2 non cert*ificauit* vnde

in forma
pau*peris*

ex*communicatur*° d*imittitu*r | 30

kirkbye
°ad agnoscend*um*
Coram M*agist*ro
I. Gan. T. H.°

pau*per*

d*imittitu*r

Will*el*mus Humberstone *p*resented vt supra/ °2o Maij 1638.° q*uesitus* &c vijs in *p*roximum° °vltimo maij 1638 Cit*ato* preconizatus non co*m*paruit ex*communi*catur° °6o ffeb*ruar*ij 1638 com*paruit* & f*acta* fide abs*oluitu*r & fass*u*s est vnde h*ab*et ad agnoscend*um* & cert*ificauit* in 2 extun*c* est cert*ificandu*m & d*imittitu*r° 35

[kirkbye]
Tumbye

Brandon Lobley *p*resented vt supra °2 Maij 1638 com*paruit* Apparitor & fass*u*s est vnde h*ab*et ad agnoscend*um* & cert*ificauit* in 2. non cert*ificauit* 40

1/ *Citato* … *Citato*: *first occurrence redundant*

vnde ex*communicatur°*

...

KIRTON IN LINDSEY

1565–6
St Andrew's Churchwardens' and Corpus Christi Guild Accounts
  LA: KIRTON IN LINDSEY PAR/7/1
f 20   *(11 March 1564/5–17 March 1565/6)*
...
Item to a drynking iij s. iiij d. & ⌈to⌉ [ij] players [x] ⌈xiiij d.⌉ iiij s. vj d.
...

1606
Bill of Complaint in Hickman v. Willoughby, Tourney, et al
  TNA: PRO STAC 8/168/31

See Gainsborough 1606

Libellous Ballad in Hickman v. Willoughby, Tourney, et al
  TNA: PRO STAC 8/168/31

See Gainsborough 1606

c 1608
Interrogatories for Defendants in Hickman v. Willoughby, Tourney, et al
  TNA: PRO STAC 8/168/31

See Gainsborough *c* 1608

1608
Depositions by Defendants in Hickman v. Willoughby, Tourney, et al
  TNA: PRO STAC 8/168/31

See Gainsborough 1608

LEVERTON

1525–6
St Helen's Churchwardens' Accounts   LA: LEVERTON PAR/7/1
f 22*   *(Reckoned 16 December) (Expenses)*
...
paid to Maister holand of Swynsed [of S] & ye

plaers of the same town whan thei rood & cryed
thare bayns att Leue*rton*   iij s. iiij d.
paid for bread & Ayle at the same tyme to cause
them & *yer* company to drynke   viij d. ob.
...   5

1545–6
St Helen's Churchwardens' Accounts   LA: LEVERTON PAR/7/1
f 45   *(Reckoned 11 July) (Expenses)*
...   10
It*em* for ale to dawns*eres* y*at* cam to ye church   ij d.
...

1565–6
St Helen's Overseers of the Poor Accounts   LA: LEVERTON PAR/13/1   15
f 10v*   *(Reckoned 30 June) (Payments)*
...
Item p*ai*d & given to the rep*aracion* of Borene
churche when they declared their Bane   v s.
...   20

1574–5
St Helen's Overseers of the Poor Accounts   LA: LEVERTON PAR/13/1
f 24   *(Reckoned 10 July) (Payments)*
...   25
Item gyven to certen players   xij d.

1577–8
St Helen's Overseers of the Poor Accounts   LA: LEVERTON PAR/13/1   30
f 29v   *(Reckoned 14 July) (Payments)*
...
Item geuen to ye waytt*es* of Boston   ij s.
...

                                                                             35
1594–5
St Helen's Churchwardens' Accounts   LA: LEVERTON PAR/7/1
f 80   *(Reckoned 17 December) (Charges)*
...
Item p*ai*d for playinge in the churche   iij s. viij d. 40
...

f 80v   *(Expenses)*

…

Item paid to the apparitor for sufferinge a plaie
in the church   iij s. viij d.

…   5

LINCOLN

c 1236
Bishop Robert Grosseteste's Letters and Mandates   10
Letter 32*

Robertus Dei gracia Lincolniensis episcopus dilectis in Christo filijs Willelmo
decano et capitulo Lincolnie salutem graciam et benediccionem. Cum domus
Dei, testante propheta Filioque Dei, domus sit oracionis, nefandum est eam in 15
domum iocacionis, scurilitatis, et nugacitatis conuertere locumque Deo dicatum
diabolicis adinuencionibus execrare. Cumque circumcisio Domini nostri Iesu
Christi prima fuerit nec modicum acerba eiusdem passio, signum quoque sit
circumcisionis spiritalis qua cordium prepucia tolluntur et omnes carnales
voluptates sensuumque libidines amputantur, execrabile est circumcisionis 20
Domini venerandam solempnitatem libidinosarum voluptatum sordibus
prophanare. Quapropter vobis mandamus in virtute obediencie firmiter
iniungentes quatinus festum stultorum, cum sit vanitate plenum et voluptatibus
spurcum, Deo odibile et demonibus amabile, de cetero in ecclesia Lincolnie die
venerande solempnitatis circumcisionis Domini nullatenus permittatis fieri. 25

1274
Hundred Roll   TNA: PRO SC 5/LINCS/TOWER/17A
mb 4*

                                                                         30

…Item dicimus quod walterus bek constabularius Castri Lincolnie apropriat
castro predicto per potestatem domini Henrici de lacy .viij. annis elapsis unam
placeam terre continentem ij acras & plus que vocatur la batailplace ubi
homines de lincolnia solebant ludere fratres predicare & alia aisiamenta habere
& ubi homines de patria solebant habere commune passagium cum carettis 35
& pecoribus ad ciuitatem in magnum preiudicium regis & dampnum ciuitatis
per annum .ij. s. & plus quo warranto nescimus Et valet per annum .iij. s.….

…

Letter 32 collation: 13 Willelmo] We. *C*   22 Quapropter] Cui*us propter C*
22 firmiter] *C omits*   25 circumcisionis] cirumcisionis *A*

15/ testante … Dei: *cp Is 56.7, Jer 7.11, Mt 21.13*

Late 13th century
Liber Niger   LA: Dean and Chapter A/2/1
ff 7–7v
...

Die natal*is* domini ad *vesper*as ad *pro*cessionem diaconor*um*.   5
Diaconus *per*sona deb*et* habere cereum de una libra ceteri *per*sone diaconi
cereum de dimidia libra. ceteri canonici diaconi cereos. *scilicet*. iiij^{or} de
libra. reliqui diaconi viij^{to} de libra & habebunt h*uius*modi ceros tam ad
*vesper*as quam ad ultimum responsorium ad matutinas i*n* festo s*anc*ti
steph*ani* consimiles cereos habebunt. Sacerdos *per*sona & alij *per*sone ecc*lesie*   10
& canonici & vicarij & alij presbiteri ta*m* ad *vesper*as q*uam* ad matut*inas*.
In festo s*anc*ti Iohan*n*is. epi*scopus* puerorum in festo s*anctorum* innocentiu*m*
h*abe*re debet unum cereum ponderis dimidie libre. cet*er*i pueri habebunt
candelas *par*uas *pro* | uoluntate sacriste.
...   15

1308–9
Dean and Chapter Common Fund Accounts   LA: Bj/2/4
f 45v*   *(15 September 1308–21 September 1309) (Gratuities and payments)*

                    20
...Item in cirotecis & sotularib*us* emptis *pro* do*m*ino Will*elm*o le venur in
ludo fact*o* in ecc*les*ia die Lune in septiman*a* pasch*e* .viij. d....
...

1313–14   25
Dean and Chapter Common Fund Accounts   LA: Bj/2/4
f 96v*   *(16 September–15 September) (Church and house costs)*
...
...Item in emendac*i*one baculi pastoralis *pro* Epi*scop*o puer*orum* .xij. d....

                    30
1317–18
Dean and Chapter Common Fund Accounts   LA: Bj/2/4
f 132   *(18 September–17 September) (Gratuities)*

...It*em* vicarijs ecc*les*ie Linc*ol*nie *pro* solemp*n*itate *per* eos facta die   35
Ep*iph*an*i*e do*m*ini circa Ludu*m* triu*m* Regu*m* .xviij s. ij. d....
...

8/ de libra: *for de dimidia libra (?)*
9/ festo: fes *and* to *written on either side of a hole in the parchment*
22/ die Lune ... pasche: *31 March 1309*

1321–2
Dean and Chapter Common Fund Accounts   LA: Bj/2/5
f 47v   *(20 September–19 September)*   *(Expenses noted)*

...Item in expensis factis tempore paschali in ludo de sancto Thoma didimo   5
.ix. s. .ix. d. In vno capite Laneo pro capite Regis in festo Epiphanie .viij. d.
...

Liber Niger   LA: Dean and Chapter A/2/1
ff 26v–7   *(19 January)*   *(Distributions to cathedral clergy)*   10
...

...de oblacionibus beati Hugonis singulis Canonicis qui magnam residenciam
in dicta ecclesia fecerint anno precedente festum translacionis eiusdem beati
Hugonis & in eodem festo presentes fuerint/ ac custodi altaris beati Petri/
sex solidi & octo denarij facturis vero residenciam in anno subsequente &   15
presentibus in ipso festo/ tres solidi & quatuor denarij . Vicarijs similiter qui
intersunt seruicio eiusdem diei ad distribuendum inter eos/ tresdecim solidi
& quatuor denarij. Pauperibus clericis eodem modo presentibus .xxij. d. Pueris
.xviij. d. Portantibus habitum non vicaribus presentibus? cuilibet .I. d. Sacriste
.v. s. pro eo quod ceteris plus laborat. Clerico suo .ij. d. Clerico commune | 20
.xij. d. Clerico Capituli .vj. d. Magistro scolarum gramaticalium .v. s. Magistro
scolarum cantus .xij. d. succentori .vj. d. Clerico ducenti columbam in festo
Pentecostes .xij. d. Accendenti candelas .vj. d. Duobus excitantibus populum
.xij. d. Duobus seruientibus precedentibus incensantem .xij. d. in eodem festo
translacionis annis singulis persoluantur?...   25

1323–4
Dean and Chapter Common Fund Accounts   LA: Bj/2/5
f 66   *(18 September–16 September)*   *(Expenses noted)*
...   30
...In ∧⌈expensis⌉ factis tempore paschali in Ludo De sancto Thoma didimo
.v. s. .viij d....

1326–7
Dean and Chapter Common Fund Accounts   LA: Bj/2/5   35
f 93v*   *(21 September–20 September)*   *(Expenses noted)*
...
...In expensis factis die Lune in septimana Pasche pro Ludo sancti Thome
apostoli in Naui ecclesie videlicet in pane vino & ceruisia. vj. s. vj. d....
...   40

38/ die Lune ... Pasche: *13 April 1327*

c 1330–3
John de Schalby's Book   LA: Dean and Chapter A/2/3
ff 30v–1*   *(Distributions to cathedral clergy)*

…

In distribucione autem pentecostis percipiet quilibet Canonicus residens   5
& in villa die distribucionis existens. iiij. s. & vj d. & ad vinum ij. s. Item
Custos altaris beati petri prepositus sacrista & clericus ecclesie habebunt
similiter singillatim. iiij. s. vj. d. de integra summa oblata & ij. s. de communa.
Item | Clericus Capituli ij. s. Item ij custodes magni Altaris iiij. s. similiter
quilibet ij. s. Item clericus sacriste. vj. d. Clericus ducens columbam vj denarijs.   10
Hostiarius vj. d.…

…

1332–3
Dean and Chapter Common Fund Accounts   LA: Bj/2/5   15
f 137v   *(20 September–19 September) (Expenses noted)*

…

…In pane empto pro ludo sancti Thome Apostoli die Lune in septimana
Pasche .xij. d. In vino .v. s. In ceruisia .ij. s.…

20

1368–9
Dean and Chapter Common Fund Accounts   LA: Bj/2/6
f 6v   *(17 September–16 September)*

…

Ludus sancti   Item computat soluisse in pane vj d. in ceruisia ij s. vj d. in vino ij s. vj d.   25
Thome   Summa v s. vj d.

…

1383–4
Dean and Chapter Common Fund Accounts   LA: Bj/2/7   30
f 119v*   *(20 September–18 September)*

…

Expense circa   In primis domino Iohanni louth pro factura vnius stelle x s. ix d. Item Willelmo
ludum die   Sadiler pro factura trium coronarum pro Regibus ij s. xj d. Item in vino empto
Epiphanie &   videlicet iiij lagenis pro ludo resurreccionis ij s. viij d. Item in Ceruicia vj d.   35
Resurreccionis   Item in pane vj d.
                                                     ☙ Summa xvij s. iiij d.

18–19/ die Lune … Pasche: *5 April 1333*

1384–5
Dean and Chapter Common Fund Accounts   LA: Bj/5/3b
f 15v*   *(18 September–17 September)*

Expensis circa
ludum Epiphanie

Expensis
circa ludum
Resurreccionis

(blank)   5
(blank)
...

1386–7
Dean and Chapter Common Fund Accounts   LA: Bj/2/7   10
f 181   *(16 September–15 September)*

Expense circa
ludum die
Epiphanie &
resurreccionis

In primis in emendacione coronarum Regum/ stelle/ ac in conduccione
furrurarum pro regibus & aliis expensis neccessariis xix s. vj d. In vino ceruicia
& pane emptis pro ludo resurreccionis iij s. iij d. ob.   15
                           ℭ Summa – xxij s. ix d. ob.
...

1389
Certificate of Minstrels' and Entertainers' Guild   TNA: PRO C 47/41/156   20
single sheet

Certificacio ffraternitatis Minstrellorum & histrionum infra Ciuetatem
Lincolnie patet in hec verba

                                                                                                                          25
In primis ordinatum & statutum est inter fratres & sorores fraternitatis
predicte quod debent semel in Anno conuenire apud Lincolniam in quodam
loco certo congruo & honesto & ibi debent sursum leuare vnam magnam
Candelam & candelam predictam debent portare vsque ad Matricem ecclesiam
beate Marie lincolnie cum maxima processione gaudio & honore & hoc die   30
Mercur⟨...⟩ in septimana pentacostes ⟨...⟩ & ibidem quilibet eorum debet
offerre vnum denarium Assemblias ⟨...⟩ congregaciones non faciunt nisi
semel in anno & hoc causa potacionis & disposicionis candele supradicte
Sacramentum inter se non faciunt nisi ad sustentandum & inueniendum
lumenare predictum Terras & tenementa mortificata seu non mortificata   35
nulla habent nec catalla aliqua ad opus fraternitatis supradicte

31/ Mercur⟨...⟩: *for* Mercurij
31/ ⟨...⟩²: *10mm hole in sheet*
32, 34/ faciunt: *for* faciant *(?)*
36/ habent: *for* habeant *(?)*

Certificate of Cordwainers' Guild of the Blessed Virgin Mary
TNA: PRO C 47/41/152
single sheet*

…

…Et quicumq*ue* homo qui op*er*atur in villa de illa arte qui ˄⌈est⌉ extra 5
fra*ter*nitatem soluet in anno sex ⟨…⟩arios ad ludu*m* vel ad candelam …
Duodecima ordinacio est q*uod* gracemania fr*atres* & sorores p*redict*e gilde
ibunt in p*ro*cessione ad monasteriu*m* cu*m* maria Ioseph s*ancto* Blasio & ij
angelis assig*n*a*t*is…

10

1389–90
Injunctions at the Archbishop of Canterbury's Sede Vacante Visitation
LA: Dean and Chapter A/2/7
f 38v   *(12 May)* *(Given at Croydon Manor)*

15

xjᵃ   …Et quia in eade*m* visitac*i*o*n*e n*os*tra cora*m* nobis A non*n*ullis fidedignis
delatu*m* extitit q*uod* v*j*carij & *c*lerici ip*s*ius ecclesie in die circu*m*cisionis
d*omi*ni induti veste laicali p*er* eor*um* strepitus truffas garulac*i*o*n*es & ludos
quos festa stultor*um* co*m*mu*n*it*er* & ˄⌈co*n*⌉uenient*er* appellant diuinu*m*
officiu*m* multiplicit*er* & co*n*suete impediu*n*t tenore p*rese*nciu*m* Inhebemu*s* 20
ne Ip*s*i vicarij qui nunc su*n*t vel erunt p*ro* tempore talib*us* vti de cet*er*o no*n*
p*re*sumant n*ec* idem vicarij seu quiuis alij [ecclesie] ecclesie mi*n*istri publicas
potac*i*o*n*es aut insolencias [c*aus*as] alias in ecclesia que domus [*est*] orac*i*o*n*es
existit co*n*tra honestate*m* eiusde*m* faciant quouismodo…

25

1390–1
Dean and Chapter Common Fund Accounts   LA: Bj/2/8
f 31v   *(18 September–17 September)*

…

Exp*ense* facte
p*ro* salutac*ione*
die Nat*alis*
d*omi*ni & p*ro*
ludo in
sept*iman*a
Pasche

In p*ri*mis d*omi*no Ioh*ann*i Louth p*ro* expe*n*s*is* p*er* eu*m* apposit*is* circa stell*am* 30
& colu*m*bam ij s. vj d. It*em* in expe*n*s*is* fact*is* p*er* sacrista*m* eod*em* tempo*re*
p*ro* salutac*i*o*n*e vj s. ij d. ob. It*em* p*ro* expe*n*s*is* fact*is* circa ludu*m* in septimana
Pasch*e* iij s. xj d.
                          ℭ S*um*ma xij s. vij d. ob.

…

35

6/ ⟨…⟩arios: *for* denarios
17/ v*j*carij: *first* j *corrected over other letter*
20/ Inhebem*us*: *for* Inhibemus
21/ Ip*s*i: I *corrected over other letters*
23/ orac*i*o*n*es: *for* oracionis

1393–4
Dean and Chapter Common Fund Accounts   LA: Bj/2/8
f 74v   *(21 September–20 September)* *(Expenses noted)*

...Item in iij par*ibus* cirothecarum empt*is* pro Maria Elizabet & angelo die   5
Nat*alis* d*om*ini in aurora ad matutinas iij d....

Bishop John Buckingham's Register   LA: Bishop's Register 12
f 477v*   *(19 June)* *(Detections and comperts against the dean and chapter)*

10

Visitation proceedings held before Bishop John Buckingham in the chapter house
in the presence of the dean and chapter
...
...Item dicitur qu*o*d decanus transiuit ad palustres comunes et spectac*u*la
publica in Ciuitate et extra et quasdam luctac*io*nes fecit publicas in claustro   15
ecclesie lincoln*ie* ac in palacio et iux*t*a hospit*a*le sancti egidij in quibus
personalit*er* int*er*fuit et remunerator seu arbitrator ludi fuit dando dat*um*
suu*m* videl*ice*t kat of ye montteyns melius luctanti ... Item decan*us*
voluptuosas expensas fecit fieri de co*mmun*i opere et fabrica ecclesie in
tripudijs in campanili et picturis et istrionib*us* ac alijs superfluis eciam ad   20
summa*m* C marcar*um*...
...

1394–5
Dean and Chapter Common Fund Accounts   LA: Bj/2/8   25
f 96v   *(20 September–19 September)* *(Expenses noted)*

...Item in iij par*ibus* cirothecar*um* empt*is* pro Maria angelo & Elizabet die
Nat*alis* d*om*ini in Aurora iiij d....

30

1395–6
Dean and Chapter Common Fund Accounts   LA: Bj/2/8
f 119*   *(19 September–17 September)* *(Expenses noted)*

...Item in iij par*ibus* cirothecar*um* empt*is* pro Maria angelo & Elizabeth die   35
Nat*alis* d*om*ini in aurora iiij d....

f 119v*

...Item Solut*um* I. Tetford pro reparacione cordar*um* et alior*um* neccessarior*um*   40
pro columba & angelo in festo Pent*ecostis* xij d....

1396–7
Dean and Chapter Common Fund Accounts   LA: Bj/2/8
f 144   *(17 September–16 September) (Expenses noted)*

...Item in Cerotecis emp*tis* p*ro* Maria & angelo in die Nat*alis* d*o*m*i*ni ij d.   5
Item in ij par*ibus* cerotecar*um* emp*tis* p*ro* duobus p*ro*phe*tis* eodem die iiij d....

1397–8
A   *List of Mayors, Bailiffs, and Sheriffs*   LA: Diocesan Miscellaneous Roll I
mb 4*   10
...

		Ioh*annes* Hoghton	
a*n*no xxj°	Ioh*annes* Toreley. Maior	Nicholaus Hoddelston	ball*iui*
	Ioh*annes* Seu*er*by elect*us*	Ric*ar*dus Staynfeld	
	es*t* i*n* offic*ium* maioris °ludus		15
	de pat*er* noster ho*c* a*n*no.°		

...

1399–1400
Dean and Chapter Common Fund Accounts   LA: Bj/2/10   20
f 11   *(21 September–19 September) (Expenses noted)*

...Et in Cerotecis emp*tis* p*ro* Maria Angelo & p*ro*phe*tis* in aurora Nat*alis*
d*o*m*i*ni vj d....

                                                                          25

1401–2
Dean and Chapter Common Fund Accounts   LA: Bj/2/10
f 59   *(18 September–17 September) (Expenses noted)*

...Et in Cerotecis emp*tis* p*ro* Maria Ang*e*lis & duob*us* p*ro*phe*tis* in Aurora   30
Nat*alis* d*o*m*i*ni vj d....

1402–3
Dean and Chapter Common Fund Accounts   LA: Bj/2/10
f 81   *(17 September–16 September) (Expenses noted)*   35
...
...Et in cirotec*is* emp*tis* p*ro* Maria & ang*e*lo in aurora Nat*alis* d*o*m*i*ni
vj d....

30/ Ang*e*lis: *for* Angelo (?)

1403–4
Dean and Chapter Common Fund Accounts   LA: Bj/5/9/10
f [1v]*   *(16 September 1403–21 September 1404) (Expenses noted)*

...Et in cerotecis emp*tis* pro Maria & Angelo ac prophetis in aurora ·   5
Natiuit*atis* do*mi*ni vj d....

1404–5 or 1405–6
Dean and Chapter Common Fund Accounts   LA: Bj/2/10
f 111v*   *(Expenses noted)*   10

...Et in cerothecis emp*tis* pro Maria angelo & ij prophe*tis* in aurora Nat*alis*
do*mi*ni vj d....

1406–7   15
Dean and Chapter Common Fund Accounts   LA: Bj/2/10
f 127v*   *(19 September–18 September) (Expenses noted)*

...Et in cerothecis emp*tis* pro Maria & Angelo & duob*us* prophe*tis* in aurora
Nat*alis* do*mi*ni ex consue*tudi*ne vj d....   20

1408–9
Dean and Chapter Common Fund Accounts   LA: Bj/2/10
f 147   *(16 September–15 September) (Expenses noted)*

                                                                                                25
...Et in serothecis emp*tis* pro Maria Angelo & duob*us* prophe*tis* in Aurora
Nat*alis* do*mi*ni vj d....

1410–11
A   *List of Mayors, Bailiffs, and Sheriffs*   LA: Diocesan Miscellaneous Roll 1   30
    mb 5

    ...

    A*n*no xij°. Wille*l*mus Kyrkby. Maior. { Henricus Dradshewe } vice*comites*
                 °ludus Pater Noster°   { Henricus Thorwurth }   35

    ...

1417–18
Dean and Chapter Common Fund Accounts   LA: Bj/5/10/6(3)
f [1]*   *(19 September–18 September) (Expenses noted)*   40

...Et in den*arijs* solut*is* in natali pro sirothec*is* ad prophe*tas* Maria*m* &
ange*lu*m vj d....

1420–1
Dean and Chapter Common Fund Accounts   LA: Bj/2/11
f 9v   *(15 September 1420–21 September 1421)*   *(Expenses noted)*

...Et in cerothecis emp*tis* p*ro* Maria Angelo in Aurora Nat*alis* d*om*i*n*i &   5
duob*us* p*ro*phetis vj d....

1421–2
Civic Register ·   LA: L1/3/1
f 4v*   *(21 April)*   10

Ordinac*io*
p*ro* lib*er*atis
Ministrallor*um*

It*em* ordinat*um* & concordat*um* est q*u*od decet*er*o non allocet*ur* alicui maiori
p*ro* lib*er*atis aliquor*um* ministrallor*um* nisi tantomodo p*ro* lib*er*ata cuiuslibet
ministralli octo solidos Ita q*u*od su*m*ma lib*er*atar*um* ministrallor*um* p*re*dictor*um*
p*ro* tempore existenciu*m* su*m*mam viginti quatuor solidor*um* non excedat Et   15
octo solidos p*ro* nuncio Co*mmun*i si aliquis talis nuncius decet*er*o h*a*beat*ur*
...

1423–4
Dean and Chapter Common Fund Accounts   LA: Bj/2/11   20
f 31v   *(19 September–17 September)*   *(Expenses noted)*

...Et in Cirote*c*is p*ro* Maria & a*n*gelo & ij p*ro*phet*is* ad matutinas in aur*or*a
Nat*alis* d*om*i*n*i vj d....

25

1424–5
A   ***List of Mayors, Bailiffs, and Sheriffs***   LA: Diocesan Miscellaneous Roll 1
mb 5
...

A*n*no iij° ⦗ Ioh*ann*es Lokken. Maior {Semanus Grantham } vic*ecomites*   30
     °Ludus Pat*er* Noster And their {Ioh*ann*es Thetilthorpe}
     was discencion bytwyx the
     cardynall of wynchester And
     the duke of Glocester°   35
...

1426–7
Dean and Chapter Common Fund Accounts   LA: Bj/5/10/3a
f [2]*   *(15 September 1426–21 September 1427)*   *(Expenses noted)*   40
...
...Et in Cirothe*c*is emp*tis* p*ro* mari*a* & angelo vj d....
...

1431–2
Dean and Chapter Common Fund Accounts   LA: Bj/5/9/12
f [6]*   *(16 September 1431–21 September 1432) (Expenses noted)*

...Et in cirotecis pro maria & Angelo vj d....   5

1433–4
Dean and Chapter Common Fund Accounts   LA: Bj/5/9/13
f [7]*   *(20 September–19 September) (Expenses noted)*

                                                                                   10
...Et in cirotecis emptis pro Maria Angelo & prophetis erga Natalem
domini vj d....

1434–5
Dean and Chapter Common Fund Accounts   LA: Bj/5/10/3c   15
f [2]*   *(19 September–18 September) (Expenses noted)*
...
...Et in cirethecis pro Maria et angelo vj d....

1440–1   20
Dean and Chapter Common Fund Accounts   LA: Bj/2/12
f 10v*   *(18 September–17 September) (Expenses noted)*

...Et in Sirotecis emptis pro Maria & angelo & prophetis in aurora Natalis
Domini vj d....   25
...

1441–2
A   *List of Mayors, Bailiffs, and Sheriffs*   LA: Diocesan Miscellaneous Roll 1
mb 6   30
...

Anno xx.º Iohannes Hedon. Maior $\left\{ \begin{array}{l} \text{Ricardus Papilwike} \\ \text{Robertus Burgh} \end{array} \right\}$ vicecomites
          °ludus Sancti laurencij./°
...   35

1442–3
Dean and Chapter Common Fund Accounts   LA: Bj/2/13
f 30   *(16 September–15 September) (Expenses noted with customary payments)*
...   40
Et in Sirotecis emptis pro Maria & Angelo in Aurora
Natalis domini   vj d.
...

1443–4
Dean and Chapter Common Fund Accounts   LA: Bj/2/13
f 63v*   *(15 September 1443–20 September 1444)*   *(Expenses noted)*

…

C Et in Ciroticis empt*is* pro Maria & Angelo ex   5
con*suetudine* ecclesie in Aurora Nat*alis* d*om*ini   vj d.

…

1445–6
Dean and Chapter Common Fund Accounts   LA: Bj/2/14   10
f [14v]   *(19 September–18 September)*

…

Et in criroti*cis* empt*is* pro Maria & Angelo ex
consuetud*ine* in Aurora Natal*is* d*om*ini   vj d.

…   15

1446–7
Dean and Chapter Common Fund Accounts   LA: Bj/2/14
f [36]   *(18 September–17 September)*   *(Customary payments)*

…   20

Et in ciroche*cis* empt*is* pro Maria & Angelo ex
consuetudine in Aurora Nat*alis* d*om*ini   vj d.

…

1447–8   25
A **List of Mayors, Bailiffs, and Sheriffs**   LA: Diocesan Miscellaneous Roll I
mb 6

…

An*n*o xxvj.º Iohannes Carberton. M*aior* ⎰Robertus Bukley ⎱ vic*ecomites*
                                                           ⎱Robertus Skupholme⎰   30
          ºludus Sanc*t*i Susanni./º

…

Dean and Chapter Common Fund Accounts   LA: Bj/2/14
f [63]   *(17 September–15 September)*   35

…

⟨…⟩ari⟨.⟩ ⟨…⟩g⟨…⟩ ex c⟨..⟩suetudi*ne* in Aurora
nat*alis* d*om*ini   vj d.

…

13/ criroti*cis*: *for* cirotecis
31/ Sanc*t*i Susanni: *for* sancte Susanne

1448–9
Dean and Chapter Common Fund Accounts LA: Bj/2/15
f [13]* *(15 September 1448–21 September 1449) (Customary payments)*
...

Et in Ciroticis emptis pro Maria & Angelo ex
consuetudine in Aurora natalis domini vj d.
...

1449–50
Dean and Chapter Common Fund Accounts LA: Bj/2/15
f [39v] *(21 September–20 September) (Customary payments)*
...

Et in Ciroticis emptis pro Maria & angelo ex
consuetudine in aurora natalis domini vj d.
,,,

1450–1
Dean and Chapter Common Fund Accounts LA: Bj/2/15
f [65v]* *(20 September–19 September) (Customary payments)*
...

Et in siroticis emptis pro maria & angelo ex
consuetudine in aurora natalis domini vj d.
...

1452–3
A ### List of Mayors, Bailiffs, and Sheriffs LA: Diocesan Miscellaneous Roll 1
mb 6
...

Anno xxxjᵒ Robertus Buckley. Maior. {Ricardus wake / willelmus Chapman} vicecomites
°Rex Henricus fuit lincolnie
ijª vice
Et ludus de kynge Robert
of Cesill°

...

Dean and Chapter Common Fund Accounts LA: Bj/2/16
f 14 *(17 September–16 September) (Customary payments)*
...
...Et in Serotecis emptis pro maria & Angelo ex consuetudine in Aurora
Natalis Domini hoc Anno vj d....
...

1453–4
Dean and Chapter Common Fund Accounts   LA: Bj/2/16
f 44v   (16 September–15 September)   (Customary payments)
...

...Et in Sirotec*is* empt*is* pro Maria & angelo ex con*suetudi*ne in Aurora   5
Natal*is* do*mi*ni ho*c* an*n*o vj d....
...

1454–5
A   ### List of Mayors, Bailiffs, and Sheriffs   LA: Diocesan Miscellaneous Roll I   10
mb 6
...

An*n*o xxxiij° will*el*mus Haltham. M*aior* $\begin{Bmatrix} \text{Ioh}annes \text{ Parker} \\ \text{Will}elmus \text{ Smyth} \end{Bmatrix}$ vic*ecomites*
°Bellu*m* ad s*anctu*m Albanu*m*.   15
ij*a*. die mai.
Ludus de S*anct*o Iacobo°
...

Dean and Chapter Common Fund Accounts   LA: Bj/2/16   20
f 79   (15 September 1454–21 September 1455)   (Customary payments)
...
...Et in sirotec*is* empt*is* pro maria et angelo ex con*suetudi*ne in aurora
Natal*is* do*mi*ni vj d....
...   25

1455–6
A   ### List of Mayors, Bailiffs, and Sheriffs   LA: Diocesan Miscellaneous Roll I
mb 6
...   30

An*n*o xxxiiij.° Iohannes Hoddelston. M*aior* $\begin{Bmatrix} \text{Ioh}annes \text{ Wodeman} \\ \text{Rad}ulphus \text{ ffo} \end{Bmatrix}$ vic*ecomites*
°ludus de S*anct*a Clara.°
...

35

Dean and Chapter Common Fund Accounts   LA: Bj/2/16
ff 106v–7   (21 September–19 September)   (Customary payments)
...
...Et in sirotec*is* empt*is* pro maria et angelo ex con*suetudi*ne in Aurora |
Natal*is* do*mi*ni vj d....   40
...

1456-7

A   *List of Mayors, Bailiffs, and Sheriffs*   LA: Diocesan Miscellaneous Roll 1
mb 6

…

Anno xxxv.º willelmus Horn. Maior. $\left\{\begin{array}{l}\text{Robertus Crabden}\\\text{Iohannes Taliour}\end{array}\right\}$ vicecomites   5
ºTerre motus in vigilia Sancti
Thome apostoli ad
horam iijª. Et ludus de
Pater nosterº   10

…

Dean and Chapter Common Fund Accounts   LA: Bj/2/16
f 136   *(19 September–18 September) (Customary payments)*
…   15
…Et in Sirotecis emptis pro maria & angelo ex consuetudine in Aurora
Natalis domini vj d.…

…

1457-8   20
Dean and Chapter Common Fund Accounts   LA: Bj/2/16
f 170v   *(18 September–17 September) (Customary payments)*
…
…Et in sirotecis emptis pro Maria & Angelo ex consuetudine in Aurora
Natalis domini vj d.…   25

…

1458-9

A   *List of Mayors, Bailiffs, and Sheriffs*   LA: Diocesan Miscellaneous Roll 1
mb 6   30

…

Anno xxxvijº Iohannes wylliamson Maior $\left\{\begin{array}{l}\text{Thomas Martyn}\\\text{willelmus Bukenell}\end{array}\right\}$ vicecomites
ºludus de Pater Noster
Bellum apud ludlaweº   35

…

Dean and Chapter Common Fund Accounts   LA: Bj/2/16
f 202v   *(17 September–16 September) (Customary payments)*
…   40
…Et in sirotecis emptis pro Maria & Angelo ex consuetudine in Aurora
Natalis domini vj d.…

…

f 207   *(Allowances)*

...

...Et in regardo dat*o* Ioh*ann*i hanson p*ro* labor*ibus* suis *ha*b*it*is circa
Assenc*ionem* fact*am* in ecclesia Cath*edrali* v*l*timo A*nn*o xxvj s. viij d. Et in
consimili regardo dat*o* Steph*ano* Bony vic*ario* p*ro* eius labor*ibus ha*b*it*is   5
circa visionem fact*am* in Choro in die Nat*alis* d*om*ini vj s. viij d. Et will*elmo*
Muskham vic*ario* p*ro* ei*us* labor*ibus* circa colu*m*ba*m* & vexill*am* in choro
ac orrilogiu*m* v*l*timo Anno iij s. iiij d....

1459–60   10
Dean and Chapter Common Fund Accounts   LA: Bj/2/16
f 233   *(16 September 1459–21 September 1460)* *(Customary payments)*
...

...Et in sirotec*is* empt*is* p*ro* Maria & Angelo ex con*suetudi*ne in aurora
Nat*alis* d*om*ini vj d....   15
...

f 238   *(Allowances)*
...

...Et in quod*am* regardo dat*o* ∧⌜Ioh*anni* hanson Capellano⌝ p*ro* labor*ibus* &   20
diligencia sua circa assu*m*pc*ione*m & visus fact*os* in ecclesia in festo *s*anct*e*
Anne xij s. iiij d....
...

1460–1   25
Dean and Chapter Common Fund Accounts   LA: Bj/2/16
f 262v   *(21 September–20 September)* *(Customary payments)*
...

...Et in sirotec*is* empt*is* p*ro* maria & Angelo ex con*suetudi*ne in· Aurora
Nat*alis* d*om*ini vj d....   30
...

1461–2
Dean and Chapter Common Fund Accounts   LA: Bj/2/16
f 288v   *(20 September–19 September)* *(Customary payments)*   35
...

...Et in sirotec*is* empt*is* p*ro* maria & Angelo ex con*suetudi*ne in Aurora
Nat*alis* d*om*ini vj d....
...

                                                                                            40
f 293   *(Allowances)*
...

...Et in consi*m*ili Alloc*acione* fact*a* Ioh*ann*i hanson p*ro* occupac*io*ni*bus*

habitis circa Assupcıonem hoc A*nno (blank)* Et Ioh*ann*i Bradley p*ro* |lab|
custu*bus* per ip*s*um fact*is* in Aur*ora* Nat*alis* d*om*ini circa stellam & cordulas
p*ro* eadem vt p*atet* per billam *suam (blank)*...

1462–3   5
Dean and Chapter Common Fund Accounts   LA: Bj/2/16
f 314   *(19 September–18 September)* *(Customary payments)*

...Et in Ciroteci*s* empt*is* p*ro* maria & angelo ex con*s*uetud*in*e in aurora
Nat*alis* d*om*ini vj d....   10
...

f 318   *(Allowances)*
...
...Et Allo*catur* ei p*ro* ⌐*expensis* et⌐ quod*am* regardo dato Ioh*ann*i hanson   15
Cap*ella*no hoc anno p*ro* labor*e* suo h*abi*to [s] circa Assenci*on*em x s....
...

1463–4
Dean and Chapter Common Fund Accounts   LA: Bj/2/16   20
f 338v   *(18 September–16 September)* *(Customary payments)*
...
...Et in Ciroteci*s* empt*is* p*ro* maria & Angelo ex con*s*uetud*in*e in Aurora
Nat*alis* d*om*ini vj d....

                                                                                25
f 343   *(Allowances)*

...Et in Alloc*acione* fact*a* d*om*ino Ioh*ann*i Hanson p*ro* labor*e* suo h*abit*o
circa Ascenci*on*em hoc Anno x s....
...
                                                                                30

1464–5
Dean and Chapter Common Fund Accounts   LA: Bj/2/16
f 361   *(16 September–15 September)* *(Customary payments)*

                                                                                35
...Et in ciroteci*s* empt*is* p*ro* maria & angelo ex con*s*uetud*in*e in Aurora
Natal*is* d*om*ini vj d....
...

1/ Assupci*on*em: *for* Assumpcionem; *abbreviation mark missing*
2/ per: p *corrected over another letter*

f 364v   *(Allowances)*

...

...Et in allocac*i*one fact*a* Iohann*i* hanson p*ro* labore suo h*a*bito in ecclesia
circa Ascencionem in Naui ecclesie ex gr*a*c*i*a & curialitate d*o*min*or*um hoc
anno x s....   5

...

1465–6
Dean and Chapter Common Fund Accounts   LA: Bj/2/16
f 382   *(15 September 1465–21 September 1466)* *(Customary payments)*   10

...

...Et in Cirotec*is* empt*is* pro maria & Angelo ex con*suetudi*ne in Aurora
Natal*is* d*o*m*i*ni vj d....

...

15

1467–8
Dean and Chapter Common Fund Accounts   LA: Bj/5/6(2)
f [9]   *(20 September–18 September)* *(Customary payments)*

...Et in Cirotec*is* empt*is* pro maria & Angelo ex con*suetudi*ne in Aurora   20
Natal*is* D*o*m*i*ni vj d....

...

1468–9
Dean and Chapter Act Book   LA: Dean and Chapter A/2/36   25
f 35   *(29 July)*

...

decret*u*m pro   Die sabb*a*ti capit*u*lar*i* videlic*et*/ xxix° die Iulij Anno d*o*m*i*ni Mill⟨...⟩
expen*sis* in   CCCClx*mo* Nono/ Mag*iste*r Robert*us* fflemmyng Decan*us* Hugo Tapton
die *sanct*e   Cancellari*us* Robert*us* Ayscogh Subdecan*us* Robert*us* Wymbyssh/ Th*o*mas   30
Anne circa   Alf⟨...⟩ & Ioh*annes* Graveley can*o*nici Resid*enci*arii ecclesie cath*e*dr*alis*
assu*m*psionem   linc*o*l*nie* In domo capit*u*la⟨...⟩ eiusd*em* capit*u*li con*g*regati vt dixerunt/
D*o*mine m*a*rie   decreuer*u*nt vnanimi con*sensu* ⟨...⟩ vt sumptus & expense nup*er* p*er* d*o*min*um*
                   Ioh*annem* Hanson Capella⟨...⟩ circa visu*m* Assumpcion*is* be*a*te Marie i*n*
                   festo *Sanct*e Anne vltimo p⟨...⟩ in Naui d*ict*e ecclesie fact*i* vna cu*m*   35

28/ Mill⟨...⟩: *for* Millesimo
32/ capit*u*la⟨...⟩: *for* capitulari
33/ d*o*m*i*num: *6 minims in* MS
34/ Capella⟨...⟩: *for* Capellanum
35/ vltimo p⟨...⟩: *for* vltimo preterito *(?)*

Regardo ipsius domini Iohannis ‸⌈in hac parte fia⟨...⟩ &⌉ ⟨...⟩ de integro
denariorum proueniencium de Apertura Magni Altaris pro termi⟨..⟩
Natiuitatis Sancti Iohannis Baptiste vltimo preterito coram canonicis
‸⌈ibidem⌉ in proximo faciend⟨.⟩

5

1470–1
Dean and Chapter Common Fund Accounts   LA: Bj/5/6(3)
f [4v]   *(16 September–15 September)* *(Customary payments)*

...Et in cirotecis emptis pro maria & Angelo ex consuetudine in Aurora   10
Natalis domini vj d....
...

1472–3
A   *List of Mayors, Bailiffs, and Sheriffs*   LA: Diocesan Miscellaneous Roll 1   15
mb 6
...

Anno xij.º   Iohannes Elston. ⌈armiger⌉ { Iohannes holway } vicecomites
                                          { Thomas Bryde   }
              Maior.   20
              °ludus Corporis Christi°
...

1473–4
Dean and Chapter Common Fund Accounts   LA: Bj/5/7   25
f [48]   *(19 September–18 September)* *(Customary payments)*
...
...Et in cerothecis emptis pro maria & angelo ex consuetudine in aurora
Natalis domini vj d....

...   30

f [51v]   *(Allowances)*
...
...Et allocatur computanti vt pro tot denarijs per ipsum solutis ⌈ad manus
Iohannis Slak⌉ pro Iantaculo Canonicorum in festo Corporis christi vt patet   35
per billam de parcellis inde xviij s. j d. ob....
...

1/ fia⟨...⟩: *for* fiantur *(?)*

1474–5

A *List of Mayors, Bailiffs, and Sheriffs*   LA: Diocesan Miscellaneous Roll 1
mb 6*

...

Anno xiiij.º   Oliuerus Franke. M*aior* $\left\{\begin{array}{l}\text{Iohannes Sparowe}\\ \text{Edwardus Brown}\end{array}\right\}$ vic*ecomites*   5
the kyng*e* went   °hoc anno fact*us* fuit le
to Amyas & the   bisshop brig*e*
kyng*e* of frau*n*ce Et ludus de corp*o*ris   °graunted to pay to
                      Christi.°   kyng*e* edward xj M^l   10
                                                    li.°

...

Dean and Chapter Common Fund Accounts   LA: Bj/5/7
f [70]*   *(18 September–17 September)* *(Customary payments)*   15

...Et in ceretecis emptis p*ro* Maria & Angelo ex consue*tudi*ne in Aurora
Natalis d*omi*ni vj d....

...

20

f [70v]*   *(Gratuities)*

...

...[Et in quod*am* regardo dat*o* ludentib*us* lusum Corporis chr*ist*i hoc Anno
n*ihi*l] ... Et in p*r*andio d*omi*nor*um* Canonicor*um* in festo Corporis Chr*ist*i
videnc*ium* ludu*m* hoc anno xvj s. ij d.   25

...

1475–6
Dean and Chapter Common Fund Accounts   LA: Bj/5/7
f [13]   *(17 September–15 September)* *(Customary payments)*   30

...

...Et in ceretecis empt*is* p*ro* Maria & Angelo ex consue*tudi*ne in Aurora
Natalis d*omi*ni vj d....

...

35

f [13v]   *(Gratuities)*

...

...Et in p*r*andio d*omi*nor*um* Canonicor*um* in festo Corporis Chr*ist*i
videnc*ium* ludum hoc Anno xviij s. vj d.

...

40

9/ corp*o*ris: *for* corpore

1477–8
Dean and Chapter Common Fund Accounts   LA: Bj/5/7
f [29]*   *(21 September–20 September)*   *(Customary payments)*

...

...Et in Ceretecis empt*is* p*ro* Maria & Angelo ex consuetudine in Aurora   5
Natalis d*om*ini vj d....

...

f [29v]*   *(Gratuities)*

...   10

...Et in Conuiuio Cano*n*icor*um* existen*tium* Ad vidend*um* ludum Corporis
Chr*ist*i in Camera Ioh*ann*is Sharpe infra Cl*ausu*m [v*l*t*ra* *(blank)* alloc*atos*
Clerico co*mmun*e tam in officio Clerici ffabrice q*uam* in Officio suo in Anno
p*re*ceden*ti*] °xvij s. iij d. ob.°...

...   15

1478–9
Dean and Chapter Common Fund Accounts   LA: Bj/3/1
f 8   *(20 September–19 September)*   *(Customary payments)*

...   20

...Et in Ceretecis empt*is* p*ro* Maria & Angelo ex consuetudi*n*e in Aurora
Natal*is* Dom*i*ni vj d....

...

f 8v   *(Gratuities)*   25

...Et in conuiuio Cano*n*icor*um* existen*tium* Ad vidend*um* ludum Corporis
Chr*ist*i in Camera Ioh*ann*is Sharpe infra Cl*ausu*m xvij s. xj d.

...

                                                                                                    30

1480
Civic Register   LA: L1/3/1
f 59*

...

Off sent Thomas day the apostyll be for Crystemes when the mayr of this   35
Cite be his officers hathe p*ro*clamyd the p*ri*walege. gyrth & ye solempnite
of ye fest of ye byrth of our lord that then after the sayd p*ro*clamacion
made eu*er*e franchest man & denyssen in habite wi*th* in yis Cite schall
haue free liberte & sayffegarde in honeste mirthe & gam sportis to goo or
doe what hym pleys. And nogth to be attachyd or arrestyd be any officer   40
of yis Cite for any accion p*er*sonele wi*th* owt the kyng be parte or s*er*uyd
be the kyngis wryt And this to be obseruyd & kept to twelff. day callyd

the fest of ye. Epyphany be past & then euere man take thayr awantage in the law. &c ∴∴

1480–1
Dean and Chapter Common Fund Accounts LA: Bj/3/2
f 10 *(17 September–16 September)* *(Customary payments)*
...

...Et in Ceretacis emptis pro Maria & angelo ex consuetudine in aurora Natalis domini vj d....
...

f 10v *(Gratuities)*
...

...Et in conuiuio Canonicorum existencium Ad videndum ludum Corporis christi in Camera Iohannis Sharpe infra clausum nihil ˏ⌈hoc anno⌉...
...

1481–2
Dean and Chapter Common Fund Accounts LA: Bj/3/2
f 33v *(16 September–15 September)* *(Customary payments)*
...

...Et in Ceretacis emptis pro Maria & angelo ex consuetudine in aurora Natalis domini vj d....
...

1482–3
Dean and Chapter Common Fund Accounts LA: Bj/3/2
f 56v *(15 September 1482–21 September 1483)* *(Customary payments)*
...

...Et in Ceretacis emptis pro maria & Angelo ex consuetudine in Aurora Natalis domini vj d.
...

f 60* *(Allowances)*

...Et solutum domino Henrico Botery pro factura mediate coronacionis beate Marie in ecclesia Cathedrali beate Marie lincolnie era festum Sancte Anne xlvij s. ˏ⌈vj d.⌉ Et solutum pro iantaculo dominorum existencium ad lusum vocatum pater noster play cum xv d. solutis pro expensis eorundem dominorum secundo die eiusdem lusi xvij s....
...

37/ era: *for* erga

5

10

15

20

25

30

35

40

Chapter Act Book   LA: Dean and Chapter A/2/37
f 17*   *(7 June)*
...

die Sabb*ati* Capit*u*lari vij° v*idelicet* die Iunij anno d*o*mini Mill*esi*mo
CCCC*mo* octog*esimo* tercio. In alto Choro ecclesie Cath*edralis* beate   5
Marie lincoln*ie* post Completoriu*m* illi*us* diei finitum d*ominus*
decan*us* cu*m* confr*atrib*us suis v*idelicet* precentore Cancell*ario*
Thes*aurario* & alford vna simul ante occid*entalem* ostiu*m* chori iuxta
solit*os* stantes & de p*ro*cessi*one* s*an*c*te* anne in p*ro*xi*mo* festo eiusd*em*
futur*o* p*er* Ciues lincoln*ie* fiend*a* comm*un*icant*es*/ vna simul   10
decreuerunt q*uod* illud ludu*m* siue serimoniu*m* de assumpc*ione* ∧⌐siue
coronac*ione*⌐ beat*e* Mari*e* erga dict*um* festu*m* de nouo rep*aratum* &
p*re*parat*um* hab*e*re volu*er*unt ac [lusu*m*] ∧⌐ludificatu*m*⌐ & ostensu*m* in
p*ro*cessi*one* p*re*dict*a* p*ro*ut cons*ue*tu*m* fu*er*at in Naui d*ic*te ecclesie.
|motu*m*|∧⌐interrogatu*m*⌐ q*ue* eciam fuit int*er* eos quoru*m* sumptibus   15
fieret huiusmodi op*us* dix*er*unt q*uod* sumptib*us* illor*um* qui ad [huc]
illud *con*tribuere ∧⌐vel aliquid donare⌐ volu*er*unt Et in casu q*uod*
huiusmodi *con*tribuci*o* siue donaci*o*. huiusmodi su*m*ptus p*er*ficere
nolu*er*it q*uod* tunc totu*m* residuu*m* inde tam p*er* commun*am* qua*m*
p*er* ffabrica*m* equal*iter* supp*or*taret*ur* ordinauer*un*tque tunc ib*idem*   20
d*o*minu*m* Thes*aurarium* & *Magistrum* Thoma*m* alford in mag*is*tros
superuisores d*ic*ti op*er*is d*o*mino Subdecano p*ro*tunc p*re*posito d*ic*te
ecclesie in turno suo p*re*positure ex*t*ra existen*te*
...

                                                                                   25

1483–4
Dean and Chapter Common Fund Accounts   LA: Bj/3/2
f 78v   *(21 September–19 September)* *(Customary payments)*
...
...Et in Cerothec*is* empt*is* p*ro* maria & Angelo ex consuetudi*ne* in Aurora   30
Natal*is* d*o*mini vj d....
...

1484–5
Dean and Chapter Common Fund Accounts   LA: Bj/3/2   35
f 99v   *(19 September–18 September)* *(Customary payments)*
...
...Et in cerothec*is* empt*is* p*ro* maria & Angelo ex consue*tudi*ne in Aurora
Natal*is* d*o*mini vj d....

...   40

1485–6
Dean and Chapter Common Fund Accounts   LA: Bj/3/2
f 120v   *(18 September–17 September)*   *(Customary payments)*

…

…Et in cerothec*is* empt*is* pro maria & Angelo ex consue*tudi*ne in aurora   5
Natal*is* d*om*ini vj d.…

…

f 123v   *(Allowances)*

    10

…Et sol*utum* Henr*ico* Butt*ere* Cap*ell*ano p*er* mandat*um* d*om*ini prepositi
p*ro* ostenc*ione* Coronac*ionis* beate M*ar*ie in ffesto s*anc*te Anne v s.…

…

1486–7   15
Dean and Chapter Common Fund Accounts   LA: Bj/3/2
f 141v   *(17 September–16 September)*   *(Customary payments)*

…Et in cerothec*is* empt*is* p*ro* maria & ang*e*lo ex consue*tudi*ne in aurora
Nat*a*l*is* d*om*ini vj d.….   20

…

f 144v   *(Allowances)*

Et sol*utum* p*ro* expen*sis* [*om*nium] d*om*inorum ⌜canon*i*corum⌝   25
Residen*ciariorum* existen*cium* ad lusu*m* Corp*or*is chr*is*ti xxviij s. iij d.…

…

1487–8
Dean and Chapter Common Fund Accounts   LA: Bj/3/2   30
f 161v   *(16 September 1487–21 September 1488)*   *(Customary payments)*

…Et in Cerothec*is* empt*is* p*ro* maria & ang*e*lo ex *consue*tudi*ne* in Aurora
Nat*a*l*is* d*om*ini vj d.…

…   35

f 164v   *(Allowances)*

…Et in expen*sis* o*m*nium d*om*inorum residen*ciariorum* existen*cium* ad
lusu*m* Corp*or*is chr*is*ti xxij s. iij d. ob.…   40

…

1488
Chapter Act Book   LA: Dean and Chapter A/3/1
f 58v*   *(13 September)*
...

aduocacio
vnius cantarie
de burton

Et eodem die iidem canonici concesserunt Domino Thesaurario presentare &   5
nominare ad illam cantariam in Burton quam dominus Robertus clerke in
presenti obtinet quecumque idoneum capellanum quandocumque contigerit
ipsam Cantariam proxime vacare et ipsum dominum Robertum secum retinere
pro eo quod est ita [ingcs] ingeniosus in ostensione & lusu vocato assensionem
vsitato singulis Annis in festo sancte Anne &c   10
...

1488–9
Dean and Chapter Common Fund Accounts   LA: Bj/3/2
f 182v   *(21 September–20 September)*   *(Customary payments)*   15

...Et in Cerothecis emptis pro maria & Angelo ex consuetudine in Aurora
Natalis domini vj d....
...
  20

1489–90
Dean and Chapter Common Fund Accounts   LA: Bj/3/2
f 203v   *(20 September–19 September)*   *(Customary payments)*

...Et in Cerothecis emptis pro maria & Angelo ex consuetudine in Aurora   25
Natalis domini vj d....
...

f 204   *(Gratuities)*
  30
...Et in expensis factis in Iantaculo canonicorum videncium ludum de le
pater noster pley xx s. I d.
...

f 206v   *(Allowances)*   35

...Et allocatur ei pro denarijs solutis Roberto Clerke capellano pro laboribus
suis circa coronacionem beate Marie in Navi ecclesie in festo sancte Anne
ij s.
...
  40

7/ quecumque: *for* quemcumque

1490–1
Dean and Chapter Common Fund Accounts   LA: Bj/3/2
f 224v   *(19 September–18 September) (Customary payments)*

...Et in [cho] ∧⌜Se⌝rothec*is* empt*is* p*ro* maria & Angelo ex co*n*suet*udi*ne in   5
Aurora Natal*is* do*m*ini vj d....

...

f 227v   *(Allowances)*

10
...Et in den*arijs* sol*utis* do*m*ino Roberto Clark p*ro* labore suo in festo s*a*nct*e*
Anne circa coronac*i*o*n*em be*a*te Marie ij s....

...

1491–2   15
Dean and Chapter Common Fund Accounts   LA: Bj/3/2
f 247v   *(18 September–16 September) (Customary payments)*

...Et in Serothec*is* empt*is* p*ro* Maria & Angilo ex co*n*suet*udi*ne in Aurora
Natal*is* do*m*ini vj d....   20

...

1492–3
Dean and Chapter Common Fund Accounts   LA: Bj/3/2
f 268v   *(16 September–15 September) (Customary payments)*   25

...Et in Serothec*is* empt*is* p*ro* Maria & Angelo ex consuet*udi*ne in aurora
Natal*is* do*m*ini vj d....

...

30
1493–4
Dean and Chapter Common Fund Accounts   LA: Bj/3/2
f 289v   *(15 September 1493–21 September 1494) (Customary payments)*

...Et in serothec*is* empt*is* p*ro* maria & Angelo ex consuet*udi*ne in aurora   35
Natal*is* do*m*ini vj d....

...

(Gratuities)
...Et sol*utum* do*m*ino Roberto Brown laborant*i* circa coronac*i*o*n*em marie   40
in ffesto s*a*nct*e* Anne Anno p*ro*ximo preced*enti* p*ro* eo q*u*od prius no*n*
allo*cabatur* ij s. Et eidem p*ro* hoc Anno ij s....

...

1494–5
Dean and Chapter Common Fund Accounts   LA: Bj/3/2
f 310v   *(21 September–20 September)* *(Customary payments)*

...Et in serothecis emptis pro maria & Angelo ex consuetudine in Aurora   5
Natalis domini vj d....

...

1495–6
Dean and Chapter Common Fund Accounts   LA: Bj/3/2   10
f 331v   *(20 September 18 September)* *(Customary payments)*

...Et in serothecis emptis pro maria & Angelo ex consuetudine in Aurora
Natalis domini vj d....

...   15

(Gratuities)
...Et in expensis dominorum Canonicorum existencium Ad ludum Corporis
christi vna cum aliis nobilibus multis secum existentibus Ad gentaculum &
cenam liiij s. ix d. ob.   20

...

1501–2
Dean and Chapter Common Fund Accounts   LA: Bj/3/3
f 9v   *(19 September–18 September)* *(Customary payments)*   25

...Et in serothecis emptis pro maria & angelo ex consuetudine in aurora
Natalis Domini vj d....

...

30

f 10v   *(Allowances)*

...Et allocatur ei vt in denarijs solutis Iohanni barne ex precepto Capituli
pro laboribus suis circa Assumpcionem in festo Sancte Anne ij s....

...   35

1502–3
Dean and Chapter Common Fund Accounts   LA: Bj/3/3
f 31v   *(18 September–17 September)* *(Customary payments)*

40

...Et in Serothecis emptis pro maria & angelo ex consuetudine in aurora
Natalis domini vj d....

...

f 34v   *(Allowances)*

...Et allo*catur* ei vt in denar*ijs* solut*is* Ioh*ann*i baron ex pre*cepto* Capit*u*li p*ro* labor*ibus* su*is* circa assump*cionem* be*ate* marie in festo *Sancte* Anne ij s....

...   5

1503–4
Dean and Chapter Common Fund Accounts   LA: Bj/3/3
f 51v   *(17 September–15 September)* *(Customary payments)*

10

...Et in serothe*cis* empt*is* p*ro* maria & ang*e*lo ex consue*tudi*ne in aurora Natal*is* d*o*m*i*ni vj d....

...

f 54v   *(Allowances)*   15

...*E*t allo*catur* eid*e*m vt in denar*ijs* solut*is* Ioh*ann*i baron ex pre*cepto* d*o*m*i*no*rum* decani et capit*u*li p*ro* labor*ibus* suis circa Assumptione*m* in festo s*ancte* Anne f*act*am in Naui ecc*le*sie ij s....

...   20

1505–6
Dean and Chapter Common Fund Accounts   LA: Bj/3/3
f 71v   *(21 September–20 September)* *(Customary payments)*

25

...Et in serothe*cis* empt*is* p*ro* maria & ang*e*lo ex consue*tudi*ne in aurora Natal*is* d*o*m*i*ni vj d....

...

1506–7   30
Dean and Chapter Common Fund Accounts   LA: Bj/3/3
f 91v   *(20 September–19 September)* *(Customary payments)*

...Et in serothe*cis* empt*is* p*ro* maria & ang*e*lo ex consue*tudi*ne in aurora Natal*is* D*o*m*i*ni vj d....   35

...

f 94v   *(Allowances)*

...Et allo*catur* eid*e*m in denar*ijs* solut*is* Ioh*ann*i baron ex pre*cepto* d*o*m*i*no*rum* 40

34/ &: *obscured by fold*

Capituli pro labore suo circa Assumpcionem in festo sancte Anne factam in
naui ecclesie tam pro hoc Anno quam pro Anno preterito iiij s....

...

1507–8   5
Dean and Chapter Common Fund Accounts   LA: Bj/3/3
f 111v   (19 September–17 September)   (Customary payments)

...Et in serothecis emptis pro maria & angelo ex consuetudine in aurora
Natalis domini vj d....   10

...

f 114v   (Allowances)

...Et allocatur eidem in denarijs solutis Iohanni baron ex precepto dominorum 15
capituli pro labore suo circa Assumpcionem in festo sancte Anne factam in
naui ecclesie ij. s....

...

1508–9   20
Dean and Chapter Common Fund Accounts   LA: Bj/3/3
f 131v   (17 September–16 September)   (Customary payments)

...Et in serothecis emptis pro maria & angelo ex consuetudine in aurora
Natalis domini vj d....   25

...

f 134v   (Allowances)

...Et Allocatur eidem pro denarijs solutis Iohanni barons ex precepto   30
dominorum capituli pro labore & expensis suis circa Assumpcionem in
festo sancte Anne factam in navi ecclesie ij. s....

...

1509–10   35
Dean and Chapter Common Fund Accounts   LA: Bj/3/3
f 153v   (16 September–15 September)   (Customary payments)
...
Et solutum pro serothecis emptis pro maria et Angelo
ex consuetudine in aurora Natalis domini   vj d. 40

...

f 154   *(Gratuities)*

...

Et Ioh*anni* baron Ianitori cl*ausi* ei dat*um* in Regard*o* p*ro*
orilegio et Coronac*ione* beate Marie in ffesto sancte Anne
et p*ro* laboribus et expen*sis*   x s.   5

...

Dean and Chapter Act Book   LA: Dean and Chapter A/3/4
f 6v   *(1 December)*

concernit
Ioh*anne*m
Barne

...   10

Die Sabbati cap*itula*ri primo vi*delice*t die mensis Decembr*is* Anno d*omi*ni
M*i*llesim*o* Quingentesim*o* nono d*omi*nus Thes*aurarius* Archi*diaco*nus
Lincoln*iensis* & Roston cano*nici* residenc*iarii* in domo cap*itula*ri cap*itula*riter
congr*egati* M*agistro* precentore Archi*diaco*no Stowe & ffizherbert recedentib*us*
a loco cap*itula*ri quicquid in illo cap*itul*o *per* eos actum fu*er*it ratum expresse   15
h*a*bentib*us*/ Post tractatu*m* inter p*re*fatos Thes*aurarium* Archi*diaco*num
lincoln*iensis* & Roston de & super ₐ⌐labore et⌐ deligencia annuati*m* continuata
& in futur*o* continuand*a* *per* Ioh*anne*m Barne[s] inter cetera circa columba*m* [in]
& lez [orlez] orlege in septimana pent*ecos*tes ac eciam circit*er* assumpc*ion*em
be*a*te marie in festo s*anct*e Anne simili*ter* in die natalis d*omi*ni in p*re*parando   20
stella*m* in aurora & in septima*n*a passionis cu*m* vexilla. vnanimit*er* [conr]
concesseru*nt* n*om*i*n*e cap*itul*i *pre*fato Ioh*anni* Barne p*ro* omnib*us* suis
laborib*us* & diligencijs circa p*re*missa in futur*o* de anno in annu*m* exhibend*is*
quamd*a*m annuitatem viginti solidor*um* eidem a*n*nuatim quamdiu cap*itul*o
placu*er*it in forma sequen*ti* soluend*am* vi*delice*t x s. *per* clericum comm*u*ne &   25
x s. *per* cl*er*icum fabrice annuati*m* ad ben*e*placitum cap*itul*i soluendo*s*

...

1510–11
Dean and Chapter Common Fund Accounts   LA: Bj/3/3   30
f 172v   *(15 September 1510–21 September 1511)* *(Customary payments)*

...

Et sol*utum* p*ro* Cerothec*is* empt*is* pro Maria et Angelo
ex consuetudine in Aurora Natalis d*omi*ni   vj d.

...   35

f 173   *(Gratuities)*

...

Et Iohanni baron Ianitor*i* cl*ausi* dat*um* eid*em* in Regardo

24l annuitatem: *first* t *written as correction over another letter*

pro orilogio et Coronacione beate Marie in festo sancte
Anne pro laboribus & expensis x s.

...

1511–12
Dean and Chapter Common Fund Accounts   LA: Bj/3/3
f 194v   *(21 September–19 September)*   *(Customary payments)*
...

Et solutum pro Cerotecis emptis pro maria et Angelo ex
consuetudine in Aurora Natalis domini vj d. 10

...

f 195   *(Gratuities)*
...

Et Iohanni baron Ianitori Clausi ei datum in regardo 15
pro [ol] orilogio et Coronacione beate marie [pro] in
festo sancte Anne pro laboribus & expensis x s.

...

1512–13 20
Dean and Chapter Common Fund Accounts   LA: Bj/3/3
f 216v   *(19 September–18 September)*   *(Customary payments)*
...

Et solutum pro Cerothecis emptis pro maria et Angelo ex
consuetudine in Aurora Natalis domini vj d. 25

...

f 217   *(Gratuities)*
...

Et Iohanni Baron Ianitori Clausi datum in regardo pro 30
orilogio & Coronacione beate marie in festo sancte
Anne pro laboribus & expensis x s.

...

1513–14 35
Dean and Chapter Common Fund Accounts   LA: Bj/3/3
f 239v   *(18 September–17 September)*   *(Customary payments)*
...

Et solutum pro Cerothecis emptis pro maria & Angelo
ex consuetudine in aurora Natalis domini vj d. 40

...

f 240   *(Gratuities)*

...

Et sol*utum* Ioh*anni* baron Ianitori Cl*ausi* dat*um* eid*em*
in Regard*o* p*ro* orilogio & Coronac*i*one be*ate* marie in
fest*o* sancte Anne p*ro* laborib*us* & expens*is*   x s.   5

...

1514–15
City Council Minute Book   LA: L1/1/1/1
f 35   *(14 October)*   10

also in this p*resent* Com*men* Concell Thomas Burton late maier off this
Citie the last yer past delyu*er*id to M*aster* maier y*at* now is iij keys ⌜[off
Syluer ffor ye wayt*es*]⌝ & the Seale off the office of maraltie which is made
off Syluer also iij Colers off Syluer ffor iij weyt*es*   ⌐15

also ⌜the seid⌝ iij Colers off Syluer ffor the wayt*es* [off wych] one hath xxiij^th
lynk*es* w*ith* a Skochyn and other hath xxviij^th [Skochyns] ⌜lynk*es*⌝ w*ith* a
Scheld The iij^de Coler hath xxvj^th lynk*es* and a Scheld
...   20

f 42*   *(25 July)*
...

also it is agreid y*at* willi*am* ffox of lincoln Sadyler Schall haue in fferme the
colecc*i*on of The Townez villages & hamlett*es* for the ffraternyte off Scaynt   25
anne Gild off this Citie off lincoln ffor the Terme off vj^s yer & he to haue
my lord off lincoln auctoritie p*ur*chest ffre to hym vnder the ordynary Seall
at the Cost*es* & Chargez off M*aster* Graceman & the Brethern off ye Seid
Gild at ye ffurst yer Begynnyng & Thother yers To be at hys awne Cost*es*
payng yerly therfore to ye g*ra*ceman & Brether*n* off ye Same dewryng the   30
Seid Terme of yers vj li. xiij s. iiij d. p*ro*vyded alwey That he Schall haue no
Colecc*i*on [& to haue his wrytyng made afore mychelmes Then next Comyng]
off Thenhabytaunt*es* w*ith*in The Citie off lincoln ffor the Same nor Suburbz
off the Same & and to haue his wrytyng afore mychelmes Then next Comyng
p*ro*uided alwey y*at* iff any vesture or garment be byquethed to thoner off   35
god & the Seid Gild by any p*er*son or p*er*sons w*ith*in the Seyd Dyaces the
Seid willi*am* ffox Schall deliu*er* or Cause To be delyuerd to ye Seid g*ra*ceman
& Brethern Sutch garment or vesture So byquethyd and the Seid willi*am* ffox
p*ro*mysis in This p*re*sent*es* to ley downe off his ffirst yer rent xl s. aforehand
to the purchesyng off the Seid ordinary Seale   40
...

f 42v

°Relious
bustage°

also in This presentes it is agreid That wher diuers garmentes & other
he⌈a⌉riormentes is yerly boroyd in the Cuntrey ffor the arryeyng off ye [page]
pagentes off Saynt anne gyld now ye knyght & gentylmen be ffreyd with   5
the plage So yat the graceman Can borowght non Sutch garmentes wherfore
euery alderman Schall prepare & Setfoorth in ye Seid arrey ij good gownes
and euery Scheryff pere a gowne and euery Chaumberlen pere a gowne &
the persons with Theym To weyr ye Same

                                                                          10

also it is agreid that ye Chefe Constables Schall Commaund in Master
maieres name euery vnder Cunstable To weyt vppon the arrey in pressession
bouth to kepe ye peuple ffrom ye arrey & also to Take hede off Sutch as
weyr garmentes in ye Same vppon payn off fforfeture to ye Commen
Chaumbre yat is to Sey euery Chefe Constable xl s. & euery vnder Constable   15
iij. s. iiij. d.
…

f 44   *(17 September)*
…   20
In This present Commen Concell Mr Sames Takyth hys oath off the mayraltie
To begyne at michelmes dey at none next Comyng and it is graunted To
hym Towerd hys Gret Charges To haue as other maiers haue had afore hym
yat is To Sey x li. off the Commyn Chaumbre & xxxiij s. iiij d. To gyff in
rewardes to mynstrelles & other resortyng to hym yat yer   25
…

Dean and Chapter Common Fund Accounts   LA: Bj/3/3
f 260   *(17 September–16 September)* *(Customary payments)*
…   30
Et solutum pro Cerotecis emptis pro maria et Angelo
ex consuetudine in Aurora Natalis domini   vj d.
…

f 260v   *(Gratuities)*   35
…
Et solutum Iohanni barns Ianitori Clausi datum ei in regardo
pro orilogio et Coronacione marie in festo sancte Anne pro
laboribus & expensis   x s.
…   40

1515–16
City Council Minute Book   LA: L1/1/1/1
f 50   *(5 November)*

…

Doct*ur*
Ranston

also it is agreid y*at* M*aster* maier Schall Call v or vj off hys Bretherne To   5
haue Co*mmu*nicacion w*ith* Doctur Ranston ffor the p*ro*ffyt*es* off Scaynt
anne gyld and Sutch Cost*es* as y*at* M*aster* maier doth off hym he Schalbe
allowyed it agayn off the Co*mme*n Chaumbr*e*

f 50v   10

…

also it is agreid y*at* M*aster* maier Schall haue iij weyt*es* And to gyff theym
lyu*er*ey Acordyng to Thauncyent Custom
…

15

f 56v*   *(17 April)*

…

°ffine for
dep*ar*ting from
p*ro*cession°

M*emora*n*dum* qu*od* ye xxviij^{uo} die ap*ri*lys in The p*re*sent*es* off Mr Sames
maier Roger[t] hogekynson willi*am* Irchenett Iohn pekerd Thom*as* Norton
Thomas ˄⌐Burton⌐ Robert wymark & willel*mo* pereson it is agreid [⟨.⟩] y*at*   20
wher laurens Bryght Dyer willi*am* Burton Barbo*r* Iohn M*ar*tyn Schipwryght
Chr*is*tofer Holtby fficher Richard Thomas ffycher & willi*am* Sowth fficher
& other goyng in the p*ro*cession on the assencyon Day wher Comaundyd
to weyt on M*aster* maier in the Seid p*ro*cession They off Sedicous mynd
dep*ar*tid ffrom ye p*re*sent*es* off the Seyd M*aster* maier ffor the Which it is   25
Concideryd by ther awne Confeffession y*at* ye Seid p*ar*tiez hath Disobayed
the othe off ther ffraunchese ffor which They be Co*m*maundid To ward ther
to remayne vnto fferther Concideracion be Takyn by M*aster* maier & hys
Brether*n* ffor the Same
…

30

Dean and Chapter Common Fund Accounts   LA: Bj/3/3
f 282v   *(16 September 1515–21 September 1516)*   *(Customary payments)*
…

Et sol*utum* pro Cerothec*is* empt*is* p*ro* maria & angelo   35
ex consuetudi*ne* in Aurora Nat*a*lis d*o*m*i*ni   vj d.
…

f 283   *(Gratuities)*

…   40

Et sol*utum* Iohanni barns Ianitor*i* Claus*i* in Regardo

26/ Confeffession: *for* Confession

pro orilogio & Coronacione marie in festo sancte Anne
pro laboribus & expensis Cum ij s. sibi concessis per
Capitulum pro tempore   [x s.] xij s.

Dean and Chapter Act Book   LA: Dean and Chapter A/3/3   5
f 87* (14 June)

...

pro Iohanne
Barne

Memoretur quod xiiij^mo die mensis Iunij Anno supradicto domini decanus
precentor Cancellarius Archidiaconus lincolniensis Archidiaconus Stowe
& Massingberd canonici Residenciarii capitulariter in domo capitulari   10
congregati concesserunt Iohanni Barne ij s. annuatim soluendos sibi per
clericum commune pro suis laboribus circa assumptionem beate marie in die
Anne prout ex antiquo habuit vt patet per libros computorum clerici commune
vltra xx s. eidem Iohanni ad voluntatem capituli ⌐concessas⌐ per capitulum
primo die mensis Decembris Anno domini Millesimo quingentesimo Nono pro   15
laboribus suis circa dictam Assumptionem et alias labores diuersis temporibus
anni excercendis [concessas]

1516–17
City Council Minute Book   LA: L1/1/1/1   20
f 69v (27 October)

...

°waytes°

In this present Commyn Concell it is agreid That Master maier Schall haue
iij weytes this yer as yat other maiers hath had & he To provyde yff yat he
Can ffor Sutch as yat be gud ffor the worchypp off this Citie   25

...

f 72v* (10 June)

...

also it is agreid yat Sir Robert Deuyas Schalbe Sent anne preste & he to haue   30
to ye ȝerly Sawde of the Same v li. and to begynne & entre in to the Same
at michelmes next Comyng & he to haue it for terme of hys lyfe of a gud
& lawfull beryng vnder the Comyn Seale and he promysyth in this presentes
ȝerly to helppe to ye Bryngyng Foorth & preparyng of the pageantes in
Scaynt anne gyld   35

...

Also Master maier receyvyd of Sir Robert Deuyas vj s. viij d. for the
Comyn Seale

...

2–3/ Cum ... xij s: addition and correction in red   16/ alias labores: for aliis laboribus
  ink apparently by the same hand   17/ [concessas]: cancelled in error; for concessos
14/ ⌐concessas⌐: for concessos

f 75*   *(22 September)*

...

Robert Deuyas
St an preist

also in This present*es* it is agreid y*at* *sir* Robert Devias off Lincoln prest
Schalhaue vse & ocupye And be Scaynt anne preste in the Citie off Lincoln
Dewryng hys lyffe to Syng ffor the bretherne & Systernz & ffor all the   5
benefac*tores* off the Same gyld & he to haue yerly alselong as y*at* he may
ocupie & Syng mes and helpe to bryng ffoorth & p*re*pare the p*ro*cession
& pageaunt*es* off the Same gylde in the Citie off Lincoln yerly v li. off gud
& lawfull money off englond To be p*ai*d by the hand*es* off the gr*a*ceman
off the Same gylde yerly ffor the tyme beyng   10

...

Dean and Chapter Common Fund Accounts   LA: Bj/3/3
f 305v   *(21 September–20 September)* *(Customary payments)*

...   15

Et sol*utum* pro cerothec*is* empt*is* pro maria et angelo
ex con*suetudi*ne in aurora Natal*is* d*o*m*i*ni   vj d.

...

f 306v   *(Gratuities)*   20

...

Et sol*utum* Iohanni barns Ianitor*i* Claus*i* in Regardo
pro orilogio & Coronacione marie in *festo sanct*e Anne
p*ro* labori*bus* & expens*is* Cu*m* ij s. sibi concess*is* p*er*
cap*itu*lu*m* p*ro* tempo*re*   xij s. 25

...

1517–18
City Council Minute Book   LA: L1/1/1/1
f 78v   *(26 October)*   30

...

°religeous
thing*es*°

also Thomas mytchell weyt delyu*ers* hys Coler whyth xxviij^th lynk*es* and
a Schochyn and willi*am* ffox delyu*ers* ij Colers y*at* is to Sey on off xxiiij^th
lynk*es* & a Schuchyn and Thother off xxvj^th lynk*es* & a Schochyn

...   35

ff 81–1v*   *(16 June)*

...

°Gild°

also Mr Sa*m*mes late Graceman of Scaynt anne gyld delyu*erd* to Mr p*e*reson
now graceman of the Same Gyld ahamp*er* wit*h* Iuell*es* off the Same gyld   40
by an Indent*ur* theroff made to ye byhoff of the Seyd gylde and it is agreid
that the Seyd Mr Sa*m*mes Schall make hys acompt of All Sutch p*ro*fytes &
resayt*es* as y*at* he hath resayuyd to thuse off the Seyd gyld

also it is agreid y*at* Mr Irchenett late graceman of the Same gyld Schall make
hys acompt for hys tyme the Same dey

°Religious   also it is agreid y*at* eu*ery* alderman Schall Sendfoorth a ser*uant* wi*th* a Tortch
orders°   To be lightyd in ye p*ro*cession w*ith* a rochet vppon hym abowt the Sacrement   5
                vppon payn eu*ery* off theym off forfytyng off vj s. viij d. and eu*ery* alderman
                To Sendffoorth one p*er*son wi*th* agud gowne vppon hys Bake to go in The
                p*ro*cession vppon the Seyd payn off vj s. viij d.

°cons*tables*°   also it is agreid y*at* eu*ery* vnder Constable Schall wayt on ye pageant*es* on   10
                Scaynt anne dey by vij off ye Clok in ye Seyd p*ro*cession vppon payn eu*ery*
                off theym y*at* makyth defau*t* to fforfy*t* xij d. |

                also in This p*re*sent*es* Mr pereson now graceman off Scaynt anne gyld
                Schewyth agowne off Blak Damask [Bought Indentyd w] abuue Indentyd   15
                abowte wi*th* blak veluet off the Gcyft off s*ir* Iohn Carre by hym Gyffyn to
                the thuse & hono*r* off the Seyd Gyld

                also it is agreid y*at* willi*am* ffox [Chamberlain] Schall haue the Seyd gownc
                in kepyn & leyue it to m*r* p*er*son   20
                …

                f 94v   *(14 September)*

                also in This p*re*sent*es* it is agreid y*at* wher the greyt Gyld off this Citie Callyd   25
                our lady Gyld is ffallyn in Decay and almost desolate ffor lake off gud ordyr
                & ffor reformac*i*on off the Same ther is apapur drawne by Mr Taylboie one
                off the Thaldermen off this Citie ffor hclpyng & reformyng off the Seyd
                Gyld here in this p*re*sent*es* brought ffoorth & Schewyd & here vnto anncxt
                The Seyd acte Schall by assent off all this p*re*sent*es* Stand In effect & Stablyshed   30
                To be off auctoritie ffrom this day fforward
                …

Dean and Chapter Common Fund Accounts   LA: Bj/3/3
f 328v   *(20 September–19 September) (Customary payments)*   35
…
Et sol*utum* pro cerothec*is* empt*is* pro maria & angelo
ex co*n*suetudine in aurora Nat*a*lis do*m*ini   vj d.
…

17/ the thuse: *phonetic dittography*

f 329   *(Gratuities)*

...

Et sol*utum* Iohanni barns Ianitori Cla*u*si in Regardo p*ro*
horilogio & Coronac*i*one ma*r*ie in f*esto* s*a*ncte Anne p*ro*
laborib*us* et expens*is* cu*m* ij s. sibi concess*is* p*er* capit*u*l*um*   5
pro temp*ore*   xij s.

...

1518–19
City Council Minute Book   LA: L1/1/1/1   10
f 97   *(18 June)*

...

also it is agreid y*at* eu*ery* man and woman w*ith*in this Citie beyng able
Schall be Broder & Syster in Scaynt anne gyld & to pay yerly iiij d. man
& wyf at the lest   15

...

f 97v

...

also y*at* eu*ery* occupac*i*on Schall bryng ffurth ther pageant*es* y*at* be longyng to   20
Scaynt anne gyld Sufficiently vppon payne off fforfytyng eu*ery* off theym x li.

...

Dean and Chapter Common Fund Accounts   LA: Bj/3/3
f 351v   *(19 September–18 September)* *(Customary payments)*   25

...

Et sol*utum* p*ro* cerothec*is* empt*is* p*ro* maria et angelo ex
consuetu*d*ine in Aurora Nat*a*lis d*o*m*i*ni   vj d.

...

                                                                                                    30

f 352   *(Gratuities)*

...

Et sol*utum* Iohanni barns Ianitori clausi in Regardo p*ro*
orilogio & coronac*i*one marie in f*esto* sancte Anne p*ro*
laborib*us* et expensis cu*m* ij s. sibi concess*is* p*er* capit*u*l*um*   35
pro temp*ore*   xij s.

...

1519–20
City Council Minute Book   LA: L1/1/1/1   40
f 107*   *(20 March)*

aldermen for age disabled & non chosen/†

also in This Seyd presentes it is agreid yat wher dyuers off the aldermen off this
Citie be dyseysyd with Infirmytez So yat they maynott attende off Master maier
To ffulfyll the Noumbre in procession & other tymes acordyng to The olde
honorable Custom here vsyd wherfore it is agreid yat George Browne Thomas
fforman & Iohn ffox Schalbe This day elect & Sowrne aldermen off this Citie   5
and it is Commaunded To theym to make euery off theym a Cremysyn gowne
agaynst Scaynt anne day next Comyng vppon payn off fforfytyng To the
Comyn Chaumbre euery off theym yat dooth ye Contrary xl s.

...

                                                                                10

f 113   *(23 May)*

...

also it is agreid yat wher Master ffox late maier off this Citie is now decessyd
& had the ayde off xj li. xiij s. iiij d. to hys office as other had afore hym hys
assignes & executores Schall Bryng ffoorth Scaynt anne Gyld acordyng to   15
Thancyent & lawdable Custome had ffor the Same

...

f 115   *(27 June)*

                                                                                20

also it is agreid yat proclamacion Schalbe made Thorugh This Citie yat euery
ocupacion by the ouersyght off the graceman Schall prepare & make redy
ther pageantes To be honorued as they haue bene afore Tyme vsed agaynst
Scaynt anne Day and that Day to bryng ffoorth euery ocupacion theyr
pageantes vppon payn off fforfytyng to the Commyn Chaumbre euery off   25
theym yat makyth Defaute xl s. and yat euery Constable gyff theyr attendaunce
vppon the pageantes in procession vppon Saynt anne Day vppon payn off
forfytyng euery off theym vj s. viij d. And iff any off the ocupacions lake
agraceman then ij of the most honest & off abelytie To be Charged To
bryng ffoorth ther Sayd pageantes   30

...

Dean and Chapter Common Fund Accounts   LA: Bj/3/3
f 374v   *(18 September–16 September)* *(Customary payments)*

...   35

Et solutum pro cerothecis emptis pro maria et angelo
ex consuetudine in aurora Natalis domini   vj d.

...

f 375   *(Gratuities)*   40

...

Et solutum Iohanni barns Ianitori clausi in regardo

5/ Sowrne: *for* Sworne   23/ honorued: *for* honoured

pro orilogio et coronacione marie in festo sancte anne
pro laboribus suis in eisdem cum ij s. sibi concessis per
capitulum pro tempore   xij s.
…

1520–1
City Council Minute Book   LA: L1/1/1/1
f 123   (10 October)
…

also it is agreid yat mestres Taylboys Schall haue monychion To prepare
& make redy ffor the bryngyng fforth off Schaynt anne gylde acordyng To
tholde Custom off this Citie
…

f 124v   (25 October)
…

also it is agreid yat the fferme of the ffraternytye off Scaynt anne Gylde
Schalbe lettyn to fferme To Sutch honest persons as wyll haue it Thurgh
the dyosyse off my lord off lincoln & gyff the most ffor it/// and in this
presentes It is graunted yat Iohn ffoster Schalhaue the Same ferme vnder
the Comyn Seyll ffor the terme of vj yers payng ye furst yer viij ⌈[th]⌉ li.
euery yer aftur x li. and he to begyn off the Same at mychelmes last past &
to haue the Comyn Seale ffre
…

f 125v   (19 November)

Memorandum yat ∧⌈in⌉ the presentes off Master mayer Mr Irchenett Mr
Alanson Mr Curton Mr papulwyk Mr wymark Mr Browne Robert Darlyngton
Robert louell Thomas Browne & hamond pay the Comyn Seale is opynyd
& Sette ye Indenture off Iohn ffoster ffor the fferme off the gederyng off
Scaynt anne gylde
…

f 130   (20 April)

also it is agreid yat Mr Irchenett Mr papulwyk Mr wymark & Mr fforman
Schall haue Communicacion with mestres Taylboys ffor the bryngyng fforth
off Scaynt anne Gyld & to know what answer She wyll make in yat behalff
and they to know the Same betwyx this & pentecost next Comyng
…

40/ pentecost … Comyng: 19 May 1521

ff 131–1v   *(16 July)*

...

In This present Comyn Concell it is agreid yat euery Graceman yat hath bene
off Scaynt anne gyld yat the Same gyld was lettyn To fferme To Mr ffox &
other They Schall make redy theyr acomptes euery off theym Seuerally by   5
theym Selff & it To be done in Tyme Conuenyently So yat Sutch money as
remaynyth in ther handes Tobe knowen & paid To the vse off the Same gyld |

anail ffor ye
attendaunce off
Scaynt anne
procession ffor
ye Constabulles

also it is agreid yat euery Constable Schall [haue] gyff ther attendaunce
vppon the pageantes in procession vppon Scaynt anne dey vppon payn off   10
euery of theym doyng the Contrary iij s. iiij d.
also it is agreid yat euery alderman Schall prepare one Torch & a persone In
anonest gowne To weyte abowte the Sacrement in proccssion the Same day
vppon payn off euery off Them So doyng the Contrary iij s. iiij d.

15

anail ffor the
aldermen &
Scheriferz To
ye Same

also yat euery alderman yat is away & weythnott vppon Master maier in ye
Same procession to fforfytt iij s. iiij d. To be paid without any pardon except
he haue alawfull excuse and yat euery Scheryff pere gyff theyr attendaunce
vppon payn off xx d. and yat euery off theym To weyt ⌈in⌉ the Same day at
ye hall agaynst yat Master mayer Come Theder vppon ye sam payn   20
also yat euery off theym haue a person in anhonest gowne goyng in procession
amongst ye profytes vppon ye fforfyture aforseyd

...

f 132*   25

also In This Seyd presentes George Browne one off the thaldermen off
this Citie which is elect in ye Sted off the Graceman off Scaynt anne gyld
Complaynyth yat wher the plage is reynyng in yis Citie wherfore he Cannot
gayt Sutch garmentes and other honormentes as Schauld be in ye pagentes off   30
ye procession off Scaynt anne day wherfore it is agreid yat Mr alanson Schalbe
Instantly desyryd to bowro agowne off my lady powes ffor one off the maryes
& thother mary To be arayed in the Crcmysyng gowne off veluet yat longith
to the Same gyld

35

also it is agreid yat Mr Sammes & Mr halton Schalbe Instanted To Spek with
the prior off Scaynt Kateryns To haue Sutch honormentes as yat we haue had
afore tyme to the preparyng off the Same Gyld

...

40

f 133

In this Seyd presentes wher yat Mr Taylbois late maier off this Citie Schuld

haue bene Graceman of Scaynt anne Gyld Acordyng to the old auncyent &
laudable Custom here afore made & vsyd he is now decessyd & the tyme
now drawyth nere y*at* the Sayd Gyld Schalbe prouidyd ffore Tobe brought
ffoorth & it is ambyguetie who Schalbe Graceman off the Same ffor this
pr*esent* yer It is agreid & It is agreid y*at* To ffulfyll George Browne &   5
Thomas fforman aldermen off this Citie Schalbe Gracemen Iuntly To
pr*e*pare & bryng ffoorth the Same vppon Scaynt anne day next Comyng
& iff they refusse So to do they or he So reffusyng To forfyth to the Same
Gylde xl s. To be p*ai*d wi*th*out any p*ar*don and they to haue Towerd the
Charges of the Same Sutch money as Schalbe Gederd wi*th*in the Citie &   10
pr*e*synct off the Same & they to make acounte off All Sutch as is Gederd
wi*th*in the Same & to be alowed all ther Charges & the rest To repay To
thuse off the Same Gylde

...

15

Dean and Chapter Common Fund Accounts   LA: Bj/3/4
f [19v]   *(16 September–15 September)* *(Customary payments)*
...

Et sol*utum* pro cerothec*is* empt*is* pro mar*i*a et angelo
ex con*suetudi*ne in Aurora Natalis d*omi*ni   vj d.   20
...

f [20]   *(Gratuities)*
...

Et sol*utum* Iohanni barns Ianitori claus*i* in Regardo pro   25
Orilog*io* & coronac*ione* mar*i*e in f*esto* s*anct*e anne pro
laborib*us* & expens*is* cu*m* ij s. sibi concess*is* p*er* capit*u*l*um*
pro temp*ore*   xij s.
...

30

1521–2
City Council Minute Book   LA: L1/1/1/1
f 141v   *(30 October)*
...

In This pr*esente*s M*aster* mayr Schewyth a papur off Mr dyghton delyu*er*aunce   35
made & draw*ne* ffor the ffoundac*i*on off the prest To Syng in ye Church
off Scaynt mychell vppon ye hyll ffor hym & hys ffadur moder & other
wi*th* all the brether*n* & Systers off Scaynt anne Gyld/// and they desyre y*at*

5/ It is agreid & It is agreid: *dittography*

wher it is within ye Citie & vnder the rewle of Master maier The donacion
& Gyft off the Same Schalbe ffurst by the presentment of Mr Dyghton
dewryng hys lyff and after hys deceyse To be at the Gyft off hys Executores
duryng theyr lyffes or any off theym and aftur theyr deceys it tobe At the
determonacion off the maycr & Comyns off this Citie ffor eny as yat all   5
other Chaunttres within this Citie is & euer hath byne with a prouyso
yat the Seid Chapylen Schall yerly be redy & delygent To helpp to the
preparyng & bryngyng foorth off the processyon off Scaynt anne day and
also the Seyd prest aftur Mr dyghton deceysse Tobe Callyd ffor euer Scaynt
anne prest   10

...

f 142v   (31 December)

...

also it is agreid yat the Composicion made Betwyx the prior off Scaynt   15
Katheryns & this Citie Schalbe Brought in & new to be made by Thaduyce
off booth partycs
also it is agreid yat euery alderman Schall make agowne ffor the Kynges in
ye pageantes in the procession off Scaynt anne day
also it is agreid yat pater noster play Schalbe played this yer   20

...

f 144   (13 June)

...

In This present Comyn Concell it is agreid yat the Graceman off Scaynt   25
anne gyld Schall prepare ffor the bryngyng fforth off the Same Gyld agaynst
Scaynt anne day next Comyng/// and yat euery ocupacion within this Citie
Schall prepare & make redy ther pageantes Tobe brought fforth the Same
day acordyng To Thold lawdable Custom and yat Master mayer ayde the
Graceman in the orderyng off the Same iff yat nede require and yat in euery   30
paroch ij honest persons Schalbe assignyd by Master mayr & the Graceman
Too Gedyr ye money off the brethern & Systers & To delyuer it To the
Graceman off the Same Gyld

...

                                                                                   35

Dean and Chapter Common Fund Accounts   LA: Bj/3/4
f [42]   (15 September 1521–21 September 1522)   (Customary payments)

...

Et solutum pro Cerothecis emptis pro Maria et Angelo
ex consuetudine in Aurora natalis domini   vj d.   40

...

f [42v]   *(Gratuities)*

…

Et sol*utum* Ioh*anni* Barns Ianitor*i* claus*i* in Regard*o* p*ro* ⌐h⌐orilogio et coronac*ione* Marie in *festo sancte* Anne p*ro* labor*ibus* et expens*is* cu*m* ij s. sibi concess*is* p*er* cap*itulu*m p*ro* temp*ore*

Et sol*utum* in Regard*o* eid*em* Ioh*anni* ex gr*aci*a Capit*u*li

⎫
⎬ xij s.   5
⎭

…

Will of John Sawer   LA: LCC WILLS 1520–25   10

See Thurlby 1521/2

1522–3
City Council Minute Book   LA: L1/1/1/1   15
f 159   *(28 May)*

…

and ordyn*ance*
for Scaynt
anne Gyld

also it is agreid y*at* eu*ery* alderman of this Citie Schall accordyng to anold acte afore made haue agowne ffor p*re*paryng off the kyng*es* in Scaynt anne Gyld awther off hys awne as it is afore ordynyd or els To borow one gowne   20 ffor y*at* dey vppon payn of xl s. To be forfyt off eu*ery* p*er*son y*at* Dooth the Contrary & payd and eu*ery* Scheryfpere To haue won p*er*son arayed in anhonest Gowne off Cloth Goyng among the proffyt*es* in procession off the Same Gyld vppon payn off xx s.

…   25

f 160v   *(2 June)*

…

The gederyng
ffor Scaynt
anne gyld

In This p*resent* Comyn Concell it is agrett y*at* wher eu*ery* mayer off this Citie Schall in the yer ffoloyng be Graceman off Scaynt anne Gyld as hath   30 bene by olde ordynance ⌐vsyd⌐ and now ffrom hensfoorth Sutch Graceman Schall haue booth Those p*er*sons y*at* was hys Scheryffes To be wardyns To hym To helpp hym in all hys besynes in the Same and they To see ye reseyt off ye money That is gederyd To The Same & also helpp to geder ye Same   35

also it is agreid y*at* eu*ery* Sutch p*er*son y*at* hath bene Graceman off Scaynt anne Gyld Scaynst ye sayd Gyld was lettyn To fferme schall make redy theyr acompt*es* agaynst y*at* M*aster* mayr Come home ffrom ye p*ar*leament vppon payn off fforfytyng off vj s. viij d.   40

…

f 162v*   *(26 September)*

...

In this present Comyn Concell George Browne Now elect the mayer off
this Citie ffor this next yer ffoloyng takyth hys othe off the mayraltye And
it is graunted To hym to haue acordyng to thancyent & lawdable Custom   5
off this Citie yat is to sey to The mayntenyng off his howse x li. & to
mynstrell rewardes xxxvj s. viij d.

...

Dean and Chapter Common Fund Accounts   LA: Bj/3/4   10
f [65]   *(21 September–20 September)* *(Customary payments)*

...

Et solutum pro Cerothecis emptis pro Maria et Angelo
ex Consuetudine in Aurora natalis domini   vj d.

...   15

f [65v]   *(Gratuities)*

...

Et solutum Iohanni Barns Ianitori Clausi in Regardo   ⎫
pro horilogio & Coronacione Marie in festo sancte   ⎪   20
Anne pro laboribus et expensis cum ij s. sibi Concessis   ⎬   xij s.
per Capitulum pro tempore   ⎪
Et solutum in Regardo eidem Iohanni ex gracia Capituli   ⎭

...

                                                                             25

1523–4
City Council Minute Book   LA: L1/1/1/1
f 168v   *(14 March)*

...

also it is agreid yat the Sayd auditores Schall here euery Such menz acomptes 30
as yat hath bene Gracemen of Scaynt anne gyld & hath not acompted off all
Such money as yat hath Comyn to ther handes by reason off ye Same

...

f 169   *(2 July)*   35

...

In this present Comyn Concell it is agreid yat euery alderman of yis Citie
Schalhaue agowne off Sylke awther off hys awne or off his Boroyng ffor the
kynges in Scaynt anne processyon acordyng Tho thact affore made & they
to haue theym redy iij dayes afore ye Same processyon day vppon payn off   40

39/ Tho: *for* To

fforfytyng eu*ery* off theym iij s. iiij d. to ye Comyn Chaumbre// And the
Tylers of this Citie To p*re*pare honest p*er*sons To weyr the fforsayd Gownes
The Same day/

also it is agreid y*at* eu*ery* off ye Sayd aldermen Schalhaue a Torch to weyte   5
abowte ye Sacrament in the Same p*ro*cess*i*on vppon payn off fforfyteyng of
iij s. iiij d./

f 169v

10

also it is agreid y*at* eu*ery* man y*at* hath bene graceman off Scaynt anne Gyld
Schall make redy hys acompt in a Dew fforme to be Broght affore *Master*
maier hys brethern & the audy*tores* assigned vppon wedonsdey next afore The
T*r*anslac*i*on off Scaynt Sw*i*thune next Comyng vppon payn off fforfytyng
To ye Same Gyld eu*ery* off ye Same Acomptant*es* vj s. viij d.   15
...
also it is agreid y*at* eu*ery* vndercunstuble Do hys attendaunce vppon *Master*
maier ⌐in ye p*ro*cession off Saynt anne Day⌐ off the pagent*es* in ye Same vppon
payn off fforfytyng eu*ery* off theym xij d.
...   20

f 172   *(26 September)*
...
In this p*re*sent Comyn Concell *Mr* alanson wich is elect & Chosyn To
be maier off this Citie ffor this next yer ffoloyng enteryng into ye Same   25
office at mychelmes Day at none Comyth in & takyth hys oth of marialtie
acordyng to the auncyent & lawdable Custom afore here vsyd and it is
graunted to hym to haue ffree the ffraunches off iiij honest p*er*sons To be
Takyn w*ith*out ye p*re*synct of thys Citie and it is graunted to hym to haue
off ye Comyn Chaumbr*e* off this Citie To ye releffe off hys howsekepyng   30
x li. & xxxiij s. iiij d. To rewardyng off mynstrell*es* acordyng to ye auncent
Custom off yis Citie
...

f 172v*   35
...
also it is agreid y*at* the ij weyt*es* y*at* be in this Citie Schall ocupye thys Next
yer & they to haue ther lyu*er*ez off the Comyn Chaumbr*e* and off eu*ery*
alderman in ∧⌐the⌐ yer xij d. & off eu*ery* Schiryff pere vj d. & off eu*ery*
Chaumb*er*len pere iiij d.   40
...

13–14/ wedonsdey ... next Comyng: *13 July 1524*

Dean and Chapter Common Fund Accounts   LA: Bj/3/4

f [89]   *(20 September–18 September)*   *(Customary payments)*

…

Et sol*utum* pro Cerothec*is* Empt*is* pro Maria et Ang*el*o
ex con*suetu*di*ne* in Aurora Natalis domini   vj d.   5

…

f [90]   *(Gratuities)*

…

Et sol*utum* Ioh*ann*i Barns Ianitor*i* Claus*i* in Regard*o*   10
pro hor*i*logio & Coronac*ione* mar*i*c in f*esto* san*c*te
Anne pro labor*ibus* Et expens*is* cu*m* ij s. sibi concess*is*   xij s.
per c*apitulu*m pro tempore
Et sol*utum* in Regardo Eid*em* Ioh*an*ni ex gr*ac*ia Capit*u*li

…   15

1524–5
City Council Minute Book   LA: L1/1/1/1

f 177   *(10 December)*

…   20

also it is agreid y*at* M*aster* maier Schall [Cawse] ⌈Se⌉ y*at* they lyu*er*ey*z*
Shalbe booght ffor *t*he ij wat*es* y*at* they may haue ij honest Gowns made
agaynst Crystynmes next to Come

…

                                                                                      25

f 179v   *(21 June)*

…

Scaynt anne   In this *p*resent Comyn Concell it is agreid y*at* Thold ordynance ordenyd
gyld   ffor Scaynt anne Gyld Schall Stand in effect y*at* is To Sey eu*er*y alderman a
                  Gowne off Sylke ffor preparyng off ye Kynge*s* in processyon wi*th* a man &   30
                  a Torch To weyt on ye Sacrement It*em* eu*er*y Scheryfpere To haue a man in
                  an honest Gowne To Go as profytt*es* in the Same procession vppon payn off
                  eu*er*y alderman y*at* feylyth To fforfyth iij s. iiij d. And eu*er*y Scheryfpere to
                  fforfyt xij d.

                                                                                      35

also it is ∧⌈agreid⌉ y*at* eu*er*y man y*at* is off abylytie in This Citie Schalbe
brother of the Same Gyld and to pay ther brotherhod aftur Thold custom

also it is agreid y*at* eu*er*y Constable in this Citie Schall weyte vppon the
pagent*es* in ye Same procession To Gyff Ther attendaunce in orderyng off   40
the Same vppon payn off fforfetyng eu*er*y off theym vj d.

also eu*er*y man off yis Citie in his degre To weyte on Master maier in the

same procession To the worschipp off this Citie vppon payn off euery man
to fforfytt iiij d.

also it is agreid yat euery ocupacion Schall prepare & aparell the pageantes
in all preparacion exceppt plate & Copz   5
...

f 181v   (23 September)
...

also it is Graunted To hym to haue x li. aftur Thold Custom Tuwerd releff   10
off his howse & xxxiij s. iiij d. ffor mynstrelles rewardes yat yer
...

Dean and Chapter Common Fund Accounts   LA: Bj/3/4
f [110v]   (18 September–17 September) (Customary payments)   15
...

Et solutum pro Cerothecis emptis pro Maria & angelo
ex consuetudine in aurora natalis domini   vj d.

...
                                                                                                          20

f [111]   (Gratuities)
...

Et solutum Iohanni Barns Ianitori Clausi in Regardo   ⎫
pro horilogio & Coronacione marie in festo sancte   ⎪
anne pro laboribus & expensis cum ij s. sibi concessis   ⎬   xij s. 25
per capitulum pro tempore   ⎪
Et solutum in Regardo eidem Iohanni ex gracia Capituli   ⎭
...

1525–6   30
City Council Minute Book   LA: L1/1/1/1
f 188v   (21 May)
...

ffor Scant anne   also It is agreid yat The ordynance made ffor preparyng of Schant anne
gyld   Gyld To be Brought fforth Schall Stand in effect & Stryngth acordyng To   35
                           the Old Costome made & afore vsyd
...

f 189

                                                                                                          40

Theyz be the names off the Constabulles yat puttyth Theym in Grace off

10/ hym: *Edward Smyth*

Theyr ffyne ffor non attendaunce off the proccssion off Scaynt anne Gyld
acordyng To Thold act afore made
Nicholaus ffawkenar
Iohannes Whyte
Willelmus Knott   5
Robertus Mason
Robertus Hosyer
Iohannes Isall

Thaldermen yat had no Gownes vff Sylk in The Same procession ffor   10
preparyng off the kynges acordyng To Thordynaunce Theroff made ffor
wych They haue lost Theyr fforfetur

William Robson nowther Gowne ne Tortch
Robert viry no Tortch   15
...

f 192   *(24 September)*
...
In This present Comyn Concell Comyth Thomas Burton which is Elect To   20
be mayr off this Citie ffor this next yer ffoloyng enteryng into hys office at
michelmes day next Comyng at none off ye Seyd Day & Takyth his othe off
mayraltyc & it is Grauntyd to hym to haue ye relefe off hys office As All
Other mayers aforetyme hath had yat is to Sey x li. To mayntyene hys howse
with And xxvj s. viij d. ffor ffeez off mynsterelles & Other   25
...

Dean and Chapter Common Fund Accounts   LA: Bj/3/4
f [135v]*   *(17 September–16 September)* *(Customary payments)*
...   30
Et solutum pro ccrothecis Emptis pro Maria et Angelo
ex consuetudine in Aurora Natalis domini   vj d.
...

f [136]*   *(Gratuities)*   35
...
Et solutum Iohanni Barns Ianitori clausi in Regardo   ⎫
pro horilogio et Coronacione marie in festo sancte   ⎪
Anne pro laboribus & expensis cum ij s. sibi concessis   ⎬   xij s.
per capitulum pro tempore   ⎪   40
Et solutum Parcario de Bytham hoc Anno   ⎭
...

1526–7
City Council Minute Book   LA: L1/1/1/1
f 198   *(19 July)*
…

In this present Comyn Concell it is agreyd yat wher the Graceman off Scaynt   5
anne Gyld hath vsyd yerly To haue Certen Stuff of dyuers Churchus in yis
Citie ffore the ffurnychyne of ye pageantes in ye procession ye Same Dey &
now ye parocheners off Scaynt Iohn Euangelyst in Wykford Denyeth To
leyve any off ther honormentes To ye Same It is now by Thentretye off this
presentes granted by the Seyd parochoners off euery paroch To delyuer &   10
leyve Sutch Stuff at this tyme as yat they haue vsyd in tyme past

also it is agreid That The old auncyent & lawdable Custom vsed by
Thaldrmen Scheryffpers & Chaumberlenpers Schabe vsed & Copyd And
yat euery Constable gyff hys attendaunce off ye pageantes ye Same Day   15
…

f 205   *(26 September)*
…

In This present Comyn Concell vyncent Grantham Esquyer wich is elect   20
Tobe mayr off thys Citie ffor the next yer ffoloyng enteryng into Thoffice
off mayraltie at mychelmes Day at none next Comyng Comyth afore thys
presentes & Takyth hys oth off Mayraltie acordyng to The Custom off yis
Citie and it is graunted to hym To haue off The Comyn Chaumbre towerd
hys Charge off hys howse x li. & xxxiij s. iiij d. ffor rewardes Tobe gyffyn   25
To mynstrelles & othir acordyng To thauncyent Custom Afore vsyd…
…

Cordwainers' Account and Minute Book   LA: LCL/5009
f 15v   *(17 February 1526/7–16 February 1527/8)*   *(Officers' wages)*   30
…

Item Solutum histrionibus istius ciuitatis pro feodis suis   iiij. d.
…

f 16   *(Necessary expenses)*   35
…

Item solutum pro le pageaunt Rome de Bethelem in
ecclesia ffratrum carmilitarum   iiij d.
Item solutum pro vno Iantaculo facto pastoribus in
processione gilde sancte Anne   vj d. 40
Item solutum pro vna corda ad dictum le pageaunt j d.
Et le takites j d. & pro vno speculo j d. ob. summa   iij d. ob.

14/ Schabe: *for* Schalbe

Item solutum pro em emendacione pro brachij
vnius aungeli   j d.

...

Item solutum pro vna parua le cage iiij d.

...   5

Dean and Chapter Common Fund Accounts   LA: Bj/3/4
f [157]   *(16 September–15 September)* *(Customary payments)*

...

Et solutum pro Cerothecis emptis pro maria et Angelo   10
ex consuetudine in Aurora [natalis] natalis domini   vj d.

...

f [157v]   *(Gratuities)*

...   15

Et solutum Iohanni Barns Ianitori clausi in Regardo
pro horilogio et coronacione marie in festo sancte
Anne pro laboribus et expensis cum ij s. sibi concessis   xij s.
per capitulum pro tempore

                                                                                                           20

c 1527
Cordwainers' Account and Minute Book   LA: LCL/5009
f 1*

                                                                                                           25
              The outhe of an out brother or Suster
...I shalbe redy yeerly to goo in procession with the Graceman Brether
& Susters of this ffraternite ffrom the chappell of Saint thomas of ye hy
brige in Lincoln vnto the cathedrall churche of Lincoln & ther to offer one
ffarthyng as custom is
                                                                                                           30
...

f 1v*

              The outhe to be geven to the Graceman at his elleccione
...[And At Saint Anne even or day I shalbe personally at ye dressyng and   35
arrayng of ye pageaunt of Bethelem & awaitt of ye sam in ye tyme of
procession of ye gild of ye said saint Anne ffor ye worshipe of yis Citie:
And when ye said procession is donne then I shall helpe to vnaray &
vndresse ye said pageant a gayn]...

1/ em: *10mm ink blot; false start for* emendacione

f 2*

The Outhe to be geven to the wardens of this gild
…[I shall helpe to dresse & redresse ye pageaunt of Bethelem at saint Anne
tyd And to goo in procession in saint Anne gild with master graceman ffrom   5
ye place accustomed to ye moder churche of Lincoln & so doune again]…

f 2v*

The outhe to be geven to ye Dean of yis gild   10
I schalbe meik & obbeydyent vnto master graceman of yis gild & fraternite
I shalbe reddy at all tymes to doo ye commaundment of master graceman
in ye of office of ye Deanshipe yis yeer ⌜stet⌝ [I or my deputie shall help to
ber the hers of yis gild ffrom place to place wheras any obbitt shalbe donne
for ony brother or Suster of yis gild & fraternite aganste ye dai assigned by   15
master graceman I shalbe personally at ye settyng vpe of ye hers & at takyng
doune of ye sam also I shalbe at dirge masse of euery obbitt of yis gild &
fraternite I shalbe personally at ye dressyng & redressyng of ye pageaunt of
Bethelem with master graceman at saint Anne tyd and to awaitt of the sam
with master graceman] except Seiknes or disseis lett me/ I shall dewly &   20
trewly gyve warnyng & Somons aganst ye iiij mornspiche daies and all other
daies/ by ye commaundment of master graceman to [ey] euery on of his
company & ffellaship beyng masters of this occupacion All thiez poynttes
& articles & all other vsed & accustomed to ye offyce of ye deanshipe I shall
well & trewly obserue & kepe to my power/ So helpe me god & haledome   25
all Saintes and by this bouk

f 3*
…

The pageant of Bethelem   30
Item iijre lynen clothez stened of damaske warkes for bethelem
Item a great hed gildyd sett with vii Beamez & vii glassez for ye sam and on
long beame for ye mouthe of ye said hed
Item iijre greatt stars for ye sam with iijre glassez And a cord for ye same steris
Item ij Angelles with Sencers for ye sam   35

Item one Cage for to ber dowes in
…

13/ ye of office: *for* ye office
13–20/ I or my … graceman: *lined for deletion*
37/ Item … in: *in a different ink*

1527
Lincoln Cathedral Statutes   LA: Dean and Chapter A/2/8
f 26v

...

ℂ In die vero *sancti* Iohannis post *vesperas*. E*piscopus* puer*orum* habebit vnu*m*   5
cereu*m* de dimidi*a* libr*e* . et quilib*et* alius chorista habebit vna*m* p*aruam*
candelam ad libit*um* sacriste/ et sic fiet ad matutinas sine redonaci*one*. Act*is*
dictus Ep*iscopus* cereos suos dabit succentori et Vicecancellario./

...
                                                                                10

1527–8
City Council Minute Book   LA: L1/1/1/1
f 206v   *(23 June)*

...

Saint anne gild

here is ye
indent*ur* of
ye said gild
Settled to
Mr Sames

Mem*orandum* that ye xxix*ti* Day of Iuly in ye yeer aboue said in the presence   15
of Vincencij Grantham Maier of this citie Ro*bert* alynson Th*omas* Burton
Will*i*am Sames Io*hn* papulwik Ro*bert* Smyth & th*omas* Grissyngton aldermen
of yis citie The common Seall is opponed and ye indent*ur* of ye lattyng to
ferm to Will*i*am Sames on of thaldermen of yis citie of ye Colleci*on* of Saint
anne gild & getheryng of alman*er* charitable subsidies & pr*o*ffytt*es* what so   20
eu*er* thay be gruyng & app*er*tenyng to ye Brother hed of ye said gild/ Excepte
alwaies Suche garment*es* and Iuells as shalhappen to be geven for a memoriall
of eny p*er*son to be kepte & Born in the honor of the sam gild/ To haue
& to hold as apperethe in ye indent*ur* y*er* of maid & Sealled for the t*er*me
of xxj*to* yeers and in the p*re*sence of all affornamed The Common Seall is   25
clossed agayn vnd*er* thaer Seall*es*

...

f 207v   *(26 September)*

...
                                                                                30
In this p*re*sent Comon Councell M*r* Norton which is newly elect to be maior
for this ₍ᴄnext⌉ yeer ffoloyng Takethe his othe & it is grauntted to hym To
haue of the Comyn Chambre To releiff of his office & charge*s* x li. And for
other reward*es* To Mynstrell*es* & strangers xxxiij s. iiij d....

...
                                                                                35

Cordwainers' Account and Minute Book   LA: LCL/5009
ff 22–2v   *(16 February 1527/8–21 February 1528/9) (Other necessary
expenses)*

...
                                                                                .40
It*em* sol*utum* pro Corda ad le pageaunt de Bethelem   vij d.

...

Item solutum pro faccione de handill pro le wyndowe
de le pageaunt   j. d.
…

Item solutum in expensis pro le pageaunt de Bethelem   xix d |
Item solutum pro le pageaunt Rome   iiij d.   5
…

Item solutum ad le pyper in die processionis   iiij d.
…

Dean and Chapter Common Fund Accounts   LA: Bj/3/4   10
f [175]   *(15 September 1527–20 September 1528) (Customary payments)*
…

Et solutum pro cerothecis emptis pro Maria & Angelo
ex consuetudine in Aurora natalis domini   vj d.
…   15

f [175v]   *(Gratuities)*
…

Et solutum Thome Bedale Ianitori clausi in Regardo pro
horilogio et Coronacione marie in ffesto sancte Anne pro   20
laboribus et expensis cum ij s. sibi concessis per Capitulum
pro tempore   xij s.
…

1528–9   25
City Council Minute Book   LA: L1/1/1/1
f 212v   *(25 September)*

In this present Comon Counceyll master grissyngton whiche electe to be
maior of this citie ffor this next yeer takytt his othe of maraltie acordyngt   30
to the old custom here vsed And it is grauntted to hym to haue to the charge
of his housse x li. xxxiij s. iiij d. for mynstrelles reward acordyng to as that
other maiors his predecessors haue had affor hym…
…

                                                                                             35

Cordwainers' Account and Minute Book   LA: LCL/5009
f 29v   *(21 February 1528/9–20 February 1529/30) (Officers' fees)*
…
Item solutum vno histrioni ambulanti ante processionem   iiij. d.
…   40

29/ electe: *for* is electe   39/ vno: *for* vni

(Other necessary expenses)
Item pro portacione de le pageaunt de bcthelem
in processione sancte Anne vltra omnes denarios
collectos pro eodem   xj d. ob.

...   5

Dean and Chapter Common Fund Accounts   LA: Bj/3/4
f [201]*   *(20 September–19 September)* *(Customary payments)*
...

Et solutum pro cerothecis emptis pro Maria et   10
Angelo ex consuetudine in Aurora Natalis domini   vj d.
...

f [202]*   *(Gratuities)*
                                                                                     15
Et solutum Thome watson Ianitori clausi in
Regardo pro horilogio et coronacione marie
in festo sancte Anne   xij s.
...
                                                                                     20
1529–30
City Council Minute Book   LA: L1/1/1/1
f 216   *(21 March)*
...

ffor Corpus   Also it is agreid thar euery person shalbe Contributorye To ye bryngyng   25
Christi gild   ffourthe of Corpus Christi gild and nott to deny the payment That they
shalbe Sessed to pai by such as shalbe assigned To Sess euery crafte and
other that shalhaue profytt of ye same

ffor Saint   Also it is agreid that Saint George gild Shalbe Mayntened & brought   30
George Gild   yeerly by ye aduise of master maier of yis citie for ye tyme beyng & his
bretherne
...

f 217*   *(22 September)*   35
...

Also Mr Vrry newly electe to be maier of this Citie Taykythe his othe And
itt is grauntted to hym To haue x li. To ye helpe of ye great charges of
his house & xxxiij s. iiij d. for rewardes of mynstrelles accordyng to ye old
auncyent vse & custome of this citie...   40
...

Cordwainers' Account and Minute Book   LA: LCL/5009
f 38   *(20 February 1529/30–19 February 1530/1)   (Officers' fees)*
...

Item solutum vno histrioni   iiij d.
...   5

(Other necessary expenses)
Item solutum pro portacione de Bethelem   [viij d.] x d.
...

Item solutum Certis de players in aula nostra   10
ad Conuiuium   [vj d.] iiij d.
...

Item solutum pro le pageaunt de Bethelem stando
ad whit ffrerie   iiij d.
Item solutum pro le takes & seruicia   j ob.   15
...

Dean and Chapter Common Fund Accounts   LA: Bj/3/5
p 21   *(19 September–18 September)   (Customary payments)*
...   20
Et solutum pro Cerothecis Emptis pro Maria &
Angelo ex consuetudine in Aurora natalis Domini   vj d.
...

p 22   *(Gratuities)*   25
...
Et solutum thome watson Ianitori clausure in Regardo pro
horilogio et Coronacione [b] Marie in ffesto Sancte Anne   xij s.

1530-1   30
City Council Minute Book   LA: L1/1/1/1
f 222*   *(26 September)*

...

ffor the
fyndyng of
saint anne
preste yeerly

In this present Comon Counceyll To the auncyent & ladable Custom of
this citie affor vsed Mr efford newly elect to be maier of this Citie taketh   35
his othe of maraltie and it is grauntted to hym To haue ten poundes
towardes Relyue of his house & xxxiij s. iiij d. To rewardes of mynstrelles
accordyng as other maiers haue had affor hym and itt is agreid that Saint
anne preste shall waitt vppon maister maier dayly: and ye said master
maier shall fynd ye same prest his bord and euery maier herafter to Come   40

4/ vno: *for* vni   15/ j ob.: *for* j d. ob. (?)

shall do the same: or to forfitt the ten pound*es* whiche thay haue of the Com*m*on chaumbcr

...

f 224   *(7 December)*   5

The Stok of
Saint George
gyld

Also itt is agreid that mast*er* maier shall tak the graceman of Saint George gyld beffor hym & vppon good & sufficient Suertie Delyu*er* to the said graceman the stok of the sam

...   10

Cordwainers' Account and Minute Book   LA: LCL/5009
f 46   *(19 February 1530/1–18 February 1531/2) (Officers' fees)*

...

Item sol*utum* histrionib*us* ist*ius* ciuitat*is*   [vj d.] iij d.   15

...

(Other necessary expenses)
Item sol*utum* pro emendac*i*one de le pageaunt
de bethlem   ij d.   20
Item sol*utum* pro Clauis ad idem opus   [ij d.] j d.
Item sol*utum* pro [l] pane & ser*u*icia portantib*us*
de le pageaunt   vj d. ob.
Item sol*utum* pro le pageaunt Room   iiij d.
Item sol*utum* portant*ibus* eiusde*m* le pageaunt   iiiij d.   25

...

Dean and Chapter Common Fund Accounts   LA: Bj/3/5
p 65   *(18 September–17 September) (Customary payments)*

...   30

Et sol*utum* pro cerothec*is* empt*is* pro Maria & Ang*e*lo
ex cons*ue*tud*i*ne in Aur*o*ra nat*a*lis dom*i*ni   vj d.

...

p 66   *(Gratuities)*   35

...

Et sol*utum* Thome watson Ianitor*i* claus*ur*e in
Regard*o* pro horilogio et Coronac*i*one [b] marie
in ffesto *Sanc*te Anne   xij s.

...   40

1531–2
Cordwainers' Account and Minute Book   LA: LCL/5009
f 54   *(18 February 1531/2–17 February 1532/3) (Officers' fees)*
…

Item paid to ye menstrill at procession   iiij d.   5
…

(Other expenses)
Item paid for bryngyng vp ye pageaunt of
betheleem At Saint Anne messe   xij d. 10
Item paid in expenses for ye plaiers   ij d.
Item paid to ye plaiers aboue all that was getherd   viij d.
Item for naills to ye pageaunt   j d.
Item for the Rome of ye pageaunt standyng   iiij d.
…   15

f 54v*
…
Item paid to ye plaiers   viij d.
Item paid in expenses at ye dener   xix d. 20
…

Dean and Chapter Common Fund Accounts   LA: Bj/3/5
p 111*   *(17 September–15 September) (Customary payments)*
…   25
Et solutum pro Cerothecis emptis pro Maria et Angelo
ex consuetudine in Aurora natalis domini   vj d.
…

p 112*   *(Gratuities)*   30
…
Et solutum Thome watson Ianitori Clausure in
Ragardo pro horilogio et Coronacione marie in
ffesto Sancte Anne   xij s.
…   35

1532–3
Cordwainers' Account and Minute Book   LA: LCL/5009
f 59v   *(17 February 1532/3–15 February 1533/4) (Officers' fees)*
…   40
Item to ye mynstrell   iiij d.
…

f 60   *(Necessary expenses)*

...

Item for mendyng ye pageaunt of bethleem   ij d.
Item for shepperdes deners at   vj d.
Item for ij gallons ayell & a penyworth breid   iiij d.   5
Item for takes to ye pageaunt   ob.

...

Item for the pageaunt stondyng in ye [h] whiett freris   iiij d.

...

Item paid for a lyn to ye pageaunt   ij d.   10

...

Dean and Chapter Common Fund Accounts   LA: Bj/3/5
p 151*   *(15 September 1532–21 September 1533)* *(Customary payments)*

...   15

Et solutum pro cerothecis emptis pro Maria et Angelo
ex consuetudine in Aurora natalis domini   vj d.

...

p 152*   *(Gratuities)*   20

...

Et solutum Thome watson Ianitori clausure in Regardo pro
horilogio et coronacione marie in ffesto sancte Anne   xij s.

...

                                                                            25

1533–4
Cordwalners' Account and Minute Book   LA: LCL/5009
f 66v   *(15 February 1533/4–20 February 1534/5)* *(Officers' fees)*

...

Item to the mynstrelles & players   ix d.   30

...

(Necessary expenses)
Item for mendyng the pageaunt   ij d. ob.
Item for ye Sheperdes dener   vj d.   35

...

Dean and Chapter Common Fund Accounts   LA: Bj/3/5
p [195]   *(21 September–20 September)* *(Customary payments)*

...   40

Et solutum pro Cerothecis emptis pro Maria et angelo
ex consuetudinc in Aurora natalis domini   vj d.

...

p [196]   *(Gratuities)*

…

Et sol*utum* Thom*e* watson Ianitor*i* claus*ure* in
Regard*o* p*ro* horilog*io* et Coronac*ione* marie in
ffesto Sancte Anne   xij s.   5

…

1534–5
Cordwainers' Account and Minute Book   LA: LCL/5009
f 73v   *(20 February 1534/5–19 February 1535/6)   (Officers' fees)*   10

…

It*em* to ye mynstrell for his ffee   iiij d.

…

(Necessary expenses)   15
It*em* to ye shepperds & 6 pageaunt berars   iiij d.

…

Dean and Chapter Common Fund Accounts   LA: Bj/3/5
p [239]*   *(20 September–19 September)   (Customary payments)*   20

…

Et sol*utum* p*ro* cerothec*is* Empt*is* p*ro* Maria & ang*e*lo
ex consue*tudine* in Aur*o*ra nat*a*lis d*o*m*i*ni   vj d.

…

                                                                                    25

p [240]*   *(Gratuities)*

…

Et sol*utum* Thom*e* watson Ianitori claus*ure* in Regard*o*
p*ro* horilog*io* et Coronac*ione* ∧⌈beate⌉ marie in festo
Sancte Anne   xij s.   30

…

1535–6
Cordwainers' Account and Minute Book   LA: LCL/5009
f 79*   *(19 February 1535/6–19 February 1536/7)   (Officers' fees)*   35

…

It*em* paid to the mynstrell ffor his ffee   iiij d.

…

(Necessary expenses)   40
It*em* paid to iij sheppard*es* at saint Anne gyld   xviij d.

Item paid to vj berars of ye b pageaunt in ye said gild   xviij d.
Item for bred & ayell spent in ye mynster ye sam tym   vj d.
Item for takyttes to ye pageaunt   j d.
Item for wesheyng the Awlbe & Ames that ye
prest synges in   iij d. 5
Item for a pottyll wyn geven to master Sapcottes   iiij d.
...

Dean and Chapter Common Fund Accounts   LA: Bj/3/5
p [283]*   *(19 September–17 September) (Customary payments)*   10
...

Et solutum pro cerothecis emptis pro maria et Angelo
ex consuetudine in Aurora natalis domini   vj d.
...

    15

p [284]*   *(Gratuities)*
...

Et soluti thome watson Ianitori clausure in
Regarda pro horilogio et Coronacione marie in
festo sancte Anne   xij s. 20
...

1536
Cathedral Treasurer's Inventory   LA: Dean and Chapter A/2/15/1–3
f 16v*   *(Jewels, vestments, and ornaments)*   25
...

Item a coop for chyldren of purpur colour with a orfrey of cloth of gold
valde debiles:.

1536–7
    30
Cordwainers' Account and Minute Book   LA: LCL/5009
f 86   *(19 February 1536/7–18 February 1537/8) (Allowances)*
...

Item solutum pro emendacione vnius Ale Angeli   j d.
...   35

Item solutum pro Emendacione De pageaunt
de betheleem   xviij d.
Item solutum pro ijobus speculis de le pageaunt   iiij d.
Item solutum pro le Tynffoull pro le paynttyng
faciei verniculi   iij d. ob. 40

1/ ye b: *false start for* berars, *not cancelled (?)*

Item solutum willelmo lytyll pro le paynttyng
eiusdem verniculi   xij d.
Item solutum pro vna Corda dicte le pageaunt   iiij d.
Item solutum pro pane & seruicia Datis portarijs
dicte le pageaunt in die Sancte Anne   iiij d. 5
Item solutum pro emendacione de le hers   j d.
Item solutum pastoribus et portarijs de le
pageaunt predicte   xv d. non allocatur
...
                                                                             10

Dean and Chapter Common Fund Accounts   LA: Bj/3/5
p [329]   *(17 September–16 September)* *(Customary payments)*
...

Et solutum pro cerothecis emptis pro
Maria & Angelo ex consuetudine in Aurora   15
natalis domini   vj d.
...

p [330]   *(Gratuities)*
...   20
Et solutum Thome watson Ianitori clausure
in Regardo pro horilogio et Coronacione Marie
in ffesto sancte Anne   xij s.
...
                                                                             25

1537–8
Dean and Chapter Common Fund Accounts   LA: Bj/3/5
p [369]   *(16 September–15 September)* *(Customary payments)*
...

Et solutum pro Cerothecis Emptis pro   30
Maria & angelo ex consuetudine in Aurora
natalis domini   vj d.
...

p [370]   *(Gratuities)*   35
...
Et solutum Thome watson Ianitori Clausure
in Regardo pro horilogio et Coronacione Marie
in festo Sancte Anne   xij s.
...   40

8/ non allocatur: *apparently added later, likely by the same clerk*

1538–9
City Council Minute Book   LA: L1/1/1/1
f 270v   *(22 November)*
…

peyment to ye
weytes

Item yt ys agreyde in this Comen Councell yat euery alderman within this   5
Cytty schall pay euery quarter in ye yere to the weytes of the saide Cytty so
longe as they dowe theyr trewe & delygent Servyse vj d. excepte wylliam
Sames & Robert Smythe mercer eyther of them to pay quarterly iiij d. euery
Scheryffe & Scheryffe peer iiij d. euery Chamberlyn & Chamberlyn fellowe
ij d. & euery Comoner j d.   10

plegges for ye
Collers to ye
weytes

Item in this Comon Cowncell Wylliam Knote & Robert Iohnson er be
Comyde plegges for Iohn Croston that he Schall delyuer or Cawse to be
delyueryde when he schall departe ffrom his offys a Chean of Syluer with
xxvijᵗʰ lynghes of Syluer & on Scheylde of Syluer with the fflower de luce   15
wiche was delyueryde to the said Robert Knote & Robert Iohnson

plegges

Item in this said Comen Councelle Iohne ffawcon meyer of the Cytty of
the Cytty of lyncoln And Christofer holtbe er be Comyde plegges ffor
(blank) that ₍ᴬ₎⌐he⌐ schall delyuer or Cause to be delyueryde when he schall   20
departe ffrom his office on Chean of Cyluer with xxvj lynghtes of Cyluer
[wyl] with on Scheylde of Cyluer wiche was delyueryd to Christofer holtbe

plegges

Item in this Comen Cowncell Nycolas ffawcon on of the Scheryffes of the
Cytty of lyncoln and Thomas Neyvell er be Comyde plegges for Edwarde   25
lybert that he schall delyuer or Cawse to be delyueryde when he schall departe
ffrom his offys acheyn of Syluer with xxv lynghtes of Syluer & on Scheylde
of Syluer wiche was delyueryde to the said Nycolas ffawcon

lyuereys to ye
weytes

Item in this present Comen Cowncell yt ys agreyde that the forsaide weytes   30
schall haue yche on of them alyuerey agenste the feste of the natyuyte of owre
loord good next ensuynge of the Comen Chamber

f 273v   *(18 July)*

35

Sent anne
(.)ilde

It is agreyde in this Comen Cowncell that Sent ane Guylde schall goo vppe
[s] on ye Sundey next after Sent [Agnes] Anes dey in manner & furme as yt
hathe beyn vside in tymez paste & euery on indefalte to forfeyt to ye Comen
Chamber iij s. iiij d.

18–19/ of the Cytty of the Cytty: *dittography*   37/ Sundey next … Anes dey: *27 July 1539*
37m/ (.)ilde: *edge of page missing*

perambulacion It ys Also agreyd in this that M*aste*r meyer w*ith* his bretheren & other
inh*a*bitauncez of ye Cytty schall Ryde ye p*er*ambulacyon the Tewysdey
next aft*er* Sent Anez dey aft*er* ye olde Custom & man*ne*r

...

5

Cordwainers' Account and Minute Book   LA: LCL/5009
f 95v   *(17 February 1538/9–15 February 1539/40) (Other expenses)*

...

It*em* for mendyng the paygeant of bethelem
& cord   v d. 10
It*em* for cost*es* & charges to ye mynst*er* w*ith*
ye pageaunt of Saint Anne day   [xiij d. x] iiij d.

...

It*em* to the mynstrell   iiij d.
It*em* for the pageaunt standyng in the   15
whytt ffreris   [iiij d.]
It*em* for gloves   viij d.
It*em* for makyng & waxe to the hersse Candyll*es*   iiij s. vj d.
It*em* for mendyng ye Angell*es* of ye hersse   ij d.

...

20

Dean and Chapter Common Fund Accounts   LA: Bj/3/5
p [413]   *(15 September 1538–21 September 1539) (Customary payments)*

...

Et sol*utum* p*ro* cerothec*is* empt*is* p*ro* mar*i*a et Ang*e*lo   25
ex consue*tudi*ne in Aurora na*t*alis d*om*ini   vj d.

...

p [414]*   *(Gratuities)*

...

30

Et sol*utum* Thome watson Ianitor*i* Claus*ure* in
Regard*o* p*ro* horel*ogi*o vexilla Reg*is* et stella in
Nocte Na*t*alis d*om*ini   vj s.

...

35

1539–40
City Council Minute Book   LA: L1/1/1/1
f 276*   *(12 November)*

...

It*em* yt ys also agreyde in this Comon Cowncell that the Stuffe belongynge 40

2–3/ Tewysdey next ... Anez dey: *29 July 1539*

to sent an Gyld schalb(.) leyd in the Chapell of the bryge & the howse wher
the saide stuffe lythe to be letton to the vse & profyt of the Comen Chambre
...

also yt ys agreyde in this Comen Cowncell that ther schalbe a large doer
mayde at ye layt Scowle howys that the pagentes may be Seyt in & euery   5
pagent to pay yerly iiij d. & noyschyppe xij d.

f 277v   (3 March)
...

Item yt ys Agreyde in this Comen Cowncell that the weytes Schall haue   10
lyberty to dwell within the Cytty to the ffeste of Sent mychell the archangel
and to haue the Conysaunce of the saide Cytty & at the saide fest of
mychylmeys to enter & to be waytes for the sayd Cytty
...
                                                                             15

ff 278-8v*   (2 June)
...

Item yt ys Agreyd that vj Coppes that was Gevyn by doctor lee & master
Freman to Serteyn Chyrches in lyncoln Schall holy remean ffrom hensfurthe
to Sent ane Guyld | 20

Also yt ys Agreyde that sent ane Guylde schall go forwardes as yt hathe downe
times paste and that euery alderman Schall haue a gowne & a broche &
euery Scheryffe to ffynde a gowne and euery occupacion to brynge ffurthe
theyr pagens accordyng to the old Custome & euery occupacion that haue   25
theyr padgeans broken to make them Reddy agenste the same day vppon
payn of euery pagent to forfyte xx s.
...

Cordwainers' Account and Minute Book   LA: LCL/5009   30
f 99   (15 February 1539/40–21 February 1540/1)   (Officers' fees)
...
Item paid to ye waites   iiij d.
...
                                                                             35

(Other necessary expenses)
Item payd for mendyng ye [pad] pageant   viij d.
Item paid for beryng of ye sam pageant   v d.
Item for bred & aille to ye berrars of ye sam   ij. d.
...   40
Item for a Cord to ye padgayn   iiij d.
...

Dean and Chapter Common Fund Accounts   LA: Bj/3/5
p [457]   *(21 September–19 September)*   *(Customary payments)*
...

Et sol*utum* p*ro* cerothec*is* Empt*is* p*ro* Mar*i*a et
Ang*e*lo ex consue*tudi*ne in Aurora natal*is* d*omi*ni   vj d.   5
...

p [458]   *(Gratuities)*
...

Et sol*utum* Thome watson Ianitor*i* claus*ure*   10
in Regard*o* p*ro* horilogio vexilla Regis et stella
in Nocte Natalis d*omi*ni   vj s.
...

Et sol*utum* in den*arijs* p*ro* Expens*is* circa
coronac*ionem* be*a*te mar*i*e hoc Anno   ij s. iiij d. 15
...

1540–1
City Council Minute Book   LA: L1/1/1/1
f 283*   *(4 October)*   20
...

ffor the
Lyu*e*reys and   Item it ys agreid by these Comen Councell that the waytt*es* now named and
waiges of the   appoynted schall haue suche lyu*e*reys as M*a*ster mair schall devise of the
waytt*es*   Charges of the Comen Chamber and also that they schall haue suche wages
appoynted &c   as the Cetezens & inhabitant*es* haue geven afore that is to sey eu*e*ry ald*e*rman 25
                  vj d. eu*e*ry scheryff iiij d. eu*e*ry Chamb*e*rlyn ij d. in the q*u*art*er* and they to
                  be paid q*u*art*er*ly and that they goo aswell of the holy day as of the warke day
...

A   *List of Mayors, Bailiffs, and Sheriffs*   LA: Diocesan Miscellaneous Roll 1 30
    mb 6d
    ...

Maior   Petrus Efforthe
                   W Alynson   vic*ecomites*
                   Iohn Plumtree   35
                   wiche decessyde of twelfft daye ye saym daye Electe & Chosyn for to occupye
® W. dyghton   in hys Roume as mayre for y*a*tt ʒere
                   °Also y*a*t ʒere off Saynt Laurance [day] Evyne the kyng*es* grace & ye qwene
                   kat*e*ryn w*it*h all hys riyall lord*es* ladys & also h*is* nobyll ∧⌈gerd⌉ w*it*h may
                   off ∧⌈ye⌉ gentyll men off ye Contye come Ryall to ye Cety off Lyncoln &   40

39/ may: *for* many

ther yar remanyd towe days & then and then remevyd to gynsborw & so
to 3oyrbe°

...

Cordwainers' Account and Minute Book   LA: LCL/5009   5
f 105v*   *(21 February 1540/1–20 February 1541/2)   (Other necessary expenses)*

...

Item to the waites   iiij d.

...

                                                                                          10

Dean and Chapter Common Fund Accounts   LA: Bj/3/5
p [499]   *(19 September–18 September)   (Customary payments)*

...

Et solutum pro Cerothecis emptis pro Maria et
Angelo ex consuetudine in Aurora natalis domini   vj d.   15

...

p [500]   *(Gratuities)*

...

Et solutum Thome watson Ianitori clausure in   20
Regardo pro horilogio vexilla Regis et stella in
Nocte Natalis Domini ac Alijs   vj s.

...

Book of Ceremonials   BL: Additional MS 6113   25
ff 179v–81v*   *(9 August)*

Of the Kinges Entree into lyncoln on
Tuesday the ix daye of Auguste

                                                                                          30

In Primis aftre hyt was knowen that his hyghnes was com to temple Brewer
to dynner being vij myles dystant from lyncolne The mayre of the said Cyttie
with hys bretherne Burgesys & other Comoners prepared them selfes towardes
the heyght lyke as all other Gentlemen & yeomen of lynsey coste & there
abowte dyd nere vnto the place where hys graces tentes & haylle were pytchyd/   35
Item the Gentlemen of lyncolne shere dyde arraye theyre seruantes on
horsbacke all ⌈on⌉ one syde where the Kinges maiestie shulde passe/
Master Mayre of lyncolne & his bretherne on ffote/
Item the Archedeacon of lyncolne/ lord deane prebendaries/ Vyccars with
manye other persons & prystes of the same Cytty rodde & mette the kinge   40

1/ ther yar: *for* ther yai   1/ & then and then: *dittography*

one myle withowt the lybertie of lyncolne before his hyghnes cam to hys
tentes & there dyd mak theyre propocycyon in lattyn/ presentinge his grace
with one Gyfte namyd in vitall/ resyted in theyre propocycyon/ and that don
passyd the nerest waye to the Mynster of lyncolne agayne

Item then his grace cam rydinge & entryd into hys tent/ which was pytchyd   5
at the farthest ende of [hys tente] the lybertie of lyncolne the Quenes grace
with hym in his owne tente/ And there dyd shyfte theyre Apparrell for his
grace was Apparellyd before he cam to hys tente | in Greene veluet & the
quene in Crymesyn veluet/ And then the kinge shyftyd hym into clothe of
golde & the quene into clothe of syluer/   10

Item behynde his graces tente was Another for ladyes/

Item on thother syde A good space dystante was the hayle pytchyd wherin
was the vj Chylderne of honour shyftyd & Apparellyd with clothe of golde
& Crymesyn veluet/ wherin Also was prepared & made readye/ aswell the
Kinges & queenes horssys of Estate as the horssys they rodde on/   15

Item aftre that euerye thynge was sett in good ordre the Kinges Maiestie with
the Queene were sett on horsse/ and then the heroldes of Armes put on theyre
cotes and the Gentlemen pencyoners with all other of the Kinges most royall
trayne dyd ryde in ordre honorablye accordinge to the auncyent ordre my
lorde Hastinges bearing the Swerde before his hyghenes   20

Then hys Maiestie

Then his graces horsse ledd by his master of the horsse

Then the vj Chylderne of honour yche aftre other on great coursers

Then therle of Rutland beinge the queenes Chambrelayne

Then the Queene/   25

Then the Quenes horsse of Estate/ |

Then all ladyes in good ordre

Then the Captayne of the Garde and the garde aftre hym

Then the comoners as they fell to the trayne

In proceading thus not farre fro the tentes Mr Myssleden Sergieant at lawe   30
being recourder of lyncolne with gentlemen of the Cuntry the Mayre of
lyncolne with his bretherne & other commoners at the entrye of the [Cyttie]
lybertie knealed on theyre knees & cryed too tymes Iesus saue your grace/

Item thys beinge don the Recourder dyd knele downe ij tymes on hys knee
drawinge neere vnto hys grace & redd a prococycyon in Englishe (Gentlemen   35
& the Mayre with his bretherne knelinge styll on theyre knees/ And when
he had redd, kyssyd it & rosse & delyuered it vnto the Kinge/ who toke &
gaue it to the duke of norffolke/ presentinge in lyke case one Gyfte namyd
in Vytall, resyted in theyre proposycyon

Item this don the Mayre presented the swerde & mase of the Cyttie to the   40
Kinge/ & then he was placyd agenste the Kinge at Armes namyd Clarenseaux
behynde the dukes berynge the mase in hys ryght hande/ |

35/ prococycyon: for propocycyon

Item all the Mayres Bretherne & burgessys were placyd in the fronte of
the trayne
Then Gentlemen of the Cuntry
Then Knyghtes
And then the Kinges trayne/   5
Item belles were Ronge not onlye in the Cuntrye at all Churchys where his
grace cam so sone as they had a sight of hys trayne/ and so in lyke manner
there in lyncolne & dyuersse places adyoynynge/
Item thus proceadinge at the entrye of the mynster thorowe the Cyttie/
the Mayre & his bretherne drewe them celfes aparte at theentrye of the   10
mynster gates/
Item the busshoppe of lyncolne with all thole Queere & crosse were readye
& stodde in the mynster alonge on bothe sydes the bodye of the Churche
gyvinge attendaunce/ and when his grace was alyghtid at the weste ende of
the mynster where were ordenyd & spred aswell carpett [&] as stooles/ with   15
quyssheons of clothe of golde for the kinges hyghnes, wheron was a crucyfyx
laid/ And one other on the queenes graces stoole/
Item Aftre his grace was kneelid downe the busshoppe cam forthe of the
Churche & gaue the Crucyfyx to the kinge to kysse & then to the queen |
and then censyd them/ hys myter beinge on hys head/ And thus proceaded   20
they into the Churche the kinge & queenes grace goinge vndre the Canape
[where] to the Sacrement where they made theyre prayers/ thole queere
synginge melodyouslye/ Te Deum/ And aftre this don his grace went strayght
to his lodginge and in lyke case all the trayane for that nyght
Item the master of the kinges horsse toke the carpettes & stooles for his ffee 25
Item on the morrowe beinge wenysday his grace rode at aftre none to the
Castle & dyd vewe hit & the Cyttie/
Item the fotemen toke the Canape for theyre ffee
Item his grace & the quene departyd on fryday from lyncolne to Gaynsborowghe
proceadinge forthe of the Cyttie with trumpetters heroldes & his trayne/ in lyke 30
case as his grace entryd/ savinge the Mayre/ the henchemen nor horssys of
Estate were not there
Item therle of Darbie bare the swerde that daye/

1541–2   35
City Council Minute Book   LA: L1/1/1/2
f 2   *(3 October)*
…

® The admyssion
of Richard
Cogyll for a
wayte of ye (...)ty
Ad predictam letam Ricardus Cogyll admissus fuit pro vno lez wayttes Ciuitatis
istius & ei deliberata est vnam Cathenam vocata a Cheyn argenti continens   40

24/ trayane: *for* trayne
40/ vnam Cathenam: *for* vna Cathena

xxvij lez lynkes & vnam crucem argenti & Iohannes ffalkener et willelmus
yates sunt plagii sui &c

® The admyssion
of Iohannes
lambert for
⟨...⟩ wayte ⟨..⟩
the C⟨...⟩

Aceciam ad predictam letam Iohannes lambert admissus fuit pro vno lez
wayttes dicte Ciuitatis et deliberata est vnam Cathenam argenti vocata a Cheyn   5
continens xxvij lez lynkes & vnam crucem argenti & Edwardus Dawson &
Edmundus atkynson sunt plegii sui &c

® The admyssio⟨.⟩
⟨..⟩ Richard
ableso⟨.⟩ ⟨...⟩ a
wayte of the
⟨...⟩

Preteria ad dictam letam Ricardus ableson admissus fuit pro vno lez wayttes
Ciuitatis predicte & ei deliberata est vnam Cathenam argenti vocata a [chyn]   10
Cheyn of Sylver & vnam crucem argenti continens eciam xxvj lynkes et
Edwardus Crosfeld est plegius eius &c

...

f 3v*   *(10 June)*   15

⟨...⟩nt Anne
guyld as
betyme

Item it is agreid that Mr yates and Mr Dighton schall dylygently vpon the
Sonday next after Saynt Iames day next bryng furth Saynt Anne Guyld and
that euery occupacion schall prepare them selffes for the same
...   20

Cordwainers' Account and Minute Book   LA: LCL/5009
f 109*   *(20 February 1541/2–19 February 1542/3)*   *(Charges)*
...

[Item for [br] beryng vpp of the pagyaunte of	25
saint Anne day & the morn aftur	xx d.
Item for brede & ayle to the pagiaunt berers at	
the mynster	ij d.]

...   30

Dean and Chapter Common Fund Accounts   LA: Bj/3/5
p [543]   *(18 September–17 September)*   *(Customary payments)*
...
Et solutum pro Cerothecis Emptis pro Maria et
Angelo ex consuetudine in Aurora natalis dominj   vj d. 35
...

5, 10/ vnam Cathenam: *for* vna Cathena
18/ Sonday next ... Iames day: *30 July 1542*

p [544]   *(Gratuities)*

...

Et sol*utum* thome watson Ianitor*i* claus*ure* in
Regard*o pro* horilogio et vexilla Reg*is* ac Stella
in Nocte Na*t*alis d*o*mini et Alijs   vj s.   5

...

1542–3
City Council Minute Book   LA: L1/1/1/2
f 13*   *(24 September)*   10

...

®how y*a*t Sir
w*illia*m Smyth
preis(.) &
kempe shall
ride for Saynt
Anne Guyld

Itᵉm it is agreid that Sir Willi*a*m Smyth preist and Willi*a*m Kempe schall
haue the Commen Seale of this Cetye for to gether aboute in the Countrey
yerly for Saynt Anne Guyld and schall haue & be allowed ther Cost*es* &
charg*es* of all suche Sommes ot mony as they schall gether for the same   15
Guyld and also yerly an honest Reward for ther paynes and accompte yerly
of all suche Somes of mony as they schall gether to the mayor of this Cetye
for the tyme beyng/

...

                                                                                      20

Cordwainers' Account and Minute Book   LA: LCL/5009
f 112v   *(19 February 1542/3–18 February 1543/4)* *(Expenses)*

...

[It*em* for bryyng vp the pageant of Bethelem   [xx d.] vj d.

...   25

Item for kydd*es* xx d. bred & aill at mynst*er* at
saint Anne tyd ij d.   Sum xxij d.
Item for cheis xiiij d. for iiij dossyn cayk*es* to
Chr*isto*fer brampston iiij s.   Sum v s. ij d.
Item for ij dossyn bred & a halff   ij s. vj d. 30
Itᵉm to Iames lovday for lyghttyng the gyld
candyll at mynst*er*   iiij d.
Item paid to the mynstrell*es*   iij d.]

...

                                                                                      35

Dean and Chapter Common Fund Accounts   LA: Bj/3/5
p [587]   *(17 September–16 September)* *(Customary payments)*

...

Et sol*utum pro* cerothec*is* Empt*is pro* maria &
Angelo ex con*suetudi*ne in Aurora Natal*is* domini   vj d. 40

...

p [588]   *(Gratuities)*

…

Et sol*utum* thome watson Ianitori Claus*ure*
in Regard*o* p*ro* horilog*io* et vexilla Reg*is* ac
p*ro* Stella in Nocte Na*t*alis d*o*m*i*ni et Aliis   vj s.   5

…

Et in tot den*a*rijs sol*utum* p*ro* Expens*is* circa
coronac*ionem* bea*t*e ma*ri*e hoc Anno   iij s. viij d.

…
                                                                                                         10

1543–4
City Council Minute Book   LA: L1/1/1/2
f 15v   *(20 October)*

…

® ffor Saynt
Anne Guyld

It*em* it is agreid y*at* Gregory Clerk & Iohn orwell schall haue the Com*m*en   15
Seale of this Cytye for one hole yere fro C*a*ndylmas next to gether for Saynt
Anne Guyld for xxvj s. viij d. vpon Sufficient Suortye and that ye seid
Gregory & Iohn orwell schallnot gather within the Cytye ne wi*th*in the
Subberbb*es* of the same

…   20

Dean and Chapter Common Fund Accounts   LA: Bj/3/5
p [629]*   *(16 September 1543–21 September 1544)*   *(Customary payments)*
…

Et sol*utum* pro Cerothec*is* empt*is* pro maria et   25
Angelo ex co*n*suetu*d*ine in Aurora Natalis dominj   vj d.

…

p [631]   *(Gratuities)*

…   30

Et sol*utum* Thome watson Ianitor*i* Claus*ure* in
Regard*o* p*ro* horelog*io* Et vexilla Reg*is* ac p*ro* stella
in au*ro*ra na*t*alis d*o*m*i*ni et alijs   vj s.

…
                                                                                                         35

1544–5
City Council Minute Book   LA: L1/1/1/2
f 30v   *(26 September)*

…

It*em* it is agreid in this seid Com*m*en Councell that the seid Thomas   40
Wryght mayr*e* schall haue towardes the releyff & mayntenance of his house
kepyng the tyme of his maraltye the Some of ten pound*es* & xxxiij s. iiij d.

for rewarde*s* of mynstrylle*s* and also ij ffraunchest men to be brought oute
of the libertyes of this Citye/

…

1546–7   5
City Council Minute Book   LA: L1/1/1/2
f 44v   *(13 June)*

…

It*em* it is agreid that the p*ro*cession & Sight vpon the Sonday next aft*er*
Saynt Anne Day, schalbe brought furth as haith ben in tymes past and that   10
eu*ery* occupacyon schall pay to the same as haith ben accustomed

…

f 45v   *(14 September)*

                                                                                                    15
ffirst it is agreid in this Co*m*men Congregacion that Chr*is*tofer Brampston
nowe elected & Sworn mayor of this Cytye schall haue toward*es* the
mayntenance of his house kepyng the Some of ten pound*es* & xxxiij s. iiij d.
for reward*es* of mynstrylle*s* with iiij ffraunchest men to be taiken oute of
the libertyes of this Cytye and also di. tu*n*ne of wyne of the charg*es* of   20
the Co*m*men Chambre/

…

1547–8
City Council Minute Book   LA: L1/1/1/2   25
f 47   *(3 October)*

the weytt*es*

at this p*re*sent lete or lawday Richard Cogle Alex*ander* Cogle & Thomas
Calbeck were admytted waytt*es* of this Cytye and ther lyuereys & wag*es* to
be appoynted them at the next Co*m*men Councell vpon a newe [warnyng]/   30
Commu*n*ycacion/

…

f 47v   *(10 October)*

…   35
ffor M*aste*r
mayor*es* Crye

It is agreid that M*aste*r may*o*r schall make his Crye vpon friday next/ and
y*at* eu*ery* man gyve attendance therunto accordyng to ye Custome/

…

9–10/ Sonday next … Anne Day: *31 July 1547*
36/ friday next: *17 October 1547*

f 48v*   *(5 November)*

...

Item it is agreid that Henry Sapcote alderman schall [bryg] bryng Inne
to the Guyldhall the Inuentorye of the Iuelles plate & ornamentes lately
belongyng to the procession for Saynt Anne Sight and that the same Iuelles   5
plate or ornamentes schalbe Sold to thuse of the Commen Chambre/

...

f 52v   *(14 September)*

10

ffirst it is agreid in this Commen Congregacion that George Stamp nowe
elected & Sworn mayor of this Cytye schall haue towardes the mayntenance
of his house kepyng the Some of ten poundes & xxxiij s. iiij d. for rewardes
for mynstrylles with iiij ffraunchest men to be taiken oute of the libertyes of
this Cytye and also di. tunne of wyne of the charges of the Commen chambre/   15

...

1548

A   ***Inventory of the Cathedral Vestry***   BL: Lansdowne MS 207D
f 331   20

...

Item a Cope of veluet with Rolls and Clouds ordeyn'd for the barne Bishopp,
with this Scripture The highway is best./

...

25

f 336

...

Item a Cope of Purple Colour for children with an Orfrey of cloth of gould.
Valde Debilis

...   30

1548–9

City Council Minute Book   LA: L1/1/1/2
f 62v   *(14 September)*

35

ffirst it is agreid in this Commen Congregacion that William yattes nowe
electyd & Sworn mayor of this Cytye schall haue towardes the mayntenance
of his howse kepyng the Some of ten poundes and xxxiij s. iiij d. for rewardes
for mynstrylles and di. tunne of Wyne of the Charges of the Commen
Chambre of this Cytye and also iiij ffraunchest men to be taiken oute   40

23/ The highway is best: *in bold, oversized script*

of the libertyes of this Cytye within vij yeres next after the dayte of this
Commen Congregacion/

…

Dean and Chapter Common Fund Accounts   LA: D/V/2/2a   5
f [11]*   *(16 September–15 September)* *(Gratuities)*

…

Et solutum pro Cerothecis in Aurora Natalis Domini   vj d.

…

                                                                                10

1549–50
City Council Minute Book   LA: L1/1/1/2
f 65   *(15 October)*

<table>
<tr><td>The waittes
& for ther
lyuereis &
wages/</td><td>Item it is agreid in this seid Commen Councell that Richard Cogle Edward 15
Liberd and Alexander Cogle mynstrelles schall be the waittes of this Cytye
and schall haue their lyuereis of the Costes of the Commen Chambre and
that they schall goo nyghtly from hensfurth vnto aester next and that [euery]
euery alderman of this Cytye schall pay towardes their wages for ye halff
yere xij d. euery scheryff & scheryffes pere viij d. & euery person that is 20
or haith ben Chamberland iiij d. and all other persons in abilytye to be
assessed by Master mayr for and towardes the payment of the seid wages
of the seid wayttes/</td></tr>
<tr><td>ffor the waittes
Colers/</td><td>Item it is agreid that fromhensfurth Master mayor for the tyme beyng schall 25
se furth Cummyng the iij Colers for the waittes and delyuer the same to the
next mayor at his goyng furth of his office/</td></tr>
<tr><td>Suortye for
Richard Cogle
Color</td><td>at this Commen Councell Nicholas ffawkener becommyth Suortye for Richard
Cogle Color of Sylver/   30</td></tr>
</table>

…

f 67   *(4 December)*

…

<table>
<tr><td>a lettre sent to
Mr Wryght</td><td>Item it is agreid that a Chamberland schalbe sent with a lettre to Thomas 35
wryght alderman vnto Bawtrey for his repayryng home Immedyatly. to gyve
vp the verdytt of the grett inquest & for the delyuery of ij of the wayttes
Colers whiche he haith kepyng or elles yat a ffyne to be sett vpon his heade
for the Same, whiche lettre was Immedyatly made & wryten in the seid</td></tr>
</table>

18/ aester next: *6 April 1550*
36/ Bawtrey: *Bawtry, Yorkshire West Riding*

Chambre and assigned *with* thand*es* of the seid mayor & ald*er*men *with*
other ald*er*men then p*re*sent

…

f 77v   *(14 September)*

ffor M*aste*r
mayor

ffirst it is agreid in this Co*m*men Congregacion that Edm*u*nd Atkynson
nowe elected & Sworn the mayor of this Cytye schall haue toward*es* the
mayntenance of his house kepyng the Some of ten pound*es* and xxxiij s.
iiij d. for reward*es* of mynstryll*es* and di. tu*n*ne of wyne of the Charg*es* of
the Co*m*men Chambre of this Cytye and also iiij ffraunchest men to be
taiken oute of the liberties of this Cytye/

…

1550–1

City Council Minute Book   LA: L1/1/1/2
f 85   *(14 September)*

…

It*e*m the seid dey & yere it is agreid by the seid mayor ald*er*men & others
aforseid that the seid Iohn ffawken*er* Sworn mayor schall haue toward*es* the
mayntenance of his house kepyng the tyme of his maraltye x li. & xxxiij s.
iiij d. for reward*es* of mynstryll*es* & di. tu*n*ne[e] of wyne of the Charg*es* of
the Co*m*men [Char] Chaumbre & iiij ffraunchest men to be taiken oute
of the lib*er*tyes of this Cytye/

…

1551–2

City Council Minute Book   LA: L1/1/1/2
f 89   *(8 December)*

…

ffor ij weyt*es*

It*e*m it is agreid that the ij wayt*es* schall haue ther lyu*er*eys of the Cost*es* of
ye Common Chambre & to weare ij Sylv*er* Colers So that they fynd Suortye
to restore them agayn, vnto M*aste*r mayor

f 94v   *(14 September)*

Yt is agreid in this Co*m*men Congregacion that Willi*a*m Hochynson nowe
elected & Sworn mayor of this Cytye schall haue toward*es* the mayntenance
of his house kepyng the tyme of his maraltye the Some of x li. & xxxiij s.
iiij d. for reward*es* of mynstryll*es* ffyve m*a*rkes towardes ye offic*er*s lyu*er*eys

di. tunne of Gascoyngn wyne of ye Commen Chambre & iiij ffraunchest
men to be taiken oute of ye libertyes of this Cytye/

…

1552–3
City Council Minute Book   LA: L1/1/1/2
f 97v   *(3 November)*

…

the waytes

Edward Liberd &
william *(blank)* piper ⎫ ar admytted the ij wayttes of this Cytye

The wayttes
Colers

memorandum that the seid wayttes haith received ij Colers of Sylver conteynyng
either of them xxxj^ti lynkes & one Schuycchon waying either of them iiij vnces

Suortyes for
ye Colors

Item that John Stowe toke in hand & became Suortye for ye Color delyueryd
to liberd & Robert Burgh Suortye for ye Color delyueryd to William *(blank)*
ye piper/

…

f 103v   *(14 September)*

Ytt is agreid in this Commen Congregacion that Thomas Emonson nowe
elected & sworn mayor of this Cytye schall haue towardes the mayntenance
of his house kepyng the tyme of his maraltye the Some of x li. & xxxiij s.
iiij d. for rewardes of mynstrylles ffyve markes towardes the officers lyuereis
di. tunne of Gascoigne wyne of ye Commen Chambre & also schall haue
iij of his frendes or kynsmen to haue the ffraunches & liberties of this Cyty
frely whersoeuer they dwell & [oth] iiij fraunchest men to be taiken oute
of the libertyes of this Cytye/

…

1553–4
City Council Minute Book   LA: L1/1/1/2
f 106v   *(15 November)*

…

the wayttes

ffirst it is agreid that the wayttes schall contynue & schall haue the lyuereys
of rede clothe as they had ye last yere of ye Costes of ye Commen Chambre
and also schall haue ther waiges of euery alderman scheryff & others as they
had in ye seid last yere

…

f 110   *(6 July)*

...

Saynt Anne
Guyld

ffirst it is agreid that Saynt Anne Guyld *with* corpus chr*ist*i play schalbe
broughtfurth & playd this yere and that eu*ery* Craftes *ma*n schall bryng
furth ther padgeons as haith ben accustomed and all occupacions to be   5
contributoryes in payment of ther monye toward*es* ye same as schalbe assessed

...

f 112   *(14 September)*

...   10

Yt is agreid & enacted in this Co*m*men Congregacion that Will*i*am Rotheram
nowe elected & Sworn mayor of this Cytye schall haue toward*es* the
mayntenance of his house kepyng the tyme of his maraltye the Some of x li.
& xxxiij s. iiij d. for reward*es* of mynstrylle*s* ffyve m*ar*kes toward*es* the offic*er*s
lyu*er*eis di. tu*n*ne of Gascoigne Wyne of ye Co*m*men Chambre iiij ffraunchest   15
men to be taiken oute of ye libertyes of this Cytye & iij of his frend*es* to haue
ther ffraunchesse of this Cytye frely whersou*euer* they dwell

Cordwainers' Account and Minute Book   LA: LCL/5009
f 120v*   20

                        layng owt for ye pachgan at Saint Annes
pamentes   It*em* pade to Spede ye caru*er* for makynge off ye paghan   iij s. ij d.
             It*em* pade for nall*es* & drynke to ye carver*es*   iij d.
             It*em* pade to wyll*i*am lytyll for panttyng ther off ye hede   25
             & the stare*s*   ij s.
             It*em* [Reseuyd] pade to the schep*erdes* on SantAndaye   xviij d.
             It*em* pade for drynge to ye berer*es* of ye pagane   iij d.

...
                                                                                          30

f 121*

pamentes   It*em* pade in ye seconde & thwrde [ye] yere off Ryne off owre
                 Soffarand lawarde & ladye kynge & [g] qwyene off Eyngland
                         ffransse Iarlande napyll*es* & so forthe   35
             It*em* pade to Roberte Ionsone on schant ane*s* daye laste
             paste for ye Rowme off ye paggyene all ye yre a fore past   iiij d.
             It*em* pade for berynge of ye paggane of Sant ane*s* daye last
             to vj felowe*s*   ij s.
             It*em* pade for a Corde to ye stry*s*   iiij d. 40
             It*em* pade for tak*es* & pacthrede   ij d.
             It*em* pade for dryncke & brede to ye berar*es*   viij d.

...

1554–5
City Council Minute Book   LA: L1/1/1/2
f 115v   *(25 October)*

…

contra

Item it is agreid that Thomas Wynterborn schall haue ye Cockplace in Saynt   5
Martyn parisshe & an other peice of void ground at pulterhill next the hye
way ther for suche yerly rent & for somany yeres as schalbe thought meit by
Master Mayor & ij of his brethren thaldermen of this Cytye/

…
                                                                                    10

f 116

…

the Colers/

memorandum dclyuerd thc iiij^th day of ffcbruarij annis predictis to Edward
Liberd Iohn powler & Thomas Corbeck the iij wayttes of this Cytye iij Colers
of Sylver weying xj vnces and Iohn Stowe Thomas newbye Smyth William   15
Cannock & Robert Lyneham ar Suortyes for ye seid iij Colers, the gretyst
Color conteynyng xxviij lynges & a Skuchon the other xxvij lynges & a
Skuchon & the other xxvj lynges & no Skuchon/

…
                                                                                    20

f 119v*   *(3 June)*

…

Saynt Anne
Guyld

Item it is agreid that Saynt Anne Guyld schalbe broughfurth and that Master
Mayor & the scheryffes last beying schall stond in suche sorte & bryngfurth
the same as haith ben hertofore accustomed and that Sir William Smyth   25
schall haue yerely v s. of ye Commen Chambre for his paynes yat he schall
taik aboute ye same & also schall haue v s. forgeven hym yat he owith to
this Cytye/

…
                                                                                    30

f 123v   *(24 September)*

…

ffor the mayor

Item it is agreid & enacted in this Commen Counsell that George Porter nowe
elected & Sworn mayor of this Cytye schall haue towardes the mayntenance
of his howse kepyng the tyme of his maraltye xx li. & for rewardes of   35
mynstrelles xxxiij s. iiij d. & towardes the iiij officers lyuereys ,v, markes di.
tunne of Gascoigne wyne iiij ffraunchest men oute of ye libertyes of this
Cytye and iij ffraunchest men of his frendes whersouer they dwell frely and
also the rent Corn of the Lordschip of Canwyk peying liij s. iiij d. for ye
yere [y] rent of the seid lordschip to ye Commen Chambre/   40

…

13/ iiij^th … predictis: *4 February 1554/5*   38/ whersouer: *for whersoeuer*

Cordwainers' Account and Minute Book   LA: LCL/5009
f 120v*

...

                laynges owt for ye paggane ye nyxte yere after

Item pad to ye iiij scheperdes on SantAnedaye	xviij d.
Item pade to ye bereres off ye paggan on SantAnedaye	ij s.
Item payde for takxe	j d.
Item in alle	j d.
Item ffor howsrowme for ye paggane to Ihonsone	vj d.
Item for dryngke to ye berars off ye paggane	vj d.

...

1555–6
City Council Minute Book   LA: L1/1/1/2
f 129   *(24 September)*

...

ffor the mayores
howse kepyng Item it is agreid in this Commen Counsell that Mr Iohn Hochynson nowe
elected & Sworn mayor of this Cytye schall haue for his howse kepyng the
tyme of his maraltye xx li. & for rewardes of mynstrylles xxxiij s. iiij d. & ,v,
markes towardes the iiij officers lyuerey Gownes di. tunne of Gascoigne wyne
& iiij fraunchest men to be taiken oute of the libertyes of this Cytye/ [& also]

...

1556–7
City Council Minute Book   LA: L1/1/1/2
f 132v   *(14 September)*

...

yt is agreid in this Commen congregacion that Mr Thomas Grantham
esquier nowe elected & Sworn mayor of this Cytye schall haue for his howse
kepyng the tyme of his maraltye xx li. & for rewardes of mynstrylles xxxiij s.
iiij d. & ,v, markes towardes ye iiij officers lyuereys di. tunne of Gascoigne
wyne iiij ffraunchest men to be taiken oute of the libertyes of this Cytye &
ye rent Corn of the Lordschip of Canwyk frely/ paying vj s. viij d. to ye
reparacions yerof/

1558–9
City Council Minute Book   LA: L1/1/1/2
f 147   *(22 September)*

...

what ye mayor
schall haue Item it is agreid in this Commen Counsell that William Boodknap nowe
elected schall haue xx li. of the Commen Chambre to the mayntennce of

---

41/ mayntennce: *for* maytenance; *superscript* a *omitted*

his house kepyng the tyme of his maraltye xxxiij s. iiij d. for reward*es* of
mynstryll*es* & v m*ar*k*es* toward*es* the officers lyuereys di. tu*n*ne of wyne al*ias*
Gascoigne wyne the rent Corn of the lordschip of Canwyk frely & iiij
fraunchest men to be taiken oute of ye libertys of the Cytye and the seid
will*ia*m to bestowe wi*th*in his yere vj s. viij d. of ye rep*ar*acions of ye seid   5
lordschip & pay for halff of ye dynn*er*s et ye Court*es* at Canwyk wi*th*in his
yere/ any acte hertofore made to the contrary notwi*th*standyng/

It*em* it is agreid that Mr Nicholas ffawkn*er* mayor schall pay bere or allowe
nothyng for the leace he haith in reu*er*cyons of Dygles Closes in consideracion   10
of the weghty charges he haith ben put to in house kepyng the tyme of his
maraltye [& otherwyse] but y*a*t he schall haue allowed xx li. for his house
kepyng duryng y*a*t tyme ˄⌈ouer & besid*es*⌉ [&] xxxiij s. iiij d. for reward*es* of
mynstrell*es* ,v, m*ar*k*es* toward*es* ye officers lyuercys ⌈iiij li. for di. tu*n*ne wyne⌉
ye rent Corn of ye lordschip of Canwyk & ye iiij fraunchest men and he to   15
bestowe of ye rep*ar*acions of the seid lordschip vj s. viij d. to bere ye halff
charges of ye dynn*er*s at Canwyk Court*es* for his yere, any acte hertofore made
to the contrary notwi*th*standyng/

1559–60   20
City Council Minute Book   LA: L1/1/1/2
f 149   *(14 October)*
...

for Sperryng of
Shop wyndoues
& kepyng
seruau*n*t*es* &c

It*em* that eu*er*y victualler schall Sparr Inne the Schopp*es* on the Sondays &
other holy days when the Second peile schall ryng to seruyce and y*a*t none   25
heraft*er* keip any s*er*uant*es* or other persones in ther howse at play or Idelly
ther remaynyng in the tyme of devyne seruice on the same days vpon payn
for eu*er*y tyme vj s. viij d.

...

30

f 156v   *(14 September)*
...

M*aste*r Mayor/

ffirst it is agreid in this Co*m*men congregacion Martyn hollyngworth nowe
elected & Sworn Mayor of this Cytye schall haue xx li. of the Co*m*men
Chambre to the mayntenance of his howse kepyng the tyme of his maraltye   35
xxxiij s. iiij d. for reward*es* of mynstrell*es* ,v, m*ar*k*es* toward*es* the officers
lyu*er*eys di. tu*n*ne wyne called Gascoigne wyne the rent Corn of the lordschip
of Canwyk & iiij fraunchest men to be taiken oute of the lybertys of this
Cytye and the seid mayor to bestowe wi*th*in his yere vj s. viij d. of the
rep*ar*acions of this seid lordschip & pay for halff of ye dynn*er*s at Canwyk   40
Court*es* to be holden wi*th*in his yere/

1560-1
City Council Minute Book   LA: L1/1/1/2
f 158v   *(10 October)*

...

The mayors   Item it is agreid that the proclamacion of this Cytye called the Mayors Crye   5
crye/   schalbe proclamed on Friday cumme fortnyght and yat attendance be geven
                    at the same/ accordyng to the custome of this Cytye/

...

concernyng   Item it is agreid that the wayttes schall goo accordyng to the custome yat is
the wayttes/   to sey/ from the feast of all halows vnto Candylmas and they to haue ther   10
                    lyuereys of the Charges of the Commen Chambre & suche wages of others
                    as haue ben vsed

...

f 162v   *(14 September)*   15

...

Master Mayor   ffirst it is agreid in this Commen Congregacion that Richard mylner nowe
                    elected & Sworn Mayor of this Cytye schall haue xx li. of the Commen
                    Chambre to the mayntenance of his howse kepyng the tyme of his maraltye
                    xxxiij s. iiij d. for rewardes of mynstrelles ,v, markes towardes the officers   20
                    lyuereys. di. tunne of Gascoigne wyne the rent Corn of the lordschip of
                    Canwyk & iiij fraunchest men to be taiken oute of the libertyes of this Cytye
                    and the seid mayor to bestowe within his yere vj s. viij d. of the reparacions
                    of the seid lordschip & pay for halff of the dynners at Canwyk Courtes to
                    be holden within his seid yere/   25

...

1561-2
City Council Minute Book   LA: L1/1/1/2
f 163*   *(2 October)*   30

...

ffor the waites   Item it is agreid yat the wayttes schall goo [et] ⌈&⌉ schall haue ther liuereys
                    of the Commen Chambre and they to begyn to go yerely herafter the next
                    mornyng after the leit Courte next after michelmas & to goo contynually
                    to our ladye day thanuncyacion yerly & to have yerely for ther wages of   35
                    euery alderman xvj d. of euery scheryff & Sheryff peare xij d. & of euery
                    chamberland & chamberland peare viij d. the one halff to be paid at Crystmas
                    & ye other halff at our ladye day thanuncyacion yerely

...

6/ Friday cumme fortnyght: *25 October 1560*

f 173v*   *(19 September)*

...

Item it is enacted in this Counsell that the seid willi*a*m Kent nowe Sworne
mayor schall haue xx li. of the Co*m*men Chambre to the mayntenance of
his howse kepyng ye tyme of his *m*araltye xxxiij s. iiij d. for reward*es* of   5
mynstrell*es* v m*a*rk*es* toward*es* the officers lyuereys di. tu*n*ne of gascoign wyne
the rent Corn of ye lordschip of Canwyk for one yere & iiij ffraunchest men
to be taiken oute of the lib*er*tyes of this Cytye & the mayor to bestowe
wit*h*in his yere vj s. viij d. of the rep*a*racions of the seid lordschip & pay for
halff of the dynn*er*s at Canwyk Court*es* to be holden wit*h*in his seid yere/   10

...

Dean and Chapter Common Fund Accounts   LA: Bj/3/6
f 125v*   *(21 September–20 September) (Costs and expenses)*

...   15

Et in de*n*arijs solut*is* Ioha*n*ni Plumbe pedagogo scole
gram*m*atical*is* p*ro* regardo suo qua*n*do discipule sui
Ludcbant commodum coram do*mi*no deca*n*o & alijs   x s.
Et in de*n*arijs solut*is* p*ro* Regardo dat*o* tam lusor*ibus*
do*mi*ne Regine ⌜xiij s. iiij d.⌝ quam ducisse suff*olcie* ⌜vj s.   20
viij d.⌝ *per* concens*um* totius cap*itu*li   xx s.

...

1562–3
City Council Minute Book   LA: L1/1/1/2   25
f 181   *(25 September)*

Item it is enacted in this Counsell y*at* Richard Carter nowe Sworn mayor of
this Cytye schall hauc xx li. of the Co*m*men Chambre to the mayntenance
of his howse kepyng the tyme of his maraltye xxxiij s. iiij d. for reward*es*   30
of mynstrell*es* ,v, m*a*rk*es* toward*es* the officers lyuerey gownes di. tu*n*ne of
Gascoigne wyne the rent Corn of the lordschip of Canwyk for one yere &
iiij fraunchest men to be taiken out of the lib*er*tyes of this Cytyc hc paying
wit*h*in his yere vj s. viij d. toward the rep*a*racions of the seid lordschip &
also paying for halff of the dynn*er*s at ye Court*es* at Canwyk to be holden   35
wit*h*in his yere

...

17/ discipule: *for* discipuli

f 184   *(13 November)*

...

It*em* it is agreid in this Counsell y*at* ye offic*er*s of this Cytye called the
mayors offic*eres* schall haue ther lyu*er*ey gownes as haith ben accustomed
and no lyu*er*ye Cotes and y*at* ther schalbe no mo Cote lyu*er*eys given to   5
the waitt*es* but iij, any acte vse or custome hertofore made to the contrary
notw*ith*stondyng/

...

Dean and Chapter Common Fund Accounts   LA: D/V/2/2b   10
f [5v]*   *(20 September–19 September)* *(Costs and expenses)*

...

Et solut*um* p*er* mandat*um* cap*itu*li s*er*uien*tibus* et
lusor*ibus* tam d*om*ini Roberti dudley x s. q*uam*
d*om*ini comit*is* oxon*iensis* v s. p*ro* Regard*o* eis   15
dat*o* in toto   .   xv s.

...

1563–4
City Council Minute Book   LA: L1/1/1/2   20
f 185*   *(4 March)*

...

It*em* agreid y*at* a standyng play of some Storye of ye bibell schall be played
ij days this Som*mer* tyme and y*at* M*aste*r mayor schall appoynt Mr ffulbeck
Mr Cokkyt Mr Scolefeild Mr beu*er*ley Mr halleley & Mr wynt*er*born to   25
gather what eu*er*y p*er*son wyll gyve to ye same play and the seid Mr ffulbeck*es*
advise Counsell & aide first to be taiken for the same/

...

f 188v   *(16 September)*   30

...

Item it is agreid y*at* Thomas ffulbeck ald*er*ma*n* schalbe allowed & haue ix
li. of ye Co*m*men Chambre whiche he haith payd & leidfurth in & aboute
the staige play by hym made this yere

...   35

f 190   *(18 September)*

...

Item it is enacted in this Counsell that the seid Iohn Hochynson Sworn
mayor schall haue xx li. of the Co*m*men Chambre to the mayntenance of   40
his house kepyng the tyme of his maraltye xxxiij s. iiij d. for reward*es* of
mynstrell*es* v, m*ar*k*es* toward*es* thoffic*er*s lyu*er*eys di. tu*n*ne of Gascoign Wyne

the rent Corn of the lordschip of Canwyk for one yere paying vj s. viij d.
wit*h*in his yere to ye rep*ar*acions of th*e* s*e*id lordschip & paying for halff
the dynn*er*s at Canwyk Court*es* to be holden w*it*h*in his yere

...

f 193*

a note of the p*ar*tic⟨...⟩ the pr*o*p*er*ties of the staig⟨...⟩ played in the moneth
of Iulij, anno Sexto reg⟨...⟩ Regine Elizabeth &c in the tyme of the maraltye
of Richard Cart*er* whiche play was th*e*n played in brodgate in the s*e*id Cy*t*y
and it was of the storye of Tobias in the old testament

ffirst hell mouth wit*h* a neither Chap ⎫
Item a pr*i*son wit*h* a Coue*r*yng,   ⎬ lying at M*r* nortons house in
Item Sara Chambre   ⎭ the tenure of Will*i*am Smart

Item a greate Idoll wit*h* a Clubb   ⎫
Item a tombe wit*h* a Coue*r*yng   ⎪
Item the Citie of Ierusalem wit*h* towers & pynacles ⎪
Item the Citie of Raiges wit*h* towers & pynacles   ⎬
Item the [th] Citie of nynyvye   ⎪ remanyng in Saynt
Item the Kyng*es* palace of nynyvye   ⎬ Swythunes Churche
Item old Tobyes house   ⎪
Item the Isralytes house & the neighbures house   ⎪
Item the Kyng*es* palace at Laches   ⎭

Item a fyrmament wit*h* a fierye Clowde & a
Duble Clowde in the custodye of Thomas ffulbeck ald*er*ma*n*

Dean and Chapter Common Fund Accounts   LA: Bj/3/8
f 129*   *(19 September–17 September) (Costs and expenses)*
...
Et solut*um* ad manus m*a*gist*r*i subdecani pro
regard*o* per ip*s*um dat*o* per mandat*um* d*omi*ni
decani s*er*uientib*us* d*omi*ni Roberti dudley   vj s. ⌈exoneratur⌉ viij d.
...

8/ partic⟨...⟩: *18mm missing*
8/ staig⟨...⟩: *30mm missing*
9/ reg⟨...⟩: *20mm missing*

f 129v*

…

Et solut*um* ad manus ven*er*abilis ffrancisci
mallett decani p*er* man*datum* barth*olome*i
halley pro regard*o* dat*o* lusoribus d*omine*   5
ducisse Suff*olcie* vj s. viij d. & al*iis* lusoribus
vj s. viij d. in toto   xiij s. ⌈ex*oneratur*⌉ iiij d.

…

1564–5   10
City Council Minute Book   LA: L1/1/1/3
f 8

…

ffirst it is agreid in this Co*m*men congregacion that Thomas ffulbeck nowe
elected & Sworn mayor of this Citie schall haue toward*es* the releyff of his   15
house kepyng in the tyme of his maralty xx li. iiij s. for di. tu*n*ne of Gascoigne
Wyne xxxiij s. iiij d. for reward*es* to mynstrell*es* & iij li. vj s. viij d. toward*es*
the lyu*er*ey gownes of the Co*m*men [Clerk] ⌈Chambre⌉ of this Citie…

…

                                                                                20
A   **List of Mayors, Bailiffs, and Sheriffs**   LA: Diocesan Miscellaneous Roll 1
mb 5d   *(July)*

…

M*emorandum* Rychard Karter mayo*r*
®Wylli*am*   thys yere was the ferthys cote bryge new repracionyd & a hows in sent marys   25
 Cokkytt   p*ar*yche porchaed & the claslyth chambre new repraonyd the claslyth dore
®*Christopher*   new mayd & the lowre by brafurth new mendyd & the kawsye to Brasbryge
 Hucchynsone   new castyng & mest*er* hollynwharth thalderman dyschargyd of hys francys
                 & of all offycys & broght in agayne by the desyre of noble men to hys fredone
                 and no more at that tyme & the storye of olde thobye was playd   30

…

Dean and Chapter Common Fund Accounts   LA: Bj/3/6
f 152*   *(17 September–16 September)* *(Costs and expenses)*

…   35

Et solut*um* xiij° die ap*r*ilis 1565 p*ro* Regard*o* dat*o*
Lusoribus d*omini* comit*is* Leicestr*ie* p*er* man*datum*
d*omin*or*um* arch*idiac*oni Lincoln*iensis* et S*u*bdecani   x s.

25–30/ thys yere … was playd: *added in red ink*   26/ repraonyd: *for* reparacionyd
25/ repracionyd: *for* reparacionyd   29/ fredone: *2 minims in* MS

f 152v*

…

Et solut*um* *per* di*ctum* Receptor*em* hoc anno tam ad
manus ven*erabilis* viri arch*idiaco*ni lincoln*iensis* x s.
qu*am* ad manus ven*erabilis* viri arch*idiaco*ni Bedford   5
x s. *pro* Regardo dat*o* subpedagogo & pueris suis p*er*
ma*n*dat*um* totius capi*tu*li   xx s.
Et solut*um* ad manus di*cti* ven*erabilis* viri Ioha*n*nis
aelmer arch*idiaco*ni Lincoln*iensis* *pro* Regardo dat*o*
Lusoribus d*omi*ni Hunesdon hoc anno   vj s. viij d. 10

…

Et solut*um* d*omi*no decano p*ro* Regardo dat*o* Lusoribus
d*omi*ni Scrowpe hoc anno   v s.

…

Et solut*um* Robe*r*to Pullayn vno nu*n*ciorum capi*tu*li   15
pro Regardo dat*o* Lusoribus D*omi*ni Riche p*er* mandat*um*
m*agist*ri decani   iij s. iiij d.

…

c **1565**   20
City Council Minute Book   LA: L1/1/1/3
f 1 col 1*

…

The first Senator

1   The maker allmyghtye the ground of all grace   25
   Save this Congregation that be here pr*es*ent
   and bryng them all to the Celestyall place
   That w*ith* pacyens wyll here the effect of our intent

The Second Senator   30

2   oure intent & p*ur*pose is Auncyent customes to declare
   that haue ben vsed in this Citie manye yeres ago
   and nowe for to breake them we wysshe ye schuld beware/
   for ther be grevous ponysshment*es* for them y*at* wyll do soo

     35

The thurd Senator

3   At the tyme of Crystmas, myrthe haith ben made
   throughout all nacyons, of the Crystian faith
   and styll so to keip it, ye nede not be afrrayde
   for then, was o*ur* Savyour born as the Scripture saith   40

15/ vno: *for* vni

The first Senator

1 At that tyme saith Saynt Iohn, appeared o*ur* p*er*fight lyght
and the Saveyor of all the world y*at* faithfully trust in hym./
Saynt luke in ye second Chapitor declaryng his strenght & myght
therfore at that tyme, to be merye we wyssh ye schuld begyn/   5

The Second Senator

2 The Aungell*es* with myrthe, the Schep*erdes* did obey
when they Song, gloria in excelsis, in tuynes mystycall
The byrd*es* w*ith* Solempnytye Song on eu*er*y Spray   10
And the beast*es* for Ioye, made reu*er*ence in ther stall/

The thurd Senator

3 Therfore w*ith* a contrite hart, let hus be merye all
having a stedfast faith, & a love most, amyable   15
disdaynyng no man of power greate nor Small
for a crewell oppressor, is nothyng com*m*endable

The furst Senator

1 Whatsoeu*er* [a] oppressor wyll be cruell & not merye make/   20
schal be sore fettered in a dongion full deip
wherin is todes & nuteis w*ith* many a gret Snayk
that place is so dark you schall not se y*our* feite

Second Senator   25

2 Therfore Crystmas myrthe I wold ye schuld esteme
and to feare god & schewe ye deid*es* of Charytye, boith ma*n* & wyff/
orell*es* the people wyll assemble w*ith* weapons scherp & keene
wherfore it wyll not p*re*vaile to make any Stryff

     30

.Thurd Senator

3 aganst that holye tyme, all good people do p*re*pare
aswell kyng*es* & Quenes that is of most noble byrth
as also dukes erles & lord*es* Royally wyll faire
and Spend the tyme of Crystmas w*ith* Ioye & myrthe   35

col 2*

The first Senato⟨.⟩

1 fforsomuch as all degrees w*ith*in this r⟨...⟩
do highly esteym the tyme of Cr⟨...⟩   40
to breke y*at* hon*o*rable custom I wold none to⟨...⟩
but Spend ye tyme in hearyng & folowyng god*es* ⟨...⟩

Second Senator

2   That is the Cheiff cause hither we were sent
to gyve the people warnyng to haue all thynges perfig⟨.⟩tly
For they yat do not, breakyth Master mayors Comaundem⟨...⟩
and accordyng to the order, ponysshed must they b⟨..⟩   5

Thurd Senator

3   Therfore endeuor your selffes to haue all thynges w⟨...⟩
that no default be found neither of Riche nor p⟨...⟩
but at that tyme help your neighbures as Saint Iames d⟨...⟩   10
Refresshyng the pouertye yat Cummyth to ye do⟨...⟩

ffirst Senator

1   Breiffly we haue declared, theffect of our mynd
and I do not doubt but you wyll haue it in reme⟨   ⟩   15
one neighbor, to an other, I wyssh ye schuld be kynde
for ye tyme doith so Spend nedes we must goo for⟨...⟩

The Second Senator

2   here we cannot tarye the tyme passith ⟨...⟩   20
this mortall world is but van⟨...⟩
all magistrates & Rulers we wold ye sch⟨...⟩
walking in your va⟨...⟩

Th⟨...⟩   25

3   The eternall Lord, hau⟨...⟩
vnto other places ⟨.,.⟩
power vpon you th⟨...⟩
he, yat all thyng⟨...⟩

                                                                                         30

Am⟨..⟩

1565–6
City Council Minute Book   LA: L1/1/1/3
f 10v*   *(26 January)*   35
...

The staige play   Item it is agreid yat ye staige play of the Storye of Tobye schall go forward
& be played in whytson holye days next & the Commen Chambre to beare
iiij li. towardes charges therof & orderers of ye same to be appoynted by
Master Mayor & his brethern   40

38/ whytson holye days next: *2–8 June 1566*

Item in consideracion that all men of this Citie accordyng to the statute
may haue in a redynes ther harnes & munytion that the Watche accordyng
to the auncyent custome of this Citie may be kept the Sonday next before
thassension day with men in harnes and the Sheryffes the Cheiff Constables
& vnderconstables of this Citie to see the same done   5

...

f 15   *(14 September)*

...

In this Commen Congregacion it is agreid that Lyon Ellys nowe elected   10
& Sworn mayor of this Citie schall haue towardes the releyff of his house
kepyng the tyme of his maralty xx li. & for di. tunne of gascoign Wyne iiij li.
& for rewardes of mynstrylles xxxiij s. iiij d. and towardes thofficers iij li. vj s.
viij d. of the Comen Chambre...

...   15

Dean and Chapter Common Fund Accounts   LA: Bj/3/6
f 165v*   *(16 September–15 September)*   *(Costs and expenses)*

...

Et in regardo dato per mandatum domini decani   20
et residensiariorum eccesie predicte lusor' Iohannis
Byron militis mensis Decembris 1565   iiij s.
Et solutum willimo Saunderson pedagogi schole
grammatice tam pro regardo ei dato pro lusione
commodij cum pueris suis quam pro custibus et   25
expensis suis circa eundem supportatis ut patet
per billam   xlvij s. vj d.

f 166*

...   30

Et solutum Roberto pullayn pro regardo per ipsum dato
Lusoribus domini Strange per mandatum capituli   v s.
...
Et solutum magistro ffrancisco Malett decano ecclesie
cathedralis predicte pro Regardo per ipsum dato   35
seruientibus domine regine vocatis the quenes players
hoc anno   vj s. viij d.

...

3–4/ the Sonday ... day: *Rogation Sunday, 19 May*   21/ eccesie: *for* ecclesie
    1566   23/ pedagogi: *for* pedagogo

1566–7
City Council Minute Book   LA: L1/1/1/3
f 20   *(25 September)*

...

allowances   ffirst in this Commen Counsell it is agreid & enacted that wher Edward   5
Halleley nowe elected & Sworn mayor of this Citie for ye yere next
folowying doith inhabit in suche place in the Citie So yat it is thought
in this Commen Counsell that he schall be at greater charges in his house
kepyng then of late any mayor hath ben, that he schall haue more by x li.
towardes ye charges of his house kepyng then others the mayores of late   10
tyme haue had that is to sey xxx li. & for di. tunne Gascoign wyne iiij li.
& for rewardes of mynstrelles xxxiij s. iiij d. and towardes thofficers lyuerey
gownes iij li. vj s. viij d....

...

                                                                                                                                                     15

Archdeaconry of Lincoln Visitation Book   LA: Diocesan Vij/3
f 33*

...

willelmus Bede
⌈[I] dimittitur/.⌉ Henricus dent   20
Thomas wateman
Antonius Ellys
ludebant in domo Arthuri Wilsonne die dominica tempore diuinorum
xxijº marcij 1567 apud lincolniam dent citatus non ⟨...⟩ ceteri quesiti non
de viijs et modis/ postea dent comparuit et fatetur/ habet recognoscere die   25
dominica proxima et recitare. postea dominus cum monicione eum dimisit

1567–8
City Council Minute Book   LA: L1/1/1/3
f 22v*   *(24 November)*   30

...

a Staige play   Item it is agreid that the staige play of the Storye of old Tobye conteyned in
& ye watche   the old testament schalbe played at the feast of penticost next cummyng
and that the Citie schall beare towardes the Charges therof vj li. xiij s. iiij d.
And also that the watch yerly herafter schalbe keipt the Sonday next after   35
holy Thuresday and euery person to haue & provide harnes to be Shewed
in the same for his landes & goodes accordyng to the Statute therof made
& provided

...

33/ the feast of penticost ... cummyng: *6 June 1568*
35–6/ the Sonday ... Thuresday: *30 May 1568*

194

LINCOLN 1567–9

f 24v *(8 May)*

...

william
huddylston
graunted x s. &
an Inuentorye
to be made of
ye Implementes
vtenselles & [gr]
gere of guyldes
& plays/

Item wher william huddylston belman & Cryer of the Courtes haith ben long
sick & is nowe poore & aged & also charged with Children, it is agreid in
consideracion therof that he schall haue towerd his releyff in reward of the
Commen chambre x s., and that George porter & George Stamp william
gadknap martyn mason Iohn Welcome aldermen & the Commen Clerk
of this Citie schall viewe & make an Inuentorye of suche Implementes
^⌈vtenselles⌉ Stuff & gere as the seid william huddylston haith in custodye
of [f] any guyldes or plays/

...

f 26v *(14 September)*

...

allowance

ffirst in this Commen Congregacion it is agreid & enacted that John Walcome
nowe elected & Sworn mayor of this Citie for ye yere next folowying schall
haue all suche allowances as master mayor had graunted by Commen Counsell
towardes the greate charges of his house kepyng the tyme of his maralty that is to
sey xxx li. & for di. tunne gascoigne Wyne iiij li. & for rewardes of mynstrelles
xxxiij s. iiij d. and towardes thofficers lyuerey gownes iij li. vj s. viij d....

...

1568–9
City Council Minute Book   LA: L1/1/1/3
f 33v* *(5 March)*

...

Saynt Anne
guyld geares to
be laid in A
Chambre in ye
Hall

Item it is agreid yat all ye geares of Saynt Anne guyld remanyng in the seid
tenement schall be laid & keipt in the Lower Chambre in the guyldhall and
ye same Chambre schalbe repayred & amendyd fore the same with Spede

...

f 40 *(14 September)*

...

ffirst in this Commen Congregacion it is agreid & enacted that martyn mason
nowe elected & Sworn mayor of this Citie for the yere next folowyng schall
haue all suche allowances for his house house kepyng in the tyme of his
maraltye as master mayor yet beying had graunted in the last Commen
congregacion holden in the feast of ye exaltation of ye holy crosse anno xmo
regni Regine Elizabeth predicte yat is to sey xxx li. & for di. tunne gascoiygne
wyne iiij li. & for rewardes of mynstrelles xxxiij s. iiij d. & towardes thofficers
lyuerey gownes iij li. vj s. viij d....

...

1569–70
City Council Minute Book   LA: L1/1/1/3
f 50v   *(14 September)*

...

ffirst in this Commen Congregacion It Is agreld & enacted that John Wylson   5
nowe elected & Sworn mayor of this Citie for the yere next folowyng schall
haue for his house kepyng the tyme of his maraltye xxx li. & for di. tunne
of wyne called gascoign wyne iiij li. & for rewardes of mynstrelles xxxiij s.
iiij d. and towardes thofficers lyuerey gownes iij li. vj s. viij d....

...   10

Dean and Chapter Common Fund Accounts   LA: Bj/3/6
f 213*   *(18 September–17 September)* *(Customary payments and expenses)*

...

Et solutum ad manus magistri archidiaconi   15
Lincolniensis pro Regardo dato Lusoribus domini
comitis wigornie   vj s. viij d.

...

f 213v*   20

...

Et solutum magistro Iohanni aelmer et magistro
Todd pro Regardo dato seruientibus domine Regine
vocatis the quenes playres   xx s.
....   25

1570–1
City Council Minute Book   LA: L1/1/1/3
f 59   *(14 September)*

                                                                           30

ffirst in this Commen congregacion aforeseid it is agreid & enacted that
Thomas Sawson nowe elected & Sworn mayor of this Citie for the yere next
folowyng schall haue for his house kepyng the tyme of his maraltye xxx li.
& for halff a tunne gascoigne wyne iiij li. & for rewardes of mynstrelles
xxxiij s. iiij d. & towardes the iiij officers lyuerey gownes iij li. vj s. viij d.... 35

...

Cordwainers' Account and Minute Book   LA: LCL/5009
f 145v   *(14 February 1570/1–14 February 1571/2)* *(Expenses)*

                                                                           40

Et de pecunijs similiter per ipsos computantes solutis

pro prandio ibidem facto viz. pro xj gallinis iiij s.
tribus porculis ij s. vij d. vno quarterio le mutton x d.
vno le busshell wheate v s./ xx gallonibus seruisie iiij s.
ij d. wode & cole iij s. viij d. sewolt iij d. currens xij d.
iiij ouncijs pepper xij d. duabus libris lez Raysyns [xvj d.]   5
& duabus libris lez preynes xvj d. cloves & mace v d.
saunders j d. sugar iiij d. mustarde v d. honnye j d.
yeaste iiij d. pane vj d.   xxvj s.
Et de pecunijs similiter solutis pro prandio predicto per
predictum Iohannem Stowe viz. pro iiij gallinis xviij d.   10
iiij lez quarter mutton iiij s. iiij d. pro le beiff viij s.
vj d. salte vj d. bere iij s. cher cole vj d. wyne viij d.
pane xij d. Musicis iiij d. butire ij caikes x d. currens
iiij d. alliger j d. in toto   xxj s. vj d.
…   15

1571–2
City Council Minute Book   LA: L1/1/1/3
f 66   *(20 September)*

…   20
Item it is agreid & enacted in this Counsayle that William Kent nowe elected
& Sworn mayor of this Citie for ye yere next folowying schall haue for his
house kepyng the tyme of his maraltye xxx li. & for di. tunne of gascoigne
wyne iiij li. & for rewardes of mynstrelles xxxiij s. iiij d., and towardes the
iiij officers lyuerey gownes iij li. vj s. viij d.….   25
…

Cordwainers' Account and Minute Book   LA: LCL/5009
f 148v*   *(14 February 1571/2–14 February 1572/3)*

                                                                     30
Iidem Computantes petunt allocari de pecunijs per ipsos
solutis tam pro prandio quam alijs &c viz./ pro seruisia
apud le corriers ijabus vicibus viij d. willelmo hesill iij s.
viij d./ pro pane & seruisia alia vice xvj d. pro quatuor
anceribus iij s. iiij d./ pro vndecim galinis iiij s. viij d. duas   35
lez caykes butire x d. vnum le peck salt ⌈di.⌉ vj d./ vnum
le peck [Barley] ordei iij d. vnum le kilderkyn bere iij s.
vnum le quarter beif viij s. viij d./ pro septem gallonibus

1/ ibidem: *on the election day, 14 February 1570/1*   10/ Iohannem Stowe: *a guild master*
1, 10, 33/ iiij s., xviij d., viij d.: *subtotals in account* 32/ prandio: *held on the election day, 15 February*
    paragraph underlined   *1571/2*

seruisie ij s. iiij d. vnum modium frumenti & le gryndinge
v s. ij d./ vnum ovem & quarterium & duas libras le sewet
vj s. x d./ pro quatuor porculis iij s. x d. pro seruisie empta
de uxore Thome Gough xx d. vnum le dossen pomis xij d.
pro seruisie empta de vxore Nicholai Iroton xij d. pro spice   5
empt' de Thoma Hanson ij s. viij d. pro [gr] Musterd aleger
& candelis iiij d. pro le pewter accomodat' de Cuthberto
wilson iiij d. pro ca⌈r⌉bonibus xij d. pro bosco ij s. viij d.
& in regardo Musicis xiij d. Necnon clerico scribenti hunc
compotum vj s. viij d. in toto   lxiij s. vj d. 10

...

1572–3
City Council Minute Book   LA: L1/1/1/3
f 76   *(26 September)*   15

...

Item yt ys enacted at this commen councell that Edmund Knyght nowe
elected & sworne maior of this Citie for the yere next folowyng shall haue
towardes his house kepeyng the ryme of his maraltie xxx li. & for halff a [d]
tune of gascoigne wyne iiij li. & for rewardes for mynstrelles xxxiij s. iiij d.   20
and towardes iiij officers lyuery gownes iij li. vj s. viij d....

...

Dean and Chapter Common Fund Accounts   LA: Bj/3/6
f 245v*   *(21 September–20 September)* *(Costs and expenses)*   25

...

Et solutum magistro Iohanni Ælmer archidiacono
Lincolniensis pro regardo per ipsum datum lusoribus
domine Regine   v s.
...   30

1572–4
St Martin's Churchwardens' Accounts   LA: L1/5/12
f 19   *(16 April 1572–16 April 1574)*

...   35
Item they are likewise charged with the somme of
xvj s. by them received for the maypoull Crosse stones
& troughe &c   xvj s.

2/ duas: d *corrected over* v   36/ they: *Cuthbert Wilson and John Holden,*
3, 5/ seruisie: *for* seruisia   *churchwardens for the two years*
4/ pomis: *for* pomorum

1573–4
Inventory of Edward Hogge   LA: INV 58/215
single sheet*   *(16 August) (In the kitchen)*
...

Item certayne Instrumentes for musyke   xx s.   5
...

1574–5
City Council Minute Book   LA: L1/1/1/3
f 89v   *(24 September)*   10
...

an order
towchyng
towchyng the
allowances of
mr porter
maior elect
the tyme of
his maraltie

ffirst yt ys agreyd & enacted at this commen Councell that George porter
nowe elected & sworne maior of this Citie for the yere of his maraltie shall
haue towardes his house kepeyng this said next yere thirtie poundes and for
di. a tune of gascoigne wyne iiij li. and for rewardes of mynstrelles xxxiij s.   15
iiij d. & towardes the fower officers lyuery gownes lxvj s. viij d....
...

Dean and Chapter Common Fund Accounts   LA: Bj/3/6
f 269v*   *(19 September–18 September) (Costs and expenses)*   20
...

Et solutum Iohanni Wyncle magistro scole gramaticalis
pro penis & diligencia suis in le settinge forth of dyuerse
plays hoc anno per mandatum capituli   xxvj s. viij d.
...   25

1575–6
City Council Minute Book   LA: L1/1/1/3
f 93   *(10 December)*
...   30

lyueryes for
the wayttes

Item yt ys agreyd that there shalbe hereafter nomo lyuery cotes giffen to the
wayttes of this Citie but onely thre liuery cotes & in mony accordyng to the
anscient orders of this Citie
...

                                                                                        35

f 97v   *(24 September)*
...

master maior
his allowances

ffirst yt ys ordred at this commen Councell that mr Skolfeyld nowe elected &
sworne maior of this Citie for that this ys the secund tyme of his maraltie
shall ∧⌐haue⌐ all suche lyke allowances as mr porter nowe maior haithe or   40

13–14m/ towchyng towchyng: *dittography*

had graunted that ys to sey/ xxj quarters of barly to be bought by the
chamberlane of the southe ward & delyuered to hym within one halff yere
next after his entry to the office/ and xl li. in mony/ and also shall haue
lykewyse allowed for halff a tune of gascoigne [wyf] wyne iiij li. and towardes
the charges of mynstrelles xxxiij s. iiij d./ Towardes the officers gownes lxvj s.   5
viij d. ...

...

Dean and Chapter Common Fund Accounts   LA: Bj/3/6
f 280*   *(18 September–16 September)   (Costs and expenses)*   10

...

Et solutum magistro Gregorio Garthe Cancellario ecclesie
predicte pro regardo per ipsum dato Lusoribus domini
Comitis Essex cantantibus in choro ecclesie predicte per
mandatum domini decani   x s.   15

...

1576–7
City Council Minute Book   LA: L1/1/1/3
f 100*   *(5 December)*   20

...

<table>
<tr><td>an order
towchyng
crystenmas
myrthe/</td><td>Item yt ys agreyd that Cristenmas myrthe shalbe proclamed in ten or xij places
where the officers shall thynke mete/ And euery Alderman & other that haue
borne the office of sheryffe & chamberlane shall ryde with the officers or
elles fynd A man & a horse to ryde with the officers the same dayes in payne   25
of xij d. to be payd to the vse of the comen chamber for euery default</td></tr>
</table>

1577–8
City Council Minute Book   LA: L1/1/1/3
f 108v   *(14 September)*   30

...

<table>
<tr><td>master maior
allowances</td><td>Item yt ys agreyd at this commen Councell that mr wynterburne elected &
sworne maior of this Citie shall haue allowd of the Commen Chamber towardes
the charges & expenses of his house kepeyng the tyme of his maraltie the some
of thirtie poundes with other allowances of wyne & grane & other charges as   35
those that haue bene ons maior haue had that ys to sey/ xxj quarters of barly
bought & to be delyuered to the said maior by the chamberlane of the southe
ward in manner & furme as ys appoynted by a comen councell maid in the
tyme of the maraltie of george porter alderman. And also that the said maior
shall haue allowed iiij li. for halff a tune of gascoigne wyne for mynstrelles   40
xxxiij s. iiij d. for & towardes the charges of four lyuery gownes iij li. vj s. viij d. ...</td></tr>
</table>

...

1578–9
City Council Minute Book   LA: L1/1/1/3
f 113v   *(16 September)*

the maior his
allowances

Item it ys agreyd at this co*mm*en Councell that mr m*a*rtyne Mayson maior   5
elect shall haue for the tyme of his maraltie allowd to hym of the co*mm*en
Chamber aswell for his dyet & other his hospitalitie housekeypyng &
wynes & other charg*es* suche allowanc*es* as those that haue bene two tymes
maior of this Citie accordyng to a co*mm*en councell maid in the tyme of
the maraltie of george porter alderman that ys to sey xl li. in mony for his   10
housekepeyng xxj q*uar*ters of barly to be bought by the chamberlane of
the southe ward And also shall haue allowance for halff a tune of gascoigne
wyne iiij li. and toward*es* mynstrell*es* xxxiij s. iiij d. And toward*es* the officers
gownes lxvj s. viij d....
...   15

1579–80
City Council Minute Book   LA: L1/1/1/3
f 119   *(20 September)*

...   20

the allowanc*es*
for m*a*ster
maior elect
this yere/
1580/

ffirst it ys agreyd that mr hawk*es* nowe elected maior & sworne shall haue
allowed for this yere of his maraltie toward*es* the charg*es* of his house suche
allowanc*es* as ys sett down by co*mm*on councell in the tyme of the maraltie
of mr george porter alderman that ys to sey xxx li. in mony toward*es* the
charg*es* of his house for wynes to be layd in his house before Christemas &   25
ther to be spent in tyme of his maraltie xiiij li. viz for di. a butt of malvesy
& di. a butt of sacke x li. & for halff a tune of gascoigne wyne iiij li./ ffor
mynstrell*es* xxxiij s. iiij d. for the foure Sess*i*ones dyners liij s. iiij d. viz for
eu*ery* dyner xiij s. iiij d. for & toward*es* officers gownes lxvj s. viij d....
...   30

1580–1
City Council Minute Book   LA: L1/1/1/3
f 125   *(23 September)*

...   35

m*a*ster maior
allowanc*es*

Item yt ys also agreyd in this co*mm*en Councell that willi*a*m kent elected
maior sworne shall haue allowed for this yere of his maraltie toward*es* the
charg*es* of his house as ys sett down & agreyd vpon by co*mm*on councell
in the tyme of george porter alderman & late maior/ viz ffortie pound*es* in
mony toward*es* the charg*es* of his house/ And for wynes to be layd in his   40
house before Christenmas ^⌈this⌉ yere[ly] & ther to be spent in the tyme of
his maraltie xiiij li. viz for di. a butt of malvesey & di. a butt of sacke x li.
And for halff a tune of gascoigne wyne iiij li. also for mynstrell*es* xxxiij s.

iiij d. ffor the foure Sessiones dyners liij s. iiij d. viz for eu*er*y dyner xiij s.
iiij d. And for & towar*des* the officers gownes lxvj s. viij d. . . .

. . .

1581–2
City Council Minute Book   LA: L1/1/1/3   5
f 130v   *(26 September)*

. . .

the maior*es*
allowance

Item yt ys agreyd in this co*mm*en councell that mr Iohn Emonson nowe
elected maior & sworne shall haue allowed for this yere of his maraltie   10
towar*des* the charges of his house as ys sett down by co*mm*on councell in
the tyme of the maraltie of george porter alderman/ that ys to sey/ thirtie
poun*des* in mony towar*des* the charg*es* of his house beyng the first tyme of
his maraltie & for wynes to be layd in his house yerely before christenmas
& ther to be spent in the tyme of his maraltie xiiij li. viz. for a halff but   15
of malvesey [x li.] And halff a butt of sack x li./ And for halff a tune of
gascoigne wyne iiij li./ for mynstrelles xxxiij s. iiij d./ ffor the foure Sessiones
dyners liij s. iiij d. viz for eu*er*y dyner xiij s. iiij d./ And also for & towar*des*
the officers gownes lxvj s. viij d. . . .

. . .   20

1582–3
City Council Minute Book   LA: L1/1/1/3
f 135v   *(24 September)*

. . .   25

master maior
his allowance

Item yt ys further agreyd in this co*mm*en councell that mr Rob*er*t Rushefurthe
nowe maior elect & also sworne shall haue allowed for this tyme of his
maraltie towar*des* the charg*es* of his house kepeyng as ys lymyted & appoynted
by co*mm*on councell sett downe in the tyme of the maraltie of george porter
alderman diseased/. That ys to sey/ thirtie poun*des* in mony towar*des* the   30
charg*es* of his house beyng the first tyme of his maraltie and for wynes to
be layd in his house before Christenmas & ther Spent in the tyme of his
maraltie xiiij li. viz. for halff a butt of malvesey & halff a butt of Sack x li./
& for di. Tune of gascoigne wyne iiij li. for mynstrelles xxxiij s. iiij d. for
the foure Sessiones dyners liij s. iiij d. viz for eu*er*y dyner xiij s. iiij d./ And   35
also for & Towar*des* the officers gownes lxvj s. viij d. . . .

. . .

1585–6
City Council Minute Book   LA: L1/1/1/3   40
f 154   *(11 December)*

lyu*er*yes & badges
for the wayt*es*

. . .

2   Item yt ys agreyd also that the Waytes of this Citie shall haue foure lyveres

allowed to them besydes old liberd lyuery and also that they shall haue ther
badges & chenes of siluer in vse possession & kepeyng puttyng in sufficient
sewerties to the comen chamber for the delyuerance of the same when they
shalbe cauled for

...   5

1586–7
City Council Minute Book   LA: L1/1/1/3
ff 168v–9   *(28 September)*

...   10

Master Maior
allowances ys
as much as a
dooble mair:

Item it is agreed at this Commen Councell that mr Dennis nowe elected
Maior and swoorne shall haue allowed him for this yeare of his Maioraltie
towardes the Charges of his housse as it is setdowne and agreed vppon in
the Common Councell houlden in the time of the Maioraltie of George.
Porter somtymes Maior of this Cittie viz ffortie poundes in Monie towardes   15
the Charges of his housse and for wines to be laid in his housse this yeare
before Christenmas and ther to be spent duringe his Maioraltye the Somme
of xiiij li. viz. for di. a butt of Malmesey and for half a butt of Sack x li. and
for haulf a [But] tun of Gascoigne wine iiij li. and for Minstrells xxxiij s.
iiij d. for the fforr Sessions dynners liij s. iiij d. [and] for euery session Dinner   20
xiij s. iiij d. | and for and towardes Officers gownes lxvj s. viij d....

...

1588–9
Inventory of Edward Rockadyne, Scrivener   LA: INV 75/271   25
sheet [1]   *(6 November) (In the parlour)*
...
Item one old lute   ⟨...⟩
...

30

1589–90
City Council Minute Book   LA: L1/1/1/3
f 192v   *(19 January)*
...

No foren
Musitions
to play at
marriages in
Lincoln
without a
contribusion
to the wayts

Inprimis whereas the waytes of this Cittie haue maid sute vnto this howse   35
not onelie for the increase of the wages which they say is verie small but
also for the inhibitinge of forren musitiones to play within this Cyttie
ether at marriages or otherwise for that the same tendeth greatlie to ther
hindraunce. It is therefore agred that ∧⌈no⌉ musitions whatsoeuer except
the waytes of this Cyttie do play at any tyme hereafter at eny marriage   40

28/ ⟨...⟩: *20mm damage to right edge of* MS

within the Iurisdiccione of Lincoln except the same musitions do giuc vnto
the Waytes of Lincoln [xiij d.] ⌈ij s.⌉ for euery marriage they shall play at
within the Cittie of Lincoln & the Countie of the same. And as concerninge
ther wages yt is likewise agred that euery one that hathe borne office within
this Cyttie shall pay yerelie towardes the wages so muche money twise by   5
yere as was agred & settdowne in mr Milners tyme/.

...

1590–1

Inventory of Christopher Jackson, Musician   LA: INV 80/9   10
sheet [2]   *(10 April)   (In the kitchen)*

...

Item a baise violin and a curtell   xl s./.

...
                                                                                  15

1592–3

Dean and Chapter Act Book   LA: Dean and Chapter A/3/7
f 124*   *(21 January)*

...

®decretu⟨...⟩   Die Dominico xxjᵐᵒ mensis Ianuarij Anno domini 1592 predicti magistri   20
soluendi   decanus Precentor, Cancellarius, et Archidiaconus lincolniensis in choro ecclesie
actor⟨...⟩   cathedralis beate marie lincolnie ad paruiloquium conuenientes decreuerunt
commediam   sumam iiij li. erogandam fore bartholomeo Gryffyn et Iohanni Hylton viz
⟨...⟩   dicto Bartholomeo l s. et Iohanni Hilton xxx s. versus releuamen laborum et
                 onerum que ijdem Bartholomeus et Iohannes sustinuerunt in edendo duas   25
                 commedias per choristas et alios ecclesie istius scolares ∧⌈agendas⌉ Quodque
                 dicta summa iiij li. soluenda sit cum cingrua expedicione per receptorem
                 gcneralcm dictc ecclesie

...
                                                                                  30

1594–5

Dean and Chapter Common Fund Accounts   LA: Bj/3/8
f 321*   *(15 September 1594–21 September 1595)   (Costs and expenses)*
...

Et solutum Roberto Butler pedagogo Choristarum pro   35
chordis & alijs necessarijs pro violis vt per billam patet
[x vij s.]   xxij s.
...

20m/ decretu⟨...⟩: *20mm missing from right edge of leaf; for* decretum de *(?)*
22m/ actor⟨...⟩: *18mm missing from right edge of leaf; for* actoribus *(?)*
24m/ ⟨...⟩: *24mm missing from right edge of leaf*
27/ cingrua: *for* congrua

1596–7
City Council Minute Book   LA: L1/1/1/3
f 237   *(5 December)*

…

Bulles to be
bated before
they be killed

Item yt is agreed that eu*er*y butcher that sell eny Bull beif in Lincoln m*ar*kett   5
hereafter that the same butcher or some for hym shall bate the same Bull
vppon the m*ar*kett hill before he kill hym vppon pane to forfeit & lose for
eu*er*y Bull killed & not bated v s. and that m*aster* Sheriffe off this Cyttie
now is or that hereafter shalbe shal[be] compounde for the not batinge of
eny suche Bull vppon pane of x s. for eu*er*y suche composyc*i*one to be   10
forfeited & paid to the poore/.

…

Dean and Chapter Common Fund Accounts   LA: Bj/5/12(38)
f 34v*   15

…

Et so⟨..⟩to eode*m* die M*agist*ro Butler p*ro* denarijs
allocat*is* ei[⟨.⟩] in comp*uto* p*ro* papiro cordis violar*um*
& alijs xx s. x d. & p*ro* penc*i*one sua ei debit*a* ad festu*m*
s*an*cti Mich*ael*is Archangeli p*ro*xim*um* futur*um* xxxiij s.   20

® *(signed)*
Th*omas* Butler

iiij d. in toto   liiij s. ij d.

…

1599–1600
City Council Minute Book   LA: L1/1/1/3   25
f 250   *(28 March)*

…

Musicions
increase of
wages &
liu*er*yes &
Cognizanses

Item 'yt is agred that the wates or musitions shall from o*ur* Ladie Day last
past haue C s. yerelie towards thir wages increse & also that hereafter they
shall haue iiij Coates yerelie at *Christ*mes over & besides the Coates they   30
haue now alreddie/ & further that ther cheines & cognizancs be repared.

…

1607–8
City Council Minute Book   LA: L1/1/1/4   35
f 56   *(22 October)*

…

a lawe for no
musitions to
play in Lincoln
but the Cytties
musitions

Item it is agreed that no musitions or musition of this Cyttie or Cuntrie
elswher shall at any time hereafter vse any musicke vppon instrumentes ether
at any marriage or at or in any Inne. alehowse or victuallinge howse or any   40

17/ eode*m* die: *20 September 1597*

other place within this Cyttie or the subburbes of the same but onlie those
musitions that were the Cytties leverye without the leave & likeinge of the
Cytties musitions the assise tyme onelie excepted/.

...

Archdeaconry of Lincoln Visitation Book   LA: Diocesan Vij/11
f 48v*

...

dimittitur   Iohannes Burton for keepeing companie in his house drinking & singing
in praier time on ye saboath day [30.] ⌈28.⌉ May 1608. comparuit et se
submisit & cum monicione dimittitur

1609–10
City Council Minute Book   LA: L1/1/1/4
f 70v*   *(18 August)*

...

Iustynyan
Walwyn to
haue his
fredome

Item It is agreed that Iustynyan W[es]alwyn [Sh] the instrument maker
shall haue the fredome of this Cyttie payinge for yt C s. & in parte of
payment of that C s. ⌈to⌉ make the Cyttie a drumme for suche a summe as
mr Hollingworthe mr Goffe mr Dicconson mr Swifte & mr Wilson or the
moste part of them shall sett down or abate of the said C s. & also payinge
the rest by x s. a yere vppon good suretie any for former lawe or act to the
contrary not withstandinge/

...

Cordwainers' Account and Minute Book   LA: LCL/5009
f 201v*   *(20 February 1608/9–19 February 1609/10)*

Item for ye Clarke & his wifes dynner at the feste   xvj d.
Item to the wates   xij d.

...

Dean and Chapter Common Fund Accounts   LA: Bj/3/9
f 139   *(Cost of wax, cloth, and other things)*

...

Et solutum Thome Kyngstone Magistro Choristarum
pro coris violarum vj s. viij d. & pro sex arcubus pro
violis suis anglice bowes for theire violls vj s.   xij s. viij d.

...

22/ any for former: *for* any former   37/ coris: *for* cordis
29/ feste: *held 6 November 1609*

1610–11
City Council Minute Book   LA: L1/1/1/4
f 74v*   *(15 December)*

...

Inprimis whereas Richard Bell the musition bought his fredome in Mr yates   5
first Maraltie bought his fredome of this Cittie & payde for the same as by
Mr yates accompts dothe appeare & the entrie of his fredome is omitted
by the towne Clarke It is therefore agreed that the saide Bell shall haue
his fredome entred accordinge to the order of this Cittie & that his sonne
Richard shall haue the benefitt of his fathers fredome as foretime   10

...

f 77   *(8 June)*

...

2 musitions to   Item That ffardinando Gibbyns & *(blank)* Lockington musitians of this   15
haue lyveryes   Citie shall haue two lyveryes of this Cities Charge./

...

Cordwainers' Account and Minute Book   LA: LCL/5009
f 203v*   *(19 February 1609/10–18 February 1610/11)*   *(Payments)*   20

...

Item spent in wyne & for mrs Morrost & mrs Mason
dynner & for the wates dynner   iiij s. ij d.

...
                                                                                      25

1611–12
City Council Minute Book   LA: L1/1/1/4
f 82   *(29 February)*

...

watts Chaines   Item it is agreed that because ther are of the Cities wates fyve in nomber   30
badges & seale   that eche of them shall haue a lyverye of this Citie. And that the three chaynes
to be amended   & badges shalbee repayred for them & also one new badge & twoo chaynes
shalbee made new for them according as thother three are And also the comon
seale for lettres shalbe newly ingraven at the Cities chardge.

...
                                                                                      35

Cordwainers' Account and Minute Book   LA: LCL/5009
f 205   *(18 February 1610/11–17 February 1611/12)*   *(Disbursements)*

...

Item laied owt to the Musicons & for wine at the dynner   vij s. vj d. 40

...

5–6/ bought ... fredome: *dittography*   40/ Musicons: *for Musicions; abbreviation mark missing*
23/ wates: *at the guild feast, 5 November 1610*   40/ dynner: *held 4 November 1611*

1613–14
City Council Minute Book   LA: L1/1/1/4
f 118 *(28 September)*

...

Iustinian Walwyn [M] Instrument maker d*i*c*t*o xj°. Apr*i*lis. admiss*us* est in   5
d*i*c*t*as lib*er*ta*t*es & ffranchesias p*r*o *(blank)*

...

Cordwainers' Account and Minute Book   LA: LCL/5009
f 209v   *(15 February 1612/13–21 February 1613/14) (Payments)*   10

...

It*em* for the Clarkis dynn*er* & his wyfe   xvj d.
It*em* for wine the wat*es* & ye beder   viij s. ij d.

...

                                                                        15

1614–15
City Council Minute Book   LA: L1/1/1/4
f 122*   *(11 July)*

...

Item that the chardge m*aste*r Maior hath bene at for the int*er*tayning of the   20
Lorde Lewttenant & building of the scaffold against the horse race shalbe
allowed him at his accompt.

...

Cordwainers' Account and Minute Book   LA: LCL/5009   25
f 211   *(21 February 1613/14–20 February 1614/15) (Payments)*

...

Item sol*utum* p*r*o vno le quart sack   xij d.
Item sol*utum* p*r*o prand*ijs* Clerici & vx*or*is   xvj d.
Item sol*utum* p*r*o prand*ijs* musitions & vna pint sacke   iij s. vj d. 30

...

Dean and Chapter Act Book   LA: Dean and Chapter A/3/10
ff 150v–1   *(1 August)*

                                                                        35

Visitation of Lincoln grammar school by Roger Parker, STD, *dean of Lincoln*
Cathedral; George Eland, BA, *chancellor and canon residentiary; and John Hills,*
STD, *canon residentiary and archdeacon of Lincoln, together with the mayor and*
other officials of the city, in the presence of Thomas Stirroppe, notary public
and clerk of the cathedral chapter   40

13/ wat*es*: *at the guild feast, 8 November 1613*
30/ musitions: *at the guild feast, 7 November 1614*

Viz. di*ct*is die horis et loco di*ct*i do*m*ini decanus et Residen*ciarij* necno*n*
maior Recordator et Aldermani p*re*dict*i* in vnu*m* congregat*i* et Convenientes
post quasdam orac*i*ones siue declamac*i*ones vnam vi*delice*t grece p*er* quendam
Sowth et alteram Latine p*er* quendam Kent pronun*n*ciatas ac post p*re*ces
divinas eodem in Loco finitas obiecerun*t* m*agist*ro Iohanni Phipps gimnasiarche   5
et willi*el*mo walkwood hipodidasculo coni*u*nct*i*m et di*ui*si*m* ar*ticu*los
infrascriptos eos*que* et quosdam de scholastic*is* p*re*dict*is* sigillatim et simul
exa*m*inarun*t* (nullo delato iura*m*ent*o*) sup*er* eisdem ar*ticu*lis Et quia tunc et
ib*ide*m liquide et manifeste eisdem visitatoribus constabat di*ct*um willi*el*mum
walkwood esse ˄⌐et⌐ p*er* no*n*nullos an*n*os p*re*teritos fuisse crasse culpabilem   10
dicti Maior Recordator et Aldermani cu*m* consilio di*ct*oru*m* Decani et
Residen*ciariorum* p*re*dict*orum* et cuiusda*m* Roberti Morecroft alterius Aldermani
tunc etiam p*re*sent*is* decreverun*t* di*ct*um willi*el*mum walkwood amovend*um*
fore ab officio hipodidascul*at*e in di*ct*a schola et nihilominus p*re*dict*i* Decanus
et Residentiar*ij* maior Recordator et Aldermanu charitat*is* intuitu erga eunde*m*   15
walkwood com*m*oti vnanimis suis consensu et assensu concordarun*t* | Sum*m*am
iij li. vj s. viij d. ex revenc*i*onibus Com*mun*nie Canonicor*um* Residen*ciarum*
di*ct*e ecclesie cath*edral*is et iij li. vj s. viij d. ex revenc*i*onibus Comunis Camere
Civitatis Lincoln*i*e et vj li. viij s. iiij d. ex stipendio hipodidasculi futuri
anuatim t*em*poribus soluend*arum* vadiar*um* Ludimag*ist*ri et Hipodidasculi   20
p*re*dict*orum* prius consuetis) equis porc*i*onibus di*ct*o walkwood in eius et famile
sue alimentac*i*one*m* Donec et quovs*que* de competenti beneficio aut salario
ecclesiastico p*ro*vis*us* fuerit) soluend*am* et contribuend*am* in p*re*sentia di*ct*i
m*agist*ri walkwood se in p*re*miss*is* eorum grac*i*æ submitten*tis* ingentes eis dant*is*

25

Item di*ct*i Decanus Residen*ciarij* maior Recordator et Aldermani qu*o*d in
posterum nullo modo [I⟨…⟩] licebit di*ct*is scholastic*is* excludere gimnaziarcham
aut hipodidasculu*m* di*ct*e schole Aliquo Anno ante festum o sapientiæ xvj°
vi*delice*t die mens*is* Decembris
…   30

1615–16
City Council Minute Book   LA: L1/1/1/4
f 132   *(18 September)*
…   35

Iur*atus*   20. Novembr*is*
10   Thomas Becket filius Iacob*i* Becket Apprentic*ius* Ric*ard*o Bell Musition p*ro* viij
annis A p*ri*mo die Novembr*is* An*n*o R*egni* R*egis* Iacob*i* nunc Angl*ie* xiij° & xlix°/.
…

7/ sigillatim: *for* singulatim *(?)*   22–3/ Donec … fuerit): *opening parenthesis omitted*
20–1/ t*em*poribus … consuetis): *opening parenthesis*   24/ submitten*tis*: *for* submittentis et gratias
  omitted   26/ qu*o*d: *for* statuerunt quod

Cordwainers' Account and Minute Book   LA: LCL/5009
f 213   *(20 February 1614/15–22 February 1615/16) (Payments)*

...

Item in vino ad festum	iij s. ij d.
Item pro prandiis musicorum	ij s. vj d. 5

...

Item solutum ad Beadle	iiij d.
Item pro prandijs Clerici & vxoris	xvj d.

...

10

1616–17
City Council Minute Book   LA: L1/1/1/4
f 136v*   *(14 January)*

fforen musition   Item. that no forren musition whatsoeuer not being one of the wates of   15
this Citie (Contrary to the lawdable vse & custome of this Citie tyme out
of mynde vsed) shall play offer or present his musicke for money or gayne
at any wedding time or other ressort or meeting within the said Cirie
suburbs or liberties therof. If the wates of the said Citie for the tyme being
shalbe willing thear to play & present their musick vnlesse it be the musitions   20
of some noble man to their owne maister onely at his house or lodging
onely vpon payne of euerie house keeper receaving such forren musition
or musitions to forfeit to the said waites for the time being ij s. & euery
forren musition offending to forfeit v s. to thuse of the said Company of
wates And that it shall & may be lawfull to & for the said Company of   25
wates in & by the name of the maisters felowes & Company of wates of
the Citie of Lincoln to sue the [offender] offenders & delinquentes for all
or any the said forfeiture by action of debt in any Courte within the said
Citie in which action no esson wager or protection shalbe allowed. Or els
the same to be levied by distresse & sale of the delinquent & offendors goodes   30
by any the maior or [sheriffs] Sheriffs officers within the said Citie for the
tyme being

...

A present for   Item that ther shall be a present provided by master Maior & his brethern
the king.   of towardes the Kinges Maiesties coming to this Citie of his intended   35
progresse holde and to be presented by them vnto his Maiestie that present
and value therof to be left to ther discretions & to be allowed them out of
this Cities revenews

...

4/ festum: *held 6 November 1615*

f 138v   *(20 February)*

...

Item that euerie inhabitant within this Citie & suburbs of the same aswell
freemen & Citizens as foreners shall cause their houses & fences with their
pentices & other groundes in & against the highe to be repaired dressed   5
[paint] & made decent & hansome & also cullor & paint their houses
needefull before & against his Maiesties coming to this Citie vpon paine
of tenne powndes a piece to be forfeit & paid by euerie offender for euery
offence to the vse & benefit of the Corporacion of this Citie...

...   10

f 139   *(25 February)*

...

Item ther shalbe soe much of the xliij li. xiij s. iiij d. in the Clarkes hand
deliuered to master Maior towardes his extraordinary charge of housekeping   15
at the kinges Maiesties coming to this Citie & towardes the fees of the Kinges
officers [& master Maiors house keeping & expenses during] that tyme as
master Maior shall please to call for the same not exceding xl li./

ff 139v–42*   *(7 March)*   20

...

Inprimis it is agreed at this comon Counsell that master Maior & his
brethren Master Recorder Master Sheriffes the towne Clarke & euery man
els which hath bene sheriffes of this Citie hereafter namid vizt. Mr Lawson
Mr Iohn Dawson Mr Burgh Mr Yates mr Somerby Mr Longston Mr Okley   25
mr Robert Beck mr Ricrost, Mr Kendall Mr Anton Mr Cumberland mr
Bishop mr Thomas Dawson Mr Whitbie & Mr Smyth. shall euery of them
provide himselfe a horse & ffoote cloth of black with black bridles & all
thinges els sutable & decent against his Maiesties coming to the Citie And
shall also provide themselfs apparrell good & decent for men of their degrees   30
and callinges and so attend & well provided shall all together decently & in
order euery one obseruing his degree & keping the same meete his Maiestie
at the owt skertes of the County of this Citie or els where. And that Master
Maior shall provide to attend on himselfe twoo men with ether of them a
liueray cloake & euery Alderman & euery sheriffe & towne Clarke aforesaid   35
shall also haue & provide[s] to attend on him ther a man [&] in a liverey
cloake well decently & in good order appointed. And that Master Maior
& his brethren shalbee all in their scarlit gownes & those which haue bene
Maiors in velvet Tippites as they vse to weare, the sheriffes in gownes of
purple in grayne the towne clarke in [some] a gowne of some fine stuffe   40

14/ soe much: s *written over another letter*

decently trymed & all others aboue named which haue bene sheriffe to bee
in black gownes garded with velvet or velvet lace playne on the back on the
Citizins facion. vpon paine that euery one that shall make defalt to forfeit
lose & pay xl. to thuse of this Corporation & what other penalty this house
shall thinke fit. All which fines paines penaltys | & forfeitures [yat] shall from   5
time to tyme by any the Maiors officers for the tyme being of the said City
be sued for by action of debt in any his Maiesties Courtes of record or any
Court within the said City to be holden wherein no wager or esson or other
protection shalbe allowed the defendant. Or otherwise shalbe bound by
distresse & sale of goodes of euery or any such offender or delinquent by any   10
officer of the Maior or sheriffs within the said City for ye tyme being

...

Memorandum that his Maiestie being to come to this Citie the macebearer
was sent to the Lord Chamberlaine at Grantham for directions when where
& in what manner master Maior & the Citizens should mete his Maiestie   15
who retorned answer that his Maiestie was intended that night to rest at
St Caterins & the day following to come into the Citie & that therefore the
sheriffes with some nomber of Cizins in gownes should meete his Highnes
at the skirtes of the Countie & so the day folowing the Maior & his breathern
with convenient company of Citizins to mete him at the Barr yate and then   20
& not before to haue some spech to his Maiestie for that his Hignesse did
not love longe speches. wheruvpon the xxvijth day of Marche 1617 anno xvo
Regni Regis Iacobi. King Iames did come from Grantham to Lincoln But
the appointed place for meeting his Highnes at the skirtes of the County
was not observed by reason his Maiestie hunted along the heath & came   25
not the highway And so the sheriffes & Citizins removed from that place &
they with either of them a white staff in his hand clad in Cloth gownes of
purple in grayne & on horsback with foot cloaths together with all of note
which had bene sheriffes on horseback with foote cloaths & black gownes all
of the auncientest facion & all that had bene chamberlaines of note on | on   30
horse back in their gownes of one facion on violetes cullor without foote
cloaths & diuerse other Citizins in cloakes of like cullor booted & spoored
on horse backe ‸⌜all with new cloakes⌝ with new Iaffelinges in their handes
frenged with red & white (being set in order by one of his Maiesties officers,
who came before his Maiesties coming to that end) two & twoo in a rancke   35
[where] weare appointed to stand in the highway near the Crosse of the cliffe
whear his Maiestie coulde not misse of them the sheriffes being hindmost And
when his Maiestie drewe neare them the twoo sheriffes onely lighted, & way
made for them they both went to his Maiesties in his Caroche & keeling

18/ Cizins: for Citizins   39/ Maiesties: for Maiestie
21/ Hignesse: for Highnesse   39/ keeling: for kneeling
30/ on on: dittography

the elder sheriff deliuered his staffe first & the king deliuered it him agayne
& the other sheriffe did the like. & so both tooke horse agayne & rydd both
beare headed before the Caroche the high sheriff [& his] of the County &
his men by the kinges officers then were put by & the other Citizens in

their degrees before the sheriffes Rid all bare headed before his Maiestie   5
conducting & attending him to his lodging at St Catherins: on the next
day his Maiestie coming to the Baryate in his Caroch hee thear lighted &
tooke his horse caparisone of state being most riche wheare the Maior the
Recorder & his bretherne the sheriffes & other Citizins afore named in
their ranck & attire as aforesaid attended him on horsback & footecloths   10
the Maior & aldermen in their scarlet robes with euery of them a man to
attend him on foote in [C] Civill livereys much what all alike: His Maiestie
came towardes the Maior & Recorder who were both lighted & on foote
hard vnder the houses on the west side of the street within the Barr yates

And the Maior reddily on his knee kneeling tendered the sword to deliuer   15
it vnto his Maiestie But his Maiestie[s] put the sworde back with the back
of his hand with all grace refused to take it from the Maior Then the kinges
Maiesty asked the Maior if he had any speech to deliuer who answered no
but this gentleman who is our Recorder hath one & the king willed say on

so the Recorder keeling all the time on his kees vttered his speech which his   20
Maiestie harde willingly & with great comendacions which ended the Maior

deliuered his Maiestie a goodly Inamiled & guilt silver cup of a full klue [hie]
in hight in wheight a C markes in siluer or ther aboutes which the kinge
tooke with great delight & content & moving his hat thanked them &
deliuered it to one of his foote men to carry openly in his hand all the way   25

to the Minster & thence conveyed it to his lodging After the cup deliuered
the Maior mounted with the sword in his hand & placed betwixt the twoo
seriantes at mace did beare the sword befor the king to the Minster & the
Earle of Rutland being lieuetenant of the Cuntrie did beare the kinges sworde
all the said Aldermen Sheriffes & other | Citizins in their ranckes yongest first   30
did ride two & two together vp the high streete through the Bale vnto the
Minster yates at the west end therof where the kinge kneeled downe on a
quishion which was thear prepared & praied a shorte praier & so vnder a
cannapie which was held over him by 4 or 6 prebends in surplosses went into
the quier the Maior still bearing the sworde aldermen & other Citizins in   35
their gownes going before him vnto the quier & thear sat by the Bishops pue
hanged about with rich hanginges in a chaire all prayer tyme Master Deane
saying prayers & the Maior holding vp sworde before him all praier tyme

After praiers done his Maiestie went about the Church to see the auncient   40

18/ Maiesty: M *corrected from* gr   20/ kees: *for* knees
20/ keeling: *for* kneeling

monument*es* therof & so went into the Chapter house to see it & from
thence to his Caroch & thearin went toward*es* his lodging at St Caterins
downe Potergate head M*aste*r Maior bearing the sworde vntill he tooke
Caroche aswell through Bale Close as Church. when he tooke caroch his
owne sword & all armam*entes* was put vp. the Maior aldermen & Citizins   5
in their ranck*es* as aforesaid rid all before the caroche Attend his Ma*ies*ties
on horse back to saint Caterines house wher his Ma*ies*ties at the dore put
of his hat & dismissed them

On sonday being the xxx^th of March his Ma*ies*tie went to the Minster in   10
his Carach & at the west dore met him there bishops & the deane &
Chapter who made a short spech M*aste*r Maior & his bretherne sheriff*es* &
other Citizins in their gownes did thear (as was directed them by the Lord
Chamberlayne & his officers from whome they had [⟨…⟩] directions for
all their cariag*es* & doing*es*) did get in their degrees before his Ma*ies*tie by   15
twoo & two in a ranck vntill the formost came at the quier door then they
did devide their rancke & one stood still of one side & an other turned &
stood on the oather & so made a faire lane & way for his Ma*ies*tie to keepe
him from the presse of the people And for order sake firstt the towne Clarke
then the twoo sheriffes & after them the Aldermen in their ranck by twoos   20
went along (betwixt the Citizins in the way they made) before his Ma*ies*tie
into the quier whear the Bushop of Lincoln preached after w*hi*ch sermon
ended the kinge healed to the nomber of fiftie p*er*sons of the king*es* evell.
when he had so done the Citizins went before him | In order as aforesaid
vnto the Bushops pallace whear he dyned and after dynner his Ma*ies*tie went   25
in his Caroch in privat vnto saint Catherins againe

On tuisday being the first of Aprill Mr Ealand one of the Masters in the
Church p*re*ched before his Ma*ies*tie in his Chamber of p*re*sens whear after
s*er*mon his Ma*ies*tie did heale liij of the king*es* evill.   30

On wedensday being the second of Aprill his Ma*ies*tie did come in his Caroch
to the signe of the George by the stanbowe to see a Cocking thear where
he appointed fouer Cock*es* to bee put on the pitt to gether w*hi*ch made his
Ma*ies*tie very merie And from thence he went to the Spreadeagle to see a [p*ri*]   35
Prise plaied thear by a fensor of the City & A servant to some attendant in
the Courte who made the Chalenge where the fenser & scollors of the [ha]
City had the better on w*hi*ch his Ma*ies*tie called for his Porter who called
for the sworde & buckler & gave & receaved a broken paite & others had
hurt*es* The King then entred his Caroche at the Inne yate whear the Maior   40
& Aldermen did crave answer to the piticon they deliu*er*ed at the king*es*

coming from the Cocking to whome the king torning gave his hand to
Master Maior & Mr Hollingworth Alderman who kissed the same & so
rid forwardes to St Catherins

On thursday thear was a great horserace on the heath for a Cupp where his   5
Maiestie was present & stood on a Scaffold the Citie had caused to be set vp
& withall caused the Race a quarter of a mile longe to be ruled & corded
with ropes & stoops on both sides whereby the people were kept out & the
horses which ronned were sene faire/

10

On friday ther was a great hunting & a race by the horses which rid the seut
for a golden Snafle And a race by three Irishmen & an English man All which
his Maiestie did behold The Englishman wonne the race |

On saterday after dynner his Maiestie went from St Katherins to Newarke   15
at whose departure from st Caterins Master Maior & his brethren did give
attendance at his coming forth of the presence & when hee tooke his Caroch
in the hinde Courte at St Caterins hee gave forth his hand to the Maior all
the Aldermen & the towne Clarke who all kissed the same then hee thanked
them all saying that if god lent him life hee would see them oftenner & so   20
tooke his Caroch & went foreward that night to Newarke Master Sheriffes
riding before his Caroche in their gownes with their white staffes & footcloaths
& men with Iafflinges but no Citizins vntill the hither end of Bracebridg
whear they likewise tooke their leaves & hee moved his hat to them & then
the high sheriff & his men receaved him at the further end of the bridge   25
beyonde the water & so conducted him on his Iorney

f 144*   *(2 September)*

...

A tenement at   Item that Iustinean Walwyn shall haue a lease of his dwelling house &c for   30
bower hill to   xxxj yeres to comense at the surrender end or forfeiture of the lease in off
Iustinian   tholde rent which proviso to set it in sufficient repaire & so to vphold &
Walwyn./   leave yt. ffyne a Cover for a drume

...

35

Cordwainers' Account and Minute Book   LA: LCL/5009
f 214v   *(22 February 1615/16–17 February 1616/17) (Payments)*

Item the Clarke & his wifs dynner   xvj d.
Item in wine at the dynner   ij s. vj d.   40

18/ hinde: *4 minims in MS*   40/ dynner: *held 4 November 1616*

Item for ye wates dynner   ij s. vj d.
Item for Thomas Greene & Simsons dinners   xij d.
Item to the Beadle   iiij d.
...
5

Inventory of John Lions   LA: LCC ADMONS 1616/253
single mb   *(17 October)* *(In the great chamber)*
...
Item i pare virginales   iij li.
...
10
                          In Instermentes
Item ij banndores   xl s.
Item i viall de gambo [&]   xx s.
Item i base violin   xx s.
Item i bandore   xvj s. 15
Item i tener violin   x s.
Item iij treble violines   xvj s.
Item i sithern   viij s.
Item i githern   iij s
Item i sagbut   xl s. 20
Item ij tener Cornittes   xvj s.
Item iiij treble Cornittes   xx s.
...

Inventory of Edmund Sandye, Musician   LA: LCC ADMONS 1616/343(a) 25
single mb   *(5 November)*
...
Item certaine old Instrumentes   iij s. iiij d.
...

30

Letter of Thomas Lake to Sir Ralph Winwood   TNA: PRO SP 14/90
f [1]   *(29 March)*

Sir. This lettres is chiefly to convey th'enclosed one to the lord Carew which
is a chiding for the cartes made at the Towre which proue very weak in their 35
axletrees and in the harnos. and you shall doe well to healpe to Chide for
his maiestie is very angry. Another is a packett of my lord chamberlain which
his lordship desireth may be saffely deliuered.
But withall I haue a commandement to putt you in mynde of that which
I did from Burly of the Proclamation for persons of quality to repaire into 40
the cuntry as was agreed before his maiesties comming forth. And likewise

2/ dinners: *4 minims in* MS   34/ This lettres: *for* This lettre

for the establishing of Provost Marshals in the neighbor shires to London.
his ma*iestie* hath receaud information that in Middlesex it is don, but wold
haue it so in other places.

yesterday his ma*iestie* made his entry into this city with as good a shew as we
heare could doe. My lo*rd* Rosse spake with him yesternight, and so shall again   5
this day at his ma*iesties* return from hunting.

My lo*rd* chief Iustice of Ireland is comed hither but hath not yet been with
his ma*iestie*. So I rest.

> Yours to doe you seruice
> *(signed)* Tho*mas* Lake   10

Lincoln this. 29. March
1616.

1617–18
Cordwainers' Account and Minute Book   LA: LCL/5009   15
f 216   *(17 February 1616/17–19 February 1617/18)* *(Payments)*

It*em* for the Clarke & his wife dynner	xvj d.
It*em* for wine at the dynner	ij s. vj d.
It*em* for the wates dennar	ij s. 20
It*em* to the beadle for keping the dore	iiij d.

…

1618–19
Cordwainers' Account and Minute Book   LA: LCL/5009   25
f 217v   *(19 February 1617/18–18 February 1618/19)* *(Payments)*
…

In pr*i*mis for wine at the dynner	iij s.
It*em* for the clarke & his wifis dynner	xvj d.
It*em* to the Musitions	ij s. vj d. 30
It*em* for Tho*mas* Grene dynner	vj d.
It*em* for Tho*mas* Dale dore keper	iiij d.

…

1619–20   35
City Council Minute Book   LA: L1/1/1/4
f 169v   *(20 September)*
…

3 Iulij 16〈..〉

…   40

7/ comed: *for* come (?)	28/ dynner: *held 2 November 1618*
19/ dynner: *held 3 November 1617*	

Iuratus   Antonius Okley filius Willelmi Okley Apprenticius Iustiniano Walwyn pro
7. annis & 8º vt Iorneman primo Augusti Anno Regni Regis Iacobi &c xvijº
& liijº

Cordwainers' Account and Minute Book   LA: LCL/5009   5
f 219   *(18 February 1618/19–24 February 1619/20)   (Payments)*
…
for wyne at the dynner   iij s.
for the wates the bedle & Thomas Grene dinners   iij s. vj d.
for the Clarkes dynner & his wife   xvj d.   10
for a potle of sack at the second day dinner   ·   ij s.
to the beadle for the dore keping   vj d.
…

1620–1   13
Cordwainers' Account and Minute Book   LA: LCL/5009
f 221*   *(24 February 1619/20–22 February 1620/1)   (Payments)*
…
for the wates denner   ij s. vj d.
Thomas Greene Thomas Dale & Richard   20
Hewetson denners   xiiij d.
for wyne at the feast   v s.
…

1621–2   25
Cordwainers' Account and Minute Book   LA: LCL/5009
f 223*   *(22 February 1620/1–21 February 1621/2)   (Payments)*
…
Item the Clarkes dynner at the feast   xvj d.
Item for wyne at the dynner   iiij s. iiij d.   30
Item for the wates dynners   iij s.
Item to the comon Beadle   iiij d.
…

1623–4   35
City Council Minute Book   LA: L1/1/1/4
f 196v*   *(22 April)*
…
A new Wate   Item that George Moone shall be admitted of the company of Wates of this
City so alwaies as he doe by lettre or otherwise conveniently satisfie master

8/ dynner: *held 8 November 1619*   29/ feast: *held 5 November 1621*
22/ feast: *held 6 November 1620*

Maior that now is & his brethern that he ⌈is⌉ lawfully comed from the
service of the right honorable the Earle of Rutland

...

f 199   *(25 September)*   5

...

9 ffebruar*ij* 1623

...

admiss*us* Thome Becket filius Iacobi n*uper* app*r*entic*ius* Ricard*i* Bell musicion p*r*o 7.
annis admiss*us* & Iur*atus* &c   10

...

Inventory of Humphrey Wilkinson, Musician   LA: INV 128/124
single mb   *(14 June)*

...   15

Im primis ⟨.⟩ Chist & his app*a*rell in it, & his
Instrument*es* of musique   xxx s.

...

1624–5   20
Cordwainers' Account and Minute Book   LA: LCL/5009
f 224v   *(16 February 1623/4–21 February 1624/5) (Payments)*

...

It*em* for mutton bred bere & other charg*es* at eating of
the Venison sent to the Company & to the messenger   vj s. viij d. 25
It*em* disbursed at the speaking of the feast   xij d.
It*em* at the bidding of the feast spent   ij s.
Item for wyne at the feast   iij s. iiij d.
It*em* for the dynn*er*s of v wat*es* & the beadle   iij s.
Item for Tho*mas* Peachell & Tho*mas* ffeild   30
daughter dinn*er*s   xvj d.
It*em* to the Beadell for keeping the dore   viij d.
It*em* for making vp the shot at the dynn*er*   xviij d.

...

                                                                               35

1626–7
Cordwainers' Account and Minute Book   LA: LCL/5009
f 226v   *(20 February 1625/6–19 February 1626/7) (Payments)*

...

It*em* c*um* invitabant fest*um*   iij s. viij d. 40

16/ ⟨.⟩: *malformed letter, probably* a   31/ dinners: *4 minims in* MS
26/ feast: *held 8 November 1624*   40/ festum: *held 6 November 1626*

Item pro carbonis Anglice Charcoles   iiij d.
Item pro vino ad festum   ij s. viij d.
Item pro prandio Clerici & uxoris   xvj d.
Item musicionibus Bedallo & Thome Grene   iiij s. iiij d.
...   5

1627–8
Cordwainers' Account and Minute Book   LA: LCL/5009
f 228v   (19 February 1626/7–21 February 1627/8)   (Allowances)

                                                                            10
Item ad invitacionem festi   ij s.
Item pro prandijs Clerici & uxoris ad festum   xvj d.
Item pro prandijs musicorum & Bedelli
ad festum   iij s.
Item pro poto ad festum   v s.   15
Item pro pro vino ad festum   vij s. iiij d.
Item pro igne ad festum [& alijs temporibus]   [vj d.] xix d.
...

Inventory of Richard Bell, Musician   LA: INV 134/49   20
single sheet*   (15 October)
...
Item one Sittorn with the casse and one recorder   iij s. iiij d.
...

                                                                            25

1628–9
Cordwainers' Account and Minute Book   LA: LCL/5009
f 230v   (21 February 1627/8–19 February 1628/9)   (Allowances)
...
Item expenditum circa appunctuacionem &   30
invitacionem festi   iiij s. viij d.
Item pro vino ad festum   iiij s. iiij d.
Item pro optimo poto ad festum   iij s. iiij d.
Item pro prandijs musicorum & Bedelli &
feodo bedelli   iij s. iiij d. 35
...

11/ festi: held 5 November 1627
16/ pro pro: dittography
31/ festi: held 3 November 1628

1629–30
Cordwainers' Account and Minute Book   LA: LCL/5009
f 232   *(19 February 1628/9–18 February 1629/30)*   *(Allowances)*

...

Item expendit*um* circa invitac*i*onem &	5
appunctuac*i*onem festi	[iij s.] v s.
Item p*ro* vino ad festu*m*	vj s.
Item pro feod*o* bedelli ad festu*m*	iiij d.
p*ro* cervitia ad festu*m*	vj s. viij d.
Item p*ro* prandio Cl*e*rici	viij d. 10
It*em* p*ro* prandijs musicor*um* ad festu*m*	ij s. vj d.
It*em* ad soluc*i*onem p*ro* prandijs ad	
festu*m* solut*am*	vj d.
Item p*ro* cervitia ad noctem ad festu*m*	xij d.

...   15

1631–2
City Council Minute Book   LA: L1/1/1/4
f 151   *(27 September)*

...   20

Iur*atus*   Ioh*anne*s Read filius Ric*ard*i appr*enticius* Iustineani walwen instrum*ent* maker
a festo s*anc*ti Martini Ep*iscop*i in hyeme p*roximo* ante dat*am* Indentur*e* scili*cet*
xiijº die Ianuarij [163] a*nno* Caroli vj 1630 p*ro* 7. annis & p*ro* viijº a*nno* vt
le iourney man xxjº die Novembr*is* 1631

...   25

1632–3
Cordwainers' Account and Minute Book   LA: LCL/5009
f 236v   *(23 February 1631/2–21 February 1632/3)*   *(Allowances)*

...   30

It*em* expendit*um* in invitacione co*mmun*is festi	
huius consortij	iij s.
It*em* expendit*um* in Cervitia ad festu*m* illud	v s. iiij d.
It*em* expendit*um* p*ro* prandijs musicor*um* & bedelli	ij s. viij d.
It*em* expendit*um* in vino ad festu*m* illud	v s. iiij d. 35
It*em* dat*um* ex mun*e*re bedello	iiij d.

...

6/ festi: *held 2 November 1629*
31–2/ co*mmun*is festi huius consortij: *held 5 November 1632*

1634–5

Cordwainers' Account and Minute Book   LA: LCL/5009
f 240   *(21 February 1633/4–19 February 1634/5)   (Allowances)*

...

Item solut*um* musicis bedell*o* & Ioha*nn*i Nicholson	5
ad festu*m*	iij s.
Item pr*o* vin*o* ad festu*m*	xviij d.
Item in expens*is* in invitac*i*one ad festu*m*	xij d.
Item pr*o* Cervisia ad soluc*i*one*m* pr*o* festo	xiiij d.

... 10

Item pr*o* prandijs Wille*h*mi [Pea*c*] E*nr*ie alder*ma*ni
& Thome Peachell ad festu*m*   xvj d.

...

1635–6   15

Will of John Morton, Musician   LA: LCC WILLS 1635i
f 15*   *(13 January; proved 27 January 1635/6)*

In dei nomyny amen I Iohn morton of the sittie of lincolne mvsvtion do
ordayne constatvte and make this my last will and testament in manner and   20
forme following ... I give my son Iohn morton and my brother Richard
morton all my bovckes be twixt them// and I put my brothere henry bell
to be the sales man of all my Instruments...

...

25

1636–7

Cordwainers' Account and Minute Book   LA: LCL/5009
f 243*   *(18 February 1635/6–23 February 1636/7)   (Allowances)*

...

Item expens*is* ad invitac*i*onem festi	iij s. 30
Item ad festu*m* pr*o* poto	xx s.
Item pr*o* prandijs m*agi*stroru*m* ˄⌜Roberti⌝ Morcroft	
Wille*h*mi Watson & Thome Peachell ad festu*m*	ij s.
Item pr*o* prandijs musicor*um* & bedell*i* & Ioha*nn*is	
Nicholson	[xx d.] iiij s. iiij d. 35

...

6/ festu*m*: *held 3 November 1634*
30/ festi: *held 7 November 1636*

Inventory of Thomas Bishop, Clerk   LA: INV 144/257
single mb *(7 January)*

...

Item one Truncke & one Tennor viol   xx s.

...   5

1637–8
Cordwainers' Account and Minute Book   LA: LCL/5009
f 244 *(23 February 1636/7–22 February 1637/8) (Allowances)*

...   10

Item in expensis in poto in preparacione festi
in invitacione & ad festum   ix s. vj d.
Item pro prandio magistri Watson ad festum   viij d.
Item pro prandijs musicorum bedellorum &
Iohannis Nicholson ad festum cum iiij d. ex   15
dono datis bedellis   iij s. x d.

...

1638–9
Cordwainers' Account and Minute Book   LA: LCL/5009   20
ff 245–5v *(22 February 1637/8–21 February 1638/9) (Allowances)*

...

Item expensis ad invitacionem festi   vj s.
Item expensis in cervitia ad festum   x s.
Item pro prandio willelmi watson aldermani   25
ad festum   viij d. |
Item pro prandijs musicorum bedellorum &
Iohannis Nicolson ad festum   iij s. vj d.
Item ex dono dato bedellis   iiij d.

...   30

1639–40
Inventory of Henry Bell, Musician   LA: INV 150/6
f [1]* *(21 April) (In the other chamber)*

...   35

Item 8 winde Instruments & a Vialinne   4 0 0

...

11/ festi: *held 6 November 1637*
23/ festi: *held 5 November 1638*
29/ ex: *corrected from* pro

1641–2
Cordwainers' Account and Minute Book LA: LCL/5009
f 248v *(18 February 1640/1–24 February 1641/2) (Allowances)*

...

Item expenditum ad preparacionem festi ij s. ad   5
invitacionem festi ij s. viij d. & [ad] in Cervitia
ad festum xxj s.   xxv s. viij d.
Item pro prandio willelmi watson aldermani
ad festum   viij d.
Item pro prandijs musicorum bedelli & Iohannis   10
Nicholson ad festum   v s. iiij d.
Item ex dono dato bedello   iiij d.

...

1642–3   15
Cordwainers' Account and Minute Book LA: LCL/5009
f 250 *(24 February 1641/2–23 February 1642/3) (Allowances)*

...

Item in expensis ad preparacionem prandij pro festo
huius consortij   ij s. vj d. 20
Item pro consimilibus expensis ad invitacionem
ad festum   ij s.
Item pro prandijs ad festum willelmi watson aldermani
& clerici huius consortij   xvj d.
Item pro prandijs musicorum ad festum   ij s. vj d. 25
Item pro prandijs bedelli & Iohannis Nicholson   xvj d.
Item pro Cervitia ad festum   xiiij d.

...

LONG SUTTON   30

1542–3
St Mary's Churchwardens' Accounts LA: SUTTON ST MARY PAR/7/1
f 5* *(16 April 1542–1 April 1543) (Payments)*

...   35

Item payd in reward to the Bayne of freston in
[Bred and] ale   ix d.

...

5/ festi: *held 8 November 1641*
19–20/ festo huius consortij: *held 7 November 1642*

f 11*

...

In *pri*mis payd to freston playars whan thay cryed
ye bane here   v s.
It*e*m gyuen in rewarde to framton players whan   5
they were here   v s.
It*e*m payd for brede & ale than   vj d.

...

1543–4   10
St Mary's Churchwardens' Accounts   LA: SUTTON ST MARY PAR/7/1
f 15v   *(1 April 1543–20 April 1544) (Payments)*

...

It*e*m payd to the playar*e*s at chrystmes   xx d.
...   15

1547–8
St Mary's Churchwardens' Accounts   LA: SUTTON ST MARY PAR/7/1
f 35   *(17 April 1547–8 April 1548) (Payments)*

...   20
It*e*m p*a*yd to the playerz in the churche   ij s.
...

1550–1
St Mary's Churchwardens' Accounts   LA: SUTTON ST MARY PAR/7/1   25
f 39v*   *(13 April 1550–5 April 1551) (Payments)*

...

It*e*m to the players for playnge   iiij s.
...

                                                                             30

f 42v*

...

It*e*m to my ladi[s] svffolks plaiars   vj s. viij d.
...

                                                                             35

1554–5
St Mary's Churchwardens' Accounts   LA: SUTTON ST MARY PAR/7/1
f 56v   *(1 April 1554–21 April 1555) (Payments)*

Item paid to the players of walsoken in cristmas   iij s. iiij d.   40
...

f 57v*

...

Item paid to the players that came first   ij s.

...

5

1555–6
St Mary's Churchwardens' Accounts   LA: SUTTON ST MARY PAR/7/1
f 60   *(21 April 1555–13 April 1556) (Payments)*

...

Item paid to the players on the sonday   10
in shrofttyde   iij s. iiij d.

...

f 61v

...

15

Item paid to the players at Christmas   ij s. iiij d.

...

1556–7
St Mary's Churchwardens' Accounts   LA: SUTTON ST MARY PAR/7/1   20
f 64v   *(13 April 1556–25 April 1557) (Payments)*

...

Item payd to the players vpon saynt mathewe day   ij s.

...

25

1559–60
St Mary's Churchwardens' Accounts   LA: SUTTON ST MARY PAR/7/1
f 75*   *(2 April 1559–21 April 1560) (Payments)*

...

Item paid to the players that came frome   30
bullyngbrooke   iij s. iiij d.

...

f 75v*

...

35

Item payd to the dawncers of Spalldynge   v s.

...

10–11/ the sonday in shrofttyde: *16 February 1555/6*

1560–1
St Mary's Churchwardens' Accounts   LA: SUTTON ST MARY PAR/7/1
f 77*   *(21 April 1560–13 April 1561)* *(Payments)*

...

Item paid to ye players that played vpon   5
Trynytie sonday   vj s. viij d.

...

f 77v*

...   10
Item paid to ye players in Cristmas   v s.

...

Item paid to ye players the fryday after
Candelmas day   iiij s.

...   15

1561–2
·*St Mary's Churchwardens' Accounts*   LA: SUTTON ST MARY PAR/7/1
f 80   *(13 April 1561–5 April 1562)* *(Payments)*

...   20
Item paide to the players of Twelft daye in
ye church   iiij s.

...

f 80v   25

...

Item payde to the players of wisbich the monday
in easter weke   vj s.

...

                                                                                  30

1562–3
St Mary's Churchwardens' Accounts   LA: SUTTON ST MARY PAR/7/1
f 82   *(5 April 1562–18 April 1563)* *(Payments)*

...

Item payd to ye players   vj s. 35

...

Item paid to ye playars of ye hye countrey   vj s.

...

6/ Trynytie sonday: *9 June 1560*
13–14/ the fryday after Candelmas day: *7 February 1560/1*
27–8/ the monday in easter weke: *7 April 1561 or 30 March 1562*

f 83*

...

Item paid to ye bayne of Du*n*nyngton	vj s. viij d.
Item paid to Agnes Durbag for cakes beare then	xx d.
Item paid to the mawrice Dauncers of spalldynge	ij s. 5
Item paid to the mawrice Dauncers of Whaplode	vj s. viij d.
Item paid to a play of fowre boyes beynge straungers	v s.

...

1563–4

St Mary's Churchwardens' Accounts   LA: SUTTON ST MARY PAR/7/1   10
f 85*   *(5 April 1563–9 April 1564)* *(Payments)*

...

Item paid to the bayne of Leake the so*m*me of	x s.
Item paid more for breade & drynck than	xiiij d. 15
Item paid to ye bayne of boston	x s.
Item paid more for breade & drynck than	xj d.

...

Item paid to my Lorde riches players ou*er* & besydes	
y*a*t was gathered	xxij d. 20

...

f 86*

...

Item paid to the players of Bullynbrooke	v s. 25

...

Item paid to the players of Spalldynge	vj s. viij d.
Item paid to the players of Ipswych ou*er* & besydes	
y*a*t was gathered	v s.

...   30

1564–5

St Mary's Churchwardens' Accounts   LA: SUTTON ST MARY PAR/7/1
f 87*   *(9 April 1564–29 April 1565)* *(Payments)*

...   35

Item paid to the bayne of Kyrton	x s.
Item paid more for bread & drynck than	xviij d.

...

Item paid to the douches of Suffolck*es* players toward	
their paynes	ij s. ij d. 40
Item paid to the children of wisbich whan they played here	vj s. vj d.

...

f 88v*

…

Item paid to M*aste*r Vicar for that that he laied out
more then coulde be gathered whan the lorde Rob*ertes*
players did play here   ij s.   5

…

1565–6
St Mary's Churchwardens' Accounts   LA: SUTTON ST MARY PAR/7/1
f 90*   *(29 April 1565–21 April 1566) (Payments)*   10

…

Item paid to ye players of Gosbertowne. ye xxix of Iune   vj s.

…

Item paid to Sir Iohn Gaskens players ye xviij^th
of nouember   v s.   15

…

Item paid to ye players of Mowlton/ ye xviij
of december   vj s. viij d.

…

Item paid to the players of Nottyngam/ ye xviij   20
of february   vj s. viij d.

…

f 90v*

…   25

Item paid to the players of bullynbrooke   vj s. viij d.

…

Item paid to the players vpon moonday in Easter weke   vj s. viij d.

…

                                                                                30

1569–70
St Mary's Churchwardens' Accounts   LA: SUTTON ST MARY PAR/7/1
f 94v*   *(17 April 1569–2 April 1570) (Payments)*

…

Item to the players that came out of Keston   iiij s./. 35

…

f 95*

…

Item p*ai*d to certaine players the xx of November   x d. 40

…

28/ moonday in Easter weke: *15 April 1566*

Item paid to the players the xxijth of Ianuary   xx d./.

...

1570–1

St Mary's Churchwardens' Accounts   LA: SUTTON ST MARY PAR/7/1   5
f 98   *(2 April 1570–22 April 1571)* *(Payments)*

...

Item paid to certayne players the iiijth daye
of Maye   xiiij d.

...   10

1571–2

St Mary's Churchwardens' Accounts   LA: SUTTON ST MARY PAR/7/1
f 104   *(22 April 1571–13 April 1572)* *(Payments)*

...   15

Item paid to certaine players that camme
from Lincoln   xviij d.

...

f 106   20

...

Item paid to the players which played in the
church vpon Mydlent sonday   xvj d.

...

                                                                          25

1572–3

St Mary's Churchwardens' Accounts   LA: SUTTON ST MARY PAR/7/1
f 109v   *(13 April 1572–29 March 1573)* *(Payments)*

...

Item paid to the players at the request of parte of   30
ye towne the weeke before mydsomer   xj d.

...

Item paid to certaine players vpon all sainctes day   ij s. iij d.

f 111*   35

...

Item paid to Mr Sampals men   v s./.
Item paid to the children of Spaldinge   xx d./.

...

23/ Mydlent sonday: *16 March 1571/2*
31/ the weeke before mydsomer: *17–23 June 1572*

LOUTH

1422–3
Trinity Guild Accounts   LA: Goulding 4A/1/2/1
single sheet   *(7 June–31 May)* *(Expenses)*   5

...

...Item xij d. fistolatorib*us*...

...

AC
1430–1   10
Louth Court Roll   LA: Goulding 4B/5/1
f [2]*   *(18 December)*

...

The bailiff presents that John Smyth bocher killed and sold corrupt flesh
in the lord's common market, to the great danger and nuisance of all the   15
people. Therefore he is in mercy 3 d.
And the same John came into court and acknowledged that he killed a bull
not baited, contrary to the ordinance and custom of the lordship hitherto
in vogue. Therefore let the steward be rewarded (onoretur) with the [skin]
⌜hide⌝ of the same according to the usage   20

AC
1431/2
Louth Court Roll   LA: Goulding 4B/5/1
p c*   *(3 March)*

...   25

The lord's bailiff is ordered to distrain John Bryght bocher to deliver to
the lord one male full of divers instruments of play, with the other goods
contained in the same male, of a certain man called Hanse who made flight
beyond the lordship, which male the said John acknowledged to the steward
[were] was left in his custody and at his inn. And the said John was allowed   30
ₐ⌜to say⌝ why he had not delivered and refused to deliver. And the said
John comes into court and says that he never did acknowledge the aforesaid
male with the appurtenances aforesaid to the steward, nor did he ever have
it in the custody of his inn. This he puts upon the lord's favour. In mercy
6 d.   35

...

14, 26/ bocher: *underlined by Goulding*
19/ onoretur: ur *underlined by Goulding*
27/ male: *all four occurrences underlined by Goulding*

1446
Louth Court Roll   LA: Louth Museum, Louth Court Rolls, Box 1
mb [1]   *(7 November)*

…

balllvus ex offıcıo suo presentat quod Robertus ⌈ıj d.⌉ de Coxhıl⟨.⟩ Willelmus   5
⌈ij d.⌉ Fleschewer et Iohannes ⌈ij d.⌉ Wryght quinto die Novembris
vltimo die Novembris vltimo preterito quendam taurum absque fatigacione
interfecerunt contra communem ordinacionem ville de Louth ideo ipsi
in misericordia

…   10

1500–1
St James' Churchwardens' Accounts   LA: LOUTH ST JAMES PAR/7/1
p 14*   *(26 April–18 April)* *(Church repairs)*

…   15

Item paid to the chyld byschop att cristynmes for 1 paire
⌈j d.⌉ cloffes nayles ⌈ob.⌉ to Thomas ⌈ij d.⌉ couper. Iohn
bradpull. ⌈ij d.⌉ Summa ⌈makyng his see⌉   vj d.

…
                                                                                                   20

1501–2
St James' Churchwardens' Accounts   LA: LOUTH ST JAMES PAR/7/1
p 32   *(18 April–3 April)* *(Church repairs)*

…

Item paid for one child bischop. j paire cloffes nayles.   25
makyng his See   vj d.

…

1502–3
St James' Churchwardens' Accounts   LA: LOUTH ST JAMES PAR/7/1   30
p 50   *(3 April 1502–23 April 1503)* *(Old debts unpaid)*

…

Also paid to the child byschop for det the yer afor   vj d.

…
                                                                                                   35

p 54   *(Church repairs)*

…

nota   Item paid in expenses of Iohn glouer. ⌈iiij d.⌉ [And for
the child byschop the yer Afor And this yer Summa   vj d.]

…   40

6–7l die Novembris … Novembris vltimo: *dittography*   33l for … afor: *apparently added later*

Item paid to the child byschope at Cristynmes for
a yere in paymentt of his expenses   vj d.

...

1503–4   5
St James' Churchwardens' Accounts   LA: LOUTH ST JAMES PAR/7/1
p 69   *(23 April–14 April)*   *(Payments for workmen)*
...
Item paid to the childe byschop at cristynmes   vj d.
...   10

1505–6
St James' Churchwardens' Accounts   LA: LOUTH ST JAMES PAR/7/1
p 115*   *(30 March 1505–19 April 1506)*   *(Church repairs)*
...   15
Item paid for makynge the childe bischope See   vj d.
...

1506–7
St James' Churchwardens' Accounts   LA: LOUTH ST JAMES PAR/7/1   20
p 130   *(19 April–11 April)*   *(Church repairs)*
...
Item paid the chylde bischope at crystynmes   vj d.
...

                                                                      25
1507–8
St James' Churchwardens' Accounts   LA: LOUTH ST JAMES PAR/7/1
p 141*   *(11 April 1507–30 April 1508)*   *(Receipts for ringing the great bell)*
...
Item same day Alexander Tisson harper   xx d. 30

...

Item ij Sonday lentyn Alexander Tisson harper   xx d.
...

1508–9   35
St James' Churchwardens' Accounts   LA: LOUTH ST JAMES PAR/7/1
p 164   *(30 April–15 April)*   *(Church repairs)*
...
Item paid for the child byschope   vj d.
...   40

30/ same day: *Septuagesima Sunday, 20 February 1507/8*
32/ ij Sonday lentyn: *19 March 1507/8*

p 167*   *(Debts owed the church)*

...

also Iohn Spencer a harpe

...

1509–10
St James' Churchwardens' Accounts   LA: LOUTH ST JAMES PAR/7/1
p 178   *(15 April–7 April)* *(Church repairs)*

...

...chylde bischop. ⌐vj d.⌐...

...

1510–11
St James' Churchwardens' Accounts   LA: LOUTH ST JAMES PAR/7/1
p 190   *(7 April 1510–27 April 1511)* *(Repairs)*

...

...To the childe byschop at cristynmes. ⌐vj d.⌐...

1511–12
St James' Churchwardens' Accounts   LA: LOUTH ST JAMES PAR/7/1
p 200   *(27 April–18 April)* *(Church repairs)*

...

...Child bischop at cristynmes. ⌐vj d.⌐...

...

1512–13
St James' Churchwardens' Accounts   LA: LOUTH ST JAMES PAR/7/1
p 211*   *(18 April–3 April)* *(Old debts)*

...

also ressauyd Dauy for a harpe ⌐xx d.⌐

...

p 216*   *(Payments)*

...

...Chylde bischope. ⌐vj d.⌐...

...

1513–14
St James' Churchwardens' Accounts   LA: LOUTH ST JAMES PAR/7/1
p 233   *(3 April 1513–23 April 1514)* *(Payments)*

...

...for the childe bischap at cristynmes of childermes day. ⌐vj d.⌐...

...

1514–15
St James' Churchwardens' Accounts   LA: LOUTH ST JAMES PAR/7/1
p 248   *(23 April–15 April) (Allowances)*

...

Item paid at cristynmes for child bischope   vj d.   5

...

1515–16
St James' Churchwardens' Accounts   LA: LOUTH ST JAMES PAR/7/1
p 264   *(15 April–23 March) (Allowances)*   10

...

Item paid for child bischope   vj d.

...

p 267*   *(18 October)*   15

...

Memorandum of Saynt Leuke day the Euangelist that I Iohn Cawed laid
all theis bokys and with oder dyuers ewidence in the rode lofte In Anew
Ambre wich oure lady gild paid ⌜vj s. vij d.⌝ for. The yer of our lord Gode.
Millesimo CCCCC. xvj   20

...

also hole Regenall of corpus christi play

...

1517–18   25
St James' Churchwardens' Accounts   LA: LOUTH ST JAMES PAR/7/1
p 299   *(19 April–11 April) (Allowances)*

...

...for childe bischope at cristynmas. ⌜vj d.⌝...

...   30

1518–19
St James' Churchwardens' Accounts   LA: LOUTH ST JAMES PAR/7/1
p 285   *(11 April 1518–1 May 1519) (Allowances)*

...   35
...Childe bischope at cristynmes. ⌜vj d.⌝...

...

1519–20
St James' Churchwardens' Accounts   LA: LOUTH ST JAMES PAR/7/1   40
p 306   *(1 May–15 April) (Allowances)*

...

...iiij. men beryng payentes to saynte mary kirke. ⌜iiij d.⌝ ... child bischope
at cristynmes. ⌜vj d.⌝...

1520–1
St James' Churchwardens' Accounts   LA: LOUTH ST JAMES PAR/7/1
p 315   *(15 April–7 April)* *(Allowances)*

…

…childe bischope at crystynmes. ⌈vj d.⌉…   5

…

1521–2
St James' Churchwardens' Accounts   LA: LOUTH ST JAMES PAR/7/1
p 326   *(7 April 1521–27 April 1522)* *(Allowances)*   10

…Childe bischope at cristynmes. ⌈vj d.⌉…

1522–3
St James' Churchwardens' Accounts   LA: LOUTH ST JAMES PAR/7/1   15
p 336   *(27 April–12 April)* *(Allowances)*

…Childe bischope at cristynmes. ⌈vj d.⌉…

…

20

1523–4
St James' Churchwardens' Accounts   LA: LOUTH ST JAMES PAR/7/1
p 344*   *(12 April–3 April)* *(Allowances)*

…Childe bischope at cristynmes. ⌈vj d.⌉…   25

…

1525–6
A   ***Trinity Guild Accounts***   LA: Monson 7/28
p 106*   30

…

…Will*iam* Foster p*art* of his wags vj s. viij d. … Paid to Will*iam* Foster for
part of the Costs of the Pagent iij s. iiij d.

…

35

1527–8
St James' Churchwardens' Accounts   LA: LOUTH ST JAMES PAR/7/2
f 3   *(28 April–19 April)* *(Allowances)*

…

…The players of Gremysby whan thay thay spake theire bayn of thaire play.   40

40/ thay thay: *dittography*

⌜ij s. viij d.⌝ … William ffoster for rynges agayn corpus christi day to hannge clos of haros in hey qwere. ⌜viij d.⌝…

f 3v

…A smyth makyng ij cais to corpus christi huche. ⌜vj d.⌝…

f 4
…
…ffor beryng pagentes. ⌜iiij s. iiij d.⌝…

Trinity Guild Accounts   LA: Monson 7/2
f 238*   *(29 September–29 September)*   *(Payments)*
…
…willelmo fforster ad facturam ⌜vj. s. viij. d.⌝ le pagentes…

f 238v*
…
It is aggreed by the hole body of the Towne of louth that the pagentes yerely of Corpus Christi day shalbe brought forth as the Course is of the Costes & charges of Trinite gild ⌜vj. s. viij. d.⌝/ Corpus Christi ⌜vj. s. viij. d.⌝ gild/ sanct petur gil⟨.⟩ ⌜vj. s. viij. d.⌝ gild/ sanct Michyll ⌜vj. s. viij. d.⌝ light/ and the Reist of our lady gild how muche so euer it cost

1528–9
Trinity Guild Accounts   LA: Monson 7/2
f 232*   *(29 September–29 September)*
…

⟨.⟩vlpynlayn

Item the layth where the pagentes standes ther	x. s.
And for the hous & chambre in the ende same	ij. s.
Summa	xij. s.

f 236   *(Repairs of guild properties)*

…William ffaner careyng tymber fro clay pyttes ⌜xvj d.⌝ to pagent layth…
…

f 237*   *(Decays)*
…
Item in Gulpyn lane the laith wher pagentes standes   iij. s. iiij. d.

1/ corpus christi day: *20 June 1527*

Item in the Chaumbres and house for a store house   ij. s.

...

f 241v   *(Wages, expenses, and payments)*

...   5

...Et in denarijs datis willelmo forster ad educacionem paginarum ⌈vj s. viij d.⌉
in processione

...

f 242v*   *(Repairs)*   10

...

Item paid to the forseid Ranyer for thekyng vpon the
pagent lathe by the space of v days & di. to meite
& wages   iij s. j d.
Item to his server by the same space   ij s. j d. 15

1530–1
St James' Churchwardens' Accounts   LA: LOUTH ST JAMES PAR/7/2
f 15*   *(24 April–16 April)* *(Church expenses)*

...   20

Item to Thomas preston for mendyng harrowes clothes
belongyng to the kirke   iij s. viij d.

...

1534–5   25
St James' Churchwardens' Accounts   LA: LOUTH ST JAMES PAR/7/2
f 30   *(12 April–4 April)* *(Church expenses)*

...

Item for removyng the pageandes   xxj d.
...   30

1535–6
St James' Churchwardens' Accounts   LA: LOUTH ST JAMES PAR/7/2
f 35*   *(4 April 1535–23 April 1536)* *(Expenses)*

                                                                                         35

Item to robert bayly for stuff takyn off hym for the
pageandes agaynst corpus christi tyde   iij s. viij d.

...

12/ Ranyer: *a thatcher from Manby*
37/ corpus christi tyde: *27 May–3 June 1535*

1539–40
St James' Churchwardens' Accounts   LA: LOUTH ST JAMES PAR/7/2
f 50*   *(13 April–4 April)* *(Church expenses)*

It*em* in p*ar*te of a rewarde to certayn ⌈viz. fabule   5
actorib*us*⌉ of my lorde of Suffolcke seruant*es* being
in the town   xxiij d.
...

1541–2   10
St James' Churchwardens' Accounts   LA: LOUTH ST JAMES PAR/7/2
f 56v   *(24 April–16 April)* *(Expenses)*
...
It*em* payd to a [beruard] bereward   xx d.
...   15

1543–4
St James' Churchwardens' Accounts   LA: LOUTH ST JAMES PAR/7/2
f 65   *(1 April 1543–20 April 1544)* *(Expenses and repairs)*
...   20
It*em* In a reward to ye kyng*es* beerward   xx d.
...

1547–8
St James' Churchwardens' Accounts   LA: LOUTH ST JAMES PAR/7/2   25
f 80*   *(17 April–8 April)* *(Allowances and expenses)*
...
It*em* payd for a pot of aylle when wyderne bayne
was her   vij d.
It*em* payd to wyderne play   vj s. viij d. 30
...

1552–3
St James' Churchwardens' Accounts   LA: LOUTH ST JAMES PAR/7/2
f 101*   *(24 April–9 April)* *(Payments and allowances)*   35
...
It*em* pa*i*ed to Rychard Curson for mony y*at* he
paied to the players   iiij s.
...

1553–4
Town Wardens' Accounts   LA: Louth Grammar School B/3/1
p 9

...

...Item paid to the mynstrelles xij d....   5

...

1555–6
Town Wardens' Accounts   LA: Louth Grammar School B/3/1
p 16*   *(2 June–24 May)*   10

...

Item paid for wyne when mr hennage was at the play   ij s. iiij d.
Item paid to mr goodale for mony laid furthe by him
at the playes   xiij s. iij d.

...   15

1556–7
Town Wardens' Accounts   LA: Louth Grammar School B/3/1
p 24*   *(24 May 1556–6 June 1557)* *(Payments)*

...   20

Item paid to william Iordayne & other ij mynstrelles for
ther paynes at the playe   ij s.

...

St James' Churchwardens' Accounts   LA: LOUTH ST JAMES PAR/7/2   25
f 124v*   *(21 April–12 April)* *(Payments)*

...

Item paid to ye quenes maiesties seruantes whenas they
plaied in ye churche   xij s.

...   30

1557–8
Town Wardens' Accounts   LA: Louth Grammar School B/3/1
p 29*   *(6 June–29 May)* *(Payments and allowances)*

...   35

Item paid to mr goodall for certeyn mony by him laid
furth for the furnishing of the play played in the Markit
stede on corpus christi day the yere before my entring   xvj d.

...

38/ corpus ... entring: *4 June 1556*

1567–8
Town Wardens' Accounts   LA: Louth Grammar School B/3/1
p 126*   *(18 May 1567–6 June 1568) (Payments)*
...

Item gevenne to mr pelsonne by assent of the wardoune and Assistent*es*   5
toward*es* his charg*es* of an enterlude he Set out the somme of v s....
...

1571–2
Town Wardens' Accounts   LA: Louth Grammar School B/3/1   10
p 146   *(3 June–25 May) (External receipts)*
...

It*em* he Chargeth himself wi*th* iij s. x d. for the licens by him gevenne for
batinge of bull*es*...
...   15

1577–8
Town Wardens' Accounts   LA: Louth Grammar School B/3/1
p 174   *(26 May–18 May) (External receipts)*
...   20
...for bayting of bull*es* vj s....
...

1579–80
Town Wardens' Accounts   LA: Louth Grammar School B/3/1   25
p 182   *(7 June–22 May) (External receipts)*
...

...It*em* he chargith himself wi*th* money by hym Receyvid of ... Iohn dalton
for licens to bate a bulle viij d....
...   30

1584–5
Town Wardens' Accounts   LA: Louth Grammar School B/3/1
p 210   *(7 June–30 May) (External receipts)*
...   35
...for killinge two bull*es* vnbayted ij s....

1588–9
Town Wardens' Accounts   LA: Louth Grammar School B/3/1
p 235   *(26 May–18 May) (External receipts)*   40

It*em* wi*th* money for lycens to kyll bull*es* unbayted   ij s.
...

1589–90
Town Wardens' Accounts   LA: Louth Grammar School B/3/1
p 243   *(18 May 1589–7 June 1590) (External receipts)*
...

Item of Iohn Braysforthe for the baytinge   5
of A Bull   xij d.
...

1591–2
Town Wardens' Accounts   LA: Louth Grammar School B/3/1   10
p 252   *(23 May–14 May) (External receipts)*
...

Item he chargeth him self with monie receaved ... of peter Smith butcher
for lyence to kill a bull unbayted xij d....
...   15

1592–3
Town Wardens' Accounts   LA: Louth Grammar School B/3/1
p 256*   *(14 May 1592–3 June 1593) (External receipts)*
...   20
Receavid for bulls vnbayted   iiij s.
...

1593–4
Town Wardens' Accounts   LA: Louth Grammar School B/3/1   25
p 261*   *(3 June–19 May) (External receipts)*
...
Item for licence for to kill [three] ⌈foure⌉
bulls vnbayted   iiij s.
...   30

1596–7
Town Wardens' Accounts   LA: Louth Grammar School B/3/1
p 277   *(30 May–15 May) (External receipts)*
...   35
Receavid of Thomas Ambler for lycencing him
not to bate a bull.   xij d.
...

37/ not: *apparently added later*

1598–9
Town Wardens' Accounts   LA: Louth Grammar School B/3/1
p 299   *(4 June–27 May) (External receipts)*

Off Iohn Skelton and Iohn hanson for ∧⌜not⌝   5
baytinge two bulls   ij s.
...

1599–1600
Town Wardens' Accounts   LA: Louth Grammar School B/3/1   10
p 305   *(27 May–11 May) (External receipts)*

Item he Receaved ... of william Hanson for a lycence for killinge a bull
vnbayted xij d....
...   15

1603–4
Town Wardens' Accounts   LA: Louth Grammar School B/3/1
p 323   *(12 June–27 May) (External receipts)*
...   20
Item that he Receaved of butchers for killinge
bulles vnbayted   ij s. vj d.
...

1604–5   25
Town Wardens' Accounts   LA: Louth Grammar School B/3/1
p 328   *(27 May–19 May) (Rent arrears)*
...
Item that he receaved theis Arrerages of rentes following ... of Martine myles
for a howse late wates. v s....   30

p 329   *(Receipts)*
...
Item receaved for bulles vnbayted ij s. ij d....
...   35

1605–6
Town Wardens' Accounts   LA: Louth Grammar School B/3/1
p 339*   *(19 May 1605–8 June 1606) (Payments)*
...   40
Item layd owt att our second Sessions for our dynners xiij s. vj d. for the
Constables dynners & the bayliffes ij s. vj d. to the Townes waytes. ij s.

for mr Massingberd ffee x s.

...

Item for the bull ringe mendinge   xij d.

p 341   5

...

Item layd owt att our third Sessions for our dynners.
xj s. for wyne. ij s. for the Constables & the Bayliffes
dynners iij s. to our waytes. ij s.   xviij s.

...   10

p 342

Item for sixe powndes of lead for settinge fast the
bull ringe   vj d. 15

...

1606–7
Town Wardens' Accounts   LA: Louth Grammar School B/3/1
p 348   *(8 June–24 May) (Wages and fees)*   20

...

Item for the charges of the dynners att the foure
quarter Sessions   iij li. ix s. vj d.
Item given to the waites att the same dinners   vj s.

...   25

1607–8
Town Wardens' Accounts   LA: Louth Grammar School B/3/1
p 355   *(24 May–15 May) (External receipts)*

...   30

Receaved of dyvers Butchers for bulles vnbayted
by them   iiij s. iiij d./

...

1608–9   35
Town Wardens' Accounts   LA: Louth Grammar School B/3/1
p 361   *(15 May 1608–4 June 1609) (External receipts)*

...

Item of Certaine Butchers for bulles vnbayted   iij s. x d.

...   40

p 365*   *(Payments)*

...

Item given to my L*o*rd of darbye his s*e*rvant*e*s (not
sufferinge them to playe) att Maday fare   v s.

...   5

1609–10

Town Wardens' Accounts   LA: Louth Grammar School B/3/1
p 371   *(4 June–3 June) (External receipts)*

...   10

of three butchers for killing iij bulles unbayted.   iij s.

...

1610–11

Town Wardens' Accounts   LA: Louth Grammar School B/3/1   15
p 385   *(3 June–12 May) (Payments)*

...

It*e*m to the musitions at the iiij sessions dinn*e*rs   vj s.

p 386   20

...

Item for fetchinge the Buck from Tattershall, w*h*ich
Mr Allington gave   v s.
It*e*m to the keep*e*rs for theire paynes & ffee, beinge
well served   viij s. 25
It*e*m spent at Mr Chamb*e*rlaynes, at the eatinge of
p*a*rte of the venson, for viij gentlewemen, & other
gentlemen strangers, for theire suppers   xvij s. viij d.
Item for ix pottels of Clarett & iiij pottles of sacke   xix s.
Item given to the Musitians   ij s. 30

...

1611–12

Town Wardens' Accounts   LA: Louth Grammar School B/3/1
p 391   *(12 May 1611–31 May 1612) (Fines and quarter sessions receipts)*   35

...

Item rec*eiue*d of diu*e*rs Butcher*e*s for licencinge
them to kill Bulls vnbaited   x s.

...

1612–13
Town Wardens' Accounts   LA: Louth Grammar School B/3/1
p 394   *(31 May–23 May)* *(Fines)*
...

ffor Bulles vnbaited   vj s.   5
...

p 395   *(Quarter sessions payments)*
...

Item the musick for 3 Sessions   iiij s. vj d.   10
...

1613–14
Town Wardens' Accounts   LA: Louth Grammar School B/3/1
p 399   *(23 May 1613–12 June 1614)* *(Receipts)*   15
...

Item of Bayly Scicisson & an other Butcher for
Bulles vnbaited   iij s.
...

                                                                                    20

p 402   *(Fees and gifts)*
...

Item to Marloe chargdes about the Bull ringe   iij s. viij d.
...

                                                                                    25

p 403   *(Wages, gifts, and payments)*
...

Item iiij^or Sessions dinners wine & Musicke   vj li. j s. ij d.
...

                                                                                    30

1614–15
Town Wardens' Accounts   LA: Louth Grammar School B/3/1
p 409   *(12 June–28 May)* *(Quarter sessions dinners and fees)*
...

Paid vnto mr Chamberline for iiij Sess*ions* dinners   35
for our owne table the foure Counstables the baliefe &
for wine as app*er*eth by the p*ar*ticulers   iiij li. xij s.
given the weight*es* in reward att the same dinners   vj s.
...

1615–16
Town Wardens' Accounts   LA: Louth Grammar School B/3/1
p 417   *(28 May–19 May)* *(Quarter sessions receipts)*
...
Item for Bulles vnbaited   ij s.   5
...

p 420   *(Payments, gifts, and fees)*
...
Item given the waites at iiij^{or} Sessions   viij s.   10
...

1616–17
Town Wardens' Accounts   LA: Louth Grammar School B/3/1
p 427   *(19 May 1616–8 June 1617)* *(Payments, gifts, and wages)*   15
...
Item Musick at Sessions   viij s.
...

1617–18   20
Town Wardens' Accounts   LA: Louth Grammar School B/3/1
p 434   *(8 June–24 May)* *(Quarter sessions fines)*
...
Item for Two bulls vnbated   xviij d.
...   25

pp 435–6   *(Payments, gifts, and wages)*
...
Item for the Venison feast   iiij li. viij s. vj d.
Item for wine   xliiij s.   30
Item for the keepers fee   v s. vj d.
Item Sugar two poundes   iij s.
Item to the musitions   ij s. vj d.
...
Item for four sessions dinner   v li. iiij s. iiij d. | 35
Item for wine   xxxij s. iiij d.
Item for Sugar   v s. viij d.
Item for Musicke   viij s.
...

30/ xliiij: *corrected from* xliij

p 437

...

Item for Mayday ffeast	v li. xvij s. iiij d.
Item for wine & sugar	xliiij s. viij d.
Item to the musitions	ij s. 5

...

1618–19

Town Wardens' Accounts   LA: Louth Grammar School B/3/1

p 446   *(24 May–16 May)* *(Amercements)*   10

...

Item received for foure Bulls vnbated	iiij s.

...

p 448   *(Payments, gifts, and wages)*   15

...

Item for the sessions dynner at Mr Egglestones the vj^t of Iuly	0	xx s.	0
Item for wyne & suger & for the Constables & baly	0	xiiij s. viij d.	20
Item to the Musitions at the same dynner	0	ij s.	0

...

p 449   25

...

...& for Ale owinge by Mr Iackson at Midsommer Sessions given the Musitions	0	ij s	0
...			
Item to Mr Eglestone for the Graves feast dynner at Michaelmas	vij li.	v s.	vj d. 30
Item to the wates at the same tyme	0	ij s.	0

...

p 450   35

...

Item to William Wright that he gave the Musitions at Michaelmas Sessions & that he otherwais laid out	0	iiij s.	vij d.
...			
Item to Mr Eglestone for the Sessions dinner houlden the xxv^th of Ianuary	0	xviij s.	0 40
Item for wyne & sugar	0	vij s.	0
Item to the wates	0	ij s.	0

...

p 451

…

Item to the Musitions   0   ij s.   0

…

5

1619–20
Town Wardens' Accounts   LA: Louth Grammar School B/3/1
p 455   *(16 May 1619–4 June 1620)   (Arrears)*

…

Item of Richard Wheat for one Bull vnbated   0   0   xij d. 10

…

p 458   *(Payments, gifts, and wages)*

…

Item to the waits at the Graves feast*es* &   15
foure Sessions   0   xij s.   0

…

1620–1
Town Wardens' Accounts   LA: Louth Grammar School B/3/1   20
p 467   *(4 June–20 May)   (Disbursements)*

…

Item to a soldier & a Trumpeter redeemed from
the Turkes by Captaine Lambert   xij d.

…   25

p 468

…

Item forgotten w*hich* was given to musitions   vj s.

…   30

1621–2
Town Wardens' Accounts   LA: Louth Grammar School B/3/1
p 474   *(20 May 1621–9 June 1622)   (Disbursements)*

…   35

Item paid for the iiij Sessions dinners   viij li. vj s.
Item paid to the wait*es*   viij s.

…

p 475   40

…

Item paid for the Bull ringe mendinge &
settinge & the Bull ringe mendinge   iij s.

…

p 476

...

Item paid to the players at Easters Sessions   iij s. iiij d.

...

                                                                                            5

1622–3
Town Wardens' Accounts   LA: Louth Grammar School B/3/1
pp 482–3   *(9 June–1 June) (Payments)*

...

Item paid for supper for mr Stutt & the   10
three scholemaisters   iiij s. |
Item paid the wait*es*   iij s.
Item paid to the Cooke   ij s.
It*em* paid for wine & sugar & stronge beere
at supper   iiij li. v s. iiij d. 15

...

p 484

...

Item paid for vj yerd*es* of Stammell for Coot*es*   20
for the wayt*es*   iij li. xvj s.

...

p 485

...   25

Item to the wayt*es* at the Sessions   vj s.
Item paid for the Sessions dinners   vj l. xiiij s.

...

1623–4   30
Town Wardens' Accounts   LA: Louth Grammar School B/3/1
p 489   *(1 June–16 May) (Receipts)*

...

Item rec*eiued* of Butchers for Bulls vnbayted   iij s.

...   35

p 491   *(Payments)*

...

Item paid to the wayt*es*   viij s.

...   40

1624–5
Town Wardens' Accounts   LA: Louth Grammar School B/3/1
p 496   *(16 May 1624–5 June 1625)   (Money laid out)*

...

Item giuen to the showe on Whitson munday   xx s.   5

...

Item paid at Midsommer dinner for wine suger
beere & musicke   xlviij s. x d.

...
                                                                          10

p 497   *(Payments)*

...

Item paid at Michaelmis Sessions for the dinner   xxxj s. viij d.
for wine & musike   xvij s. viij d.

...   15

Item Christmas Sessions dinner   xxxiiij s. viij d.
Item wine & musicke   vij s. x d.
Item Easter Sessions dinner   xxxij s. viij d.
for wine & musicke   xiij s. x d.

...   20

Item iron worke for the well & the bull
chaine mendinge   iiij s. viij d.

...

p 498*   25

...

Item for sendinge to Sir Thomas Grantham
aboute the proclamation for kinge Charles   ij s.
for wine and sugar after the proclamacion   xij s. x d.
to the Musike   xij d. 30
ffor a hoggshead of ale   xvij s.
for vj dozen of bread   vj s.
Item to Dicke Hill for drumminge   xij d.
for j l. of powder   xviij d.
Item for wood for the boonefire   iij s. vj d. 35

...

Item for mendinge the drumme   xiiij d.

1625–6
Town Wardens' Accounts   LA: Louth Grammar School B/3/1   40
p 502   *(5 June–28 May)   (Fines at 12 January 1625/6 sessions)*

...

Receiued of Henry ffisher for a bull not bated   vj s.

...

p 504   *(Payments and allowances)*

…

Item payde for the sessions dinner att midsom*er*
& for wine   xlj s. x d.
Item to the wates then   ij s.   5

…

p 505

…

Item payde Will*i*am wardaile for the supper att   10
the venison feaste   lv s.
Item for wyne the same nighte   xvij s. x d.
Item to the Waites   ij s.

…

Item for 4 yeards & a halfe of Stam*e*ll for the   15
waites at 13 s. the ye*a*rd   lviij s. vj d.

…

Item payde for the Sessions dinner the vj° of
Octobr*e* & for wine   xliiij s. ij d.
Item to the waytes   ij s.   20

…

p 506

…

Item for the sessions dinner the xij° of Ianuary   25
& for wyne   xliij s. 4 d.
Item to the Waites   ij s.

…

1626–7   30
Town Wardens' Accounts   LA: Louth Grammar School B/3/1
p 512   *(28 May–13 May)* *(Payments)*

…

It*e*m p*a*id Mr Egglestone for the dinn*er* at
Midsomm*er* Sessions   xliij s. viij d. 35
Item to M*is*tris Wood for wine   xj s.
Item to Iohn Rodesby for wine   vij s. vj d.
It*e*m to the Waites   ij s.

…

Item paid Mr Egglestone for the Sessions dinn*er*   40
at Mich*ae*l*m*is & for wine   liij s. vj d.
It*e*m to the musicke   ij s.

…

p 513

...

Item for the Sessions dinn*er* at Christmas	liiij s. vj d.
Item to the Waites	ij s.

...

Item for the Sessions dinn*er* att Easter	liiij s. vj d.
Item to the waites	ij s.

...

1627–8

Town Wardens' Accounts   LA: Louth Grammar School B/3/1
p 517   *(13 May 1627–1 June 1628)*   *(External receipts)*

...

Item for two bulls vnbayted	ij s.

...

p 518   *(Ordinary disbursements)*

...

Item to our musicke for attendinge at ij Sess*ions*	iiij s.

...

1628–9

Town Wardens' Accounts   LA: Louth Grammar School B/3/1
p 524   *(1 June–24 May)* *(Disbursements)*

...

payd for the Sessions dynner wyne & Musick	l s. viij d.
payd for the like at Mighellmas	lix s. vj d.
payd for the like at Chrismes	lvj s. vj d.
payd for the like at Easter	iij li. v s.

...

p 526   *(Repairs)*

payd for the Bull cheane mending	xx d.

...

1629–30

Town Wardens' Accounts   LA: Louth Grammar School B/3/1
p 531   *(24 May–16 May)* *(Quarter sessions fines)*

...

Item receaved for Bulls vnbaited	iiij s. x d.

...

p 532   *(Disbursements)*

Item payd for the fower Sessions dynners &
for mewsicke   xj li. iiij s.
...   5

1630–1
Town Wardens' Accounts   LA: Louth Grammar School B/3/1
p 538   *(16 May 1630–24 May 1631)* *(Quarter sessions fines)*
...   10
Receaved of Buchers for Bulls vnbated   vj s.
...

p 541   *(Payroonts)*
...   15
payd for mending the Bull ch[e]eane   xvj d.
...

1632–3
Town Wardens' Accounts   LA: Louth Grammar School B/3/1   20
p 553   *(20 May 1632–9 June 1633)* *(Disbursements)*
...
Item paid to the Musicions at Mid*summer* Sessions   ij s.
...
                                                                                     25
p 554
...
Item paid for the Bull Chaine mending   iiij s.
...
                                                                                     30
p 555
...
Item paid more to the Musicions at ye Sessions   vj s.
...
                                                                                     35
p 557   *(Allowances)*
...
ffor the Waytes Coates   iij li.
...

1633–4
Town Wardens' Accounts   LA: Louth Grammar School B/3/1
p 560   *(9 June–25 May)* *(Disbursements)*
...
Item paid to the waites at the 4 Sessions   viij s.   5
...

1634–5
Town Wardens' Accounts   LA: Louth Grammar School B/3/1
p 563   *(25 May–17 May)* *(Receipts)*   10
...
Item receiued for a bull that was vnbaited   xij d.
...

pp 564–5   15
...
Item paid to Sergeant Boddington for two Sessions
dynners wee had there with wine sugar and Tobacko   ix li. vij s. x d. |
Item to mr Ed: Price & his brother for the other
2 Sessions dynners   viij li. x s. ij d. 20
Item paid to the waites for their service done at
all the Sessions   viij s.
Item paid to the harroldes at Armes in money xxx s.
& in wine and Sugar ij s.   xxxij s.
...   25
Item paid to Mauborne for nailing downe the
markett well & mending the bull teame   xvj d.
...
Item paid for 4 yerdes 3 quarteres of cloth for the
waites Coates at 13 s. 4 d. per yerd   iij li. iij s. iiij d. 30
...

1635–6
Town Wardens' Accounts   LA: Louth Grammar School B/3/1
p 570   *(17 May 1635–5 June 1636)* *(Receipts)*   35
...
Item received for one Bull vnbaited   xij d.
...

p 571   *(Allowances)*   40
...
Item to the Musicions   vj s.
...

1636–7
Town Wardens' Accounts   LA: Louth Grammar School B/3/1
p 576   *(5 June–28 May)* *(Quarter sessions fines)*
...

Received for three Bulles vnbated   iij s.   5
...

p 577   *(Payments)*
...
paid to the Waytes   vj s.   10
...

p 578
...
paid for mending the bull teame   xij d.   15
...

1637–8
Town Wardens' Accounts   LA: Louth Grammar School B/3/1
p 583   *(28 May–13 May)* *(Receipts)*   20
...
Item Bulls vnbated   ij s.
...

p 584   *(Allowances)*   25
...
Item paid to the waites for a yeare wages   viij s.
...

1638–9   30
Town Wardens' Accounts   LA: Louth Grammar School B/3/1
p 593   *(13 May 1638–2 June 1639)* *(Quarter sessions fines)*
...
Item receiued for a Bull vnbated   xij d.
...   35

p 594   *(Allowances)*
...
Item paid the waites for a yeare   viij s.
...   40

p 595
...
Item paid for fiue yeardes of Stammell for
the Waites Coates   iij li. vj s. viij d.
...   5

p 597
...
Item paid to Mawborne for Iron-work about
the Bull-ring and Boultes   iiij s.   10
Item paid William ffenwick for takeing it vp
and setting it downe againe   xviij d.
...

1640–1   15
Town Wardens' Accounts   LA: Louth Grammar School B/3/1
p 615   *(24 May 1640–13 June 1641) (Allowances)*
...
To the Waites for their yeres wages   viij s.
...   20

p 616
...
ffor the Bull teame mendinge   vj d.   25
...

p 619
...
ffor Cloth for Coates for the waytes   iij li. x s.   30
...

MAREHAM LE FEN

1608   35
Archdeaconry of Lincoln Visitation Book   LA: Diocesan Vij/11
f 160*

Presentments made during the visitation of Horncastle, Hill, and Gartree deaneries
...   40
°*dimittitur*°   Egremona filia Iohannis Scarburgh
°*dimittitur*°   Elizabetha woodthorpe famula Iohannis Skarburgh

°*excommunicatur*° Katherina fil*ia* Io*hannis* Graye

[S]

for being w*ith* Cut*b*ert Scofeild on[e] Careing sonday ∧⌈playing⌉ on his
instrument in *se*rvice time. °21. Iunij 1608. ap*ud* Lincoln*iam* coram m*agist*ro
Ingram &c citat*is* d*ic*t*is* Egremona & Elizabetha n*ullo* m*od*o &c d*omin*us   5
ex*communicauit certis causis &c commisit vices suas m*agist*ro Corie *Rec*tori
de Maram ad aud*iendu*m & ter*mi*nandum &c et ad *cert*i*ficandu*m proximo
apud Lincoln*iam* pro d*ic*ta Katherina vijs &c in proxim*um* 1. Julij. 1608.
d*ic*ta Katherina cit*ata* per vijs &c ex*communicatur.*° °14. No*vembris* 1608.
certificat*um* fuit dict*as* Egremonam & Elizabetham crimi*na* sua hui*usmod*i   10
fass*as* fuisse & ea*sdem* penituisse v*n*de dimit*tuntur.*°

°Tumby°

°*dimittitur/*° Stephen ffletcher ∧⌈alias [hit] Otley⌉ pro con*simili* °.21. die Iunij 1608.
°*excommunicatur.*° apud Lincoln*iam* &c vijs in proxim*um* .1. Iulij 1608. cit*atus* per vijs. &c
ex*communicatur* 24. Se*ptembris* 1608 iuramento &c absolvitur & cum   15
mon*ici*one dimi*ttitur/*°

...

MARKET DEEPING

20

1573–4
St Guthlac's Vestry Book   LA: MARKET DEEPING PAR/10/1
f C3v*   *(25 December–25 December)* *(Dike reeves' payments)*
...
Item to the erle of Worseter*es* [s] pleyar*es*   xvj d. 25

f C4*
...
Item to the pleyar*es* att the Churche   x d.

30

1603–4
St Guthlac's Vestry Book   LA: MARKET DEEPING PAR/10/1
f D17v*   *(10 January–9 January)* *(Bailiffs' accounts)*
...   35
Item p*ai*d to Mr Thornes for a dru*m*m at ye
pro*c*lamacio*n* of ye K*inges* Maiestie   iij s. vj d.
...

3/ Careing sonday: *13 March 1607/8*

1605–6
St Guthlac's Vestry Book   LA: MARKET DEEPING PAR/10/1
f D21*   *(13 January–7 January)*   *(Bailiffs' accounts)*

...

Item paid to Richard Heynes for ye towne drumme   ij s. vj d.   5

...

MARSH CHAPEL

1621   10
Bill of Complaint in Dawson v. Mumby   TNA: PRO STAC 8/114/12
mb 74*   *(7 November)*

                    To the kinges most excellente maiestie.//
In all humblenesse sheweth vnto your moste excellente maiestie your   15
highnesse faithfull obedient and quiett disposed subiecte Thomas dawson
of Marshchappell within your maiesties Countye of Lincoln yeoman that
wheareas your said subiecte and Marye his wife have lived in greate love
and to theare mutuall good Contente and in good name and faire reputacion
love and respecte amongst theare neighboures for the space of these eighte   20
yeares laste paste duringe which time and after your said subiectes former
greate losses & crosses itt hath pleased god of his greate goodnesse and
mercies to blesse your said subiecte in his estate whereby your said subiecte
and his wife have bene better able and willinge accordinge to theire poweres
and abilityes to be charitable and helpefull to the poor distressed & needye,   25
and alsoe to be beneficiall to theare kindred and in a competente measur
able to provide for theire familie, and posteritye. And wheareas your said
subiecte for the greatest parte, of the said time, has bene humbled with the
gratious visitacions and mercifull Correccions of sickenesse and infirmityes
sente vnto him from almightye god; wheareby your said subiecte by reason   30
of his oulde age, and through extreamitye of paine, and weakenesse, hath
bene inforced to keepe his bedd, for the greatest parte of three yeares laste
paste, and compelled to live in a stricte phisicall course of life & diett:
which your said subiecte, and his said wife, thanckefullye, chearefullye, and
contentedly indured, knowinge that the said Crosse came vnto them, from   35
god theare mercifull father. Butt soe itt is may itt please your moste excellente
maiestie, that one Thomas Mumbye of Marshchappell aforesaid yeoman,
Gabriell Baylye of Laceby in the said Countye of Lincoln yeoman, Arthur
dawson of Marshchappell aforesaid yeoman and Iohn Browne of Marshchappell
aforesaid Labourer *(blank)* and diverse otheres, altogeather vnknowe vnto   40

5/ drumme: *7 minims in MS*   40/ vnknowe: *for vnknowne*

your said subiecte, whose names your said subiecte doth moste humblye
desyer may be inserted hearein when they shalbe discovered, by your said
subiect or some of them, envyeinge the contented prosperitye, and happines
of your said subiecte, and his said wife, inioyed, and that mutuall comforte,
which each of them received from thother, by the concorde they lived in,   5
and by that trulye loveinge opinion, each of them, reciprocallye had of
thother, out of a malitious minde, and divelish disposicion, to putt debate,
and striffe, betwixte your said subiecte, and his said wife, and to lessen theire
love, and good likeinge, each to thother, and to scandalize them, or one of
them, in theire good names, and reputacions. and as much as in them was,   10
to laye a perpetuall blott, and ignominy vppon them your said subiecte,
and his said wife, and theire posteritye; and to cause them to be hated and
detested of theire lovinge honest vertuous, and well disposed neighboures
aboute the moneth of Iulye laste paste att Marshchappell aforesaid, did
combine Complott and confederate themselves. to and with the said other   15
vnknowne persons; whose names your subiecte desyereth may be hearein
inserted; and moste malitiously, disgracefullye and ignominiously; then and
theare did forge, make, contrive, compose write, and publish, or did helpe,
cause assiste knowe of or procuer to be forged, made, contrived composed,
written or published two false, vntrue, ignomous scandalous scurrilous and   20
infamous libelles, in verse or meeter thone was as followeth. Physick ô
Physick, for the dawes sonnes sicke. And straight desyeres an Æsculapius.
The dawes wife tooke Hippocrates by the prick not knowinge Galen from a
Priapus, It is noe matter howe she takes a purge, when such as Binynsbye
with his pill doth vrge, Shees small shees propper and beyond demure; yett   25
make her husband singe, the Cuckoos note Shees purus puteus like the
female pure, Her masteres pinnesse yett the shippe in boyes boat Or rather
like these prisoneres of the Lowes whose Calfes Cow-tongue spoke and soe
overthrewe vs. Rames Hornes and tupp stones ô I am in a sowne dawson
with guiftes, is proved a mightie magnes, fore hee bestowinge on Ramsey   30
one poore gowne; vsurps and will still his moste lovinge Agnes, Rather then
th' mother shalbe lefte vndone, Heel give a coate vnto Besse Kirkbyes sonne.
Amongst the Crowd, which haunte the holy crewe, Pilkin comes toning of
his wives disgrace *(blank)* is knowne in every place yett in this Corporacion
fynde I few, which cann his wifes faultes hide though shewes his owne, what   35
can be hid from husbandes iealous growne the said other [said] libell, or

6/ reciprocallye: o *corrected from* i *by erasure and overwriting*
20/ scurrilous: *followed by 10mm of line filler*
28/ Lowes: *followed by 7mm of line filler*
33/ toning: *for* tening; *written over erasure and followed by 6mm of line filler*
34/ disgrace: di *corrected over other letters by erasure and overwriting*
36/ said other [said]: *95mm erasure partly written over and the rest covered by line filler*

scandalous verses or meeter was intituled ∧⌐°by the *said* co*n*federates or some
of them°⌐ in some Coppie or Coppies published as aforesaid Thoma Rober*ti*
Harrison, in other*es* Thema and was as followeth Mrs. dawson is pr*o*pp*er*
and small Shee makes him, Cuckold aboue them all, Will Collingwood w*i*th
his righte hand will take ∧⌐her⌐ by the cu*n*t whe*n*s pricke will stand; The   5
Kitching phisicke is the beste, Theare Brasby kisses aboue the reste, And
the said Thomas Mumby Arthur Dawson, Gabryell Baylye and Iohn Browne
(blank) and other vnknowne p*er*sons whose names yo*u*r said subiecte humbly
desyereth may be inserted, when they shalbe made knowne, or some of them,
did of theire further envye, and malitious hatred w*hi*ch they did beare vnto   10
your said subiecte, & his said wife, moste scandalouslye and wickedlye,
knowinge the same to be twoe libells, and infamous song*es*, wheareby your
said subiecte, and his said wife, or one of them, was scandalized and traduced,
did in the said moneth of Iulye laste paste att Marshchappell aforesaid and
other places publish the same by readinge singinge or giveinge Coppies   15
theareof to sundry of yo*u*r ma*ie*sties subiect*es*; to the greate disgrace, and
defamac*i*on of your said subiecte, and his said wife; By w*hi*ch infamous
libelles or scurrelous verses, the said Thomas Mumby Arthur Dawson,
Gabryell Baylye & Iohn Browne; *(blank)* and other*es* vnknowne, whose names,
your said subiecte, humbly desyereth may heareafter be inserted hearein,   20
or some of them, denoted and notoriously intended yo*u*r said subiecte, his
wife, and one Marke Pillington whoe had marryed the daughter of your
said subiecte; by w*hi*ch notorious abuse, and slander, the good names, and
Creditt*es*; of your said subiecte, his wife, and sonne in lawe, is privatelye,
and closely abused and iniured to the greate offence and scandall, of your   25
ma*ie*sties pr*e*sente peaceable, setled governemente, established in this land &
to the greate discouragemente and distaste of the friend*es*, and kindred of
your said subiecte, and his said wife, and of all other*es* that wished well to
them, or conceaved well of [eather] ⌐any⌐ of them, and tendeth alsoe to the
incouragemente of the said offender*es* and other*es* of like lewde course of   30
livinge, if the said misdemeanor*es* shoulde not be moste sevearely punished.
And further may itt please your moste excellente ma*ie*stie the said Thomas
Mumby in a further manifestac*i*on of his his said malice, againste yo*u*r said
subiecte, and his said wife, and to hinder (as much as in him laye) the
discoverye of any the author*es* contriver*es*, or publisher*es*, of the said false,   35
and scandalous libells, or verses, after your said subiecte aboute the moneth
of Auguste laste paste, had pr*o*cured a warrante from S*i*r Adrian Scrope
knighte, one of your highnesse Iustices of peace w*i*thin the p*ar*tes of the
said Countye, wheare the said offendor*es* did inhabitt and dwell, w*hi*ch said

1/ was: *written over erasure*   26/ &: *apparently inserted later*
21/ denoted: n *corrected over another letter, possibly* v   33/ his his: *dittography*

warrante was directed to the Cunstable of Marshchappell aforesaid, for the
apprehendinge, of the said Iohn Browne and to bringe, him the said Browne
before him the said S*ir* Adrian Scrope or some of his fellowe Iustices in
regard your said subiecte conceived the said Browne to be a greate agente
in contriveinge, and publishinge, the said infamous libelles and verses and   5
indeavoured, by all lawfull meanes, he coulde, for the discoveringe of the
author*es*, and publisher*es* theareof; and the said Mumbye knowinge, of the
said warrante, or feareinge that the said Browne woulde discover the same
if he weare lawfullye theareof examined hid the said Browne in his owne
house, and in other secrett, and vnknowne places. and sethence hath   10
convayed him, to some place altogeather vnknowne, to your said subiecte
wheareby the said Browne, coulde never sethence, his said ∧⌈secrett⌉
convayeinge away by the said Mumby be discovered by your said subiecte;
and the said Mumby aboute the said moneth of Auguste, laste beinge asked
of the said Browne, and wheare he was (well knowinge that he was not   15
in probabilitye to be found by your said subiecte) wheare vppon the said
Mumby conceaved an absolute concealemente of the said iniurious
vnchristianlike, and, vnlawfull doinges, and practises to the greate discreditt
of your said subiecte) in the heareinge of manye your ma*ie*sties loveinge
subiect*es* vttered these or the like word*es* Lett dawson and the divell, and   20
∧⌈the divell and⌉ dawson (intendinge your said subiecte) doe what he cann,
and all his Cubbs, he shall not have itt out before Michelmas (meaneinge
the feaste of St Michaell Tharchangell laste) whoe made the said infamous
libell or scandalous verses (soe contrived and published as aforesaid) for he
that made itt was att Lincoln, and itt was a woman that writt it, and he   25
(meaneinge your subiecte) will not live to gett itt out, thinckeinge the greate
age, and infirmitye, of your said subiecte, to be such as these, said offences,
shoulde by the meanes of your said subiect*es* death goe vnpunished. In tender
Consideraci*on* thearefore of the p*re*misses, and for that the said offences,
weare all latelye committed sethence yo*ur* ma*ie*sties laste moste gratious   30
generall, and free pardon and are ∧⌈all⌉ directlye and expresselye Contrarye
to the lawes, and statutes of this realme, and to your ma*ie*sties p*re*sente moste
excellente, and peaceable governemente theareof. May itt thearefore please
your moste excellente ma*ie*stie to graunte vnto yo*ur* said subiecte, your
ma*ie*sties moste gratious writt of Sub pena vnto the said Thomas Mumby,   35
Gabryell Baylye, Arthur Dawson, and Iohn Browne *(blank)* and thother
vnknow*ne* p*er*sons (when they shalbe discovered) to be directed commaundinge
them, and everye of them theareby, p*er*sonallye to be and appeare before your
ma*ie*stie, and the righte hon*our*able Lord*es* and other*es* of your highnesse

1/ warrante: war *corrected over erasure*   17/ conceaved: *for* (having conceaved
15/ he was¹: *apparently written over erasure*

privie counsell in your maiesties high Courte of Starr Chamber att a certaine
day and vnder a certaine paine thearein be limitted, and expressed; then and
theare personally to answeare vnto the premisses ∧⌐and the said Mumby to
declare wheare the said Browne is and to be ordered to bringe him forth⌐
and to abide and performe, such further order and sensuer as to your   5
maiestie said honourable privie Counsell shalbe adiudge to stand with equitye
and good Consciences; and your subiecte accordinge to his bounden
dutye; shall dayly pray for your maiesties longe life & prosperous raigne
over vs./

                                                                                   10

(signed)   Fr. Harvey
             Rt. mey

Defendant's Answer in Dawson v. Mumby   TNA: PRO STAC 8/114/12
mb 73   *(8 November)*   15

        The answere of Thomas Mumby one of the defendantes to the bill of
                Complaynt of Thomas Dawson Complaynant./
The sayd defendant savinge to himselfe now and att all tymes hereafter
all advantage of exception to the Incertaintie & insufficiency of the sayd   20
Informacion for answere to soe much thereof as concerneth this defendant
to make answere vnto sayth that about the moneth of Iuly last one Alice
Hutchinson this defendantes servaunt did as she affirmed to this defendant
find in this defendantes yard a paper sealed with wax being as this defendant
taketh it of the effect of the Two libels in the Informacion mencioned which   25
she brought and shewed to this defendant who opened the same and
indeavored to read the same but could not but here and there a part and
afterwardes this defendant being called before Sir Adrian Scroope Knight
one of his Maiesties Iustices of peace within the County of Lincolne by the
Comaundement of the sayd Sir Adrian did deliver the same writinge to him   30
but this defendant never saw any other libell but that which he delivered to
the sayd Sir Adrian And as to all the [⟨…⟩] ⌐°forginge makinge deuisinge°⌐
contrivinge[s] Composinge writinge or publishinge of the libels in the
Informacion mencioned or eyther of them And as to all the Combynacions
Complottinges confederacies devisinges and other misdeamenors and   35
offences in the bill of Complaynt laid to the Charge of this defendant and
punishable in this Honorable Court this defendant ∧⌐°sayth that he°⌐ is not

2/ be: *for* to be
6/ adiudge: *for* adiudged (?)
32/ [⟨…⟩]: *108mm of text crossed out*
33/ Composinge: C *corrected over another letter*

of them or any of them guiltie in such manner and forme as in and by the
Informacion they are sett forth and declared ⌈°agaynst him°⌉ without that
that any other matter or thinge in the sayd bill of Complaynt conteyned
materiall or effectuall in the law to be answered vnto by this defendant
and not herein well and sufficientlie answered vnto confessed and avoyded   5
traversed or denied is true All which matters and thinges this defendant is
ready to averre and prove as this Honorable Court shall award and prayeth
to be hence dismissed with his reasonable Costes and Charges in this behalfe
most wrongfully susteyned./
(signed) Leuinge   10

MORTON

1607

Episcopal Visitation Book   I A: Diocesan Vj/19   15
f 53   *(6 August)*

*Presentments at the visitation of Corringham and Gainsborough deaneries during
the bishop's triennial visitation*
...   20
Richard Lilly of Morton for prophaning ye sabaoth by keeping a piper &
sufferinge him to play in his hous in euening praier time vpon ye 19 daie
of Iulie 1607
...

                                                                                 25

PINCHBECK

1552
Letter of Richard Ogle to Sir William Cecil   TNA: PRO SP 10/15
f [1]*   *(27 October)*   30

Pleasith yt your Mastershyp to be aduertysed that by force of the commyssyon
of Sewers wherin you toke [payn] payn suche dykyng hath bene made in
the cvntry [that] ∧⌈as⌉ shalbe to the vniuersall welth of the [cvuntre] ∧⌈the
same⌉ yet som parte ys to be doon whych I trust shall hereafter be doon by   35
the labour & payn that my ffrend Iohn Burton hath taken & woll take
therin for the whych he hath had and sustayned dyspleasure but yet never
cessed to se thynges doon accordyng to the effect of the decrees/ sir mr welly
& I have sent a feyned lycence to the councell whych we toke ffrom players/
a thyng moche to be loked too and the offendours worthy punysshement yf   40
your Mastershyp thynk conuenyent to deliuer the letter to the councell
thys berer shall deliuer the letter & the box or elles to be orderd as to your

Mastershyp shall seme good/ very requysyte yt ys to have a generall commyssyon
ˌ⌈of Sewers⌉ as was sewed/ for the savegard of the hole contrey whych [we]
I referre to your Mastershyp dyscressyon I have the commyssyon & the bokes
that you sat vppon in my hendes/ & the sayd Burton shall shewe to you
the lawes by vs deuysed vppon your remembrances and notes referryng   5
the reformacion therof to your dyscressyon/. ferther requyryng you to
geve credyt to the berer thus ye almyghty have you [h] in hys kepyng in
honour & helth to endure to hys pleasure ffrom pynchebek the xxvij of
octobre 1552
per your seruant Richerd   10
Ogle

1582/3
Inventory of Hugh Artle, Piper   LA: LCC ADMONS 1582/21
single sheet*   *(2 February) (In the parlour)*   15
…
Item ij pare of pypes   ij s.
…

POTTERHANWORTH   20

1618
Episcopal Visitation Book   LA: Diocesan Vj/24

See Branston 1618   25

RIPPINGALE

1611
Episcopal Visitation Book   LA: Diocesan Vj/21   30
f 122v   *(13 September)*

*Presentments made during the visitation of Aveland and Lafford deaneries held
in the parish church of Sleaford by Otwell Hill, LLD, vicar general and official
principal of William Barlow, bishop of Lincoln*   35

dimittitur
Thomas Markernes for haueing musitions & dancing in his house vpon the
saboath day in time of divine praier & did dance himselfe °30 Octobris 1611
citatus &c comparuit et obiecto &c negat et habet ad purgandum &c 4. in   40

proximum postea fatetur &c et d*imittitu*r cum monic*ione*°

...

ROUGHTON

5

1609
Archdeaconry of Lincoln Visitation Book   LA: Diocesan Vij/12
pp 75–6   *(29 April)*

Presentments made during the visitation of Horncastle deanery held in the   10
parish church of Horncastle by Otwell Hill, LLD, commissary and official of the
archdeacon of Lincoln

...

d*imittitu*r   Rob*er*t Barber for plainge in Christmas Tyme in prayer time one St Stephens
day °6. Oc*tobris* 1609. ques*itus* &c vijs &c/° °20 oc*tobri*s 1609 [quesi*tus*   15
&c] ⌐cit*atus* p*er*⌐ vijs &c/ *suspenditur*° °vlt*imo* ffebr*uarij* 1609 d*ic*tus
Rob*er*tus Ba*r*ba*r* in p*er*so*n*a Rich*ar*d*i* yongre iuratus absoluitur et cum
monic*ione* d*imittitu*r°

d*imittitu*r   Chr*is*tofer Barber Iunior p*ro* consimili °18º Iul*ij* 1609. cit*atus* &c comp*aru*it   20
& obiec*to* a*r*ticu*lo* fate*ur* & cu*m* monic*ione* d*imittitu*r/° |

d*imittitu*r   Launc*elot* ∧⌐Hodgson⌐ Servant vnto Willia*m* Andrew p*ro* consimili
°18º Iul*ij* 1609. cit*atus* &c comp*aru*it & obiec*to* a*r*ticu*lo* fate*ur* & cu*m*
monic*ione* d*imittitu*r/°   25

suspenditur   Iohn Russells for beinge then pres*en*t °18º Iul*ij* 1609 ques*itus* &c vijs &c°
°6. Oc*tobris* 1609. cit*atus* p*er* vijs & *suspenditur*°

d*imittitu*r/   Chr*is*tofer Bowlton for harboringe of them in his howse ye same daye in   30
prayre time °18º Iul*ij* 1609. cit*atus* &c comp*aru*it & obiec*to* a*r*ticu*lo* fate*ur*
& cu*m* monic*ione* d*imittitu*r/°

...

SAXILBY   35

1555–6
St Botolph's Churchwardens' Accounts   LA: SAXILBY PAR/7/d
f 7v*   *(1 January–1 January)* *(Expenses)*

...   40
Item to the pypur   vj d.

...

SIBSEY

1601
Archdeaconry of Lincoln Visitation Book   LA: Diocesan Vij/10
f 92v   *(1 April)*

*Presentments made during the visitation of Bolingbroke deanery held in the parish
church of Horncastle by Thomas Randes, the archdeacon of Lincoln's official*
…

d*i*m*i*ttuntu*r*
gard*iani* ibi*de*m for not presenting certaine [rude and] p*er*sons w*i*thin that
p*a*rishe wh*i*ch are make*re*s and publishe*re*s of rymes tending to the discredit
of some of the p*a*rishione*re*s there making therof a co*m*mon practize and in
a braving and boasting manner. [saeth] saieng they will doe yt and for not
p*re*senting the wief of *(blank)* mawley for not receyving the holie co*m*mun*i*on
at Easter last past nor eny tyme since 30 die Ianuar*i*j 1601 citati comp*a*rue*ru*nt
et a*r*t*i*cul*o* objecto allegar*u*nt that as yet they knowe of noe suche matte*re*s
[vnde d*o*min*u*s] sed petie*ru*nt tempus competens ad inquirend*um* et ad
p*re*sentand*um* &c vnde d*o*min*u*s ipsos monuit [t] iuxta [monuit] petic*i*onem et
ad cer*ti*f*i*cand*um* citra 25. Marcij prox*imum* 2. Apr*i*lis 1602 ex*hi*bit*um* est
cer*ti*f*i*cariu*m* vnde dimittuntur

SILK WILLOUGHBY

1623
Archdeaconry of Lincoln Visitation Book   LA: Diocesan Vij/18
f 227v*   *(1 October)*

*Detections exhibited during the visitation of Lafford and Aveland deaneries by
John Hills, STD, archdeacon of Lincoln, at a session held in the church of Sleaford
and presided over by John Farmery, LLD, the archdeacon's official*
…

det*ectio* clerici   d*i*m*i*ttitu*r*
Iohn Tayler p*re*sented for that vpon the nameinge, let us goe singe a Psalme,
in mockerie began a ribaldrye songe amoungst manie on the saboath daye
15 *nou*embris 1623 cit*atus* &c. comp*a*ruit Magiste*r* Hawen nu*ncius* &c. et
fa*te*tu*r* &c. submisit &c. vnde h*a*b*et* ad agn*o*scend*um* &c et cer*ti*f*i*cand*um*
inde prox*imum* 29. *nou*embris 1623 ex*hi*bi*t*o Certificario d*i*m*i*ttitu*r* °29:
No*ue*mbris 1623. loco cons*i*st*o*riali coram d*o*mino Canc*e*ll*a*rio prese*n*te R*e*gistra*r*io
comp*a*rue*ru*nt Iosep*h*us Thirlby Wi*l*lelm*us* Leake Thomas Yates [Aug*u*stin*us*
Iessup] & wi*l*lelm*us* Cooper et affirm*a*uer*u*nt that the s*a*id Iohn Taylor George
Beckwell & Io*h*n Iessopp were the ringlead*er*es in this [buss] abuse and

[did] Iohn Taylor did begyn to sing & Iohn Iessop was the next principall offendor.°

Dimittitur

detectio clerici

George Beckwell presented for lettinge a great fart at the same tyme with laughinge and shoutinge of manie there 15. nouembris 1623. habet vt supra eodem die

...

dimittitur

Iohn Ieesup presented for the like 15 nouembris 1623. citatus &c comparuit et dominus ei obiecit That he with others did meet together vpon an vnseasonable tyme of vpon the saboath daye & then did much prophane & [abu] the ∧⌜same⌝ [saboath daye] & abuse themselues by singinge baudye & ribauldrye songes in mockerye vpon the nameing of singing a Psalme respondet et dicit That he this respondent was then in companie with those that did so offend & was culpable therein as well as they et vlterius dicit That there was then and there in companie blameable as abouesaid Ioseph Thirlbye William Leake Thomas Yates Austin Ieesup. William Cooper Nicholas [se] seruant to Richard Sprat & Robert Kime all of Silkewilloughbye parish °& diuers others whose names he nowe remembreth not Et se submisit &c vnde habet ad publice confitendum &c in ecclesia ibidem prout in schedula et ad certificandum in 2dam sessionem et dominus decreuit omnes alios prescriptos citandos fore in proximum &c 11. decembris 1623 dictus Ieesup exhibuit certificarium de penitencia dicte confessionis &c vnde dimittitur./°

f 228v

monitus ad
soluendum
feodum

Ioseph Thirlbye

ffor that he with otheres did meet together vpon an unseasonable tyme of saboath daye and they did much prophane the same and abuse themselues [by] ∧⌜by yeelding their ⟨...⟩nere & companie with divers that were⌝ singing baudye & ribauldrye songes in mockerye vpon the nameinge of singinge of

their orders
are executed
& received [q]
since their
suspension.

A Psalme 29. Novembris 1623. citatus &c preconizatus comparuit cui obiecto articulo fatetur et submisit &c vnde habet ad agnoscendum &c et certificandum inde proximum °11 decembris 1623. dictus Thirlbie preconizato &c non comparendo nec certificando &c vnde suspenditur.°

similiter

William Leake for the like 29: Nouembris 1623. fatetur vt supra °11. decembris 1623. vt supra suspenditur.°

similiter

Thomas Yates for the same 29: Nouembris 1623. fatetur vt supra °11. decembris 1623. vt supra suspenditur°

23   Austin Ieesup pro consi*mi*li 29: Nouembris 1623. cit*atus* pre*conizatus*
     com*paruit* M*agist*er Hawen nu*n*cius &c et fa*tetur* eius no*mine* obiect*um* et
     submisit vnde h*abet* ad agnoscend*um* &c et cer*tific*and*um* inde pr*oximum*
     °11. decemb*ris* 1623. fa*cta* pre*conizacione* &c *pro* d*icto* Iessup no*n* com*paruit*
     nec cer*tific*and*o* &c vnde sus*penditu*r./°   5

similiter   Willi*a*m Cooper pro eadem culpa 29: Nouembris 1623. cit*atus* &c
     pre*conizatus* com*paruit* et h*abet* ad agn*oscend*um* et cer*tific*and*um* inde
     pr*oximum* °11. decemb*ris* 1623. vt sup*ra* sus*penditu*r°   10

     Nicholas *(blank)* famul*us* Rich*ard*i Sprat vt supra 29: Nouembr*is* 1623.
     ques*itus* &c vijs &c in pr*oximum* °xj° die decemb*ris* 1623. cit*atus* vijs &c
     pre*conizatus* &c no*n* com*paruit* vnde sus*penditu*r°

     Rob*er*t Kime pro consi*mi*li 29: Nouembr*is* 1623. ques*itus* vijs &c in   15
     pr*oximum* °11. decemb*ris* 1623. cit*atus* vijs &c pre*con*izatus &c no*n*
     com*parui*t vnde sus*penditu*r°

SLEAFORD

                                                                                    20

1476–7
Trinity Guild Accounts   BL: Additional MS 28,533
f 1   *(16 June–8 June)*

…

Item payd to ye mynstrels   xiiij d. 25
Item payd to ye mynstrels of corpus day p*er*   iiij d.
Item payd for ye ryngyng of ye same day   ij d.

…

1479–80   30
Trinity Guild Accounts   BL: Additional MS 28,533
f 2*   *(c 13 June–11 June)*

…

Item payd to Robert Appylby for viij planck*es*
& warkema*n*shyp of y*em*   ij s. ₐ⌜iiij d.⌝ 35
Item payd to the mynstryls   xij d.
Item payd for the Ryginall of ye playn/ for the
ascenc*ion* & the wrytyng of spechys & payntyng
of a garme*n*t for god   iij s. viij d.

…   40

1482–3
Trinity Guild Accounts   BL: Additional MS 28,533
f 3v*   *(16 June–15 June)*

...

Item ffor Beryng of ye Bancr to ye mynstrell   vj d.   5

...

SOUTH KYME

1601   10
Bill of Complaint in Lincoln v. Dymoke, Bayard, et al
TNA: PRO STAC 5/L1/29
sheet [21]*   *(23 November)*

To the Queenes most excellent Maiestie/   15

Complayning sheweth and enformeth your excellent Maiestie your highnes
faythfull and loyal Subiecte Henry Earle of Lincoln, That whereas your
Royall Maiestie in the whole Course of your happie and flourishing Reigne,
as also your Highnes noble and worthie progenitoures in their Reigne and   20
goverment haue ever had a gracious Regarde of the honour and estate of the
Nobility and Peeres of this your Highnes Realme, and men of more inferiour
Condicion to them haue Caryed such respective and due observance to the
Nobles of this kingdome as they haue not once presumed to scandalize or
deprave their persons and place by publique scornes & reproches yet nowe   25
soe it is (most dread Soveraigne) That one Talbois Dymmocke a Common
Contryver and publisher of Infamous pamphletts and Libells Roger Bayard
of Kyme in your Highnes County of lincoln ˄⌈yeoman⌉ Iohn Cradocke
thelder and Iohn Cradocke the younger of kyme aforesaid yeomen and other
their accomplyces intending as much as in them consisted to scandalize and   30
dishonor your said Subiect and to bring him into the scorne and Contempte
of the vulgar people of his Country haue of late and since your maiestics
last free and generall pardon by the direction Consent or allowance of Sir
Edward Dymocke in your Highnes said County of Lincoln knight Contryved
published vsed & acted these disgracefull false and intollerable slaunders   35
reproches scandalous wordes Lybells and Irreligious prophanacions ensewing,
And first the said Talbois Dymocke being a man of a very disordered and a
most dissolute behaviour & Condicion about the Twelfth Daie of August
in the one & ffortith yeare of your Highnes Raigne passing thoroughe the

27/ Roger: *corrected over erasure*   38–9/ the Twelfth Daie ... Raigne: *12 August*
30–1/ and dishonor: d dis *corrected over erasure*   *1599*

Towne of Tattershall in the said county of lincolne where your Subiect
now & then inhabited did resort to the Doore of the howse of one william
Hollingehead there dwelling in the said towne of Tattershall & then & there
stayed a while against the doore of the said howse sitting on his horsebacke
Att which tyme with a lowde voyce in the ⌐then¬ presence and hearing of   5
divers & sondry persons he vttered & spake to Anne Hollenghead wyfe of
the said william Hollinghead these wordes ensewing. That is to say Commend
me (sweete Harte) to my Lord of Lincoln and tell him that he is an Asse &
a foole (meaning your said Subiect) Is he my vncle and hath no more witte?
I would to God he had some of my wytte for I could spare him some   10
which speaches he then ∧⌐& there¬ vttered and published in Contemptuous
malicious and scornefull manner to the great discontentment of the hearers
and to the disgrace and ignominy of your said Subiect And the said Talboys
Dymocke persuing his former bould and insolent purposes and Courses
against your said Subiecte after sondry plottes and Conferencye had betwene   15
the said Sir Edward Dymocke and him the said Talboys Dymocke howe to
scandalize deprave and disgrace your said Subiecte the said Talboys Dymocke
with the privity procurement and allowance of the said Sir Edward Dymocke
in or about the Moneth of August in the xliij.th yeare of your Highnes Raigne
did frame and Contryve one Infamous Lybell or Stage play which the said   20
Sir Edward Dymocke and Talboys Dymocke tearmed and named the Death
of the Lorde of Kyme and to the end that the whole hundred and wapentage
adioyning should resorte therevnto and be behoulders thereof: Notificacion
was thereof publiquely made and Divers persons and neighboures adioyning
were sent vnto and invited by some of the servantes of the said Sir Edward   25
Dymocke to be at kyme vppon Sonday being about the last Day of August
at Dinner there to take parte of some venison and to see a play in the
afternoone of the same day: All which was done by the then procurement
& direction of the said Sir Edward Dymocke and Talboys Dymocke, Att
which day divers of the inhabitantes thereaboutes (videlicet) Edward Newlove   30
of Helpringham in your highnes said County. gentleman william Garewell
of Hold in the said county yeoman Robert Iackson of Asgarby Thomas
whelpdale of Howell in the said County yeoman and Divers others to
your said Subiect vnknowen did resorte to kyme aforesaid and were there
enterteyned at the howse of the said Iohn Craddocke thelder of Kyme   35
aforesaid yeoman servant vnto the said Sir Edward Dymocke accordingly
and in the afternoone of the said Day the said Talboys Dymocke Roger
Bayard Iohn Cradocke the elder and Iohn Cradocke the younger vppon a

9/ Is he: *corrected over erasure*
15/ Conferencye: encye *corrected over erasure*
19/ August … Raigne: *August 1601*
26/ Sonday … August: *probably Sunday, 30 August 1601*
37/ Roger: *corrected over erasure*

Grene neere adioyning to the howse of the said Sir Edward Dymocke at
kyme aforesaid hard by A Maypole standing vppon the said greene did then
and there present and acte an enterlude or play by the then procurement and
privity of the said Sir Edward Dymocke dyveres persons of the Neighbour
Townes therevnto adioyning and of the howsehould servantes of the said   5
Sir Edward being then ᴀ⌈&⌉ there assembled to heare & see the same In
which play the said Talboys Dymocke being the then principall actour therein
did first then & there Counterfeite and tooke vppon him to represent the
person of your said Subiecte and his speaches and gesture and then & there
in the said play tearmed & named your said [Subiecte] Subiect the Earle of   10
lincolne his good vncle in scornetull manner and as an actor then tooke
vppon him to represent the person of your said Subiect and in such sorte
representing the person of your said Subiecte in the said play was there
fetcht away by the said Roger Bayard who acted and represented then &
there in the said playe the person and place of the divell And the said Roger 15
Boyard in an other parte of the said playe did then and there acte & represent
the parte of the ffoole and the parte of the vyce in the said playe and then
and there actinge the said parte did declare his last will & testament and
then & there in the hearing of all the persons assembled to see and heare
the said playe did bequeathe his woodden dagger to your said Subiecte by   20
the name of the Earle of lincolne and his Cockscombe & bable vnto all
those that would not goe to Hornecastle with the said Sir Edward Dymocke
against him at which Towne of Hornecastle the said Sir Edward [D⟨...⟩] had
vnlawfully and ryotously by such as he had there vnto appointed vppon the
xxvjᵗʰ day of Iulie last being the Sabath daie made a Ryotous entrye into   25
the personage howse there and Claymed divers duties of right belonging
to your subiect, to belonge to him and where his servantes and such as he
had appointed for that purpose contynued that force in parte of the said
personage howse of Hornecastle aforesaid before and at the tyme of the said
playe and in the said enterlude [and] ⌈or⌉ playe and as a parte thereof there 30
was also by the then like procurement and direction of the said Sir Edward
Dymocke a Dirige songe by the said Talbois Dymocke ᴀ⌈Marmaduke
dicconson Roger Bayard Iohn Cradock the elder and Iohn Cradock the
younger.⌉ and other the then actors of the said playe wherein they expressed
by name most of the knowen lewde & licencious woemen in the Citties of   35
london & lincoln and Towne of Boston concluding in their songes after
every of their Names. Ora pro nobis After which Dirige so songe as aforesaid
the said Iohn Cradocke thelder towardes the end of the said playe in scorne
of Religion and the profession thereof being attyred in a Ministers Gowne

14, 15/ Roger: *corrected over erasure*   23/ [D⟨...⟩]: *erasure mostly obscured by line filler*
17/ ffoole: *corrected over erasure*   24/ ryotously: *first y written over another lette*

and having a Corner Cappe on his head and a booke in his hand opened
did then and there in a Pulpitte made for that purpose deliver and vtter a
prophane and irreligious prayer: which was framed and devised by the said
Sir Edward Dymocke & Talboys Dymocke and did then & there reade a
Text out of the booke of Mabbe as he then reade yt during which tyme of   5
the action and continuance of the said playe the said Sir Edward. being
then in his said howse att Kyme aforesaid, sent from tyme to tyme by his
servantes and others directions to the said actoures what they should doe.
And further enformeth your Maiestie your said Subiecte That whereas your
said Subiecte about two yeares past had purchased. A Messuage and certeyne   10
landes in Kyme aforesaid of the yearely value of Twenty poundes of one
Ambrose Marshe: the said Sir Edward Dymocke and Talbois Dymocke
dispightinge most maliciously your said Subiect have nowe of late Contryved
and made of your said Subiecte this pasquill, lybell, or Ryme in wrytinge
ensewing That is to say The Bandogge nowe Tom Bull comes to our Towne.   15
And sweares by Hamboroughhe Marshe and much a doe: To seigniorize to
seate and sitt him downe: This Marshe must marshall him and his whelpes
to, but let him headd Tom Bull, ffor yf they sturr, Ile make yt but a kennell
for a Curr. And afterwardes did publiquely fix and sett the same vnto and
vppon the said maypole to the veiwe of a nomber of your Highnes Subiectes   20
& caused a Bull being the Armes of the said Sir Edward Dymocke. to be
pictured and sett herevppon a little aboue the said Lybell and the said libell
directly vnder the picture of the said Bull. In which malicious and scornefull
lible by the said bull therein mencioned The said Edward and Talboys
dymocke did meane and intend the said Sir Edward Dymocke who giveth   25
the Bull for his Creste or Cognizance And by ˄⌜the⌝ Bandogg and Curr they
meant and intended your said Subiecte who giveth the white Greyhounde
as the Creste and Cognizance of your said subiecte to the great scandall and
reproche of your said subiecte being one of your highnes Peeres and to the
great Contempt of persons of like estate and quallity All which reproches   30
scandalls lybells pasquills Interludes playes and other the misdemeanoures
aforemencioned were committed and done longe since your Maiesties last
free and generall pardon. In Consideracion whereof. and forasmuch as the
said reproches scandalls libells interludes Pasquills Playes and other the said
misdemeanoures doe tend to the great disgrace and contempt of your Highnes   35
Nobilytie and the great dislike and discontentment of your Maiesties well
Disposed and Civill Subiectes and be offences merely against your Highnes
police and good and godly lawes. And doe further tend to the wilfull
Contempte of your most gracious goverment and of your Crowne and
dignity and to the daungerous ymboldning & pernicious example of other   40

16/ sweares: ares *corrected over erasure*

like lewde and evill disposed persons to committ the like offences vnles some
severe and Condigne punnishment be executed vppon the said intollerable
offendoures May it therefore please your Maiestie to grante your highnes
writtes of Subpena to be directed to the said Sir Edward Dymocke Talboys
Dymocke Roger Bayard Iohn Cradocke the elder and Iohn Craddocke the   5
younger Commaunding them and every of them thereby at A Certeyne Daye,
and vnder a Certeine payne therein to be lymitted to be and personally to
appeare before your highnes in your Maiesties most honorable Courte of
Starrchamber then and there to answere the premisses and to abide such
further order therein as by the said honorable Courte shalbe thought fitt   10
and convenient And your Highnes said Subiecte shall dayly pray for your
Maiesties most happy Reigne long to continewe over vs./.
(signed) Crewe

Interrogatories for Tailboys Dymoke, John Craddock the elder, and John 15
  Craddock the younger   TNA: PRO STAC 5/L1/29
sheet [29]   (before 7 December)
...

1   (..) primis whither were yow at Tattershall in the County of Lincoln where
the Complaynant now Dwelleth on or about the xijth Daie of August in the 20
xljth yeare of her Maiesties reigne, And whiche Did you ther at your beinge
in or then passinge through the said towne, resorte to the Dore of the howse
of one William Hollinegheid then Dwellinge in the same Towne of Tattershall
and whyther Did yow staie a while against the Dore of the said howse sytting
on horsebacke, and whither did yow then or at any time sithens, speak to   25
Anne wyfe of the said Hollenghed or to anie other person or persons, or in
the presence & hearinge of any person or persons and what be thare names,
these wordes followinge (that is to say) commend me sweete harte to my
lord of Lincoln and tell him that he is an Asse, and a foole, is he my vncle
and hath no more witt I would to god he had somme of my wittes for I could 30
spare him soomme, Did yow speake all the saide wordes or some parte of
them ∧⌈& which of them⌉ or wordes to the like effecte & what were those
wordes yow so spake

2   Item whither did yow your self, or did yow or anie other by the helpe privitie 35
or solicitation of Sir Edward Dimocke Knight or of anie other and by whome
in or aboutt the moneth of August last or at anie time sithence frame and
contrive one libell or stage plaie, which yow and the said Sir Edward Dimocke
or some of yow, tearmed and named the Death of the lord of kime or not,
whither was theire anie notification publiquely mad of the said libell or   40

5/ Roger: *corrected over erasure*

stage plaie, and diuers persons sente vnto and solicited or invited, and by
whome and by whose Commaundment to be at kime on sondaie beinge
about the last of August aforesaid at dynner, there to take parte of somme
venison, and to se a plaie in the after noone of the same Daie what were
the names of the parties that wer⟨.⟩ so solicited or invited to be there yat   5
sondaie or at anie time since.

3   Item whither was the said libell or stage plaie after the makinge thereof acted
and plaied at kime aforesaid, and where & in what place, was the same acted
and plaied & by whome and by what persons, was the same acted and plaid,   10
whither was yt acted and plaied vppon agrene, nere adioyninge to the howse
of the said Sir Edward Dimocke at kime aforesaid, hard or nere by the
maypoole, then standinge vppon the said grene, whither was the same Donne,
by the solicitation privitie or procuerment, of the said Sir Edward Dimocke,
and what number of persons were assembled there, at the actinge of the said   15
libell or stage plaie, and what were the names of asmanie as yow do knowe.

4   Item whither in the actinge of the said libell or stage plaie, did anie person,
and what is his name, counterfett and take vppon him, the person of the
said Earle of Lincoln complaynant, and his speches and gesture, naminge the   20
Complaynant his good vncle & whither was the same done in scornefull
manner or not,

5   Item whither in the said libell or stage plaie, was there not one that acted
and plaied the parte of the Devill, and what was his name, and whither did   25
not the partie, so actinge and playinge the parte of the Devill, fetch and carie
awaie, the partie that represented the person of the Complaynant or not./

6   Item whither in the said libell or stage plaie, was there not one person that
acted the parte of the vice or foole, in the said plaie, and then and there   30
actinge the said parte, did Declare his last will and testiament, and then and
there in the hearinge and ye presence of the people there assembled, to here
the said plaie, did bequeath his woodden dagger to the Complaynant, and
his Cockescome and bable vnto all those that would not goe to horncastle with
the said Sir Edward Dimocke againste the Complaynant, and whither had   35
the said Sir Edward Dymock the xxvjth of Iulie then past made a forceble
enterie into the messuage called the parsonage howse of hornecastle aforesaid
vppon the possession of the Complaynant or not, and whither was the said
messuage kept by force by the said Sir Edward Dimocke, or his confederates
at the time of the actinge of the said plaie as you knowe./ or haue heard./   40

32/ ye: *apparently added later in space between* and *and* presence
35/ had: *corrected over erasure*

7   Item whither in the actinge of the said libell or stage plaie, was there not a
     Dirige songe by the actors of the said plaie, or some of them, and by which
     of them, and whither in the said Dirige, were not the names of some knowne
     lewde and licencious, women in the Cyty of lincoln and towne of Boston,
     and some women of Credit and good behaviour named therein, Concludinge   5
     in there songe after euerie of there names, ora pro nobis, and what moved
     yow to name women never detected or defaymed, amongste women suspected,
     and who advised yow to name them or anie of them, and whither was *Sir*
     Edward Dimocke made privie there as yow knowe or haue hard./

                                                                                10

8   Item whether in the endinge of the said plaie was theire not one *person*, and
     who was the said *person* that was atired in a garment like a ministers garment,
     havinge a corner cap on his head and a booke in his hand opened, whither
     was not there a poulpett made of purpose and did not the said *person*
     representinge a minister in the said pulpitt Deliuer and vtter a prophane   15
     and irreligious praier, and what was the said praier, and who was the inventer
     & maker thereof, and did not the said *person* representinge the *person* of
     the minister, reade a text out of [the] ⌈A⌉ book, which text as he said was
     taken out of the booke of Mabb, and what was the text he so redd, and
     whether Did not the said pretended minister Devid his pretended text, into   20
     three *partes* (viz.) the first the loders stone in Bullingbrooke fferme,
     the second Byard*es* leape of Ancaster heath, and what was the third he
     said he could not tell, but bad them goe to *Mr* Gedney of ancaster he
     could tell./

                                                                                25

9   Item whither Duringe the time of the said Stage plaie, did not diuers of the
     servaunt*es* and frendes of the said *Sir* Edward Dimocke and others then goe
     and come from the howse of the said *Sir* Edward, in kime aforesaid to the
     said stage plaie, how farr Distant was the said *Sir* Edward*es* howse, from the
     place where the plaie was plaied, and whither was *Sir* Edward privie to the   30
     intercourses of his ffrend*es* and servaunt*es* so passinge to and from the said
     plaie, and whither might not anie be in the howse of the said *Sir* Edward,
     and se the said plaie plaid or not, and is not the greene where the said plaie
     was plaied, next adioyninge to the vtter Courte of the said *Sir* Edward
     Dimockes howse, and whither was he then within the said howse or no,   35
     And is not the said Tailbois dimocke brother to the said *Sir* Edward, and
     was he not bothe before and since most commonly resiant within his howse,
     & hath not the said Tailbois Contrived manie libelles [the] of and againste
     the Complaynant and others by the directio*n* helpe counsell or pryvitie of
     the said *Sir* Edward Dimocke./   40

8/ *Sir:* corrected over the
38–9/ [the] ... others: *corrected over erasure*

10   Item do you knowe or haue yow hard whither the Complaynant about one
      yeare past purchased a messuage and certaine lands in kime aforesaid, of
      the yearlie valewe of xx li. or thereaboutes of Ambrose marshe, whither was
      there not sithens the Complaynantes purchase, a pasquill libell or rime made
      of the Complaynant or not and what was the said libell or ryme or the effecte   5
      thereof, did not the said libell conteyne these or the like wordes followinge,
      The bandog now Tom Bull comes to our towne and sweares by Hamborough
      Marshe and much a do, to Seignoriz to seate and sitt him downe this marshe
      must marshall him and his whelpes to, but let them heede Tom bull, for yf
      they sturr, Ile make yt but a kenell for a Curr/ whither was the said pasquil   10
      or rime fixed, or sett vnto or vppon the said may pole to the vew of the
      persons then present, And whither was there not a bull pictured and sett
      vppon the said maypole a little aboue the said libell, and the said libell
      directly vnder the picture of the said bull, and whither was the said libell
      and picture of the said bull, made and sett vpp by the said Sir Edwardes   15
      privitie or by whome or by whose devise was the same don, And whither had
      yow not the helpe of the said Sir Edward about the Contrivinge of the said
      Pasquill or libell or some parte thereof, or who by name Contrived and made
      the same, and whither was not the premisses donne in malice scorne and and
      Disgrace of the said Complaynant, and whither Dothe the said ∧⌈Sir⌉ Edward   20
      Dimocke give the bull in his Conizans or creste, and whither doth the
      Complaynant give the white greyhound in his Conizans or Creste with a
      coller & a slippe about him./

11   Item whither haue yow heretofore written framed Contrived and made anie   25
      pamphelittes libelles or bookes eyther touchinge the Complaynant or anie
      other, and what did yow tearme them, and whither did yow meane or intende
      to touch the Complaynant in anie of them or not, when were they and
      euerie of them made, by whose privitie or with whose allowance were they
      or anie of them donn, whither Did your brother ∧⌈Sir⌉ Edward Dimocke   30
      Ioyne with yow, or was privie to or about the [matters] ⌈makynge⌉ or
      publishinge of them or anie of them./

12   Item whither sithens you came to the Cyttie of London last or after yow were
      served with subpena & had vewed or hard the effecte of this bill exhibited   35
      against yow [whither] Did yow vse these speches (viz.) that yt was treue
      that yow acted the parte of the Earle of Lincoln meaninge the Complaynant
      and that yow were fetcht away, whilest yow acted the same by Byard who
      played the parte of the Devill, or what speaches vsed yow to that or the
      like effecte./   40

19/ and and: *dittography*   28/ in: *corrected over erasure*

13   Item whither doth S*ir* Edward Dimocke beare your Charges and mainteine
       _∧⌜these your⌝ seutes [here] yea or no, and whither Did yow give anie ffee to
       Bawtrie yea or no, and whether Dothe Bawtrie followe your seute without
       ffee yea or no and whither is he appointed by S*ir* Edward Dimocke to
       mainteigne theise and the like caus*es* against the Compla*y*na*n*t yea or no./   5

Examinations of Tailboys Dymoke and John Craddock the elder and the
   younger, Defendants   TNA: PRO STAC 5/L1/29
sheets [5–8]*   (7 December) (Examination of Tailboys Dymock, gentleman,
   of South Kyme)   10
...
To the 1 Interro*gatory* this def*endant* saieth that he was ⌜in ye companie
of Iohn ffisher esqu*ier* Robert Banwell esqu*ier* & Brian Eland esqu*ier*⌝ att
Tatershall in the Countie of Lincoln where the now Complainant _∧⌜dwelleth⌝
on or about the xij^th day of August in the 41th yere of her maiesties Raigne   15
& passinge through that towne on horsebacke _∧⌜he this def*endant*⌝ did call
for drinke at the dore of the house of Willi*a*m Hollingshed mencioned in
this Interro*gatory* being a Tipplinge house & at that tyme _∧⌜Anne⌝ the wife
of the *said* willi*a*m Hollingshead brought forth drinke to this def*endant* &
his *said* companie as they sate on horsebacke at the dore of the *said* house   20
& then he this def*endant* vsed some speches to the *said* Anne about a
fortification w*hich* the now Compl*ainan*t had made about his Castle at
Tatershall to this effecte viz. what a foolish fortification is this my Lord saieth
that I am a foole but I would to God he had had a little of my witte in
the making of it for this is the most foolish thing that ever I sawe But this   25
def*endant* saieth that he did not vse the *said* word*es* followinge viz. Commend
me sweete harte to my Lord of Lincoln & tell him that he is an Asse & a
foole, is he my vncle & hath no more witt I would to God he had some of
my witte for I could spare him some Neither did this def*endant* vtter anie
oth*er* word*es* in effecte then he hath before declared   30

To the 2. Interro*gatory* he saieth that in or aboutes the moneth of August last
past he this def*endant* of himself w*ith*out the helpe privitie or sollicitac*i*on
of S*ir* Edward dymock knight or any other did frame & make a stage play
to be plaied [in] for sporte & merriment at the setting vp | of a Maypole in   35
⌜Southe⌝ kyme w*hich* play he this def*endant* of himself termed the death of
the Lord of kyme because the same day should make an ende of the Sommer
Lord _∧⌜game in South⌝ [in] kyme for that yeare And saieth that he this
def*endant* did publiquely notifie & make knowne to some of the p*a*rishe of
kyme that there then was such a stage plaie to be plaied & he this def*endant*   40

38/ yeare: y *corrected over* t

did also appointe [Iohn Cradock thelder &] Iohn Cradock the younger
Roger Bayard & two oth*er*s to play & haue part*es* in that play But neither
he this def*endant* nor anie other p*er*son by his p*ro*curement consent or
privitie did send vnto sollicite or invite anie other p*er*sons to be at kyme on
Sonday about the last of August aforesaied at dynner there to take p*ar*te of   5
some venison & to see the s*ai*ed play in the afternoone of the s*ai*ed day nor
at anie tyme since

To the 3. he saieth that vpon a Sondaie in the afternoone after eveninge
praier beinge the last day of August last as this def*endant* taketh it the saied   10
Stage plaie was plaied & acted in [the] a grene[⟨.⟩] in the towne of kyme
nere the Maypole [by] ∧⌐& that he⌐ this def*endant* ⌐marmaduke⌐ [Iohn
Cradock] ∧⌐Dickinson⌐ [thelder] Iohn Cradock the younger Roger Bayard
& two others whose names this def*endant* doth not now re*mem*ber were all
the p*er*sons that acted & plaied the same And that the saied grene is about   15
a stones cast from the s*ai*ed S*ir* Edward dymock*es* house But this def*endant*
saieth that the same was not done by the sollicitacion privitie or p*ro*curement
of S*ir* Edward dymocke as is supposed neither did the s*ai*ed S*ir* Edward
knowe thereof vntill after the same was done And saieth that one Anthonie
Baily Antho*nie* Malyn *(blank)* Scotchye *(blank)* Willoughbie Antho*nie*   20
Newlove serv*antes* & Reteyners to the now Comp*lainan*t & Iohn Pagett | hugh
Hoskins m*r* willoughby [Campanett] T⟨...⟩ Shac⟨.⟩ Iohn Bradshaw & diuers
other p*er*sons whose names this def*endant* doth not now certenly remember
& divers women & children were present & beholders of the saied Play

                                                                                                 25

To the 4. Interr*ogatory* he saieth that in the actinge of the saied plaie no
p*er*son did ∧⌐counterfyett &⌐ take vppon him the p*er*son of the Earle of
Lincoln & his speaches & gesture naminge the now Comp*lainan*t his
good vncle But in that play he this def*endant* did represent ∧⌐& take
vpon him the title & terme of Lord Pleasure her & did Calle⌐ the Lord   30
of North kyme (being another So*mm*er Lord that yeare) [calling him]
my vncle Prince But the same was not done in scornefull manner of the
now Comp*lainan*t

To the 5 Interr*ogatory* this def*endant* saieth that in the s*ai*ed Stage Plaie the   35
afores*ai*ed Roger Bayard did plaie the p*ar*te of the devill & that the s*ai*ed
Bayard so actinge & plaienge the p*ar*te of the devill did fetche & carrie away
this def*endant* who represented the title & terme of Lorde Pleasure her in
the s*ai*ed Play

                                                                                                 40

To the 6. Interr*ogatory* he saieth that the s*ai*ed Roger Bayard did also in

22/ T⟨...⟩ Shac⟨.⟩: *top edge of* MS *frayed and damaged*

the saied Play acte the parte of the vice or foole & then & there acting that
parte did declare his last will and testament & then & there in the hearinge
& presence of the people assembled to heare the saied Play did bequeath
his woodden dagger to the Lord of North Kyme because he had the day
before called the Lord of South kyme Pyebald knave, But this defendant   5
ₐ⌐saieth⌐ that the now Complainant was not so much as once named in
that matter Neither did the saied Bayard bequeth his Cockscomb & bable
vnto all those that would not goe to Hornecastle with the saied Sir | Edward
dymocke against the now Complainant as is supposed Neither doth this
defendant knowe that the saied Sir Edward dymock had the xxvj daie of   10
Iulie then past made a forcible entrie into the messuage called the parsonage
house of Hornecastle aforesaied vpon the possession of the saied Complainant
as is also supposed Neither doth this defendant know nor hath crediblie
heard that the saied messuage was kept by force by the saied Sir Edward
dymock or anie his Confederattes at the tyme of the Actinge of the saied   15
Plaie as is also supposed by this Interrogatory

To the 7. Interrogatory this defendant saieth that in th⟨.⟩ Actinge of the saied
Plaie there was a ₐ⌐lattin⌐ dirige songe by ₐ⌐Marmaduke dickinson And that
he¹ this defendant & other the Actors in the saied Play answered therevnto   20
Amen And that the Names of some lewd & licentios wemen in the Citie
of Lincoln Towne of Boston & ₐ⌐some of⌐ London were named therein
concludinge in the songe after euerie of their Names Ora pro nobis But no
wemen of Creditt & good behaviour were named therein which were never
detected or defamed as is supposed Neither was Sir Edward dymocke made   25
privitie vnto the doinge of the matters aforesaied but whatsoever was done
therein was by this defendantes owne advice & device

To the 8. he saieth that in the endinge of the saied Plaie Iohn Craddocke
thelder [being] ₐ⌐was by this defendantes request & direccion⌐ attired in a   30
blacke garment or gowne & having a corner capp on his head & a booke in
his hand opened did stand in a thinge ₐ⌐of wainscott⌐ made like a Pullpitte
made of purpose for the saied Play & did represent | the person of a Minister
or Preiste & did then & there vtter these wordes & speaches viz. the marcie
of Musterd seed & the blessinge of Bullbeefe ₐ⌐& the peace of Pottelucke⌐   35
be with you all Amen, of which speches he this defendant was the Inventer
& maker And at the same tyme the saied person did reade a text which
he saied was taken out of the Hytroclites in these wordes viz Cesar dando,
sublevando, ignoscendo gloriam adeptus est & did englishe ₐ⌐it⌐ this viz.
Bayardes leape on Ancaster heathe the Bownder stone in Bollingbrookes   40
[⟨..⟩] fenne I say the more knaves the honester Men And the saied person

38–9/ Cesar … est: cf Sallust de Catilinae coniuratione 54.3

then devided his texte into three partes viz. the first a colladacion of the
auncient plaine of Ancaster heathe the second an auncient storie of Mabb
as an appendix & the third concludinge knaves honest menn by an auncient
story of the [⟨..⟩] ffriar & the boye And also at the same time the saied
person told a Tale of Bayardes leape which he saied was taken owt of the   5
booke of Mabb & then willed the people to goe to one Mr Gedney of
Ancaster & he could tell it better

To the 9 Interrogatory he saieth that duringe the time of the saied Plaie
some of the servauntes & freindes ∧⌜of Sir Edward dymock⌝ were at the   10
saied Play & beholders thereof as others were but whether they did during
that tyme goe & com or not this defendant doth not know for he did not
marke it And saieth that the house of the saied Sir Edward is distant aboutes
a stones cast from the Place where the saied Play was plaied And this
defendant well knoweth that the saied Sir Edward dymock | was not privie   15
to the intercourse of his ffreindes & servauntes passing to & from the saied
Plaie ∧⌜Neither might any as this defendant thinketh⌝ [but whether any
might] be in the house of the saied Sir Edward dymocke & [haue] see the
saied Play plaied But if they might see the same this defendant is assured
that they could not ∧⌜heare⌝ [see] it Neither is the greene where the saied   20
Play was plaied next adioyning to the utter courte of the saied Sir Edward
dymockes house Neither was the saied Sir Edward within his house whiles⟨.⟩
the saied Play was in plaienge to this defendantes knowledge And further
this defendant saieth that he is brother to Sir Edward Dymock & Was
before & since most commonlie rasyant within the saied Sir Edward   25
Dymockes house & that he this defendant hath not at anie tyme contrived
anie Libells of & against the Now Complainant & others by the direccion
help councell or privity of ⌜the saied⌝ Sir Edward dymocke as is supposed
by [these] this Interrogatory

30

To the 10. Interrogatory he saieth that the now Complainant aboute one
yeare past did purchase a Messuage & certen Landes in Kyme aforesaied
of the yerely value of xx li. or thereaboutes of Ambrose Marshe but the
defendant doth not knowe that since the saied Complainantes purchase
there was a Pasquill Libell or Ryme made of the saied Complainant But   35
saieth that he ∧⌜this⌝ defendant in the last Sommer at the tyme that the saied
May game sportes were vsed in ∧⌜South⌝ kyme aforesaied did make & write
a ryme to this effecte & in these wordes followinge viz. The Bandogge now
Tom Bull comes to our towne, and sweares by Hamborough Marche and
much a doe, to seigniorize to seate and sitt him downe, This Marche must   40
marshall him & his whelpes to, But let them heed | Tom Bull for if they
stirre, Ile make yt but a kennell for a Curre: And the same Ryme he this

defendant himself did fixe & naile vpon the Maypole of kyme aforesaied
And saieth that the picture of a bull beinge the cognezaunce of the towne
of kyme was pictured & sett ^⌈by the defendant⌉ vppon the saied May pole
a little aboue the saied ryme & the saied ryme directly vnder the picture of
the saied Bull, And that the Lord of the saied May game did subscribe to   5
the saied Ryme with these wordes Lord Cradock And this defendant saieth
that neither the saied Ryme nor picture of the saied bull was so sett vpp by
the privitie of the saied Sir Edward dymocke as is supposed but the same
was done by this defendantes owne device in a merriment at the tyme of
the saied May games And [further] this defendant saieth that he had not the   10
helpe of the saied Sir Edward about the contrivinge of the saied ryme or
anie parte thereof Neither was the same done in malice scorne & disgrace
of the saied Complainant as is supposed And further saieth that the saied
Sir Edward dymocke doth give the bull in his Cognizaunce or Crest & the
now Complainant doth give the white greyhounde in his Conizaunce or   15
Creste with a coller & a slippe about him

To the 11. Interrogatory this defendant saieth that he [doth] hath not
heretofore written framed contrived & made anie pamphlettes libells or
bookes either touchinge the saied Complainant or anie other Neither did   20
this defendant intende or meane to touche the now Complainant in anie
matters | done by this defendant [as is] Neither did ^⌈this defendantes
brother⌉ Sir Edward dymocke ioyne with this defendant nor was privie [vn]to
or about the makinge or publisshing of anie such matters done by this
defendant as is supposed by this Interrogatory   25

To the 12 Interrogatory this defendant saieth that he did not since he
came to the Citie of London last nor after he was served with Subpena
& had viewed or heard of theffecte of this bill exhibited against this
defendant vse these speaches viz. That it was true that this defendant   30
acted the parte of the Earle of Lincoln meaninge the now Complainant
& that this defendant was fetcht away whilest he acted the same by
Byard who plaied the parte of the devill But the defendant ^⌈hath saied⌉
[saieth] that whilest he plaied the parte in the saied play of the Lord
Pleasure her, that this defendant was fett away by Bayard who plaied the   35
parte of the devill in that play

To the 13. Interrogatory this defendant saieth that the matters of this
Interrogatory are as he thinketh alltogether impertinent to the misdemeanours
wherewith he is charged by the now Complainantes bill in this honorable   40
Courte & there fore taketh himself not bound to make aunswere therevnto
                    (signed) Taylboyes Dymok

sheets [9–9v]*   *(Examination of John Craddock the younger)*

...

To the 2. Interrogatory he saieth that in or about the moneth of August last
past Mr Talbois dymock one of the now defendantes did make [and] frame
& contrive a [stage] Play or speache which he termed the death of the Lord   5
of Kyme And that before the same was plaied it was reported that vpon
the last day of August last the same should be plaied And ⌈farther saiethe⌉
that Iohn Cradock thelder this defendantes father did invite divers of his
acquaintances & ffreindes ∧⌈viz. Anthony Malyn Thomas Whelmdale
Edward Newlove William Callis & [others] diuers others whome he doth   10
not now remember to come to him to his house at kyme⌉ [to com to him]
to dynner where they had ⌈some little⌉ venison vpon the saied last day of
August but no persons to this defendantes knowledge were sollicited or
invited to be there that Sonday [or at anie tyme since to see], to see a play in
the after noone of the same day And more he cannot say to this Interrogatorie   15

To the 3. Interrogatory he saieth that vpon Sonday the last day of August
last the saied Play was acted & plaied in the greene of South Kyme nere the
Sommer pole a prety good distaunce from the house of Sir Edward dymocke.
And that mr Talboys dymocke ∧⌈Marmaduke Dickinson⌉ [Iohn Cradock   20
the elder] Roger Bayard [Marmaduke Di] & he this defendant were Actors
therein And yat in that play he this defendant [plaied] (being before the
Sommer Lord of Kyme) & acting that parte ∧⌈in the saied Play⌉ was feyned
to be poisoned & so carried forth of the saied play And this defendant doth
not knowe yat the same play was made or acted & plaied by the sollicitacion   25
privitie or procurement of Sir Edward dymocke as is supposed. But saieth
that [din] the ⌈saied⌉ persons which dyned at this defendantes ffathers house
were present at the l saied Play & most of the parish of kyme were then also
presente & more he cannot certenly depose to this Interrogatory

...   30

sheets [10–10v]

...

To the 8. he saieth that in the ending of the saied [sta] Play Iohn Cradocke
thelder this defendantes ffather was attired in a ∧⌈blacke⌉ garment ∧⌈but not⌉   35
like a Ministers ∧⌈garment but as an ordinary⌉ [garment] gowne [∧] having
a corner capp on his heade but whether he had a book in his handes or not
this defendant doth not remember & that a place ∧⌈like a pulpitt⌉ was made
at the saied May pole for him to stande in [⟨...⟩nd not representinge the
person of a Minister] But what ∧⌈prophane⌉ prayer or what other matter he   40

21/ were: *corrected over* was

[this d] there vttered this defendant cannot certenly depose but he spake
somethinge there of the booke of Mabb And further to this Interrogatorie
this defendant saiethe he cannot depose anie thinge

To the 9 he saieth that he doth not know that duringe the tyme of the saied   5
Plaie | divers of the servauntes and freindes of the saied Sir Edward dymocke
& others did then goe & com from the house of the saied Sir Edward in kime
aforesaied to the saied [Stage] Plaie but the house of the saied Sir Edward
dymocke is a good distance from the place where the saied [stage] play
was plaied, And this defendant doth not knowe that anie might bee in   10
the house of the saied Sir Edward & see the saied plaie paied but the grene
where the saied play was plaied is ∧ᶦin parte therecofᶦ adioyninge to the
stables which stande in the vtter Courte ∧ᶦor yardeᶦ of the saied Sir Edward
dymockes house...

15

sheet [11]   *(Response to the tenth interrogatory)*

...And further saieth that also at the same tyme there was a bull pictured
& sett vpon the saied May pole a little aboue the saied ryme & so it hath
ben vsed to sett the picture of a Bull & a tyme vnder ∧ᶦvpon the Maypoleᶦ   20
in other yeres before, at such tyme as a May pole hath ben sett vpp in
Kyme aforesaied...

...

sheets [11v–12]   *(Examination of John Craddock the elder)*   25
...
To the 2. Interrogatory he saieth that ... in the last Sommer Talboys dymocke
one of the now defendantes & no other person to this defendantes knowledge
did make a Play or speache which was ∧ᶦplaiedᶦ vppon a Sonday the last
Sommer after eveninge praier [plaied] in the grene of Kyme ∧ᶦaforesaiedᶦ   30
by the saied Talboys dymocke & some others ... but vpon the saied Sonday
[Antho] Edward Newlove Anthony Malyn william willoughby Iohn Rastrick
Thomas whelpdale Robert Iackson william Scotchy & diuers others to ye
number of aboutes xlᵗⁱᵉ persons came to dynner to this defendantes house as
they or manie of them had vsually done in other yeares before, because he   35
this defendant is bailiffe of the Wapentake where the saied persons dwell And
after they had | dyned at this defendantes house some of the saied persons
went to see the saied Play hearinge thereof at that tyme.
To the 3 he saieth that the saied Plaie was vpon the saied Sonday plaied
in a grene almost a bowshoote from the house of Sir Edward dymock in   40
kyme aforesaied & that the same was plaied as this defendant thinketh by

Talboys dymock Roger Bayard Iohn Cradocke the younger & Marmaduke
dickinson [as this def*endant* thinketh] But he this def*endant* was not present
whilest the s*aie*d play was in plaienge but came thither ymediatly· vpon the
endinge thereof...

...   5

sheets [12v–13v]*

...

To the 8. Interrog*atory* this def*endant* saieth That after the endinge of the
saied Play the afores*aie*d Talboys Dymocke [verie m] came vnto this def*endant*es   10
house & verie much vrged him to com vnto the s*aie*d Greene & there to
deliver an old idle speache w*hi*ch | was made about 2. or 3. yeres before
by the saied Talbois Dymocke as this def*endan*t thinketh, w*hi*ch speech was
written in a paper booke And al the same tyme the s*aie*d Talbois caused this
def*endant* to putt on a black gowne of the ordinary making but ∧⌜the same   15
was⌝ not like a Ministers gowne, & also to putt on a corn*er* Capp w*hi*ch
the s*aie*d Talbois had caused to be brought vnto this def*endant*, and he also
deliu*er*ed to this def*endant* the booke wherein the s*aie*d speach was written
and so caused this def*endant* to com ∧⌜with the s*aie*d booke in his hande⌝
vnto the s*aie*d greene where the saied May pole stoode diu*er*s people being   20
then there, and then he this def*endant* went vp into a place representinge a
pullpitt w*hi*ch was placed nere the s*aie*d May pole & ∧⌜then &⌝ there he
this def*endant* did vtter & reade owt of the s*aie*d booke word*es* to this effecte
viz. de profundis pro defunctis lett vs pray for o*ur* deere Lord that died this
present day Now blessed be his body & his bones I hope his legg*es* are hotter   25
then gravestones And to that hope letts all conclude[e] it then, both Men &
Woemen pray & say amen And further this def*endant* saieth that he did then,
vtter some other word*es* w*hi*ch he doth not now ∧⌜certenly⌝ re*mem*ber And
that the s*aie*d Talboys Dymocke was the Inventer of the matters afores*aie*d
And that he this def*endant* at the tyme afores*aie*d did read a text w*hi*ch he saied   30
was taken out of the 22 chapter of the booke of Hetroclites w*hi*ch text was
Cesar dando, sublevando, ignoscendo gloriam adeptus est & the same he
this def*endant* | devided into three p*art*es viz. ∧⌜the first⌝ Bayard*es* leape ∧⌜on⌝
[of] Ancaster heathe ∧⌜the second⌝ the Bolders stone in Bullingbrooke ffenne
And the third the more Knaves the honester Men And at the same tyme also   35
he this def*endant* in merrie termes made mention of mr Gedney of Ancaster
But he this def*endant* did not say that his Text was taken owt of the booke
of Mabb [nor doth furth*er* ⟨...⟩] as is supposed.

...

31/ Hetroclites: *first* e *corrected over* i

sheet [14]   *(Response to the tenth interrogatory)*

…But in this last Sommer there was a ryme (which was made by Talboys
dymocke as this defendant thinketh) sett vpp vpon the May pole in kyme
and likewise in other yeres before this defendant hath knowne at some   5
tymes one Ryme and at some tymes another Ryme sett vp vpon the May
poles in kyme…

1601/2
Interrogatories for Witnesses ex parte Lincoln   TNA: PRO STAC 5/L34/37   10
sheets [7–7v]   *(before 18 February)*
…

1   Imprimis whither were you at Kyme in the Countye of Lincoln in or
     about the moneth of Awgust last past, and on what day of Awgust to your
     remembrance were you, and diuers others, invited to kyme to a venison   15
     feast there, and by whome, were you and they so invited at whose howse
     were you intertayned in kyme to eate your venison, whither was the same
     on a Sonnday or not, to what end were you and others so invited, as veryly
     thinke was yt not of purpose to see a play played there that day. by Tailbos
     dymock & others. yea or no/?   20

2   Item whither did Tailbos dymock come to you and others ∧⌈so then & there⌉
     assembled at Kyme at one Cradokes howse whilst you were at dynner and
     told you and thothers, that you shold see A play played that daye in the
     afternoone/ whither was yt so played or not, who by name were present at   25
     the acting theireof or who were actors therein and howe many persones and
     to what number were that day assembled to see the said play. whither did
     you heare some so assembled or whoe by name, and seing the said play
     to dislike greatly thereof in respect the Earle of Lincoln was to planely
     demonstrated represented or named therein, or what words did they or any   30
     of them then vse, did not they or some of them, then hold vppe their hands
     and say the play was to bad, & to playne and did not they then departe
     before the play was ended as seeming to be ashamed to heare the same,
     and what be their names

                                                                             35
3   Item where was the said plaie acted, and whoe by name acted the same, &
     in what place in the said Towne, how nere vnto Sir Edward dymockes howse
     in kyme, was the said play acted whether might soch as were within the
     said Sir Edwards howse there look ⌈to⌉ the place or see or heare the said
     actours play their partes, whither was Sir Edward and his Lady then at   40
     kyme house, whither did any or whoe by name did come from them, or
     ether of them, to the said players, or was their any that caried message, or

intercourses betwixt the said *Sir* Edward or his Lady, and the said Act*ours* during the act*ours* of the said playe

4   Item whith*er* did Tailbos dymock bring into the Company of you and oth*ers* being at dynner at kyme vppon the said Sonday one yong Crawdok sonne   5 to the said Iohn Cradoke yo*ur* host arrayed in a piebald Cote. And did not the said Tailbos then vtter theis speeches or the like in effect vid*elicet* that the said Cradok*es* sonne was he whome his the said Tailbos good vnkle (meaning the Earle of Lincoln,) had called Piebald knave, at Conesbye w*i*thin a shorte tyme before. And whith*er* do you knowe or haue you heard, that   10 there was some riott misrule or misdemeano*ur* comitted at Conesbye w*i*thin a shorte tyme then before by the said Tailbos dymock yong Crawdoke and others And was not the said yong Craddoke then likewise apparreled in a piebald cote or not & was not the said riott misrule & misdemeano*ur* so by them comytted [the] at Conesby on a sonnday likewise as you knowe   15 or haue heard.

5   Item what p*ar*te did the said Tailbos dymock plaie in the said play, what speech did he vse therein did he not therein towche the compl*ainant* in diu*ers* qualityes, naming hym by name, & did not the said Tailbos ther Counterfeyt   20 the manner speeche [&] gesture & behauio*ur* of the compl*ainant* saying he was like vnto hym/ and was not the said Tailbos so representing the said Compl*ainant* in the said play fetched away by one Byard who played the devill*es* p*ar*te in the said play/ yea or no/

25

6   Item what p*ar*te did the said Byard play in the said play. whith*er* did he act the devill*es* p*ar*te or not and the fooles p*ar*te also, And in playing the fooles p*ar*te did he not make his will & gyue his wooden dagger to the nowe Compl*ainant* by name, and his cockscombe and bable to those that were afraid to goe to horncastle yea or noe/ And whith*er* haue you heard, or do   30 you knowe, that the said Byard since the acting of the said play, reported to Antony malyn & oth*ers* in heckington, that *Sir* Edward dymock & Tailbos dymock were a seuinnight or a fortnight together about the pennyng of the said play. or what word*es* did the said Byard vse to that or the like in effect   35

7   Item what p*ar*te played the said Iohn Cradock theld*er*, in the said play whith*er* was there a pulpitt errected and fixed vnto A maypoole sett vppe in the grene where the said play was acted whith*er* did the said Cradoke playe the p*ar*te of a mynester, and was arrayed in a black gowne and had a Corn*er* capp &   40

2/ actours: *for* acting (?)   33/ seuinnight: *7 minims in* MS

a counterfeyt beard yea or no/ whether had the said Cradock a pott of Ale or
beare for his hower glasse what speeches did he vtter to your rememberance
what was his text, how was the same devided, or howe much thereof do you
nowe remember/

8   Item was there not a speeche or dirge song by one dicconson and by the
     other actours in the said play what was theffect of the said dirge, was not the
     names of diuers weomen of good fame, as well as women of lewd behauior
     therein recyted, & did not the said actours at the Concluding of euerye name,
     sing ora pro nobis or what can you remember therof/

9   Item whither haue you not sene At the tyme of the play and synce a pasquill
     or libell writen vpon a bord fixed to the maypoll what was theffect of the
     libell, whither was there not the picture of the bull paynted ouer the said
     libell, or not/ whither doth Sir Edward giue the bull for his crest, or cognizance,
     and the complainant the greyhound for his crest or cognizance. And haue
     you not heard that the Complainant, a litle before, bought a howse & certeyne
     groundes of Ambrose marshe in kyme aforesaid |

10   Item whither are you Anthony newlove willie Skotchey Anthony Malyn and
     william willughby or any of you or euer were followers seruantes or retayners
     to the Complainant or hold any land of hym yea or no/ And haue not you
     or some of you bene threatned by Sir Edward dymock or some other of his
     name or by his appoyntement since the acting of the said play for devulgating
     thereof or for that yow haue spoken in dislike thereof/ yea or no

11   Item do you knowe that Sir Edward dymock orre Tailbos dymock at any
     tyme heretofore haue published framed or deuised any prophane writing
     Cartell libell or bookes ether against the nowe Complainant, or any other
     & against whome by name where were the said Cartelles Prophane writinges
     or libelles or any of them sett vppe, or caused to be sett vppe & published
     & by whome & by whose direction

12   Item haue you not seen nor heard of a prophane Sermon or libell hertofore
     contryved and published by the said Sir Edward & Tailbos dymock where
     was the same published howe long synce and by whome was yt published
     what was theffect thereof was not the said prophane speeche Sermon or
     libell and the dirge and other irreligious ⌈actes⌉ in this play formerly
     conteyned in theis interrogatories all one and the same in substance as you
     veryly beleue

5

10

15

20

25

30

35

40

10/ ora pro nobis: *written in display script*

Depositions of Witnesses ex parte Lincoln   TNA: PRO STAC 5/L34/37
sheets [1–4v]   *(18 February) (Deposition of William Scotchye, aged 40,
yeoman, of Heckington)*

...

1   ∧⌐To the first¬ Interrogatorie ∧⌐he¬ saith That he ⌐this dep*onent*¬ & divers   5
others were at Kyme in the Countie of lincoln vpon A Sabothe Daye in
August laste past to the whiche place he this ∧⌐dep*onent*¬ [Examinate]
Amongst divers others [were] ∧⌐was¬ Invited to one Iohn Cradocks howse
thelder ∧⌐[being]¬ ∧⌐servant to S*ir* Edward Dymocke¬ [bay] bailiffe of the
wapentake of Aswardhorne¬ to A venison feast & as he this ∧⌐dep*onent*¬   10
[Examinat] thinketh to se the playe which was Played the Same Daye after
Dinner by Taylboys Dymoke & others

2   To the second Interrogatorie this [Examinate] ∧⌐dep*onent*¬ saithe that ⌐mr¬
Tailboys Dymoke Did Come vnto him & others ∧⌐so¬ Assembled at Cradocks   15
howse in Dinner time on the said Sondaye & there tould this [Examinate]
∧⌐dep*onent*¬ & the Rest that they should se the Deathe of the lorde of kyme
playd that Daye | which was playd the same Daye accordingly & there
were pr*esent* at it will*ia*m willoughbie Antony malin Edward newlove Iohn
Raystridge Thomas wheldayle one Mr Shute one Mr Campanitt one lowrence   20
white of louthe he this [Examinat] ∧⌐dep*onent*¬ & thre or foure Hundred
others besydes as he this [Examinat] ∧⌐dep*onent*¬ thinketh & Also this
[Examinat] ∧⌐dep*onent*¬ saith that he did heare some of the Assembly *videlicet*
will*ia*m willoughbie Antony malin Iohn Raystige Edward newlove Thomas
Wheldale of howell & others speak these & suche lyke words ∧⌐*videlicet*¬ .   25
ffye for shame this is to bad, & to playne, yf therle of lincoln take this he
will take Any thinge, & more to this Interrogato⟨...⟩ he Cannot Depose

3   To the third Interrogatorie this ∧⌐dep*onent*¬ [Examinate] saith that the saide
play was acted by ∧⌐mr¬ Taylboys Dymoke Iohn Cradoke thelder Iohn   30
Cradoke the yonger Roger byard ∧⌐&¬ Marmaduke Diconson vpon A grene
neare | vnto S*ir* Edward Dymoke his Howse & that S*ir* Edward Dymoke
was ∧⌐then¬ at home in his Howse as this ∧⌐dep*onent*¬ [Examinate] was
Informed & more to this Interrogotorie he Cannot Depose

35

4   To the ffourthe Interragotorie this ∧⌐dep*onent*¬ [Examinate] saith that ∧⌐mr¬
Taylboys Dymoke & Iohn Cradoke the yonger did Come in to the saide
Cradoks howse this ∧⌐dep*onent*¬ [Examinat] & others beinge at Diner (the
said yonge Cradoke beinge in A pybald Cote) ∧⌐& that¬ the said Taylboys
then vsing ∧⌐vsed¬ these speyches ∧⌐viz.¬ this is he which my good vncle   40

27/ Interrogato⟨...⟩: *letters at edge of page missing*

therle of lincoln Called pybald Knave at Cunesbie [A shorte time before &
further saithe] ∧⌜[said And sayth] And further this dep*onent* sayth⌝ that he
did heare that there was verie ill Rule at Conisbie on A Sondaye before &
that yonge Cradoke was there in A pybald Cote & that [one Mr Pagett]
∧⌜the s*aid*⌝ Compl*ain*ant did there Cale the said Cradoke pybald knave for   5
that they did hinder the said Compl*ain*ant to Ryde on his waye by Reson
of there drumes & other noyes ∧⌜as this [Examit] ⌜dep*onent*⌝ was Informed⌝
& further to this Interragotrie he Cannot depose |

5   To the fifte Interragatorie this [Examinat] ∧⌜dep*onent*⌝ saith that [the] Taylboys   10
     Dymoke Did play A p*art*e in the said play in which p*art*e he named therle
     of lincoln ∧⌜&⌝ Conterfeatid the said Earle in speche gesture & behavior
     ∧⌜to the vnderstading of this ∧⌜dep*onent*⌝ ⌜[Exam*in*at]⌝⌝ [defendant] saing
     ∧⌜also⌝ he was lyke vnto the Compl*ain*ant ⌜And⌝ [&] that the said Taylboys
     dymoke after he had ended his said speche was fetched Awaye by one byard   15
     who then ∧⌜plaid⌝ [pl*a*yd] the Devills p*art*e in the saide play & further to
     this Interrogatorie he Cannot Depose

6   To the Sixt Interrogatorie this [Examinat] ∧⌜dep*onent*⌝ saithe that the said
     byard Did play the Devils p*art*e & allso the fooles p*art*e & in playinge the   20
     fooles p*art*e did make his will & therby did bequeath his wooden dagger
     ∧⌜to⌝ the Earle of lincoln by name & his Coxcombe & babble to all those
     that were Afraide to go to Horncastell ∧⌜And⌝ [&] this ∧⌜dep*onent*⌝ [Exam*in*at]
     further saith that Antony malin of heckenton tould him this [Examinat]
     ∧⌜dep*onent*⌝ that the Aforsaid byard Confessed to ∧⌜hym⌝ the said Antony   25
     malin Sins the Acting of the said play that S*ir* Edward dymoke & ∧⌜mr⌝
     Taylboys dymoke were A ∧⌜sevenight⌝ [sennett] or | more in peninge of
     the said play & further to this Interragat⟨...⟩ he Cannot Depose

7   To the seventhe Interragatori this ∧⌜dep*onent*⌝ [Examinat] saith that the said   30
     Iohn Cradoke thelder did play ∧⌜& counterfaite⌝ the p*art*e of A minister in
     the said play beinge Arayed in A blacke gowne & having A blacke [Conerd]
     ∧⌜Cornered⌝ Capp & A Counterfeat beard & standing in A pulpitt fixed to
     the maypole ∧⌜on kyme greene⌝ having [t] then & there A pott of Ale or
     beare hanginge by him in steade of an hower glase wherof the said Cradoke   35
     Did Drinke at the Concluding of Any poynte or p*art*e ∧⌜of his speech⌝
     having also A booke in his hand wheron he did Read A text whiche was

3/ Conisbie: *4 minims in* MS
12/ Conterfeatid: id *corrected over* ing
13/ vnderstading: *for* vnderstanding; *abbreviation mark missing*
27/ peninge: *4 minims in* MS

taken as he said owt of the [heterocles] ⌈heteroclites⌉ or the booke of mabb
whiche text this [Examinat] ⌈dep*onent*⌉ dothe not nowe Reme*m*ber but
saith the said Caradoke devided it into thre p*ar*ts viz. the first the loder stone
in bullingbrocke fenn the Second byard leape on Ancaster heathe the third
the more knaves the honester men wherin he spake | of ould gedney of   5
Ancaster & Henrie of bullingbrooke & further to this Interrogatorie this
[Examinat] ₌⌈dep*onent*⌉ Cannot Depose

8   To the eight Interrogatori this [Examnte] ₌⌈dep*onent*⌉ saith that Marmaduke
Diconson with ₌⌈mr⌉ Taylboys Dymoke & the Rest of the Actors Did sing   10
A Dirge wherin they Reconed vp as it semed Divers lewd women in ₌⌈&
about london⌉ [london] Lincoln & boston ₌⌈with some other ₌⌈also⌉ of
good fame & reporte⌉ Concluding After Everie one of there names ora
pro nobis & further to this Interrogatori this ₌⌈dep*onent*⌉ [Examinate]
Cannot Depose   15

9   To the ninthe Interrogatori this ₌⌈dep*onent*⌉ [Examinat] saith that at the time
of the said play & [Sins] synce, he hath sene A Cord fixed to the maypole
wheron was written these words ffollowing viz
the bandoge now tom bull Comes to our towne   20
and sweares by Hambroughe Marche & muche Adoo
to ₌⌈signorize⌉ [seignorize] to seate & sitt him downe
this marche must marshall him & his whelpes too |
But lett them Heed tom bull for yf they sturr
ile make it but A Kennell for A Curr   25

[&] ₌⌈And⌉ Also this [Examinat] ₌⌈dep*onent*⌉ saithe that there was A white
bull paynted vpon the same bord over the said verses & further this [Examinat]
₌⌈dep*onent*⌉ hath Credibly heard that the said Earle of lincoln About that
time did ₌⌈buy⌉ [by] Certen Howses & grownds of one Ambrose marshe   30
in kyme Aforsaid [⟨.⟩] ₌⌈And⌉ further to this Intorgatori this ₌⌈dep*onent*⌉
[Examinat] Cannot depose

10 · To the tenthe Interrogatorie this [Examinat] ₌⌈dep*onent*⌉ saith that nether
him selfe ₌⌈nor⌉ Antony malin nor Antony newlove are Servants Reteners   35
₌⌈vnto⌉ nor ₌⌈ever did⌉ hould Any land of therle of lincoln to his Knowledge
& further saith that will*ia*m willoughbie Reteneth to Mr Rob*er*t Carre of
Aswarbie Esquire & further this [Examinat] ⌈dep*onent*⌉ saith that since the
Acting of the said play ₌⌈he this [Ex*amina*t] ₌⌈dep*onent*⌉ hath byn enformed
that⌉ one Rob*er*t horsman hath Reported to Antony malin Aforsaid &   40

13–14/ ora pro nobis: *written in display script*

others that [this] he | the said horsman would not be in this [Examinat]
ᴧ⌜deponentes⌝ Cote for xl li. with other threatning words Aledging that Sir
Edwarde Dymoke was Informed that ᴧ⌜he⌝ this [Examinat] ᴧ⌜deponent⌝ was
the only man that had [aiquanted] ᴧ⌜acquainted⌝ the said Earle of lincoln
with the maner of the said play [&] ᴧ⌜And he sayth⌝ also yat one Iohn   5
Goodyeare & ᴧ⌜Divers others⌝ [hath] ᴧ⌜haue⌝ given owt threatnynge speches
Agaynst ᴧ⌜hym⌝ this [Examinat] ᴧ⌜deponent⌝ lykewyse ᴧ⌜to that effect⌝ by
Reson wherof he [is de] ᴧ⌜this deponent⌝ verily thinketh that he hath bene
Iniuriously dealt withall ᴧ⌜of late in the Countrie⌝ & is Afrayde of further
danger hearafter & further [this Examinat] to this Interrogatori ᴧ⌜he⌝ [ht]   10
Cannot Depose

(signed) william Scochye

sheets [5–5v]   *(Deposition of Robert Hychcock, aged 50, cleric, of Quarrington)*   15
…
To the xjʳʰ Interrogatory ᴧ⌜he⌝ sayeth that he this ᴧ⌜deponent⌝ [examinate],
abowt vj yeres since [or there abowte], did see sett vpp & fastened, vppon
the Sessions Dore at Slyford, one the markett Day & Sessions Day there, A
bill of defyaunce, (As he this [examinate] ᴧ⌜deponent⌝ conceived & collected   20
vppon some circumstaunces) to bee against the nowe Lord Clincton, in
which bill (to the nowe remembraunce) of this ᴧ⌜deponent⌝ [examinate])
the intended person of the said bill was called Cockoldes bratt, bastard, the
sonne of a whore or to such purpose, ᴧ⌜with⌝ other most vild termes. And
farther this tumultuous bill, did give the lye to some intended person, &   25
chalenged the feeld to fight with him, & this bill was subscribed with the
name of Sir Edward Dymock/ Also this ᴧ⌜deponent⌝ [examinate] heard
credibly, that the like bill was sett vpp at louth/ Lastly this ᴧ⌜deponent⌝
[examinate] did heare credibly that Talboys Dymock, Did come vppon [vppon]
a tyme abowte three yeres since, when the preacher was in the pulpitt, praying 30
& preaching, At A place called Billing borowe, & Did then much disturb the
preacher, by speaking to him many opprobrious wordes, viz. why doest thow
not pray for the good Erle of lincolne he hath as much nede to bee prayed
for as any other, to the greate disquiett of the preacher & congregacion &
more this ᴧ⌜deponent⌝ [examinate] cannot saye to this Interrogatory | 35

To the xijᵗʰ Interrogatory this ᴧ⌜deponent⌝ [examinate] sayeth that he heard
yt Reported by Mr Rychard Enderbye at Dynner tyme in Mr Edward kinges
howse A iustice of peace in lincolneshire, abowte Christmas last past was

2/ threatning: *3 minims in* MS
22/ remembraunce) … [examinate]): *first*) *superfluous*

two yeres/ That S*ir* Edward Dymock together with Talbois Dymoock had
contrived, & fframed A fabulous matter in forme of A Sermo*n*, & that the
same was preached at Screlesby in the presence of the said S*ir* Edward,
& A nomber of gentleme*n* there assembled in A pulpitt by A minister as he
remembreth or one that counterfayted ˄⌈to be⌉ a minister/ whereat many   5
well affected in religio*n*, were much offended & supposed that S*ir* Edward
did yt in derysio*n* of preaching. And this [examin*a*t] ˄⌈dep*onent*⌉ verely
thincketh; & hath heard that the same Sermo*n* was in many thing*es* like vnto
another Sermo*n* w*hi*ch was since made one Kyme Greene, many circu*m*stances,
concurring to induce him this ˄⌈dep*onent*⌉ [examinate], soe to thinck &   10
namely amongst others, for that they were both of the storye of mabb &
of Ankaster heath, & of old Gedney/ Bysides this ˄⌈dep*onent*⌉ [examinate],
did at the same tyme, see in the said mr Enderbyes handes, A coppye of the
said former Sermo*n*, w*hi*ch he the said mr Enderbye did openly shewe forth
at the table, in mr King*es* house aforesaid All w*hi*ch manner of counterfaicting,   15
was by many godly ministers held to bee very blasephemous & manifest
abuse of the word of god, & religio*n* nowe established/. And more to this
Interrogatorye this ˄⌈dep*onent*⌉ [examinate] cannot say/
(signed) Robert Hickcock

                                                                                  20

1602

Interrogatories for Sir Edward Dymoke   TNA: PRO STAC 5/L1/29
sheet [17]*

        …

1   Imp*ri*mis whith*er* doe you knowe that in or about the moneth of August   25
    last past there was an Enterlude libell or stage play acted at Sowth kyme in
    the Countye of Lincoln by Tailbos Dymock Iohn Crawdoke theld*er* Iohn
    Crawdock yong*er* marmaduke dicconson Iohn Byard & others, or by whome
    was the said plaie or interlude so played, and what was theffect thereof to
    yo*ur* nowe remembrance   30

2   It*em* whither did you knowe or had notice or intelligence of the same
    play or was pryvye to the making framing or devising of the said libell
    enterlude or stage play, at any tyme before the acting & publishing thereof
    by thaforenamed Actors, or any oth*er* p*er*son or p*er*sones, their or any of   35
    their fellowes assistant*es* in the same or any oth*er*s/ and when did you first
    knowe thereof. whither did Tailbos dymock desire yo*ur* helpe or vse yo*ur*
    aduise in the Contryving of the said writing Ryme sett vpon the Maypolle,
    or in any p*ar*te of the said playe yea or no/

2/ A²: *corrected over* S
5/ counterfayted: d *corrected over* th

3   Item whither after the tyme of thacting of the said play were you at southkyme
    whither did one Richard Shute or any other resort to the said play & enforme
    you therof, whilst the said playe was in playinge, or any tyme before or after
    and what speeches were vsed to you concerning the play aforesaid whither
    did you punishe the said Actours yea or no./ for playing of the said play or   5
    setting vppe the said libell, And whither was was yt playde vpon a Sunday
    or not and whither was the same play acted with your pryvyte or concent
    or not/.

4   Item whither did you gyve venison to any person or persones to be eaten at   10
    kyme that day or gaue concent to the Invyting & drawing together of dyvers
    numbers of persones of the neghbor Townes adioyning to kyme aforesaid, to
    come to kyme, to a venison feast there, And whither was the said play acted
    in theafternone of the same day. or to what ende was the said persones so
    by you or any other by your assent invited, whither came they to kyme or   15
    not, accordinglye. .

5   Item whither did any of your seruantes during the tyme of the said play goe
    from your house to the said play and returne from thence and geue you
    intelligence of the matter and manner of the said play. And if they did   20
    whither did you alerte thereof or not./ And whye did not you forbid the
    perseuerance and furder acting of the said play. And who by name did you
    send speak to, or comand to forbyd the said Actors for playing, when you
    did heare thereof./

                                                                                    25

Interrogatories for Roger Bayard   TNA: PRO STAC 5/L1/29
sheet [18]
...

1   Imprimis whither do you knowe that there was An Enterlud or play acted
    at South kyme in or about the monthe of [of] August last past by whome   30
    was the said ˄⌈play⌉ played whither was yt plaied on a sonday or not,
    what parte or partes did you play therein, who procured you to be ˄⌈an⌉
    actor therein

2   Item whither did you report to one Anthony Malyn of Heckington or any   35
    other since the acting of the said play That Sir Edward dymock & Tailbos
    Dymock, were a sevennight or a fortnighte together about the pennyng or
    contryving of the said play And how knowe you the same to be true

3   Item what speches hath the said Sir Edward Dymock vsed to you, afore or   40

6/ was was: *dittography*   22/ who: *corrected over other letters, the first of which is R*

since the acting of the said play conc*er*ning the said playe whith*er* did Tailbos
ᴧ⌈or any oth*er*⌉ speake to you in S*ir* Edwards name, to be an actor therein,
And Did not the said Tailbos tell you that both S*ir* Edward and my Lady
Dymock wold be at the said play, to see the same acted: or not   5

4   It*em* whither did you in the acting of the said play and in playing the p*ar*te
of the foole therein, say: that he yo*ur* wooden dagger shold haue, that called
the Lord of kyme pye-bald knave, whither did the said Tailbos Dymock then
ᴧ⌈openly⌉ say that he that soe called the Lord of kyme pyebald knave, was
his the s*ai*d Tailbos good vnckle, the Earle of Lincoln, the nowe compl*ainan*t   10

5   It*em* whoe gaue the venyson, that was eaten, at a feast made that Day at one
Crawdock*es* house, whither Did S*ir* Eduard dymock knowe of the said feast
& play, [and] that shold be and was that Day, whither was S*ir* Edward pryuye
to the invityng of the guest*es* that came thither that day   15

6   It*em* whither was there a libell or writing putt vppe or clymmed vpon a bord,
that was fixed to the maypoell, that day/ who made or contryved the said
libell whither was the same made by Tailbos Dymock. and w*i*th the pryvyte
of the said S*ir* Eduard Dymock or not/ what was theffect of the said libell   20
or writing soe clymmed vppe vpon the maypowle, to yo*ur* remembrance
(whether ys yt yet vpon the said Maypoll or not/

7   It*em* whither haue you bene directed by S*ir* Edward Dymock ᴧ⌈Leon*ar*d
Bawtrie⌉ or any other, what you shold answere to theis or any other   25
Interrogatory exhibited by the Compl*ainan*t. and what instructiones did
he gyve you/

Examinations of Defendants in Lincoln v. Dymoke, Bayard, et al
     TNA: ᴘʀᴏ STAC 5/L1/29   30
     sheets [19–20]   *(7 April) (Examination of Roger Bayard, aged 31, cooper, of
     South Kyme)*
     …
1   To the first Interr*ogatory* he saieth That there was a play or Interlude (to make
ann ende of a maygame) played at Southkyme aboute the moneth of August 35
menconed in the Interr*ogatory* acted or played by this Exam*inate* Mr Talboyes
Dimock Iohn Cradock the younger and Marmaduke Dickonson and saieth
it was played vppon a sonndaye and saieth that he this exam*inate* played the

22/ (whether … not/: *virgule used as closing parenthesis*
36/ menconed: *for* men*c*ioned; *abbreviation mark missing*

Cloundes parte and the Divelles and he saieth That Mr Talbyes Dimock did procure him to be ann actor and gave him the partes

2   To the second Interrogatory he saieth that he Did not reporte to Anthony Melling of Heckinghtonn in the Interrogatory mencionid nor anie other   5 since the acting of the said play That Sir Edward Dymock & Talboyes Dimock was a seavennight or a fortenight to gether aboute the peninge & Contriving the said play and more to this Interrogatory he can not Depose

3   To the third interrogatory he saieth that Sir Edward Dimock vsed noe speches   10 to this examinate eather before the play or since the actinge therof Concerninge the saide playe And that Talboyes Dimock nor anie other did | euer speake to this Examinate in Sir Edwardes name to be an actor in the said play Neather did the said Talboyes Dimick tell this Examinate that eather Sir Edward Dimock or the Ladie Dimock wold be at the same play   15

4   To the iiijᵗʰ Interrogatory he saieth that he did vse these wordes in playinge the partes of the Clounde or foole videlicet My wodden dagger that same Lord sholl haue, that called my Lord of Kyme a pybalde knaue/ But this Examinate Denieth that he Did here Talboyes Dimock then say that he   20 that called the Lord of kyme pybalde knaue was his good vnckle the Earle of Lincoln

5   To the vᵗʰ Interrogatory he saieth he cannot Depose

   25

6   To the vjᵗʰ Interrogatory he saieth ther was not any libell[s] or writeinge sett vppon aborde with a writeinge vppon it fixed vppon the may poole that day the play was acted but there was a borde with a writeing vppon it fixed vppon the may poole when the may pole was sett vpp, but who made the libell or writeinge he knoweth not/ But he saieth that the wordes that are   30 fixed vppon the maypole to his Remembrance are these videlicet. The bandogge now Tom bull comes to oure towne, and sweres by Hambrough march & much a doe. To signorize, to seate, & sett him downe: But this march shall marshall him and his whelpes toe: But lett him heede Tom bull for yf they sturr. Ile make him but a kennell for a curr: But the said writing was not made   35 by Talboyes Dimock or by the privitye of Sir Edward Dimock to his knowledge

7   To the vijᵗʰ Interrogatory he saieth he hath not receiued anie instructions or bene Directed by Sir Edward Dimock Mr Bawtre or anye others what answers he should mak to the said Interrogatories/ or anie otheres/   40

18–19/ My ... knaue: *in display script*   31–5/ The ... curr:: *in display script*

1602/3

Interrogatories for Marmaduke Dickinson   TNA: PRO STAC 5/L1/29
sheet [28]*   *(before 11 February)*

…

3   Item whether was the said Libell or stage Play after the Making thereof   5
Acted or plaied at kime afforesaid & by what persons was the same Acted
whither was not the same Plaied vppon a Green next adioyning to the House
of the said Sir Edward dimock at kime afforesaid Neare to the maypole
then standinge vppon the said Greene, whether was ye same done by the
solitCitacion priuity, or procurement of the said Sir Edward dimock, And   10
what Nomber of Persons were assembled there at the Acting of the said
Libell, or stage Play, And what were the Names of as many as you doe knowe

4   Item whether in the Acting of the said Libell or Stage did any person and
what is his Name Counterfett & take vppon him the person of the said   15
Complainant and his speeches and gesture meaning the Complainant his
good vncle the Earle of Lincoln, And whether was the same done in scornfull
manner or Not

…

8   Item whether in the ending of the stage play was there not one person & who   20
was the said person that was attired in a garment like a ministers garment
hauing a Corner Capp on his hedd & a Booke in his hand opened whether
was not there a Pulpitt maid of Purpose, And Did not the said person
representing a Minister in the said Pullpitt deliuer & vtter a prophane
Irreligious praier: And what was the said Prayer & who was the Inventour   25
and Maker therof, And did not the said person representing ye person of the
minister reade a Text out of the Booke which Text as he said was taken out
of the Booke of Mabb And what was the text he soe Redd, And whether did
not the said Pretendid Minister, deuide his protended Text into Thre Partes,
viz. ffirst the loodes stone in Bullingbrook ffor the second Bayardes Leape of   30
Ancaster heath, And what was the third he said he Could nott Tell But Badd
them goe to Mr Gedney of Ancaster heath for he Could tell & what else did
the said pretendid Minister further say at that time speake your knowledge

9   Item whether during the time of the said stage Play did not diuers of the   35
servantes & ffreindes of the said Sir Edward dimock goe & Come from the
then house of the said Sir Edward dimock in kime, afforesaid to the said

10/ solitCitacion: *for* solicitation; *line ending divides word after* solit
14/ Stage: *for* Stage play
23, 25, 26/ a Pulpitt maid o, Irreligious praier, representing ye person o: *written over multiline erasure in*
   darker ink and smaller script
29/ protended: *for* pretended

stage Play how farr distaunt was the said *Sir* Edward*es* Howse from the
Place where the Play was plaied & whether was *Sir* E Edward Priuy to the
InterCourses of his said ffreind*es* and servaunt*es* so Passing, And whether
did any of *Sir* Edward*es* said ffreind*es* or servant*es* tell yow, that he the said
Sir Edward and his Laidy were priuy to the same Play, And whether during   5
the time of the Play or before did any of the freind*es* or servant*es* of the said
Sir Edward dimock, sett any stooles and Cushens ready for the said *Sir*
Edward and his Ladye to sitt vppon to heare the Play & whether did yow
heare any of his servant*es* or ffreind*es* say that the said *Sir* Edward and his
Laidy woulde Come furthe to heare the Play & what be their names And   10
whether might not any being in the Howse of the said *Sir* Edward see the
said play plaied or nott, And is nott the Greene where the said Play was
played next adioyninge to the vtter Court of the said *Sir* Edward*es* dimock*es*
howse or Nott:

15

10   Item whether did not Tailboys dimock deliu*er* yow the dirige in the Play a
       fortnight before the said play was played or how longe before did he deliuer
       yt to yow, And whether did not the said Tailboys Dimock will yow to gett
       the said dirige perfectly by memory, & whether did he that plaied the fooles
       parte or the Deuills part, or both say these word*es* ffollowing Viz., he my   20
       woodden dagger shall haue that Called the Lord of kime Piebald Knaue
       & whether did not Tailboys dimocke vppon thease speeches manifest &
       explaine to the People assembled that he to whome the woodden dagger
       was bequeathed was the Now Earle of Lincoln this Compl*ainan*t And whether
       did not the said Tailboys dimock Promis to geue yow money to beare yo*ur*   25
       Charges to London about this suite Yea or Noe
       ...

Examination of Marmaduke Dickinson   TNA: PRO STAC 5/L1/29
sheets [1–3v]   *(11 February)*   30
...

To the 1 Interr*ogatory* he saieth that neither this def*endant* nor to his
knowledge anie other by the helpe privity or sollicitation of *Sir* Edward
dymocke or anie other (except Talboys dymock now decesed) did frame
or contrive the [stage] play w*hi*ch was termed or named the death of the   35
Lord of kyme But the *saie*d Talboys dymocke was the onely maker &
contriver thereof for anie thinge this def*endant* knoweth

To the 2. he saieth that there was not to his knowledge anie notification
[thereof] publiquely made of the *saie*d [Stage] Play before the same was   40

2/ E: *false start for* Edward *at end of line*

plaied ∧⌈at kyme vpon the grene there⌉ But divers persons were invited by
Iohn Cradocke thelder to be at kyme vpon a Sonday being as he taketh it
the last of August 1601 to be that day ∧⌈wherein the saied Play was plaied⌉
at dynner at the saied Cradockes house but whether those persons were ∧⌈also⌉
invited to see a Play in the afternoone or not it is more then this defendant   5
doth knowe And saieth that Edward Newlove ∧⌈Thomas whelden Robert
Iackson⌉ william Willoughbie Anthonie Malyn [∧] & diuers others whose
names he doth not remember were that day at dynner at the saied Cradockes
house And more he cannot say to this Interrogatory

                                                                                       10

To the 3. he saieth that in the afternoone of the saied Sonday the saied play
was plaied on a greene in kyme next adioyning to Sir Edward Dymockes |
house [& that Talboys] nere vnto the Maypole standing on the saied grene
& that Talbois dymocke Iohn Cradock thelder Iohn Cradocke the younger
Roger Bayard & he this defendant were the Actors therein And saieth that   15
he doth not knowe that the same was done by the sollicitacion privity or
procurement of Sir Edward dymocke, But the aforesaied Talboys dymock
was the onely procurour ∧⌈& first mover⌉ of this defendant to beare a parte
in that Play & because this defendant at the first refused to meddle therewith
the saied Tailboys the rather to move this defendant therevnto then [told]   20
saied to this defendant that his brother Sir Edward dymocke would haue
this defendant to be one of them & that he & his Lady would com & see
the saied Play And further this defendant saieth that there were a bout a
hundred persons assembled at the actinge of the saied Play viz. Iohn Turner,
Iohn Pagett william welborne, Richard Thorpe, Iohn Ebbe Launcelott Newton   25
& diuers others whose names he doth not remember.

To the 4. he saieth that in the actinge of the saied Play the saied Talboys
dymocke did play a parte which did seme to represent the now Complainant,
the saied Talboys counterfeiting & taking vpon him the speches ∧⌈& gesture⌉   30
of the now Complainant And thereby the saied Talboys did as this defendant
thinketh meane the now Complainant in scornefull manner

To the 5. he saieth that the aforesaied Roger Bayard did in the saied stage Play
acte & play the parte of the devill & that he did in the saied Play fetch &   35
carry away the party that | represented the person of the now Complainant

To the 6. Interrogatory he saieth that the saied Roger Bayard did also in the
saied Play acte and play the parte of the vice or ffoole & in actinge of that
parte did declare his last will and testament and then & there the saied   40

3/ 1601: *underlined*

Bayard did bequeath in the presence of the people there assembled [bequeth]
his woodden dagger with these wordes ⌐in Ryme⌐ viz. That Lord shall it
haue which called the Lord of kyme Pibald knave, wherevnto the saied Talbois
aunswered, that the same was his good vncle the now Complainant And
also at the same tyme the saied Bayard did bequeth his Coxecomb & bable   5
vnto all those which would not goe to Hornecastle with Sir Edward dymock
against the now Complainant

To the 7 he saieth that in the acting of the saied Play there was ⌐by the
apointment of the saied Talboys dymocke⌐ a dirige songe by this defendant   10
& that in the same dirige there were the names of some wemen recited but
whether they were lewd & licentious wemen or not or where they dwelled
this defendant doth not know. And saieth that the concluding of the saied
dirige after euery of the names of the saied Wemen was ora pro nobis. and
that he this defendant onely named those wemen by the direccion of the   15
saied Talboys dymocke this defendant not knowinge whether anie of those
wemen were detected or defamed or not neither doth this defendant know
⌐nor hath certenly heard⌐ that Sir Edward dymock was in anie sort privie
therevnto And more he cannot say to the Interrogatory |

20

To the 8 . he saieth that Iohn Cradocke the elder was in the ending of the
saied Play attired in a garment like a ministers garment having a Corner
capp on his head & a book in his hand opened & that certen bordes being
sett vp close to the saied maypole in manner of a pulpitt the saied Cradock
thelder went into the same & there [⟨.⟩] he deliuered some wordes after   25
the manner of a praier but what those wordes were this defendant cannot
|certenly| depose But the Texte which the saied Cradocke then spoke of
was as he saied taken owt of the booke of Mabb & that text he devided
into 3 . partes ⌐viz.⌐ ffirst the bownder stone in Bullingbrooke ffenns, ffor
the second Bayard leape of Ancaster heath And the third he saieth he could   30
not tell but willed the people to goe to mr Gedney of Ancastre for he
could tell But what further matter the saied Cradocke then spake of this
defendant doth not know for he this defendant then departed away from
the Companie

35

To the 9 . he saieth that he doth not know whether diuers of the servantes
& freindes of Sir Edward dymock did goe & com from the then house of
the saied Sir Edward during the tyme of the saied stage play or not, And
further saieth that the house of the saied Sir Edward is distant from the
place where the saied Play was plaied two buttlengths or thereaboutes And   40

30/ saieth: th *corrected from* d

that none of the *servauntes* or ffreind*es* of the *saied* S*i*r Edward dymocke
except the *saied* Talboys dymock as is afore*saied* did tell this defe*ndant* that
the *saied* S*i*r Edward | or his Lady were *p*rivy to the *saied* play But before
the saied play some Cushions & stoles were sett at the same place w*hich* the
saied Talboys dymocke told this defe*ndant* was for S*i*r Edward dymock &   5
his Lady to sitt & see the Play but this defe*ndant* doth not know who did
sett the same there neither did anie other *p*erson besides the *saied* Talboys
tell this defe*ndant* that the *saied* S*i*r Edward or his Lady would com forth
to heare the *saied* Play And furth*er* saieth that if anie were in the topp of
the towre or ∧⌐vpper p*ar*te of the⌐ house of the *saied* Edw*ard* dymocke they   10
might from theare see the *saied* play plaied, & that the greene where the
saied play was plaied is next adioyning to the vtter Co*ur*t of the *saied* S*i*r
Edw*ard* dymock*es* house

To the 10. he saieth that the *saied* Talboys dymocke did deliu*er* this defe*ndant*   15
the dirige w*hich* this defe*ndant* songe in the *saied* play about fortnight before
the same was plaied & then willed this defe*ndant* to gett it *p*erfectly by
memory And more then is afore*saied* he cannot say to this Inter*rog*atory
saving that this tyme 12 . monethes the *saied* Talboys did [giue] promise to
giue this defe*ndant* monie to beare his charges to London about this suit   20

To the 11. he saieth that vpon Sonday the 24th of Ia*nua*ry 1601. he this
defe*ndant* did ∧⌐send worde⌐ vnto the *saied* S*i*r Edward dymocke (for that
he then lay sicke & this defe*ndant* could not speake w*ith* him) to acquainte
him that this defe*ndant* was *se*rved w*ith* a S*u*bpena for singing the dirige in   25
the *saied* Play & that this defe*ndant* was going | to London & therefore
desiered to knowe the *saied* S*i*r Edward*es* pleasure therein what this defe*ndant*
should doe And ∧⌐afterwarde*s*⌐ [therevpon] Henry woodfall *se*rvant to the
saied S*i*r Edward brought this defe*ndant* worde from the *saied* S*i*r Edward
(as the *saied* woodfall then told this defe*ndant*) that S*i*r Edward*es* pleasure   30
was that this defe*ndant* should repaire to one Parre his sollicitor & that Parre
would derecte this defe*ndant* to one mr Bawtree for this defe*ndantes* dispatch
at London in this cause

To the 12. he saieth that he did vpon a Saterday in the afternoone being the   35
xxx^th of Ia*nua*rie 1601 goe to mr Bawtrees chamb*er* in Lincolns Inne according
to the *saied* direc*c*ions given this defe*ndant* by the *saied* woodfall & there
this defe*ndant* did meete w*ith* one Lovell one of the *saied* S*i*r Edward*es*
*se*rva*ntes* att w*hich* tyme the *saied* Lovell called this defe*ndant* badd fellow
∧⌐& knave⌐ saieng that he this defe*ndant* came thither to vndoe his master   40

36/ 1601: *underlined*

& all his servantes & to bewray the doinges of his Master And vpon those
spechcs he this defendant departed from thence And more then is aforesaied
he cannot depose to this Interrogatory .

                                          (signed) marmaduke Dickenson

1610
Sentencing Notes in Lincoln v. Dymoke, Bayard, et al
  Huntington Library: EL 2733 (2)
f [1]   *(4 May)*

	Sir Edward dymocke	
Comes Lyncolne plaintiff	Talboys dymocke	et alii.
	Iohn Cradocke	defendentes

They made a stage playe on a greene before Sir Edwarde Dymockes dore
and Talboys Dymocke personated the Earle in apparell & speeche And after
their playe Iohn Cradocke beinge attyred like a minister wente vpp into a
Pulpit which they had of purpose made & fastened to the Mayepole and
havinge a Booke in his handes did Deliuer and pronounce diuers scurrulous
and vayne matters in manner of a Sermon/ And concluded with a most
blasphemous & graceles Prayer:

          To be [led] lead through westminster hall with papers, and to
          be whipped vnder the Pillorye & then to stande in the pillory

              To acknoweled their offences at the assises:
              To stande in the Pillory and bee whipped.

          Imprisoned duringe the kinges pleasure & fined at 300 li.
          a peece & bounde to good behauiour before enlardgement

       Sir Edwarde Dymocke Committed to the fleete duringe the kinges
       pleasure and fined at 1000 li. for beinge a spectator & pryvie to yt.

          Talboys dymocke was Dead and therfore not sentenced./

Sentences in Lincoln v. Dymoke, Bayard, et al
  Huntington Library: EL 2733 (1)
f [1]   *(4 May)*

          In Camera Stellata .4. Maij
          Anno. 8. Iacobi Regis.

<table>
<tr><td></td><td></td><td>Sir Edwarde Dymocke</td><td></td><td></td></tr>
<tr><td></td><td></td><td>Roger Bayarde</td><td></td><td></td></tr>
<tr><td></td><td>Comes Lincolne plaintiff:</td><td>Iohn Cradocke senior</td><td>defendentes</td><td></td></tr>
<tr><td></td><td></td><td>Iohn Cradock Iunior</td><td></td><td></td></tr>
<tr><td></td><td></td><td>Marmaduke dickenson</td><td></td><td>5</td></tr>
</table>

The offences   ffor a very infamous and libellous Stage plaie, acted on a Sabboath daie vppon a greene before Sir Edwarde dymockes house, in vewe of 300 or 400 persones purposely drawen thither. wherein they personated the said Earle in Apparell, speeche, gesture and name. [to] with much disgrace and infamy: And so grossly That the Standers by. Cryed Shame vppon yt: And after the   10 plaie ended one of them apparelled like a preacher with a booke. went vpp into a pulpitt fastened to the Maypole and vttered prophane and scurrilous matter in manner of a Sermon, Concludinge with a most [prophane] Blasphemous and gracelesse praier: and therevppon [fix] songe a diridge and fyxed a slaunderous Ryme concerninge the Earle on the Mayepole   15 and the Earles Coate of Armes over yt:/

The Sentence   Sir Edward Dymocke. 1000. li. and fleete duringe the kinges pleasure

<table>
<tr><td>Bayard</td><td>}</td><td>300 li. a peece fine: fleete</td><td>20</td></tr>
<tr><td>Cradock senior</td><td></td><td>duringe the kinges pleasure</td><td></td></tr>
<tr><td>Dickenson</td><td>}</td><td>To bee lead throughe westminster</td><td></td></tr>
<tr><td></td><td></td><td>hall with Papers &c. and bee</td><td></td></tr>
<tr><td></td><td></td><td>sett on the Pillory and whipped</td><td></td></tr>
<tr><td></td><td></td><td>To be sett on the Pillory</td><td>25</td></tr>
<tr><td></td><td></td><td>at Lyncolne assises. and</td><td></td></tr>
<tr><td></td><td></td><td>acknoweledge there offences.</td><td></td></tr>
<tr><td></td><td></td><td>to god and the said Earle.</td><td></td></tr>
<tr><td></td><td></td><td>And then be whipped</td><td></td></tr>
<tr><td></td><td></td><td>vnder the pillory</td><td>30</td></tr>
</table>

Cradock Iunior 200. li. fyne. & fleete:/

The lordes present at this Sentence

The lord Chauncelor
The Earle of Northampton   35
The lord Bishop of london.
The lord Zouch
The lord Knowles
The lord Cheiffe Iustice of Englande
The lord Cheiffe Iustice of Common Pleas   40
The lord Cheiff Baron:/

(signed) Thomas Mynall

Fines in Various Suits Involving the Earl of Lincoln and Sir Edward Dymoke Huntington Library: EL 2723

f [1]*

Termino Trinitatis Anno tercio Iacobi Regis   5

2. Comes
Lyncolne
Plaintiff
for Riottes
& other
misdeameanours./

Sir Edwarde Dymocke	M li. & vC li.	mitigated to M markes	
Valentyne Browne knight	M li.	to	vC markes
Brian Elande	C li.	to	l li.
Lionell Massingberde	C markes & x li.	to	xl li.
Thomas Pinchbecke	C markes & x li.	to	xl li.	10
Robertc Hughes	x li. & xl li.	to	xx li.
Roberte Wyldman	x li. & xl li.	to	xx li.
Iames christofer	x li.	to	v li.
Anthonie Robinson	x li.	to	v li.
Henry Woodfall	x li. & xl li.	to	xx li.	15
Iohn Browne	x li. & xl li.	to	xx li.
Iohn Lovell	x li. & xl li.	to	xx li.

Thomas Wardell   x li.
ffrauncys ffowler   x li.
Bartholomewe Roach xl li.   to   xx. markes a peece.   20
Edwarde Dymocke generosus xl li.
Iohn Carsey   xl li.
Richard Cooke   xl li.

The Some   25
mittigated   MCCCxx li.

Off this Sentence Sir Edwarde Dymocke obteyned his maiesties speciall pardoun dated. 26. Iunij .4. Iacobi Regis. aswell of the ffynes for himsclf & the rest as of the Punishmentes:/   30

Termino Pasche Anno quinto Iacobi Regis

Comes
Lyncolne
Plaintiff for
Riottes &
misdeameanours
[(.)]

Sir Edwarde Dymocke	C li.	
William Righton	C li.	35
Iohn Leachman	l li.	Theis fines were
Edwarde Righton	xl li.	mittigated &
Iohn Lovell	xl li.	(as it ∧ ⌐is⌐ said) are
Thomas Pinchbecke	xl li.	paid into the
Iames Christofer	xl li.	eschequer:/ 40
Iohn dedicke	100. li.	

Termino Pasche Anno 8.º Iacobi Regis

Sir Edwarde Dymocke.	M li.	Theis ffynes	
Roger Bayarde	CCC li.	stande [⟨...⟩]	
Iohn Cradocke senior	CCC li.	without mittigation:	
Iohn Cradocke Iunior	CC li.	at all.	
Marmaduke dickenson	CCC li.		5

Comes Lyncolne Plaintiff for a [Riotous] Libellous Stage play (marginal note)

Termino Pasche Anno .8. Iacobi Regis

Comes Lyncolne	M li.		
Iohn Richmonde	CC li.	Theis ffynes	10
Bartholomewe Dawson	CC li.	likewise stande	
Anthonie Willson	CC li.	without any	
George Warde	CC li.	mittigacons at all.	
George Thompson	CC li.		

dymock knight plaintiff for pullinge downe a house in the nighte: (marginal note)

15

SPALDING

c 1541–7

AC   *Spalding Gentlemen's Society Minute Book 1*
   Spalding Gentlemen's Society Museum: Maurice Johnson Papers   20
   f 74v*

   ...

Mommyng Plays (marginal note)

The secretary Communicated some remarkable Extracts from the Church
Wardens accounts of Spalding about the Reformation & a decre of yat Time
off a Bill of Complaints exhibited by the parishioners to ye then Prior of   25
Spalding against himself for Corrupcion & abuses, put upon the Town
against a Compoticion made with Them by his predecesors

Bill of Complaint against ye Lord Prior of Spalding by ye Parishioners (marginal note)

Also the Accounts of a Solemn Pley held in the Gore to See which many
persons of Quality all the Towns in the Neighourhood & Stamford Peterbourg
&c came, this was written & directed by one Howson a prest & was a   30
representacion of the battle between St Michael & the Devill & was a
Tournement with Some Fire Workes & Machines

   ...

A   *Description of a Play in Spalding*   Gooch: *A History of Spalding*   35
   pp 128–9*

   ...

...The following curious record made by Maurice Johnson two hundred years
ago, tells how funds were raised for that purpose in Henry the Eighth's time.

13/ mittigacons: *for* mittigacions; *abbreviation mark missing*
30–2/ this ... Machines: *written in darker ink and a smaller hand*

"In the old acts of the churchwardens of the Parish Church of the Blessed
Virgin St. Mary, in Spalding, there are, amongst others, very large acts of
some plays, which were exhibited here in the Gore against the Great Gate
of the Priory, one of which, uncertain as to time, wanting date, in three
long paper rolls appears to have been very costly and magnificent.   5

"All Lincolnshire and many great towns and much quality in the neighboring
counties, being invited to it by special messengers by billets of baines.

"From about thirty of the towns there were spectators present. It was
contributed to by the Lord Willoughby, the Lady Fitzwilliam, the Champion
Dymocke, the Lady Kyme, Mr. Mann of Bolingbroke, the Lord Bishop of   10
Peterborough (John Chambers, 1541–56), and the City of Peterborough, and
the Burghers of Boston and Stamford, from all of which many were present.

"It seems from the articles of expense such as arms, drums, and much
minstrelsy, besides the Grantham Waits, to have been a manly performance
and sort of Tournament or representation of the War in Heaven and battle   15
between St. Michael and the Devils, with machinery of heaven and hell, much
gunpowder was used in it and bows and staves, headed with iron, and it
seems to have been performed on horseback. There are large allowances for
horsemeal and shoeing horses, It was composed and ordered by Mayster
Howsun, an ingenious priest, and the guests who were foreigners and nobility   20
of the corporations, were treated by the town with comfitts and other cakes,
and with malmsey wine and claret wine.

"The inhabitants had allotments of so many first places measured | out
about the scene of action and paid largely for the same to accommodate
their families and foreign (visiting) friends. It seems to me, by all I can   25
discover, to have been towards the latter end of King Henry the Eighth's
reign, and to have lasted three days in action, besides the rehearsals which are
mentioned, and for which, to have it accurate, the players were fed likewise.

"The principal performer was one Edgoose, who I presume played the
Archangel. There is particular mention made of three tormentors with staves   30
tipped with iron. Much carving and painting, and the place seems to have
been parted off with great poles and cables and much cordage was used
about it.

"N.B. – With great part of the money collected then, the Parish Church
was cleaned and beautified. – M.J."   35

...

1604/5

Bill of Complaint in Jackson et al v. Earle et al   TNA: PRO STAC 8/186/12
sheet 9*   (*8 February*)   40

To the king*es* most excellent Ma*ie*stie
In most humble manner sheweth & informeth yo*u*r most excellent ma*ie*stie

your humble faithfull & obedient Subiect*es* Iohn Iackson of Spalding in yo*ur*
highnes County of Lincoln gent*leman* one of yo*ur* Ma*ies*ties Cheifeconstables
of the wapentake of Ellowe in the part*es* of Holland in the said Countye,
Roger Vincent of Spalding aforesaid yeoma*n* & one of the Pettyconstables
of the said towne for the yeare now last past Iohn Dale of the said towne of   5
Spalding Marcer and one of the Churchwardens of the same towne aswell
for the yeare now last past as also for the yeare now p*re*sent; That whereas
yo*ur* said Subiect*es* have alwaies heretofore lived in good name & fame &
in & w*i*th the good oppinion & creditt not onely of theire neighbours of
the said towne but also w*i*th the Gentlemen and Comission*er*s & other men   10
of the cheifest regard & place in the said part*es*. And ˄⌈whereas⌉ yo*ur* said
Subiect*es* haue not onely heretofore lived honestly in theire private conu*er*sac*i*on
but haue also in theire seu*er*all offices behaved themselues honestly & dutifully
indeavoring by all meanes (as became them) to reforme & suppresse such
vices & offenc*es* as by the dutye of theire seu*er*all offices they were bound   15
to looke vnto. Now soe it is (if it please yo*ur* most excellent Ma*ies*tie) that
one George Earle Edmund Hobson Nicholas Stanwell & Anthony Taylo*ur*
Comon Alehouse & Taverne haunters & of riotous & wastfull behavio*ur*
& condic*i*on and obstinate in theire courses & impatient of any reproofe
or rep*re*henc*i*on, and therevpon conceiuing mallice & hatred against yo*ur*   20
subiect*es* and namely against the said Iohn Iackson & Roger Vincent for that
they would not giue passage & allowance of theire disorders confederating
& combyning themselues together w*i*th diu*er*se others of like condic*i*on &
qualitye (whose names are yet to yo*ur* subiect*es* vnknowne) seeking w*hi*ch
way to deprave & defame yo*ur* said subiect*es*, they the said George Earle   25
Edmund Hobson Nicholas Stanwell & Anthony Taylo*ur* together w*i*th others
(to yo*ur* subiect*es* vnknowne) since yo*ur* ma*ies*ties last gen*er*all p*ar*don haue
devised made written & published abrode, the seu*er*all Libells & slaunderous
Rymes herevnto annexed against yo*ur* said subiect*es* & others, And namely
the said George Earle Edmund Hobson Nicholas Stanwell & Anthony   30
Taylo*ur* (together w*i*th others vnknowne) about Midsomer last past did make,
devise, put in writing publish & spread abrode one of the said Libells &
Rymes subscribed by Thomas tell troth w*illia*m wish yow well, In w*hi*ch
lybell & Ryme yo*ur* said subiect Iohn Iackson is tearmed by the name of the
great God Bacchus w*i*th other reproches therein attributed vnto him, And   35
yo*ur* subiect Roger Vincent is there termed and named by the name of Busye
& p*re*cise clowne foole & Asse & other thing*es*, And yo*ur* subiect Iohn Dale
is there noted & sett out by selling of Pinnes pointes & Laces for that yo*ur*
said subiect is a Mercer by his trade. And likewise sheweth to yo*ur* ma*ies*tie

17/ Earle: *followed by 50mm erasure covered by line filler*
25, 30/ Earle: *followed by 45mm erasure covered by line filler*

your said Subiect Iohn dale that the said George Earle Edmund Hobson
Nicholas Stanwell & Anthony Taylour together with others vnknowne in
the moneth of Aprill last past, did make devise put in writing publish &
spread abroad the other of the said Libells herevnto annexed subscribed
with these wordes per me william &c de Moulton wherein your said subiect   5
is termed by the name of ffoole Asse Pedler & other rayling & reprochfull
termes & phrases, as by the same appeareth./ And further sheweth vnto your
excellent Maiestie your said Subiectes that they the said George Earle Edmund
Hobson Nicholas Stanwell & Anthony Taylour & others vnknowne having
devised made & written the said Libells did (the better to spread abroade   10
& publish the same) not onely read them to diuerse particuler persons but
also did giue & send abroade many coppyes thereof, and did cause the said
Libells to be fixed and sett vpon diuerse doores & postes in the said towne
of Spalding and to be comonly & ordinarily songe in Alehouses & taverns
in the said towne where they did vse to resorte to drinke play & keepe   15
vnrulye & vnthriftye company./ And further sheweth vnto your excellent
Maiestie your said subiect Roger Vincent That whereas your subiect being
then Constable of the said towne of Spalding, had (by vertue of a warrant
directed vnto him from Sir Mathew Gamlyn Knight one of your Maiesties
Iustices of Peace there) the xvjth day of Iune last arrested one for suspicion of 20
fellony whom he carried before the said Sir Mathew Gamlyn to be examined
The said Edmund Hobson meeting your said Subiect (who with the said
prisoner & others were then returning from the said Sir Mathew Gamlyn)
to the intent to discourage your said subiect from that & the like service
did in scornfull & scoffing manner salute your subiect by the name of Busye   25
calling him twice or thrice Busye (by which your said subiect is also termed
& named in the said Libell) to the great disheartening & discouragement of
your said subiect in his said office & reproche before the said prisoner &
others./ And further sheweth & informeth your maiestie your said Subiectes
that the said George Earle Edmund Hobson Nicholas Stanwell & Anthony   30
Taylour, did about the feast of the Nativity of our saviour Christe in the
yeare of our Lord god 1603 devise write & publish one other infamous &
scurrilous Libell of all the Maryed Coples both men & women in the said
towne of Spalding, by theire said Libell making three sortes of women terming
some of them Strikers some others scowldes & the rest fooles whereby they   35
haue not onely slaundered and defamed many honest women but haue sett
& procured discorde & dissencion betwixt diuerse of theire husbandes &
them./ And Lastly sheweth & informeth your maiestie your said Subiectes
that the said George Earle Edmund Hobson Nicholas Stanwell & Anthony
Taylour (not satisfied with these particuler Libells but taking pleasure in   40

1, 8, 30, 39/ Earle: *followed by 50mm erasure covered by line filler*

the idlenes of theire running witt*es* & growing more bould by custome of
Rayling to goe on by degrees from few to many) did about the moneth of
August last past devise write & publish one other moste false infamous &
invectiue Libell or Ryme against one will*ia*m Browne Clarke minister of the
said towne of Spalding and A verye zealous & paynefull preacher of god*es*   5
word there, In w*hi*ch said Libell or Ryme the said will*ia*m Browne (although
his life could never ∧⌈yet⌉ be by any detected) was very slaunderously &
wrongfully abused w*i*th many vndecent vnreu*er*ent & reprochfull termes &
phrases, The content*es* & p*ar*ticulers of w*hi*ch last menconed Libells yo*u*r
said subiect*es* are not able to sett downe for that the coppyes thereof are not   10
as yet come to yo*u*r said subiect*es* hand*es* notw*i*thstanding that they are very
comon amongst theire owne confederates and comonly voyced abrode w*i*thin
the said towne of Spalding./ In tender consideraci*o*n whereof and in regard
that that vnchristean & shamlesse abuse was formerly excepted out of the
gen*er*all & free p*ar*dons graunted aswell by the late·Queene Elizabeth of   15
famous memory as also by others yo*u*r highnes renowned p*re*decessors
as being A most odious offence both to god & Man, and that all these
misdemeano*u*rs were comitted since yo*u*r ma*ie*sties most gratious gen*er*all &
free p*ar*don at yo*u*r ma*ie*sties Coronaci*o*n, and therefore worthley deserre
some exemplary punishm*ent* to be inflicted vpon the said offendors May it   20
therefore please yo*u*r Moste excellent Ma*ie*stie (the p*re*misses considered) to
graunt out yo*u*r Ma*ie*sties most gratious writt of Subpena to be directed to the
said George Earle Edmund Hobson Nicholas Stanwell & Anthony Taylor
comaunding & inioyning them & eu*er*y of them thereby at a c*er*taine day
& vnder a c*er*taine paine therein to be limitted & sett downe p*er*sonally to   25
appeare before yo*u*r most excellent ma*ie*stie in yo*u*r ma*ie*sties high Courte
of Starrechamber then & there to aunswere the p*re*misses and further to be
ordered & censured therein as shalbe by yo*u*r most excellent ma*ie*stie and
yo*u*r Counsell in yo*u*r said Courte thought meete & conveynient: And yo*u*r
said Subiect*es* (according to theire bounden dutyes) shall daylie pray vnto   30
almighty god for the p*re*servaci*o*n of yo*u*r Royall ma*ie*stie in all health &
happines long to live & raigne over vs./
…

Exhibits Attached to the Bill of Complaint   TNA: PRO STAC 8/186/12   35
sheet 7

To his ffrend*es*

5/ A: *corrected over another letter*
9/ menconed: *for* menc*i*oned; *abbreviation*
  mark missing
19/ deserre: *for* deserue
23/ Earle: *followed by 45mm erasure covered by*
  line filler

Thowe franticke asse, mad Pasquill second Mate
whose harte doth harber Malice greife and hate
whose ffolishe muse is exercised ofte tymes
onely in makinge Lybells, Ieastes and rymes

Yet ffreshe in my remembrance doth lye
the grose abuses which vnwittinglye
you in a Paper fraughte with ffoolishe lynes
conteyninge noughte but false reportes & Crymes

Not longe agoe vnto a neighber mine
did publishe in a Libell made in ryme
where thy stageringe muse was much to blame
In that on him she Causeles did Complaine

But leaveinge this suche trifles as they be
In one thinge ffrend lett mee admonishe thee
and that is this noe more to disgrace
this man which Comes of an ancient race

But if it be soe that thy floing Muse
of fforce must be ymployed in abuse
Ile sett ye downe a subiecte ffar more fitt
in whose dispraise you maiste ymploye thy witt
                        yours to replye when you begine
Knowe therefore that there dwelleth in the Towne
an Intermedlinge, and a precise Clowne
his name is buesye one of oulde Benson Breede
ffarr better for to hange then good to ffeede

His Neighbours by a Metapher him Call
Bissye, and whie because his actions all
are always bent vnto this onely end
by fflateringe and Cologinge to offend

He hath the eyes of Lincius for to prye
in all mens actions very waryly
and wheare he fyndes their dealing are not righte
he in the Sessions them will straighte indighte

This yeare hees Iacke in office and doth take
exceedinge paines even for his Conscience sake

hees soe demure soe grave and soe precise
that none muste playe yf he knowe: but he fflyes

To greate God Baccus and doth then reporte
He sawe twoe neighbours vse vnlawefull sporte   5
Tis true he saithe and bindes it with an oathe
and therefore I muste needes present them bothe

This Epicure sittes still with one attes backe
® id est magnus   to whome he saithe, boy fill me a Cupp of sack   10
homo   this nedes doth make the Masse of ffleshe more fatt
then newe milke or ffreshe ffishe will doe a Catt

But leave this humour busie, sease to trudge
for him that meanes to vse thee as a drudge   15
Leave it I saye and quickly or I sweare
Tenn shillinge will not fynde you shewes this yeare

That all men well maye knowe this fawninge asse
® Non ignoratis de. He maried hath a tricke and bonye lasse   20
quo Loquimur   The which not longe agoe I wott did dwell
with him, yat pynns, poyntes, and laeces nowe doth sell./

            yours as wee see reformations of   Thomas tell trothe
            manner   william wishe you well
                                                                            25

sheet 8

Theare is a Pedler in Spalldinge Towne
yat selles pynns and poyntes and mickell geare
he is as proude withoute a gowne   30
is in his ofice evere yeare

His mouthe is a wrye with a hoked nose
his heade is busy in every thinge
He is a brave ffellowe in his owne hose   35
and in every matter he is meddlinge

He huffes he snuffes into ayer
alonge the Streates as he doth passe
The peopell Can saye every wheare   40
yonder goeth a prodigall asse

10–11m/ id … homo: *in display script;* 'that is, a great man'
20–1m/ Non … Loquimur: *in display script;* 'you are not unaware of what we are talking about'

What is he what is he doe I saye
why man I sawe him yesterdaye
goeinge in the Markett place
with a freshe Ierkinge painted with Lace

His wealthe he standeth greatly on
alsoe vppon his Ientrye
awaye awaye foolishe Iohn
Ittes a Callinge not fitt for thee

Manners manners Iohn amend
and gett thy neighbours love againe
Lett theis ffewe lynes which I have pend
warne thee of thy foolishe vaine./

per me William et
de Molto/.

1605
Interrogatories for Defendants in Jackson et al v. Earle et al
   TNA: PRO STAC 8/186/12
   sheet 5*   (8 May)
   …

4 Item wheather did you at any tyme tell wher and of whom you had any of
the said libells, or any coppyes therof, what coppyes were ther made of the
said Libells or any of them, or who to your knowledge had any coppye or
coppyes of them? whether have yow at any time shewed or given forth to any
other any Copye or Copyes of you said libells or any of them yea or no:

5 Item wheather did you about the three and twentyth daye of Apryll last
recite or k⌈n⌉owe that the same libell or libells was recyted in the Markett
place at Spaldinge, or any parte of them or any of them and whoe recyted
the same there?
   …

7 Item wheather did you at any tyme singe or publishe or knowe that the said
libell or libells or any parte of them were sunge or published in any alehowse
or Taverne in the said towne of Spaldin⌈g⌉ or elswhere, wher was the same
sunge or published, and by whom and in whose howse?
   …

27–8/ whether … no: *apparently added later in a smaller script*
28/ you: *for ye*

Examination of George Earle   TNA: PRO STAC 8/186/12
sheet 1v   *(11 May)*

…

To the 4. Interro*gatory* he sayth that ∧⌜abowt half a yeare nowe past as he
remembreth⌝ one Mathewe Scarboroughe gent*leman* an attorney shewed   5
∧⌜& de*liuere*d⌝ vnto this defe*ndant* ∧⌜at his the s*aid* Scarboroughes owne
howse in Spalding afores*aid*⌝ the coppyes of twoe of the ∧⌜s*aid*⌝ libells [in
the bill mencioned]. And ∧⌜after⌝ this defe*ndant* [theruppo*n* dyd wryte] ∧⌜had
[taken] wrytten⌝ coppyes [⟨…⟩] of them, he [de*liuere*d vnto] redelyuered
vnto the s*aid* Scarboroghe the s*aid* coppyes w*hich* this defe*ndant* so receyued   10
of him and ∧⌜afterward*es*⌝ this defe*ndant* [hath] reported ∧⌜in pryvate⌝ vnto
some of his frend*es* the havinge of the s*aid* coppyes of the s*aid* Scarborough &
this defe*ndantes* wrytinge of the said coppyes owt againe. And this defe*ndant*
dyd ∧⌜in pryvat manner⌝ shewe [them to some of his frend*es* shewe the] one
of the s*aid* coppyes (so wrytten by the defe*ndant*) to Iohn Iackso*n* one of   15
the Pl*ainantes* & to some of ∧⌜his⌝ this defe*ndantes* frend*es* [and the same
he sayth he dyd in secrett manner] And [he] ∧⌜this defe*ndant*⌝ denyeth that
he dyd gyve or delyuer any coppyes of the s*aid* libells [or in the bill int⟨…⟩] or
any of them to any p*er*son or p*er*sons. And what ∧⌜or howe many⌝ Coppyes
were made of the s*aid* libells or further to this Int*errogatory* he cannott   20
certenly depose
To the vth Inter*rogatory* he sayeth that he this defe*ndant* dyd not to his
∧⌜vttermost⌝ remembrance about the xxiij^th daye of Aprill laste recyte or
knowe that the s*aid* libell or libells was ∧⌜or were⌝ recyted in the markett
place at Spalding or anye p*ar*te of them or anye of them   25
…

sheet 2
…

To the 7. Inter*rogatory* he sayth that he dyd not at any tyme sing or publishe   30
the s*aid* libells or any of them or any p*ar*te therof in any Alehowse Taverne or
other place ∧⌜nor did knowe that the s*aid* libells or any p*ar*te of them were sung
or published in any Alehowse or Taverne by any others⌝ But sayth that he
this defe*ndant* [hath published] dyd ∧⌜to⌝ [⟨..⟩] some of his pryvatt frend*es*
[∧]⌜[in Alehowses & Tavernes]⌝ make knowen the content*es* of the s*aid*   35
coppyes of twooe of the s*aid* libells wrytten by this defe*ndant* [as afores*aid*] owt
of the coppyes to him de*liuere*d by mr Scarborough as afores*aid* and further
sayth as he afore hathe s*aid* and more sayth not to this Int*errogatory*
…

5/ one: e *corrected over another letter, possibly* t   32–3/ ⌜nor … others⌝: *begun as interlineation and*
15/ one: *3 minims in* MS   *continued in left margin*

SPILSBY

1564
Archdeaconry of Lincoln Visitation Book   LA: Diocesan Vij/2
f 71v*   *(13 April)*   5

*Presentments made during the visitation of Bolingbroke deanery held in the
parish church of Horncastle by John Aylmer, archdeacon of Lincoln*
...

d*imittitu*r   10
d*ominus* Iohann*es* How*s*on ferebat a torche in a maske. and toke vpon him
⟨..⟩ preach vpon a cobord till in one of the maskers strake doune the cobord/
xiiijº die octobris 1564 ap*ud* Lincoln*iam* How*s*on c⟨...⟩ et fatet*ur* ad fecisse
p*er* mandatu*m* d*omin*e ducisse Suff*olcie* vnde d*ominus* e⟨..⟩ suspendebat ab
ad*ministracio*ne diuinor*um*./. iiijº die Novembri*s* 15⟨..⟩ ap*ud* Lincoln*iam*   15
comp*aruit* et d*ominus* ex c*er*tis causis eu*m* absolvit

STAINTON BY LANGWORTH

1607/8   20
Lease to Giles Farnaby, Musician   Sandbeck Park: MTD/B17/9
single sheet   *(18 February)*

This Indenture made the xviij^th daie of ffebruarie in the fiffth yeare of the
raigne of o*ur* Soueraigne Lord Iames by the grace of god kinge of England   25
ffrance & Ireland defender of the faith &c And of Scotland the one and
fortith Beweene Nicholas Saunderson of ffillingham in the countie of Lincoln
knight of the one p*ar*tie, and Giles ffarnabie of Aistroope in the said countie
gentl*eman* of the [said] other p*ar*tie Witnesseth that the said S*ir* Nicholas
Saunderson aswell for and in consideration of the good and lawfull seruice   30
to be doon by the said Giles ffarnabie vnto the said S*ir* Nicholas in teaching
his children musick as also for that he the said Giles hath given and granted
vnto the said S*ir* Nicholas Saunderson one Richard ffarnabie the sonne
of the said Giles ffarnabie to serue him for seauen yeares from the feast of
Phillip and Jacob thappostles now next ensewing and to teache and instruct   35
the children of the said S*ir* Nicholas Saunderson in skill of musick and
plaieing vppon instrument*es*. Hath demised granted leased and to ferme

13/ c⟨...⟩: *word lost in gutter, likely* comparuit
14/ e⟨..⟩: *word lost in gutter, likely* eum
15/ 15⟨..⟩: *date lost in gutter, likely* 1564
24/ This Indenture: *in display script with elaborated capitals*

letten and by these presentes doth demise grant lease and to fearme let vnto
the said Giles ffarnabie his executors and assignes all that his messuage or
tenement with thappurtenaunces and one croft therevnto adioyning in
Stainton next Langwoorth in the said countie of Lincoln togither with the
third part of one close of meadow called and knowen by the name of the   5
woodswarues containinge by estimacion fowerteene acres, one close of
meadow or pasture containing by estimacion seauen acres lieing vppon a
place called Sowthill next Langworth, and one other close of pasture called
the middle close sometyme belonging to a ferme called Greaues fearme
containing by estimacion seauenteene acres, all which said closes and messuage   10
ar now in the tenure and occupacion of Iohn Lamynge of Stainton aforesaid or
of his assignes. To haue and to hold the said messuage or tenement meadowes
and closes of pasture aforesaid with all the profittes and commodities to them
or anie of them belonginge (the wood and trees excepted) vnto the said
Giles ffarnabie his executors and assignes from the feast of Phillip and Iacob   15
thappostles now next ensewinge the date vnto the full end & tearmes of
twentie yeares from thence next ensewinge and fullie to be complett and
ended yeildinge and paieinge therefore yearlie and euerie yeare vnto the said
Sir Nicholas Saunderson his executors and assignes the some of sixteene
poundes of lawfull money of England at two tearmes or tymes in the yeare   20
that is to saie at the feast of Sainct Michaell tharchangell and thanunciation
of our Ladie Sainct Marie the virgin by even and equall porcions, and one
coople of fatt hennes yearlie att the feast of the Purification of our Ladie
Sainct Marie, And if it happen the said yearlie rent of sixteene poundes or
anie part thereof to be behind and vnpaid in part or in all by the space of   25
fowerteene daies next after anie of the said feastes or Daies wherein it ought
to be paid (beinge lawfullie demaunded) that then it shall and maie be
lawfull to and for the said Sir Nicholas Saunderson his heires and assignes
and euerie of them unto the premisses aboue demised and euerie part thereof
to reenter and the same to haue againe reposses and reenioy as in his or their   30
former estate anie thinge herein contained to the contrarie in anie wise
notwithstandinge. And the said Giles ffarnabie for him his executors and
administrators coveiniteth and granteth to and with the said Sir Nicholas
Saunderson his heires and assignes by those presentes, that he the said Giles
ffarnabie his executors or assignes shall plant and sett yearlie vppon some   35
convenient place of the premisses six ashes, and six willowes settes and the
same shall from tyme to tyme saue preserue and renew when and so often
as neede shall require, and likewise shall well and sufficientlie hedge and
ditch the groundes aforesaid, and repaire vphold maintaine and keepe all
and singuler the edifices and buildinges now being or hereafter to be vppon   40

12/ To ... hold: *in display script*   24/ And if it: *in display script*
18/ yeildinge: *in display script*

the demised premisses with all manner of necessarie reparacions whatsoeuer
and the same so from tyme to tyme sufficientlie repaired vpholden fenced
maintained and kept as aforesaid in the end of the said tearme shall giue the
leaue and yeild vpp vnto the said Sir Nicholas Saunderson his heires and
assignes with whatsoeuer buildinges shalbe made or sett vppon the premisses   5
by the said Giles ffarnabie or his assignes and shall not plashe the hedges
vppon the premisses but in convenient tyme for the needfull fencinge of the
same. Provided alwaies notwithstanding and it is fullie condiscended and
agreed by and betweene the said parties that if the said Giles ffarnabie his
executors or assignes shall at anie tyme duringe the said tearme plow vpp the   10
said closes or anie part thereof or alien sell or putt awaie the said messuage
or premisses to anie person or persons whatsoeuer vnles it be to his wife child
or children or some of them, without the consent of the said Sir Nicholas
Saunderson his heires or assignes therevnto first had and obtained in writeinge,
or that he the said Richard ffarnabie shall not continue and abide with the   15
said Sir Nicholas Saunderson his heires or assignes and do him his ∧⌐best⌐
seruice During the tearme of seauen yeares aforesaid, he the said Sir Nicholas
Saunderson givinge him necessarie and convenient meat drinck and apparell
fitt for his callinge, That then this present lease shall cease and be void and
otherwaies remaine, and be effectuall according to the grantes reseruations   20
and condicions therein mencioned and contained. In witnes whereof the
parties abouesaid to these present indentures haue interchangeablie putt
their handes & seales the daie[s] and yeare first aboue written.

...

25

STALLINGBOROUGH

1566
Inventory of Heathenish Church Goods   LA: Diocesan FUR 2
f 184v*   *(1 May)*   30

Item a crosse and   }   the crose was meltid
a crosse clothe   }   the said fyrst yeare and
                             turnd to thuse yat the candestickes
                             wear, And the crose clothe   35
                             was sold to players, who defaced it

...

4/ yeild: y *corrected over another letter*
8/ Provided: *in display script*
18/ convenient: conveni *corrected over erasure*
21/ In witnes: *in display script*
33/ said fyrst yeare: *the first year of Queen Elizabeth's reign, 17 November 1558–16 November 1559*

STAMFORD

1389
Certificate of Guild of St Martin   TNA: PRO C 47/41/173
single mb*   5

       Ordinacio gilde siue *fraternitatis sancti* Martini in ecclesia
                sancti Martini de Stamford
In honore dei & *sancti* Martini ab antiquo tempore ordinata fuit quedam
gilda siue fra*ter*nitas in ecclesia *sancti* Martini de Stamford sub tali forma q*uod*   10
*fra*tres & sorores p*redicte* gilde h*ab*erent quendam Capellanum celebrante*m* in
ecclesia p*redicta* in honore *sancti* Martini *pro* fratrib*us* & sororib*us* p*redictis*
& *pro* om*n*ib*us* benefactorib*us* suis & inuenirent c*ertum* lumen ˰⌐in⌐ eadem
ecclesia in honore *sancti* Martini et est & fuit consuetudo fra*ter*nitatis p*redicte* a
tempore cui*us* memoria non existit q*uo*d in festo *sancti* Martini [h⟨..⟩] p*redicti*   15
*fra*tres h*ab*eant, quend*am* taurum quiquide*m* taurus hutere*tur* & vendere*tur*
ad proficuu*m* fra*ter*nitatis p*redicte* & q*uo*d in eode*m* festo p*redicti* fra*tres* &
sorores conueniant ad potand*um* & ibi orent *pro* fratribus & sororib*us* suis
& om*n*ib*us* benef*a*ctorib*us* suis Et ad sustentacio*n*em & supportacio*n*em
Capellani p*redicti* & alior*um* on*erum* quid deuoti homin*es* ville p*redicte* longo   20
tempore ante statutu*m* de t*er*ris & ten*ementis* ad manu*m* mortuam dat*is*
factu*m* dederunt p*redicte* gilde siue fra*ter*nitati c*er*tos redditus ad val*orem*
xxx. s. *per* annu*m* Et quilibet fra*ter* & soror dabit in festo *sancti* Michaelis ad
supportacio*n*em oner⟨..⟩ p*redictorum* vnum bussellu*m* ordei Et p*redicti* fra*tres*
& sorores h*ab*ent quendam aldermannu*m* & alios officiarios ad colligend*um*   25
reddit*us* p*redictos* & ad ordinand*um pro* om*n*ib*us* supra*dictis* bona & catalla
non h*ab*ent nisi t*antum* ad on*erum* p*redictorum* supportacio*n*em

1427–8
St Mary's Churchwardens' Account   BL: Cotton Vespasian A.xxiv   30
f 3v*

...
Et sol*uto* Thom*e* harpmaker *pro* emendacio*n*e
de la schafte   xl d.
...   35
Et in exp*en*s*is pro* portator*i* de la schafte   viij d.
...
Et sol*uto pro* nerfis ad le schafte   i d.
...
Et pa*n*no e*m*pt*o pro* le schafte   xj d.   40
...

26/ omnibus: *followed by 35mm blank covered by line filler*

Et in dato histrionibus   vj d.

...

1440

Episcopal Visitation Book   LA: Diocesan Vj/1   5
f 83   *(21 October)* *(Presentment by the prioress, Elizabeth Weldon)*

...

At a visitation held in the chapter house of St Michael's Priory, outside Stamford,
by William Heyworth, bishop of Lincoln

...   10

Item dicit quod quedam Agnes monialis loci illius egressa est in apostasia
adherendo cuidam cithariste et dicit quod manent simul vt dicitur, in nouo
castro super Tynam

...

                                                                                 15

f 83v   *(Presentment by Sister Margaret Mortymer)*

...

Item dicit de apostata vt supra

...

                                                                                 20

(Bishop's injunctions)
Item iniunctum est priorisse quod quo commodius poterit reducat dictam
apostatam que recessit vt prefertur cum citharista nomine Roberto Abbot

...

                                                                                 25

f 81v

...

...Also we enioyne yow prioresse vndere lyke peynes þat wyth all your
diligence and hast possyble ye gar seke your suster Anneys Butyler þat is
owte in apostasye and bryng hir home to hir cloyster and so moderly trete   30
hir after your rule þat she seke no cause eftis to go in apostasye ne oþer take
non ensample be hir to trespace in lyke wyse...

...

1465   35

Corporation Hall Book I   STH: Hall Book 2A/1/1
f 5v*

Theys Be the Names of all Manner Craftes sett together in pagentes whiche
Shall within them selfes Chuys them wardeyns for to serche and ouerse All   40
Manner poyntes longyng to the same Craftes that they be Chosen of for the
welfare & woorshipe of this Sayd Towne & Boroughe and yff Any wardeyn
so Chosen fynd any Manner of Defalt within his Craft or in the Master

or *ser*uant of the same That wyll nott Be amendid by hym he shall then
Complayn to the Alderman That he and his bredern & Counseyll may
ther in Take Adewe Correccyon and Reformacyon

Draper*es* hosyer*es* Taylor*es*	} Sub duob*us* gardianis		Bower*es* fflecher*es* Stryng*eres* Turnor*es* Dyer*es*	} modo ut Supra	5
Marcer*es* Grocer*es* habardassher*es*	} simili modo				10
Baker*es* Brewer*es* vynten*eres* Myllner*es*	} Sub modo *predicto*		Scryvener*es* Glasyer*es* Peyntor*es* Steynor*es* Barbor*es* Chaundeller*es*	} ut su*pr*a	15
Shomaker*es* Cerryer*es* Cobler*es*	} si*m*ili modo		Weyver*es* Walker*es* Shermen	} Sub duob*us* gardianis	20
Bocher*es* Fyssher*es* hosteller*es* Cokys	} modo ut su*pr*a		Carpenter*es* Masons Slater*es*	} modo ut su*pr*a	25
Irenmonger*es* Smythes Saddeller*es* Bottlemaker*es* & All other*e* ham*er* men	} modo ut su*pr*a		Barker*es* Glover*es* Skynner*es* Whittawer*es*	} modo ut su*pr*a	30

...

1465-6
35

Corporation Hall Book I   STH: Hall Book 2A/1/1
f 6   *(30 September–30 September) (Session held 22 July)*

Constituc*io* de
Emp*cione* &
vendic*ione*
p*ro* om*nibus*
artificibus

Item itt is ordeynyd Statutyd & by the same Ald*er*man Bredern Comburgessez
and all the hooll Co*m*mons in this Session halden in the same hall in the   40
feast of sent Marye magdelyn In the Sext yeer of the Reigne of kyng Edward
the ffourth Stablysshid for eu*er*mor That all Mann*er* Men of Craft*es* That

ben Burgessez and ffre men of the said hall and Sworn shall occupye in Byyng
and Sellyng in lykewyse and fforme as they have done Before tyme all manner
of ware and chaffer such as shall pleas them for to By or sell att any Season
within the said Towne and Broughe

5

Constitucio
de officio
Gardianorum

Item itt is ordeynyd and by the said Stablysshed That the said Two wardens
of euery pagent of the Craftes before said shall lefellye Serche or do serche
withowt any Intervpcyon all Manner ware Chaffer or any other thyng that
is ordeynyd to be sold within hys said pagent and wardeynrye and such as
he ffyndyth ffawtye to bryng itt Tofore the alderman and his Counsell as   10
fforfitt And itt to Stond in hys Grace

...

1472–3

Corporation Hall Book I   STH: Hall Book 2A/1/1   15
f 16*   *(30 September–30 September) (Session held 1 November)*

...

Mynstrelli

willelmus Barton
christoferus Totyll   Electi sunt Minstrelli & Iurati &c
Ricardus pynder   20

1479–80

Corporation Hall Book I   STH: Hall Book 2A/1/1
f 27v*   *(30 September–30 September) (Session held 2 December)*
...   25

℃ Eisdem die & Anno Ordinatum & prouisum per Aldermanum & confratres
suos & totam comunitatem ville quod ob honorem dei & reformacionem
fidei. ludus Corporis christi instanti Anno sit publice ludendus in omnibus
sicut in Anno vltimo elapso &c

...   30

f 29*

Ministralli

℃ Henricus Haynes Ministrallus admissus pro Anno instanti per   ⎫ 35
plegium Roberti Nevour   ⎪
℃ Ricardus Pyndell consimiliter admissus pro eodem Anno per   ⎬ Iurati
plegium Ricardi Navour   ⎪
℃ Willelmus Iohnson similiter admissus pro Anno predicto per   ⎪
plegium Willelmi Tygh   ⎭ 40

...

1481–2
Corporation Hall Book I   STH: Hall Book 2A/1/1
f 33*   *(30 September–30 September) (Session held 14 April)*
...

Constitucio

C Eisdem die & Anno Ordinatum est per Aldermanum Comburgenses   5
& omnes communes In communi Aula congregatos ex eorum communi
assensu & assensu quod Amodo imperpetuum Annuatim ludus Corporis
Christi per gardianos artium & societates eorum ludatur prout alias &c
videlicet vj pagentes in festo Corporis Christi proximo futuro & residui
v pagentes in festo Corporis Christi Anno extunc sequenti sic continuando   10
huiusmodi pagentes in festo predicto per Artes prius assignatas sub pena
cuiuslibet Artis ad hoc assignate in contrarium facientis seu sic facere
recusantis quadraginta solidorum ad commodum communis Aule
conuertendorum & leuandorum

15

1482–3
Corporation Hall Book I   STH: Hall Book 2A/1/1
f 34v   *(30 September–30 September) (Session held 16 December)*
...

Admissi
Ministralli

C Henricus Hede Ministrallus admissus est pro Anno instanti   20
per plegium Roberti Navour
C Ricardus Pynder consimiliter admissus est pro eodem
Anno per plegium Ricardi ffletcher   Iurati
C willelmus Smyth simili modo admissus per plegium
Iohannis knyght   25
...

1486–7
Corporation Hall Book I   STH: Hall Book 2A/1/1
f 40v*   *(30 September–30 September) (Session held 4 December)*   30
...

Ministralli
Iurati cum
scutis per
plegios eisdem
deliberatis
saluo et secure
reliberandis

C Eisdem die & Anno Henricus Hayn ministrallus plegius
Robertus ∧⌜Navour⌝ pro scuto
C Ricardus Pynder simili modo ministrallus plegii Iohannes
Stede & Bernardus Richman   Iurati 35
C christoferus Totyll ministrallus admissus plegius Iohannes
Gybbes pro scuto
...

6–7/ communi assensu & assensu: *for* communi assensu & consensu

1494–5
Corporation Hall Book I   STH: Hall Book 2A/1/1
f 57   *(30 September–30 September)* *(5 December burgess admissions)*
…

℃ Iohannes Brandon Mynstrell*us* admiss*us* est pro laborato   5
& dabit de ffine   ij s.
…

f 59*   *(Session held 30 April)*
…   10

*(..)*lers ⟨...⟩
silv*er* ⟨...⟩chen

Mem*oran*dum At this day receyued off Raff Boweman a
coler off Syluer *with* A skochen ordeyned for A wayte
which was afore in the kepyng off Roberde Nevou*r*
sometyme of Stamford   *recepta* in
℃ Receyued also off Iohann*i* Stede a coler off syluer *with*   custodia   15
a skochen in lyke wyse &c   Alder*manni* |
℃ Receyued Also off Dauid Cicill A coler of Syluer *with*
a skochen which M*r* Iohn Dyconn*s* hadd in kepyng for
oon of the waytes
…   20

1538
Archdeaconry of Lincoln Visitation Book   LA: Diocesan Vij/1
f 69v*
                                                                                             25
*Proceedings arising from the visitation of Longoboby deanery held before John
Pope, the archdeacon of Lincoln's official*
…

parochia
sancti martini

[Lancelatus Lacy p*er*turbauit diuinu*m* officiu*m* vna vice cu*m* corno que volare
permisit ad summu*m* altare t*em*p*or*e elevacionis corporis christi/ comparuit   30
et fat*etur* Iuramento habet penitere p*er* vnu*m* diem dominicum &c]
…

1539–40
Corporation Hall Book I   STH: Hall Book 2A/1/1   35
f 131   *(30 September–30 September)* *(1 March burgess admissions)*
…

willelmus skelton Mynstrell*us* admiss*us* est ad scott*um* &
lott*um* et dabit pro fine p*er* pl*e*giu*m* Roberti Crosby &
wille*l*mi clerke   iiij s. 40
…

29/ que: *for* quem

1554–5
Corporation Hall Book I STH: Hall Book 2A/1/1
f 161v *(30 September–30 September)* *(20 November burgess admissions)*

...

Ioh*a*nnes Morrice Mynstrell*us* admiss*us* *est* ad scott*um* 5
et lott*um* et dabit *pro* fin*e* *per* *ple*gi*um* Ioh*a*nnes Moore
& Ioh*a*nnes Creche iiij s.

...

1570–1 10
Corporation Hall Book I STH: Hall Book 2A/1/1
f 199v *(30 September–30 September)* *(9 December burgess admissions)*

...

® Solvend*a* in fine   Robertus Benyson minstrell*us* *pro* consi*m*ili ij s.
nat*a*lis d*o*m*i*ni

... 15

1575–6
Corporation Hall Book I STH: Hall Book 2A/1/1
f 212 *(30 September–30 September)* *(Session held 9 February)*

... 20

An ordre for   It is this daie ordered, and agreed vnto, aswell for the restraint of vnpr*o*ffitable
Alehouse   hauntinge of alehowses, and eschewinge of loytringe ydlenes, as for the
haunt*er*z and   good attendance and applienge of laboures and woork*es*, That eu*er*y poore
ydle *persons*   handicraft*es* man, labourer, iourneyman, and servaunt vsynge alehouses or
wh*ich* leaue   Tiplinge houses and leavinge theire work*es* on the weake daye, or vsinge to goe 25
their work*es* &   ydelly or loyteringe abroade to any pastime game or plaies on the weake daies
seke pastimes   leavinge theire woorke, or on such daies doe vse or kepe them selues any
kynde of playe or pastyme (shootinge only excepted) That then eu*er*y the saide
*pa*rties so offendinge and havinge no sufficient excuse to be allowed by M*aste*r
Alderman shalbe vpon his takinge co*mm*itted to warde, And besid*es* paye for 30
eu*er*y time he shall so offende against this constituc*i*on the so*mm*e of vj d./.

...

1580–1
Inventory of John Mackreth, Musician LA: INV 65/178 (B) 35
single sheet *(In the hall)*

...

It*e*m one harpe, one bayse vyol, & A trible vyole, &
an old bayse vyol xl s.

... 40

14/ *pro* consi*m*ili: *that is, for admission to scot and lot*

1586–7
Corporation Hall Book I   STH: Hall Book 2A/1/1
f 231v*   *(30 September–30 September)*   *(29 April apprenticeship registrations)*
...

eis*dem* die & a*nn*o ven*it* Will*elmu*s Willoughby & cog*no*vit se fore Appre*n*tic*ium*   5
Thome Willoughby Musitian p*ro* te*r*m*in*o vij annor*um* vt p*er* Indent*uram*
gere*n*t*em* dat*am* 30 die octobr*is* a*n*no 28º Re*g*ine apparet
...

1588–9   10
Corporation Hall Book I   STH: Hall Book 2A/1/1
f 235v   *(30 September–30 September)*   *(2 November burgess admissions)*
...

Thomas Willoughbie musicus Ad*mitt*itur A*d* S*c*ottum
& Lott*um* & Dat pro fine   v f 15
...

1589–90
Corporation Hall Book I   STH: Hall Book 2A/1/1
f 238v   *(30 September–30 September)*   *(11 October apprenticeship registrations)*   20
...

Ad hanc Aulam ven*it* Robertus Pownder & cog*no*vit se fore Apprentic*ium*
Thome willoughb(.) musicio p*ro* vij*tem* An*n*is A tertio die novemb*ris* Anno
xx*x*[j]*mo* vsq*ue* fine*m* dict*i* Termini vt p*er* Indentur*am* gere*nt*em dat*am* die
& A*n*no supradict*is* plenius p*ar*et   25
...

1593–4
Corporation Hall Book I   STH: Hall Book 2A/1/1
f 253   *(30 September–30 September)*   *(26 July apprenticeship registrations)*   30
...

Ad hanc Aulam Henricus Bolton ven*it* et Cog*no*vit se fore apprentic*ium*
Thome willoughbie music*io*n p*ro* decem Annos a festo Annunciacio*n*is be*a*te
marie vlt*imo* preterito vt p*er* Indentur*am* gere*n*t*em* dat*am* xxº die maij Anno
xxxvj*to* Eliz*abe*the Re*g*ine plenius Apparett   35
Ad hanc Aulam Ioh*ann*es waters ven*it* et Cog*no*vit se fore Apprentic*ium*
Thome willoughbie music*io*n p*ro* Septem Annos a festo S*ancti* Michael*i*s

7/ 30 die ... Re*g*ine: *30 October 1586*
23/ musicio: *for* musici
23–4/ tertio die ... xxx[j]*mo*: *that is, 3 November 30 Elizabeth I, 1588*
33, 37/ Annos: *for* Annis
34–5/ xxº ... Re*g*ine: *20 May 1594*

vlt*imo* preterito vt p*er* Indentur*am* gerent*em* dat*am* xvj^to die Augusti Anno
xxxvj^to Eliz*abethe* R*egi*ne plenius Apparet
...

1602–3   5
Corporation Hall Book I STH: Hall Book 2A/1/1
f 273v   *(30 September–30 September)* *(17 May burgess admissions)*
...

ffranciscus Benyson musicus si*milit*er admissus et
n*ihi*l dat p*ro* fin*e* quia nat*us* fuit in villa   n*ihi*l 10

1624–5
Corporation Hall Book I STH: Hall Book 2A/1/1
f 342v   *(30 September–30 September)* *(5 April burgess admissions)*
...   15
Ad hanc Aulam Henricus Pearse Musition
admitt*itur* ad Scot*um* et lot*um* et dat p*ro* fine
quia seruiebat apprentic*iam*   n*ihi*l
...
                                                                                    20
1625–6
Corporation Hall Book I STH: Hall Book 2A/1/1
f 344v   *(30 September–30 September)* *(1 December burgess admissions)*
...
Ad hanc Aulam ffrauncisc*us* Coyney ∧⌐musi*c*ion⌐   25
admitt*itur* ad Scot*um* et Lott*um* et dat p*ro* fine
imediat*e* Ioh*an*ni Clark Camerar*io*   x s.
...

1627–8   30
Corporation Hall Book I STH: Hall Book 2A/1/1
f 348v*   *(30 September–30 September)* *(Session held 4 October)*
...
At this haule it is aggreed by m*aster* Alderma*n* togeather w*i*th the most voyces
of the Comburgeses & Capitall Burgeses or commone counsell assembeled 35
vppon the request of the Right honorable Henrye Lord Graye expressed by
his letter nowe reade in the open haule that the sayed Lord Grayes searuantes
vizt Edmunde Troupe, Willia*m* Knewstubbes Natha*n* Ash, Thomas Troupe
Willia*m* Smyth, Henry Beuisse togeather w*i*th Henry Pearce in all to the
number of seaue*n* p*er*sons shall be admitted and are from henceforth alowed 40

1–2*l* xvj^to ... R*egi*ne: *probably 16 August 35*   2*l* xxxvj^to: *for* xxxv^to *(?)*
   Elizabeth i, *1593*   9*l* similiter admissus: *that is, to scot and lot*

to be & scrue in the place of the toune waightes of Stamford. And shall haue
att theire first enterance theire Cotes & the toune badge att the charge of
the sayed toune And shall from time to time doe such searuice for the sayed
toune as waightes in other tounes are accustomed to doe and shall begine
theire searuice yearely att the Aldermans feast.   5

...

1628–9
Corporation Hall Book I   STH: Hall Book 2A/1/1
f 352   *(30 September–30 September)* *(9 October burgess admissions)*   10

Ad hanc aulam Edmund Troupe William Knewstubbes
Thom*as* Troupe *et* Nathan Ashe Musissians admitt*untur*
ad scott*um* et lott*um* et dant *pro* fin*e* q*ui*a su*n*t musicos
vill*e* predict*e*   nll 15

1629–30
Recognizance of Nathan Ash as Alehouse Keeper
LA: Stamford Quarter Sessions Book, 1629–30
item 29   *(23 January)*   20

Stamford   memorand*um* q*uo*d vicessimo tertio die Ianuarij Anno Regni d*omi*ni n*ost*ri
Burg*us* in   Caroli dei graci*a* Anglie Scotie ffranci*e* et Hibernie R*e*gis fidei defenc*oris* &c
Comitatu   quinto Coram Edmund*o* Corker Alderman*o* et Thom*a* Watson gen*eroso*
Lincolnie   Iusticiarijs dicti d*omi*ni Regis ad pacem in Burgo predicto conseruand*am*   25
              assignat*is* Robert Glouer de Stamford predicta Tallowchaundler et Thom*as*
              Troupe de eadem Weauer mannceper*un*t pro Nathan Ash de eadem mussission
              vid*e*lic*e*t vterq*ue* manucaptorum predictorum sub pena quinq*ue* lib*r*arum et
              predic*tus* Nathan Ash assumpsit pro seipso sub pena dece*m* lib*r*arum legalis
              monet*e* Anglie Quas concesser*unt* dict*o* dom*ino* Reg*i* hered*ibus* et successor*ibus* 30
              su*is* de bon*is* et Catall*is* terris et tenement*is* su*is* fiend*as* et leuand*as* sub
              Condicione sequent*i*/

The condicion of this Recognizance is such that whereas the aboue bounden
Nathan Ash is admitted & allowed by the sayed Iustices to keepe a Commone   35
alehouse or victulinge house vntill the fower & twenteth day of Aprill next
enshuinge the date hereof and noe longer in the house wherein he nowe
dwelleth in Stamford afforesayed & not elsewhere I therefore the sayed
Nathan Ash shall not dueringe the time afforesayed p*er*mitte or suffer or haue

---

14/ musicos: *for* musici   34/ The condicion: *in display script*
22/ memorand*um*: *in display script*   38/ I therefore: *in display script*
23/ defenc*oris*: *for* defensoris

any playe att dyce Cardes tables quoy*tes* logge*tes* bowles or any other vnlawfull
gaime or gaimes in his house or backsyde Nor shall suffer to be or remayne
in his house any p*er*sone or p*er*sons not beinge his ordinarye houshoulde
searuante vpon any Saboth daye or holy daye dueringe the time of deuine
searuice or searmone Nor shall suffer any p*er*sone or p*er*sons to lodge or   5
staye in his house aboue one daye or one night but such whose true name or
surname he shall deliuer to one of the Cunstables or in theire absence to some
other of the officers in the same parish the nexte daye followinge vnlesse theye
be such p*er*sone or p*er*sons as he very well knoweth and will answare for his
or theire forthcomminge Nor suffer any p*er*sone or p*er*sons to remayne in   10
his house tippelinge or drinckinge contrarye to lawe nor yet to be there
tippelinge or drinckinge after nyne of the Clocke in the night time Nor buy
or take to pawe*n* any stollen goodes. Nor willingly harboure in his sayed
house harnes stables or other wheir any Rogues vagaboundes sundrye beggers
masterlesse me*n* or other notoriouse offenders whatsoeuer Nor suffer any   15
p*er*sone or p*er*sons to vtter any beare ale or other victuall by deputacio*n* or by
cullor of his licence. And allsoe if he shall keepe the true assyse & measure
in his pot*tes* bread or otherwise in his vtteringe of his beare ale and bread
and the same beare & ale to sell by sealed measures and accordinge to the
assyse and not otherwise and shall not vtter any stronge beare & stronge ale   20
aboue the pennye the quarte and smaule beare ⟨.⟩ ale abo⟨..⟩ the halfe pennye
the quarte and soe after the same rates. And allsoe if he shall not vtter nor
willingly suffer to be offered druncke taken or tippeled any Tobacco in his
house or other place therevnto belonginge That then this p*re*sente Recognizance
to be voyde & of none effecte or else to remayne in force/   25
(signed) Edm*und* Corker alderma*n*
Thomas Watson

1632–3
Corporation Hall Book 1   STH: Hall Book 2A/1/1   30
f 369*   *(30 September–30 September)   (Session held 4 March)*
…

An order that
both the first
& seconde
companye shall
p*ro*uide theire
gownes and
attende w*ith*
m*aste*r
Alderman at
the king*es*
comminge

Att this haule it is aggreed by the Alderma*n* Comburgesses & capitall Burgesses
assembled that whoesoeuer is or shall be hereafter chosen in to the place or
companye of a Comburgesse for the entertaynemente of the Kinges ma*ies*tie   35
for the worshippe of the towne & place he houldeth shall p*re*sently before
the King*es* ma*ies*ti*es* comminge make or cause to be made one gowne of
Sadde murrie cloth furred w*ith* fine ⟨.⟩dowt*es* sutable to the Gownes of the
Alderma*n* & other of the Comburgesses to be worne vpon festifall dayes
& att other times to be appoynted by the Alderma*n* for the time beinge on   40

21/ ⟨.⟩ ale abo⟨..⟩: *some letters too faded to read*

paine of Tenne poundes of Currante English monye and imprissonmente
vntill the same shall be payed to the Alderman for the time beinge to the
vse of the sayed towne of Stamford and the partye soe offendinge to be
displaced from that companye & disfraunchesed of all libertyes belonginge
to the sayed Corporation and another to be putt in to his roome whoe   5
shall more regard the worshippe of the sayde towne
And it is further aggreed that whoesoeuer ˰⌈is or⌉ shall be hereafter chosen
to be one of the Capital Burgesses or commone counsell of the sayde towne
for the entertaynemente of the kinges maiestie the worshippe of the towne
& place he houldeth shall likewise presently before the kinges comminge   10
make or cause to be made one gowne of sadd cullered cloth or stuffe on
paine of ffiue poundes of Currante English monye and imprissonmente
vntill the same shall be payed to the Alderman for the time beinge to the
vse of the Towne & the partye soe offendinge to be displaced from that
Companye & disfraunchesed from all libertyes and priueledges belonginge   15
to the sayed Corporation and an other putt in his roome whoe will more
regard the worshippe of the sayed Towne and that all & euery of both the
sayed Companyes (if theye be well in bodye & limbes) shall attende with
the Alderman vpon his maiestie vpon horsebacke or otherwise on foote
as occasion shall requier dueinge all the time that his maiestie shall be   20
within the libertyes of Stamford vpon the seuerall penaltyes & punishmentes
afforesayed./

f 371*   (Session held 9 May)

...   25

A Constitucion
for the Towne
musicke to
waite vppon
the Kinge and
prouision made
for the better
maintayninge
of Saint
Maryes Belles

Att this halle it is aggreed that Thomas Troupe Nathan Ashe, Henry Pearce,
William Knewstubbes, & Iohn Palmer shall all of them be bounde in one
obligation of the penaltye of ffiue Markes for the safe deliuerye of the Towne
scutchions vpon demaunde and that all & euery of the sayed partyes shall
attende as the Towne waightes att the Bridge or att the Towne halle with   30
theire winde Instrumentes att the Kinges Comminge to the George and soe
likewise att his goinge through the towne

...

1636-7   35
Corporation Hall Book 1   STH: Hall Book 2A/1/1
f 384*   (30 September–30 September) (25 February burgess admissions)

...

Ad hanc Aulam ˰⌈ordinatum est quod⌉ Willelmus Mewese
Musicion nuper Apprenticius cum Thoma Willoughby nuper   40
de Stamford predicta Musicion defuncto admittatur ad

Scot*tum* et Lot*tum* pro nihilo sub condic*ione* qu*od* si
ponit duos sufficien*tes* ho*mines* obligari secu*m* in Sum*mam*
quadragint*a* libr*arum* pro securit*ate* ville p*redicte* ab onere
suo Et p*redicti* Wil*lel*mus Mewes Simon ffisher et Nathan
Ashe su*per* xxviij^um diem ffebr*uarij* Anno supra*dicto* oblig*ati*   5
Al*der*mano et Burg*ensibus* ville sive Burgi de Stamford
p*redicta* secundu*m* ordine*m* p*redictum* Ideo admit*titur* &c   ni*hi*l

1639–40
Corporation Hall Book 1   STH: Hall Book 2A/1/1   10
f 400   *(30 September–30 September) (Session held 26 October)*

...

William Mewes
& his Company
Chosen to be
the Townes
Wates

At this hall Will*i*am Mewes Music*i*on w*i*th other younge men of his
company are chosen to be the Townes Waites, and they are to haue the
vse of the scutcheons The said Will*i*am Mewes puttinge in sufficient securitie   15
to the Towne for the safe Custody and redeliu*er*y of them when they shalbe
thereunto called

...

1641–2   20
Corporation Hall Book 1   STH: Hall Book 2A/1/1
f 410   *(30 September–30 September) (Session held 2 December)*

...

At this hall it is ordered & agreed that those three Scutcheons of the Townes
and two more to be made to them, shall be deliu*er*ed into the Custody of   25
Will*i*am Mewes Music*i*on to be worne by him and the rest of his Company
as the Townes Music*i*ons, he the said Will*i*am Mewes giveinge securitie for
the safe ⌜re⌝deliu*er*y of them at his or any of their dep*ar*tures from the
place of the Townes Music*i*ons

...   30

SUTTERTON

1518–19
St Mary's Churchwardens' Accounts   Bodl.: MS. Rawlinson D 786   35
f 96v   *(4 April 1518–24 April 1519) (Expenses)*

...

Item for ye plaars rewarde of qwatlod   ix d.

...

1/ si: *redundant*
38/ qwatlod: *Whaplode*

1520–1
St Mary's Churchwardens' Accounts   Bodl.: MS. Rawlinson D 786
f 104   *(8 April–31 March)*   *(Expenses)*

...

Item payd for makynge*s* of ye [blare*s*] ˄⌈[plare*s*]   5
plaares⌉ candelles   vj d.
...

1521–2
St Mary's Churchwardens' Accounts   Bodl.: MS. Rawlinson D 786   10
f 106v*   *(31 March 1521–20 April 1522)*   *(Parcels for the church work)*

Item p*ai*d by the hande*s* off S*ir* Iohn ffor makyng the
towne wax erga festu*m* assu*m*pcio*n*is be*ate* ma*r*ie   v d.
Item p*ai*d the same tyme ffor makyng the plaars candelle*s*   vj d 15
Item p*ai*d the same tyme by ye hande*s* off ⌈S*ir*⌉ Iohn to
Iohn Alyne ffor ledy*ng* & ffeystyng*e* ye same ca*n*delle*s*   j d.
...

1522–3   20
St Mary's Churchwardens' Accounts   Bodl.: MS. Rawlinson D 786
f 110v   *(20 April–5 April)*   *(Parcels for the church work)*

...

Item p*ai*d by the hande*s* off S*ir* Iohn ffor makyng the
towne lyg*h*t & the plac*r* Candelle*s*   xij d. 25
...

1523–4
St Mary's Churchwardens' Accounts   Bodl.: MS. Rawlinson D 786
f 112*   *(5 April–27 March)*   *(Receipts)*   30
...

Item Rec*eiv*ed by the hande*s* off S*ir* Iohn off tho*m*as
Hutto*n* Rob*er*t Hutto*n* ˄⌈Rich*ar*d qwyttynggam⌉ Willi*am*
Hobso*n* & Willi*am* Beyll wi*th* other dyue*r*s off the towne
ffor i*n*creme*n*tte*s* ffor the play playd o*n* the day off the   35
assv*m*pcio*n* off o*u*r ladey   ix s. vj d.
...

f 114   *(Parcels for the church work)*

                                                                                        40
iiij d.   Item p*ai*d by the hande*s* off the sayd Willi*am* Brandon

ffor makyne com*m*one lyght*es* Anensse the ffest off the
assu*m*pc*i*on off o*u*r Ladey   iiij d.

...

f 114v   5

...

It*em* p*ai*d by the hand*es* off *Sir* Iohn ffor makyne the
com*m*one lyght   viij d.

1524-5   10
St Mary's Churchwardens' Accounts   Bodl.: MS. Rawlinson D 786
f 116   *(27 March 1524-16 April 1525) (Parcels for the church work)*

...

Item payd to the players of Swynshede for a Rewarde   iij s. iiij d.
Item [s] payde for Brede and [drykk] drynke at the   15
same tyme   vij d.

...

Item payd to the Playrers of Donygton for a Reward   xij d.

...

                                                                      20

f 116v*

...

It*em* for makyng the wax Agayn*st* owr Lad*es* day   [iiij]v d.

...

                                                                      25

1525-6
St Mary's Churchwardens' Accounts   Bodl.: MS. Rawlinson D 786
f 122v   *(16 April-1 April) (Receipts)*

...

It*em* Resauyd of Gaterynge to the plays of fframton   30
and kyrton   iij s. vj d. ob.

...

f 123*   *(Parcels for the church work)*

...

                                                                      35

It*em* payd to the players of fframton and kyrkton   vj s. viij d.

...

It*em* payd for ij li. wax to owr ladys lyght   xij d.

...

23/ [iiij]v: v *corrected over* [iiij]

1530–1
St Mary's Churchwardens' Accounts   Bodl.: MS. Rawlinson D 786
f 131   *(17 April–9 April)* *(Payments)*
…
Item payd to the playres of Whapplett When they   5
Rode ther play   vij d.
Item paid by ye hande*s* of S*ir* Iohn for vj li. wax agayn*st*
owr lady day   iij s.
Item payd by the handes off Syr Iohn Eschedayll for
makyng of [Item payd by ⟨…⟩] wax agayn*st* owr lady day   10
the assumpcyon   xiij d.
…

1531–2
St Mary's Churchwardens' Accounts   Bodl.: MS. Rawlinson D 786   15
f 132   *(9 April–31 March)* *(January receipts)*
…
Item Resauyd of the counte of the players   ij s. x d. ob.

f 133v*   *(Expenses)*   20
…
Item for maykyng of xj li. wax agayn*st* owr laydys day   viij d.
Item for maykyng of x. li. wax of owr laydys   v d.
Item for gyltynge of the same   j d.
…   25

1536–7
St Mary's Churchwardens' Accounts   Bodl.: MS. Rawlinson D 786
f 141v*   *(16 April–1 April)* *(Charges for the parish church)*
…   30
Item for vij li. wax & on half agyn*st* owr lade*s* day   v s.
…

1600–1
Archdeaconry of Lincoln Visitation Book   LA: Diocesan Vij/9   35
f 44v*   *(3 June)*

Proceedings arising from the visitation of North Holland deanery by Thomas Randes,
the archdeacon of Lincoln's official, held in the church at Donington in Holland
…   40

10/ ⟨…⟩: *24mm of cancellation illegible*

Tho*mas* Harvie
dimittituntur *willia*m wayte
for abuseng thear neighbou*r*s in making rymes vppon them 21 Marcij 1600
citati comp*aru*eru*nt* et sese submiser*un*t vnde d*omin*us ip*s*os cu*m* monic*ione*
[ip*s*os] dimisit   5

SWINESHEAD

1534
Will of Richard Lambeson, Notary   LA: LCC WILLS 1532–34   10
f 322v   *(11 April; proved 8 June)*

…Also I will that Anthony my sun shall haue one materes one cou*er*lyd one
pare of lynyn sche*tes* one bolster my best gaberdyne my beste clarycord*es* and
one cowe…   15

TATTERSHALL

1495–6
Receiver's Accounts   CKS: U1475/Q16/2   20
sheet 5   *(Choristers' expenses)*
…
Et sol*utos* Rob*er*to lounde p*ro* notac*ione* Canttus current*is*
iiij. p*arttum* vocat*i* the Cry of Caleys ⌈xj d.⌉ & alt*er*ius
Cantus vulgarit*er* nu*n*cupat*i* fflos flor*um* ⌈x d.⌉ p*er* p*ar*cell*am*   25
inde fact*um*   xxj d.
…

1498–9
Precentor's Accounts   CKS: U1475/Q19/4   30
sheet 1
…
Et R*oberto* lounde p*ro* notac*ione* iiij. ⌈ij. d.⌉ Scrowes de
audim*us* vocem Gaude de ⌈vj d.⌉ .vij. p*artibus* compilat*o*
p*er* m*a*gist*er* Bawldwyn aut*em* ⌈v d.⌉ Domine celi & t*er*re   35
de v p*artibus*/ emend*acione* ⌈iiij s.⌉ defectuum libri vo*cati*
legend*a* s*an*ctorum in om*n*ibus loc*is* diutino vsu obfuscat*i*
eid*em* p*ro* cons*imili* ⌈iij s.⌉ emendac*ione* scriptu*re* lengend*e*
temp*oralis* a principio vsque fine*m*/ notac*ione* aut*em* ⌈vj d.
ob.⌉ Salue regina de vij fol*ijs*/ vers*uum* proph*e*tie ⌈ob.⌉/   40

36/ defectuum: *5 minims in* MS
38/ lengend*e*: *for* legende

iij lectia ⌈ij d.⌉ de tenebr*is*/ leudat*i* ⌈ij d.⌉ p*ar*ui de iiij.
p*ar*t*ibus*/ triplic*i* ⌈ij d.⌉ cantus voc*ati* maydens of london/
bass*o* & tenor*i* ⌈j d.⌉ cantus voc*ati* Sec*u*lor*um* Ric*ar*di
Davy/ contratenor*i* ⌈j d. ob.⌉ eiusd*em* cantus cum alijs/ xij.
p*ar*ell*is* p*er*gameni ⌈ij s. iiij d.⌉ & R*oberto* lounde ⌈iiij s.⌉   5
p*ro* notac*ione* .vj. qua*ter*nor*um* cum diu*er*s*is* cant*ibus* int*er* se   xv s. viij d. ob.

1500–1
Impositor's, Precentor's, and Steward's Accounts CKS: U1475/Q19/6
sheet 3v *(Rewards)*   10

…

Et in den*ar*ijs p*er* manus Comp*utantis* regardat*is* hom*i*n*ibus*
ludent*ibus* ⌈xiiij d.⌉ diu*er*s*a* int*er*ludia & philippo ⌈ij d.⌉
laborar*io* deferent*i* transmissiua*m* vsque wragby hoc anno   xvj d.

…   15

1501–2
Impositor's, Precentor's, and Steward's Accounts CKS: U1475/Q19/7
sheet 1v *(Rewards)*

…   20

Et in regard*a* dat*a* lusorib*us* mimis vrsurijs & al*iis* extraneis
sup*er*uenient*ibus* hoc anno p*er* p*ar*cellam s*ic* ostens*antibus*
& apara*ntibus*   iij s. vj d.

…

                                                                                   25

1502–3
Impositor's, Precentor's, and Stewards' Accounts CKS: U1475/Q19/8
sheet 1v*

…

…Solut*os* Rob*er*to lounde Ioh*anni* pykering & Thome Asshwell p*ro* eor*um*   30
comm*un*is dietant*ibus* ext*ra* Collegiu*m* vt inferius xx li. vj s. viij d.…

…

sheet 2

…   35

Et in co*mmun*is den*ar*ijs solut*is* Iohanni Pykering ⌈v s. x d.⌉
uno alt*eri* sex Clericor*um* & Thome ⌈v. s.⌉ Asshwell Cl*er*ico
conduct*icio* pro eor*um* comm*un*is temp*ore* infirm*itatis* s*ue*
hoc anno ad vices   x s. x d.

…   40

1/ lectia: *for* lectionum   37/ uno: *for* uni
5/ p*ar*ell*is*: *for* parcellis

1585/6
Inventory of John Atkin, Musician   LA: INV 73/49
single sheet   *(19 March)*

...

Item his harpe   iij s. iiij d.   5

...

1604
Episcopal Visitation Book   LA: Diocesan Vj/18
p 62   *(18 August)*   10

*Proceedings arising from the visitation of Horncastle, Hill, and Gartree deaneries
held in the parish church of Horncastle by the commissaries*

...

+   Maria vxor Anthonij Elsman vppon a comon fame and vehement suspicion of   15
a. 4 s. 6 d.   adultrie with one Gryffen an actour in Interludes and also she to [is a] ⌐be
a⌐ common scold & a great disturber of her neighbours/ °5o octobris 1604.
citata non comparuit. suspensa° °9. Novembris 1604 comparuit dicta Maria et
iurata &c absoluitur &c et habet soluere feodum apparitoris &c°

...   20

THORPE ST PETER

1546–7
St Peter's Churchwardens' Accounts   LA: THORPE ST PETER PAR/7/1   25
p 7*   *(20 May–20 May)*

...

Item payd to ye players off candylmesse day   viij d.

...

Memorandum payd in ye same yere after we had   30
accowntyd att candylmes to ye players whytche played
her off ye sonday next after Saint mathyes day   vj d.

...

THURLBY   35

1521/2
Will of John Sawer   LA: LCC WILLS 1520–25
f 50v*   *(14 January)*

...   40

...Item I gyffe my erres to ye thylde of our lady whyche the mynstrilles

33/ ye sonday ... day: *27 February 1546/7*   41/ ye thylde: *for* the yelde *(?)*

kepe in lincoln…

…

TIMBERLAND

1638
Archdeaconry of Lincoln Visitation Book   LA: Diocesan Vij/21
f 23*

Proceedings arising from the visitation of Wraggoe deanery by Morgan Wynnterly and others

…

Bardney   Will*elm*us Boulton *presentatus* apud Timberland for fidling in the time of
A.   divine seruice & sermon./ °27. oct*o*bris 1638 comp*aruit* & submisit vnde
      h*abe*t ad agnosc*endum* & cert*ificandum* in 2° °18 Maij 1639. C*itatus*
      preconizato non com*paruit excommunicatus./*°

A.   Ra*dul*phus Colledge *presentatus* for the like/ °27. *octo*bris 1638 cit*atus*
      preconizato non C*omparuit excommunicatus/.*°
      & vide dec*anatum* de Horncastle/
      …

TOYNTON ALL SAINTS

1612
Inventory of Charles Cooke, Gentleman   LA: INV 112A/131
mb 1*   *(8 April)* *(In the parlour)*
…
It*em* one chest of viols with the bookes one bandore
one ffrench cittron on english cittro*n* with a double
payer of virgenals   x li.
…

TOYNTON (NEXT HORNCASTLE)

1637
Archdeaconry of Lincoln Visitation Book   LA: Diocesan Vij/20
f 157v*   *(5 October)*

Proceedings arising from a session held for the deaneries of Horncastle, Hill, and Gartree in the parish church at Horncastle before Morgan Wynne, cleric, archdeacon of Lincoln, in the presence of Philip Pregion, notary public and registrar

…

Willelmus Maddyson Iunior
Iohannes Waterman
gardiani for omitting to present a company of disordered persons distemperd
with drincke vpon the sunday so that they cutt off one anothers beardes and
besmeared & dawbed there faces & cloathes with soote dirt & such like matter   5
that they scare seemed like men & some of theire freindes scarce knew them.

vide librum officialem expeditur/

TOYNTON ST PETER   10

1615
Will of Ralph Knyght, Musician   LA: LCC WILLS 1615
f 89*   *(17 June)*
...   15
...All the rest of my goodes vngiuen and not bequeathed I giue to my Sister
Anne whome I make the executrix of this my will who shall see my body
honestly buryed and my Debtes payd And giue vnto my man Dixon the
worse trible violinge of two...
...   20

Inventory of Ralph Knyght, Musician   LA: INV 117/394
single sheet*   *(2 October)*
...
In primes his purse gerdell and his Aperell and   25
his Instrumentes   x s.
...

TYDD ST MARY
                                                                                 30
1616
Archdeaconry of Lincoln Visitation Book   LA: Diocesan Vij/16
f 11v*   *(1 October)*

Proceedings arising from the visitation of South Holland deanery held in the   35
parish church at Boston, before Christopher Wyvell, LLD, the archdeacon of
Lincoln's official, and Thomas Robinson, cleric, MA, his surrogate judge
...
Anthonie Thompson for misbehavinge himselfe vppon the saboth daye as
namelie in pipinge./ 30mo octobris 1616 quesitus &c vijs &c 13 Novembris   40
1616 citatus &c suspensus.

6/ scare: *for* scarce

The *said* Anthonie for not livinge with his wife./ 27 Novem*bris* 1616 cit*atus* &c *suspensus.*

...

WADDINGHAM

1566
Inventory of Heathenish Church Goods LA: Diocesan FUR 2
f 108* *(11 April) (Goods held since the death of Queen Mary)*

Examination held at Lincoln before Martin Hollingworth, commissioner
...

Item all the banner clothes and crosse clothes were cutt in peces by S*ir* Roberte Towne o*ur* p*ar*soune and he made [pal] playinge cotes for childerne of them

f 108v*
...

Item one sacringe bell w*hic*h honge at a maypole toppe and what is become thereof we knowe °nott°
...

WADDINGTON

1639
St Michael's Vestry Book LA: WADDINGTON PAR/10/1
f 11Av*
...

Item to ye muzicke   iiij d.
...
⟨...⟩he muzicke   iiij d.

WAINFLEET ST MARY

1616
Archdeaconry of Lincoln Visitation Book LA: Diocesan Vij/17
f 20/25*
...

D*imittitu*r
Stephen Gregge for mainteininge a cockfight in the churchyard. [⟨.⟩] 4 Iun*ij*

31/ ⟨...⟩he: *20mm of text missing due to tear*

1616. quesitus &c vijs &c 18ᵘᵒ Iunij 1616 citatus &c comparuit Lawrence et allegavit se esse nuncium &c & obiecto articulo fatetur & dimittitur.

Dimittitur
Richardus Smithe similiter . 4: Iunij 1616. citatus &c comparuit [& obiecto   5
articulo fatetur] Thomas Byte & allegavit se esse nuncium &c & obiecto
articulo fatetur & cum monicione dimittitur.

⟨...⟩
⟨...⟩e similiter 4 . Iunij 1616. citatus &c comparuit & obiecto articulo negat   10
& habet ad ⟨...⟩ proximam monicionem postea fatetur & cum monicione
dimittitur.

⟨...⟩
⟨...⟩ Iunij 1616. comparuit Shepherd ∧⌜& allegavit se esse nuncium &c⌝ &   15
obiecto articulo fatetur ⟨...⟩

WELTON LE WOLD

1566   20
Inventory of Heathenish Church Goods   LA: Diocesan FUR 2
f 148*   *(26 April) (Goods held since the death of Queen Mary)*
...

Item ij albes	wherof one was sold to tiiij plaiers the other likewyse
	made a coveringe for the communion table 25
Item iiij vestments	sold to the same men since christmas last/

...

WESTBOROUGH

30

1609
Archdeaconry of Lincoln Visitation Book   LA: Diocesan Vij/12
p 465*
...

suspensus   35
Iohannes Elliott for playinge on his bagpipe at Westburghe all eveninge
prayer time on sunday the ixᵗʰ of Iulij 1609. 28 Iulij 1609. citatus non
comparuit &c [excommunicatus] suspensus
...

9/ ⟨...⟩: *50mm missing*	14, 15/ ⟨...⟩: *70mm missing*
10/ ⟨...⟩e: *40mm missing*	16/ ⟨...⟩: *entire line missing*
11/ ⟨...⟩: *40mm missing*	24/ tiiij: *for iiij*

WHAPLODE

1514
Will of John Randall   LA: LCC WILLS 1520–25
f 31v*   *(31 March)*   5
...
...It*em* lu*m*ini de le dauncers xij d....
...

1637   10
Archdeaconry of Lincoln Visitation Book   LA: Diocesan Vij/20
f 239   *(1 July)*

Proceedings arising from the visitation of South Holland deanery held in the
parish church at Bourne before John Farmery, LLD, vicar general, in the presence   15
of Philip Pregion, notary public, and Mr Titloe, vicar of Bourne
...
d*imittitu*r
Ioh*an*nes Holmes for fighting cockes vpon ye sabboath day in ye time of
diuine seruice. °27 oc*tobris* 1637 co*m*p*aru*it App*aritor* & fass*us* est h*ab*et ad   20
agnoscend*um* & cer*tificandum* in 2. ex*h*ib*itum* est cer*tificariu*m & *(blank)*°

d*imittitu*r
Ioh*an*nes Higgens for ye like. °27 oc*tobris* 1637 co*m*p*aru*it App*aritor* fatetur h*ab*et
ad agnoscend*um* & cer*tificandum* in 2. non cer*tificavi*t vnde ex*communicatus*   25
28 Martij 1639 co*m*p*aru*it & f*acta* fide abs*oluitur* & d*imittitu*r°

WIGTOFT

1512   30
AC   ***Sts Peter and Paul's Churchwardens' Accounts***
   F.: 'Extracts from the Churchwardens Accompts of Wigtoft'
   p 205*
...
It*em* payd for to kyng gyrdyl   0 0 2   35
...

1519
AC   ***Sts Peter and Paul's Churchwardens' Accounts***
   F.: 'Extracts from the Churchwardens Accompts of Wigtoft'   40
   p 207*
...
It*em* Resavyd for maye   0 0 8
...

1525

AC **Sts Peter and Paul's Churchwardens' Accounts**
   F.: 'Extracts from the Churchwardens Accompts of Wigtoft'
p 216*

...   5

Item payd to Thomas Dekonson, for what spent at
swynneshed baume   0 3 4

...

1532   10

AC **Sts Peter and Paul's Churchwardens' Accounts**
   F.: 'Extracts from the Churchwardens Accompts of Wigtoft'
p 222

...

Item. to katyn deconson, for drynke and bredd at ye   15
creyeng of Spauldyng Baunne,   0 0 9
Item. payd to ye seid katyn, for drynke,   0 0 1

...

Item. payd for the cryeng of Spauldyng Bayn,   0 6 8
...   20

WITHAM ON THE HILL

1550–1
St Andrew's Churchwardens' Accounts   25
  LA: WITHAM ON THE HILL PAR/7/1
f 1v*   (25 December–25 December)

...

Item payd to the players in the Church   iij s. iiij d.
...   30

WRAGBY

1585
Episcopal Visitation Book   LA: Diocesan Vj/16   35
f 60v

dimittitur
Thomas Toniton saltauit in ecclesia °xjº die septembris 1585 apud lincolniam
citatus comparuit et negat habet ad purgandum se iiijª manu die Sabbati 40
proximo postea submisit se vnde cum monicione°

...

40/ manu: *5 minims for* nu

Religious Houses

BARDNEY ABBEY

1246
Bardney Abbey Chartulary   BL: Cotton Vespasian E.xx
ff 30v–1v*   *(23 April)*   5
…

Composicio de Iurisdict*io*ne Archid*iaconali* & p*ro*curacione eiusde*m* de
Capella o*m*nium sancto*rum* de Barton*en*si.

Omnib*us* s*an*cte matris ecclesie filijs inspectur*is* & auditur*is* presentes litteras   10
innotescat. Q*uo*d cum mota e*ss*et questio auctoritate ap*ost*olica coram decano |
eccl*es*ie sar*um* suisq*ue* collegis. Int*er* d*omi*n*um* Thomam archid*iaconum*
lin*col*niensis ex una parte. et abb*at*em & Conuentum de Bard*eneia* ex
altera. sup*er* totali Iurisdictione archidiaconali In parochia de Bard*eneia*
exercenda. & sup*er* visitacione ecclesie parochialis de Bard*eneia*. &   15
p*ro*curacione r*aci*one visitacionis s*ib*i debita. Et coram priore de strugullia
d*omi*ni pape commissario sup*er* p*ro*curacione annua ecclesie o*m*nium
s*an*ctorum de Barton*en*si. quam dicebat e*ss*e parochialem. Simil*ite*r r*aci*one
visitacionis s*ib*i debita. Quam s*cilicet* d*ic*ti abb*as* & Conuent*us* In proprios
usus possident. Et sup*er* quib*us*dam iniurijs & alijs p*er*sonalibus actionib*us*.   20
quas ponderata r*aci*one Centum libras estimabat? Tandem. amicabili reali &
In et*er*num valitura composicione? dicta questio utraq*ue* in forma subscripta
conquieuit. Videlic*et* q*uo*d d*ic*t*us* Archid*iaco*n*us* & sui successores omnes
qui p*ro* temp*or*e fuerint. Habebunt uisitacionem Ecclesie parochial*is* de
Bard*eneia*. Quaten*us* est ecclesia parochialis. & p*ro*curacion*em* annuam   25
r*aci*one visitacionis eiusdem. Et simil*ite*r habebunt plene. integre. & sine
aliq*ua* diminucione Iurisdictionem omnimodam In d*ic*ta parochia de
Bard*eneia*. Nisi in subscriptis casib*us* tantum? a dicto archid*iacono* predic*to*
Abb*at*i & successorib*us* suis concessis & expresse exceptis. Videlic*et* q*uo*d
d*ic*t*us* Abbas & sui successores retineant & habeant causas iniuriar*um*   30
illatar*um*. f*ac*to u*e*l uerbo int*er* laicos d*ic*te parochie dieb*us* festiuis. Ite*m*
causas de festis non obseruatis. Ite*m* de Cariagijs p*er* dies sollempnes. Ite*m*

de arietib*us*. & alijs spectaculis. It*em* de scothales. It*em* de luctatorib*us*.
It*em* de Coreis. It*em* de excessib*us* reg*ul*arium domus de Barden*eia*. In dicta
parochia de Barden*eia* ab ip*s*is comissis. It*em* de male decimantib*us*. & de
ale | atorib*us* Sup*er* premissis uero exceptis casib*us*? retinebunt & habebunt
d*ictus* Abb*a*s & sui successores plenam iurisdictione*m*. Ita ta*m*e*n* q*u*od si   5
fuerit ab ip*s*is Abb*a*te & successorib*us* suis in hui*us*modi appellatum? ad
d*o*min*um* archidiaconum & suos? fiat appellacio successores. & plenam
sup*er* appellacionib*us* habebunt archidiaconu*s* predict*us* & sui successores
cognicionem cum effectu. Celebrabunt aut*em* d*ictus* archid*iaco*nu*s* & sui
successores cap*itulu*m in parochia de Barden*eia* de eisdem p*ar*ochianis &   10
familia abbacie t*antu*m. In Cappella iuxta monas*ter*ium de Barden*eia*. bis
in anno. u*e*l ter. cum uiderint expedire. u*e*l in alijs capell*is* eiusdem p*ar*ochie.
de causis eiusde*m* & d*ict*e familie. Et exceptis hijs uicib*us*. in uicinis eccl*es*ijs
extra d*ict*am p*ar*ochiam cum uoluerint. Remisit aut*em* d*ictus* archidiaconu*s*
pro se & suis successorib*us* In p*er*petuu*m* d*ict*is Abb*a*ti & Conuentui &   15
eor*um* successorib*us* procuracione*m* petitam de d*ict*a ecclesia o*m*nium
s*an*ctor*um* de Barton*ensi*. Et de Barden*eia*? denarios b*eat*i petri & synodalia.
& omnes alias iniuriarum actiones & alias quascumq*ue* coram dictis iudicib*us*
motas & eciam mouendas s*ibi* temp*or*e confectionis h*uius* scripti *contra*
d*ict*os abb*at*em & Conuentu*m* de Barden*eia* competentes. quas estimabat   20
mille Marcas. omnemq*ue* condempnac*ion*em expensar*um* f*a*ct*am* apud
strugull*iam* expresse renuntians sup*er* omnib*us* premissis? omnib*us* impetratis
& inposterum impetrandis. In *cuius* rei testimonium p*re*senti scripto in
mod*o* cirographi confecto? sigilla archidiaconi & d*ict*orum Abb*at*is &
Conuent*us* vice Mutua sunt appensa. Act*a* ap*ud* freston*iensem*. Non*um*.   25
k*a*lendar*um*. Maij. Anno d*o*m*in*i M*o*. cc*o*. xl*o*. sexto….

1434
Bishop William Gray's Register   LA: Bishop's Register 17
f 202v*   30

…Similit*er* iniu*n*gimus vobis vniu*er*sis et sing*u*lis presentib*us* et futuris sub
penis supra et infrascriptis q*u*od om*n*es tam senes q*u*am iuuenes indifferent*er*
iux*t*a eor*um* posse corporeu*m* temporib*us* debitis contemplacioni vacent in
claustro omissis ludis inhonestis quos p*er* quosdam in Mon*asterio* nimiu*m*   35
ex*er*ceri consueuerunt & q*u*od nullatin*us* in antea sicut solito discurrent aut
vagent circa insolencias contra regulares obseruancias & q*u*od in p*re*missor*um*
aliquo transgredientes acrit*er* puniant*ur* secundu*m* regulam ita q*u*od pena
vnius sit omnib*us* in exemplum…

7/ & suos? … successores: *for* & suos successores? fiat appellacio *(?)*
12/ u*e*l in alijs capell*is*: *for* ibidem u*e*l in alijs capellis *(?)*

1527–8
Cellarers' Accounts   TNA: PRO SC 6/HENVIII/1986
f 17v*   *(Gifts and rewards)*

...

Item datum in Regardo ijbus Cantatoribus	
de tatershall	xx d.

...

Item datum in Regardo Cuidam Cantatori	xij d.

...

Item datum in Regardo lusoribus supervenientibus	
tempore natalis domini ⌜[ij s. viij d. viij d. xij d.	
xij d. ij s. viij d. xij d.]⌝	ix s.

...

Item datum in Regardo Thome Swan mimo	vj s. viij d.
Item datum in Regardo lusoribus ducis suffochie	v s.

...

f 18*

...

Item datum in Regardo mimo seruo domini Iohannis	
husee ⌜⟨...⟩⌝	viij d.

...

Item datum in Regardo lusoribus de Bedford	iiij d.

...

Item datum in Regardo vrsario domini Iohannis husee	xij d.

...

Item datum in Regardo vrsario ducis Richmondie	xx d.

...

Item datum in Regardo thome Swan	xx d.
Item datum in Regardo vrsario ducis suffochie	xx d.

...

Item datum in Regardo iijbus Mimis	xij d.

...

Item datum in Regardo iiijor Mimis Ciuitatis eboraci	xvj d.

...

Item datum in Regardo iiijor Mimis	xvj d.

...

f 18v*

...

Item datum in Regardo Mimo domini latemer	viij d.

...

Item datum in Regardo cuidam Cantatori seruo
domini sugges   iij s. iiij d.
Item datum in Regardo ij^{bus} Mimis   viij d.
...

Item datum in Regardo lusoribus domini Regis   iiij s.   5
...

Item datum in Regardo iij^{bus} Mimis domini Cardinalis   vij s. vj d.
...

Item datum in Regardo Cantatoribus in die
sancti oswaldi   xij s. 10
Item datum in Regardo thome Swan & alijs
mimis dicto die   iiij s. iiij d.
...

Item datum in Regardo iiij^{or} mimis domini Regis iij s. iiij d.
...   15

Item Iohanni Sawbell mimo ij s.
...

1528–9
Cellarers' Accounts   TNA: PRO SC 6/HENVIII/1986   20
f 35   (29 September–15 April) (Gifts and Rewards)
...
Item datum in Regardo ... iij^{bus} mimis ⌜vj d. vj d. iiij d.⌝
...

                                                                               25

f 35v*
...
Item datum in Regardo iij^{bus} mimis de norwiche ⌜viij d.⌝...
...

Item datum in Regardo vrsario domini ducis Richmonde   ij s. 30
...

Item datum in Regardo ij^{bus} mimis   xij d.
Item datum in Regardo Gyrsby mimo ⌜viij d.⌝ & magistro bracost/ ⌜xij d.⌝
cuidam vrsario ⌜vj d.⌝ puero mimo ⌜iiij d.⌝
...   35

14–16/ Item ... ij s.: part of a series of entries added in the left margin due to lack of space
30/ datum: d partly written over [solutum]
33/ &: corrected over ad

1529
Cellarers' Accounts   TNA: PRO SC 6/HENVIII/1986
f 42*   *(15 April– 29 September) (Payments)*

…

In primis sol*utum* 2^ob*us* mimis delib*eratum* ad p*ro*prias   5
man*us* celler*arij*   vj d.

datum
® It*em* vrsario
vestmorland
viij d.

…

datum   It*em* dat*um* in Regard*o* cuidam gestatori ⌈iiij d.⌉ & iij^{bus}
waites ⌈xij d.⌉ de lyn*coln*   ·xvj d

…   10

datum   It*em* dat*um* in Regard*o* ser*uo* vic*arij* de Barton ⌈viij d.⌉ & cuidam mimo
d*o*m*i*ni de hastyng*es* ⌈iiij d.⌉

…

f 42v*   15

datum   It*em* dat*um* in Regard*o* iiij^{or} mimis   xij d.
datum   It*em* dat*um* in Regard*o* ij^{bus} waites   viij d.

…

datum   It*em* dat*um* in Regard*o* iij^{bus} Mimis d*o*m*i*ni R*egis*   v s. 20

…

datum   It*em* dat*um* in Regard*o* iij^{bus} waites de yorke   xij d.
datum   It*em* dat*um* in Regard*o* ser*uo* d*o*m*i*ni Srope &
ij^{bus} mimis   xij d.

25

f 43*

…

datum   It*em* dat*um* in Regard*o* ij^{bus} Mimis   viij d.

…

datum   It*em* dat*um* in Regard*o* diu*er*sis mimis die *sancti* oswaldi   iiij s. viij d. 30
datum   It*em* dat*um* in Regard*o* Cantatorib*us* de tat*er*sall/
⌈vij s. vj d.⌉ de lincoln ⌈ij s.⌉ & boston ⌈iij s. iiij d.⌉   xij s. x d.

…

datum   It*em* dat*um* in Regard*o* iiij^{or} mimis d*o*m*i*ni R*egis*   iij s. iiij d.

…   35

6–8m/ It*em* … viij d.: *inserted in space left blank in right margin*
9/ de lyn*coln*: *added over filler line between* waites *and sum*
23/ Srope: *for* Scrope (?)

f 43v*

…

datum   Item datum in Regardo ij^bus Mimis domini westmorland
        & seruo vicecomitis   xvj d.

…   5

datum   Item datum in Regardo ij^bus mimis domini Cardinalis   iij s. iiij d.

…

1531
Cellarers' Accounts   TNA: PRO SC 6/HENVIII/1986   10
f 68   *(8 June)* *(Corpus Christi feast expenses)*

…

Item datum in Regardo Mimis   xij s.

…

                                                                                       15

CROWLAND ABBEY

1536
Letter to Thomas Cromwell   TNA: PRO SP 1/101
single sheet*   *(26 January)*   20

After my due commendations and thankes. Where I haue writen lately to you
two or thre tymes of sad maters: now I haue occasion to write vnto yow of
a cause of myrthe ordeyned to temper sadnes. Ye know the kinges grace hath
one old fole: Sexton/ as good as myght be. which bi reason of aige is not like   25
to continew. I haue espied one yong fole at Croland. whiche in myne opinion
shalbe muche more pleasaunt than euer Sexton was in euery poinct. and he
is not past xv yeres old./ whiche is every day newe to the herer. And albeit I
meself haue but smal delectation in folys (I am made of so hevy a mater) yet
emong a greate number whiche I haue herd speke. I haue thought this same,   30
one of the best that I haue herd and I beleue you wol so think when ye here
him. He wolbe very mete for the cort and the kinges grace shall haue muche
pleasir by such passe t⟨…⟩ shal make bothe with gentilmen and gentilwomen/
⟨…⟩ please you to send to thabbot of croland for him and h⟨…⟩ veryly. ye shal
do the kinges graces as great pleasir ⟨…⟩ may be doen in any suche thing./// 35
ffrom Spalding the xxvi day of Ianuarie.

                                        Your owne *(signed)* Thomas Bedyll

---

33/ passe t⟨…⟩: *30mm missing due to tear in sheet*   34/ h⟨…⟩: *35mm missing due to tear in sheet*
34/ ⟨…⟩: *40mm missing due to tear in sheet*   35/ ⟨…⟩: *30mm missing due to tear in sheet*

HUMBERSTON ABBEY

1440
Episcopal Visitation Book   LA: Diocesan Vj/1
f 69   *(6 July) (Charges by Abbot William West)*   5

Visitation held in the abbey's chapter house by William Alnwick, bishop of Lincoln

...

Conspiracio   ℭ Item dicit quod Willelmus Anderby & Iohannes wrauby, monachi,   10
sunt confederatores & confederatores adinuicem contra abbatem.
Anderby purgauit se de conspiracione cum ffreshney/ wrauby purgauit se
cum Anderby

Anderby   ℭ Item quod iste [Anderby] ⌜wrauby⌝ dixit publice postquam abbas receperat
mandatum domini pro visitacione ecce iam abbas non habet intromittere   15
∧⌜se⌝ de me

wrauby   ℭ Item dicit quod wrauby non intelligit nec addiscere velit

wrauby   Item dicit quod wrauby proteruiter & rebelliter respondebat abbati [quando]
cum ipsum corriperet eo quod scandebat portas quasdam ad respiciendum
fistulatores & ducentes choreas in cimiterio ecclesie parochialis & est inobediens   20
quasi in omnibus dicens quod nunquam subiret correccionem abbatis in
aliquibus Fatetur vltimam partem articuli & iurauit de peragendo penitenciam
∧⌜videlicet⌝ quod [peraga] petat veniam ab abbate quod & fecit & quod
dicat vnum nocturnum de psalterio dauitico infra septimanam proximam
& quoad primam partem articuli fatetur   25

...

f 69v*   *(Charges made by William Anderby, monk)*
...

Item dicit quod ⌜⟨...⟩⌝ abbas vendidit vnum corrodium Iohanni harden   30
harpour pro x marcis & valet xl s. in anno & stetit sic viij annis et dicit
quod tempore vendicionis abbas comminabatur conventui quod nisi
consenserint vendicioni huic ipse venderet quarterium frumenti pro ij s. &
⟨...⟩ de bonis domus abbas fatetur vendicionem sed contencionem esse
inter ipsum & quosdam de conuentu pro consensu   35
...

11/ confederatores & confederatores: *for* confederatores & conspiratores *(?)*
30/ Item dicit: *obscured by repair paper*

NUN COTHAM PRIORY

1531
Bishop John Longland's Register   LA: Bishop's Register 26
ff 218–19*   *(30 April)*   5

Iohn Longlond by the sufferaunce of god bushope of Lincoln to our
welbeloued susters in christe the prioresse and covent of nuncotton of our
dioces of Lincoln sendeth greting grace and our blessing. And forasmoche
as in our ordynary visitacion of late exercysed within yat house dyuerse   10
thinges apperyd and were detected worthy reformacion we therefore for the
honour of god and redresse of the same and mayntenaunce of good religion
ther send to you thies Iniuncions folowing whiche we will and commaund
you to kepe undre the paynes ensewing.
   …I chardge you lady priores and all the ladyes susters of your monastery   15
and your succesours hereafter to come in the vertue of obedyence and the
payne of contempte that fromehensforth ye doo and cause to be doon all
your dyvyne seruice to be treateably song vndre sobre & deuoute manner,
with good pause and punctuacion And without eny haste or festinacion.
And that ye kepe your due houres and tymes of your said dyvyne seruice   20
with all other your obseruances and your ceremonyes aswell in the cloistre,
chapitour house, fratry and dortor, as in the quere. And that ye kepe fyrme love
and charyte emonges you, without whiche charyte noo vertue can prevaile nor
religion prosper nor be acceptable to almighty god, nor merytoryous to the doer.
And chardge you lady priores ther sett in the roome as hede, ruler and   25
gouernour: to use your self as a good modre, lovingly charitably, and
indifferently to all your susters and spirituall children. And soo doing ye
shall best please god and noryshe charyte emonges them. And that ye give
nott to light credence to euery tale, whiche light credence is the norysher
of debate and uaryaunce.   30
And likewise chardge you lady priores that ye suffre nomore herafter eny
lorde of mysrule to be within your house, nouther to suffre hereafter eny
suche disgysinges as in tymes past haue bene used in your monastery in
nunnes apparell ne otherwise. And that frome hensforth ye do nomore
burden ne chardge your house with suche a nombre of your kynnesfolkes as ye   35
haue in tymes past vsed. your good | mother itt is meate ye haue aboute you
for your comforte and hirs bothe, And oon or ij moo of suche your saddest
kynnesfolkes whome ye shall thynk mooste conuenyent but passe nott.
   …
And forasmoche as by your negligent sufferaunce dyuerse of your susters   40

11/ worthy: *for* worthy of

hath wandred a brode in the world, some vndre the pretense of pylgrymages, some to see ther frendes, and otherwise wherby hath growen many Inconuenyences, insolent behauioures, and moche slaunder aswell to your house as to those susters, as by the compertes of my said visitacion doth euydently appere, I chardge you lady priores therfore and all your successours that fromehensforth ye neyer licence ne suffre eny your susters to goo out of your monastery without a grette vrgent cause by you knowen and ij of your seniour susters approved afore your said licence soo given. And that they tary nott out of the monastery in the nightes time…. '

And that ye lady prioresse cause and compell all your susters (those oonly ˄⌐excepte⌐ that be seke) to kepe the quere And nomore to be absent as in tymes past they haue been wont to use, being content iff vj haue been present, the residue to goo att lybertie where they wold some att thornton some att Newsom, some at hull some att other places att their pleasures: whiche is in the sight of good men abhomynable, high displeasur to god, rebuke, shame and reproche to religion. And due correccions to be doon according vnto your religion from tyme to tyme.

Also we chardge you lady prioresse vndre payn of excommunicacion that ye frome hensforth nomore suffre Sir Iohn warde Sir Richard caluerley Sir william Iohnson nor parson curtes ne the parson of Skotton ne Sir william Seele to come within the precincte of your monasterye, that if they by chaunce doo vnwares to you that ye streight banishe them and suffre not them ther to | tary, nor noon of your susters to commune with them, or eny of them. And that ye voide oute of your house Robert laurence And he nomore to resort to the same.

Ouerthis I chardge you lady prioresse undre the said payne that ye yerely make your accompte openly and truley in your chapitour house afore the moost parte and the senioures of your susters that they may knowe frome yere to yere the state of the said house. And that ye streight vpon sight herof dymynishe the nombre of your seruantes aswell men as women, whiche excessyve nombre that ye kepe of them bothe is oon of the grette causes of your miserable pouertye, and that ye are nott hable to mayntene your household, nouther reparacions of the same by reason whereof all falleth to ruyne and extreme dekaye. And therefore to kepe noo moo thenne shalbe iuged necessary for your said house. And that ye suffre nott eny men children to be brought vpp, nor taught within your monastery, nor to resorte to eny of your susters, nouther to lye within your monastery. Nor eny person young ne old to lye within your dorter butt oonly religious women. And that euery suster doo lye alone according vnto the lawes. And the doore of the said dorter nightly to be shite and light nightly to brenne in the same.

…

ff 219v–20*

…

Item I chardge you ladyes all undre payn of disobedyence and of the lawe, that ye and eueryche of you doo truely obserue your religion, serue god, kepe your dyuyne seruice deuoutely and all other rytes, obseruances and ceremonyes apperteyning vnto your said religion aswell within the chirche, chapitour house fratry dortre as cloistre. And that ye be obedyent in all lefull commaundementes vnto your lady priores. And obserue and kepe very charite amonges you. And to leve all discencion rancor, malice and debate, and to vnite your selues in god by clene, chaste, and religious, lyving. And nomore to wandre abrode in the contreth as ye haue vsed nouther by the pretence of pilgrymages, nor of visitacion of your frendes, whereby moche slaunder hath risen to your house and many inconvenyences. And to occupye your selues whenne your seruice is doon in some good occupacions and labours, soo to avoide ydlenes | the mother and norisher of all vice. And to flee all yll company. and noo suspecte persones to haue eny resorte to you nor ye to them And thus doing ye shall haue the blessing of god and myn

…

THORNTON ABBEY

1440
Episcopal Visitation Book   LA: Diocesan Vj/1
f 73   *(11 July)* *(Testimony of Brother John Hull)*

Proceedings of the visitation held in the chapter house of Thornton Abbey by William Alnwick, bishop of Lincoln

®Sacrista   Item quod sacrista accomodat vestamenta meliora Monasterij ludentibus ludos noxios in partibus inter laicos per quod deteriorantur & scandalum generatur Monasterio petit igitur vt in istis refrenetur accomodacione

…

f 73v   *(Testimony of Brother John Wrangle, infirmarian)*
…

Item dicit de elemosina & de pueris qui solent esse in elemosinaria vt supra & de vestimentis accomodatis vt supra

…

30/ quod: *for* quod dicit *(?)*
37/ qui: *corrected from* que

f 78v   *(Bishop's injunctions to Thornton Abbey)*

...Item iniungimus & mandamus sacriste dicti Monasterij pro tempe existenti
sub penis supra & infrascriptis ne vestimenta dicti Monasterij quecunque
ad aliquos ludos ∧[noxios] in partibus inter populares vel ad alia ludibria vel   5
spectacula quouismodo accomedare presumet cum per tales accomodaciones
multum deteriorata sunt vestimenta huiusmodi & non liceat [humanibus]
∧⌈humanis⌉ vsibus prophanari que semel deo dedicata existunt...

3/ iniungimus: *7 minims in MS*
3/ tempe: *for* tempore; *mark of abbreviation missing*
5/ ∧[noxios]: *caret added but no insertion made*
6/ accomedare: *for* accomodare

Households

ARMINE OF OSGODBY

1631/2
Letter from Thomas Tuke to Sir William Armine   sro: DD/FJ 25
f [1v]*   *(10 February)*   5
...

The common fame is that the Queen has not been at masse this month: sure
it is she was not at their play at midnight on Christmas eue, when they acted
the Virgin's deliuery & bringing to bed, & the birth of Christ, & his lying
ith manger etc. Which made some of her French followers pout. And that the   10
king has crost of late some sunday night–masking & has been heard to say he
will haue no more masking & dauncing on those nights. And there I pray God
he may continue, & incline his heart to all goodnes, & Her's also to loue the
truth, & hate the idolatries & errors, shee has been nuzzled up in, and Both of
them to study & doo such thing*es* as may tend to God's glory, & to reioyce   15
the h⟨...⟩ of all such as fear God & wish the welfare of the Church & State:
...

f [2]*

...   20
Ashwedensday

Has talkt of masking*es* & massing*es*, & whisper's something of a presse, but
when, or why, ne gru quidem. The Qu*een* would haue had the mask on sunday
night last: because of ashwed*ens*day but the ki*ng* would not, but made it be
last night.   25

16/ h⟨...⟩: *10mm missing*
21/ Ashwedensday: *15 February 1631/2*
23/ ne gru quidem: *'not even a peep'*
23–4/ sunday night last: *Shrove Sunday, 12 February 1631/2*
24/ because: *corrected over another word*
25/ last night: *Shrove Tuesday, 14 February 1631/2*

1632
Letter from Thomas Tuke to Sir William Armine SRO: DD/FJ 25
single sheet*

Easter Munday

...

When the K*ing* & Q*ueen* were at Cambridge, they heard a play ˄[at] ⌐acted by⌐
Queene's Colledge ˄⌐men⌐ a long, dull, vnseasoned piece off stuffe, & gaue
no contentment: yet it seemes the m*aste*r of the house & the vicechancel*lor*
Dr Butts (who they say had's head in it) thought & sought to haue giuen
all contentment, & therin also to haue furtherred their own thoughts &
hopes. The puritan too must be the matter of their merriment (w*hi*ch how
vnfit, specially where Papists were present,) halfe an eye might see. Now
this very day has filld the town full of a strang action Butts has acted vpon
himselfe; Court & Citty rings of this, The Vicechancellor of Cambridge
Doctor Butts has hang'd himselfe. Iudicium Dei tremendum. There went
out also (a grosse abuse) at that time I wot not how many extraordinarie
graduats, 21 Doctors they say, & so also diuerse of other degrees: & the
earle of Hol*land's* Secret*ary* Sanderson, made they say, great gaines therby:
for w*hi*ch cause one that came to mee this euen from the Court tells mee
the king has caused Holland turne away his man Sanderson, and take into
his room one Lucas that was the L*ord* Carleton's secretarye.

Easter tuesday

T'is true ynough that Butts has made such an end of his life, so as no story
speaks the like of any vicechancellor, any where.

...

single sheet verso*

Wedensday

...

The speach is that Butts & Sanderson spacking together, 21 went out Doctors,
some of them for dunsery hauing neuer been able to get to be M*aste*rs of
arts: 18 Bach*elors* of Divin*ity* 8 M*aste*rs of arts: 2: bach*elors* of Law: things so
cried againste by the more ingenuous Academicks, that it came to the k*ings*
& the Chancel*lors* ears, post factum, and therupo*n* they say the Chancel*lor*
chode the Vicechancel*lor* Besides the play that the men of Q*ueens* Col*lege*

5/ Easter Munday: *2 April 1632*	16/ Iudicium Dei tremendum: *'a terrible judgement*
7/ ˄[at]: *caret written over at*	*from God'*
13/ present,): *closing parenthesis inserted later, possibly*	23/ Easter tuesday: *3 April 1632*
intended to overwrite comma	30/ Wedensday: *4 April 1632*

played was most fulsome: the Puritans drest in Ministers Gownes, kissing
& courting of wenches: and this done too whe⟨..⟩ it's supposed 40 disguised
Iesuites & priests were, besides the Queen & her followers. And Martin, the
Bishop of London's chaplin, that preacht that so much talkt of Arminian
sermon at Pauls Crosse on good friday was present. is the Master of Queens   5
College. And no other day, as men here talk, did Butts make choyce to hang
himself on, then (last good fryday hauing sayd to his wife the Deuill was too
good for him) iust vpon easter day, making himselfe his own hangman, and
putting himself to death that day the redeemer of the world rose from death.
...   10

Letter from Thomas Tuke to Sir William Armine   SRO: DD/FJ 25
f [1v]*   (2 May)
...

Here of late [⟨.⟩]in the space of 9 daies eight died suddenly, the last of which   15
was a Player, who fell down suddenly vpon the stage in the play-house in
Salsbury court in the sight of all the spectators, wheroff diuerse were Lords,
come to hear a new play, wherin this man had his part, a lusty young fellow,
about 30 yeers of age. They carried him out into the air, but all done, they
could, he so died. This hapned vpon fryday last. I say no more but God   20
make vs all fit for his kingdome.
...

Letter from Thomas Tuke to Sir William Armine   SRO: DD/FJ 25
p 4*   (29 November)   25
...

Thursday, St Andrew's euen Nouember 29.
...

I was this euen in a stacioners shop, whether came 2 Courtiers; one of
them is now going Embassy ledger to Venice, the other a man, I haue   30
knowen well these 2⟨.⟩ yeers & more, exceptione maior: both these said
that this very day at noon they heard the king say He hop'd his brother of
Sweden was aliue & would recouer his health and mine acquaintance said,
for certain a stop is made of blacks till the king exprest himself further, &
bid the play should be plaied at Court to night. And one of the Players   35
by chance passing by where I was, one in my company, that knew him,
askt him If the play held at Cour⟨.⟩ to night? yes, quoth he, & I am now
going thither.
...

20/ fryday last: *27 April 1632*
31/ exceptione maior: *'(a witness) greater than (any) objection'*

Letter from Thomas Tuke to Sir William Armine   SRO: DD/FJ 25
p 1*   *(30 November)*

...

The Play held at Court last night: and about 10 a clock about the time the
play began, l*ett*ers were brought fro*m* Hague to the king, from the Q*ueen*   5
of Boh*emia* & the k*ings* Agent there, that the k*ing* of Sweden was aliue, and
that there was hope of his health....

...

1633/4   10
Letter from Thomas Tuke to Sir William Armine   SRO: DD/FJ 25
single sheet*   *(9 January)*

...

Lith⟨...⟩ the french dancing master said to be knighted, & was so saucy as
to tell ⟨...⟩ had spent 5000 li. in his seruice more then he got: the K*ing* bad   15
⟨...⟩ gon, & to help on gaue him a kick on the back. He is a cut ⟨...⟩
The ⟨...⟩tertained the K*ing* at Sum*erset* house on munday night with a play
& do they begin to say Shee is again w*ith* child...

...

20

BERTIE OF GRIMSTHORPE

1560
Richard and Katherine Bertie's Household Accounts   LA: 1 ANC 7/A/2
f 52*   *(December)*   25

...

To George mr Pellams man to furnishe him self lorde
of Christmas and his men in a livery   xl s.

1561   30
Richard and Katherine Bertie's Household Accounts   LA: 1 ANC 7/A/2
f 52v*   *(1 January)*

...

	To the players the first daye for my m*aste*r	x s.
repaid L g	[To the players for my L*adies* grace	v s.] 35
	To Georg trumpiter from my m*aste*r	iij s. iiij d.

...

To the ij vyolens from my m*aste*r   iij s. viij d.

...

14/ Lith⟨...⟩: *12mm missing, 5mm faded*   16/ ⟨...⟩²: *13mm faded, 3mm missing, 45mm faded*
15/ ⟨...⟩: *9mm missing, 11mm faded*   17/ ⟨...⟩: *3mm faded, 1mm missing, 10mm faded*
16/ ⟨...⟩¹: *4mm missing, 11mm faded*   17/ munday night: *6 January 1633/4, feast of Epiphany*

To George the lorde of good order for my m*aste*rs
gifte to him   x s.

…

(2 January)   5
In rewarde to one *(blank)* of borne w*hi*ch brought a
bayting bull   iij s. iiij d.
To the offeringe, Salmon being busshop by my L*adies*
grace given by my m*aste*r   vj s.
                                                                                                                       10

f 53*   *(6 January)*
…

To Robart Phillips, Thomas Bambrick Iohn Sargent,
Thomas Border, and Iohn Kyrry, the players in reward
after xv s. the man   iij li. xv s. 15
To Robart lettis and Robart Balle of godmanches*ter*
musitians [of huntington] in reward   xx s.

…

(13 January)   20
To ffrances Cowp*er* ∧⌈[vppon a bill]⌉ the xiij^th daie
ou*er* and beside*s* l s. [v d.] by my L*adies* grace and
pretie for the furniture of the lord of Christmas as
by his bill appeareth.   vj s. ij d.
                                                                                                                       25

(26 January)
To S*ir* ffraunces foskewes players w*hi*ch came to offer them
selfes to playe before my L*adies* grace the xxvj^th daye   iij s. iiij d.
…
                                                                                                                       30

f 53v   *(between 9–20 February)*
…

To one w*hi*ch played the hobby-horse before my
m*aste*r and my Ladies grace   [x s.] vj s. viij d.
To the ij musitians w*hi*ch came w*i*th him   ij s. 35
…

f 54   *(12 March)*
…

To the waytes of lincolne the xij^th daie   xx d. 40
…

14/ Thomas: T *corrected over* I

f 56*   *(between 1–17 July)*

...

To the players in reward   xiij s. iiij d.

...

5

(29 July)
To Gooes the master of fense and his companie w*hi*ch
played before her grac*e* the xxix daie mr pellam
beinge messinger   xiij s. iiij d.

...   10

f 56v*   *(between 2–14 August)*

...

To ij men w*hi*ch played vppon the puppett*es* ij night*es*
before herr grac*e*   vj s. viij d.   15

...

To mr fraunces Gwevara w*hi*ch he gave by my m*a*st*ers*
com*m*andm*en*t to the Kepers of the lions at the towre
at London in maij last ⌈v s.⌉ and to a mayde 12 d.   vij s.

...   20

f 57*   *(After 6 September)*

...

To iiij musitians and a hobby horse w*hi*ch weare at
Beleawe at the marriage of mr Carrow and demnan   xv s. x d.   25

...

f 57v*   *(September)*

...

gevin to [the] George Rafe trumpiter at Beleaw by my   30
m*a*st*ers* com*m*andem*en*t to Salmon   vj s.

...

f 58*   *(18 October)*

...   35

To my Lorde Robart dudleyes players at Grimsthorpe the
xviij^th w*hi*ch offered them selfes to playe but dyd not   x s.

...

f 58v*   *(between 1–13 December)*   40

...

To mr Rose and his daughters w*hi*ch played before [yo]
herr grace in herr syckynes   xiij s. iiij d.

(14 December)
To a servant of my Lorde willowbies which offered
to playe and singe before my master and herr grace
the xiiij^th daye by Boucher   xx d.
...   5

f 59*   *(between 25–30 December)*

...
To ij of my Lord Robart Dudleis men which came to
playe before ye vppon the drume and the phiph   vj s.   10
To my Lorde of Arrendalles players   vj s. viij d.

(30 December)
To the waightes of London the xxx daie   v s.

                                                                        15

1562

Richard and Katherine Bertie's Household Accounts   LA: 1 ANC 7/A/2
f 31v*   *(January)*
...
for a lute bought of Rose for mr Perigrine &   20
mistris Suzan   xlvi s. viij d.

f 60*   *(1 January)*

...
To the players   vj s. viij d. 25
To the trumpiter   iij s. iiij d.
To diuers noble mens trumpiters to the numbre of x   xx s.
...

(2 January)   30
To the players boye which brought cakes for my master
for herr grace & for the childrin   xij d.

(3 January)
To the Quenes trumpiters the iij daie in rewarde   xx s. 35
...

(6 January)
To roses boye vppon Twelfe daie by my Ladies
commaundment   xx d. 40
...

f 60v*   *(January)*

…

To the Quenes violens at newyers tyde	xx s.
To the Erle of warwyckes players	vij s. vj d.

…

To the minsterell*es* at mr Brownes mariage	x s.
To yo*ur* players by herr grac*e*	xl s.

…

f 32   *(February)*

…

ffor viij yard*es* of cotton lyning for the ij Goorges gownes at [the yard]	vj s.

f 62*   *(after 29 March)*

…

To Rooes when he mended mr perigrines Lute	x s.

…

f 62v   *(after 12 April)*

…

To the waites that played at herr grac*e* lodging at the Corte by Salmon	xx d.

…

f 63*   *(May)*

…

To a moresse dawnce of litle bytam the xviij^th day by my m*aste*rs comaundem*ent*	ij s.

…

f 64*   *(19–27 July)*

…

To the Qwenes players w*hi*ch played at Grimsthorpe the xix^th daie	xx s.

…

to the waight*es* of Lyncolne in rewarde for plaienge the xxj^th daie	iij s. iiij d.

…

To a [p bag b] bage piper	[xix d.] xx d.
To a Iugler w*i*th his musisioner at mr nantons mariage the xxvij^th daie	x s.

…

f 64v*   *(July)*

...

To her graces hand*es* by mr Carow to paie playe; and
to mr Peregrine and m*ist*ris Suzan   xvj d.

...

To the minsterell*es* at Roiston by herr   xij d.

...

f 65v*   *(after 21 September)*

...

To my Lord of Rutland*es* man w*hi*ch paid vppon
the Lute   vj s.

...

f 66*

...

To a bagge piper w*hi*ch played and songe before
my m*aste*r and her grace at Mr Eirsbies ∧⌐by
mr Ienye⌐   iij s. iiij d.

...

1581
Richard Bertie's Household Accounts   LA: 10 ANC 317
p 12*   *(September)* *(Gifts and rewards)*

...

It*em* gyven to the players of Borne the third day   x s.

...

1583
Peregrine Bertie's Household Accounts   LA: 1 ANC 7/A/7
f 6*   *(November)* *(Gifts and rewards)*

...

It*em* given to the Trompetors   v s.

...

Peregrine Bertie's Household Accounts   LA: 2 ANC 14/18
p 4   *(December)* *(Necessary expenses)* *(At London)*

...

It*em* payd for a lute the iiij^th day   iiij li.

...

6/ by herr: *for* by herr grace
11/ paid: *for* plaid

p 8   *(Gifts and rewards)*

Item given to will*iam* shelton the fole the third daye   x s.

...

Item given to the waytes the xxvj^th day   iij s. iiij d. 5

...

Item given to the Quenes Trompetors the xxxj^th day   xx s.

...

Between 1605–26   10
Letter from Elizabeth Bertie to Robert Bertie   LA: 10 ANC/Lot 340/1
f [1]*

My Lord I durst not let pas this messenger with out sending to you, fering
lest you wold haue condemd mee of forgetfulnes which fate I coufes I haue,   15
thouth neuer of you for soner should I forget my sealfe then remoue my
thouths of of you. I immagin by this time your Lordship hath bin at the
Court wheare you haue Courted the Ladis and danst with the Queene which
bisnes being past I presume you haue laisor to make vs so happi in the contry
as to heare from you. had I anithing worth the sending I wold not a trubbled   20
you with reding my il indited and scribling lines but asouring my sealf of your
Lordships loue and axsepttans both of them and this youre thin heare inclosed
intreating you not to estme it as athing worth the sending you but as atoken
of my loue and seruis to your Lordship. This beschsing God to giue you
health and long life and send you well to retorne and sone I rest   25
Grinsthorpe

                            your veri louing wife
                            Elizabeth Willughby.

    I beshich you com*m*and
    Mr Smith to pay morton   30
    wife for the cheare she sends me   your saruant perimus
    and withall to send me a round   misses you euing and
    french rouf the best he can get   morning and wee mis
    and another of the nowest fasion   Mr Smith diner and
    so I kiss your Lordships hands   soper   35

1614/15
Letter from Peregrine Bertie to Robert Bertie   LA: 10 ANC/Lot 338
f [1]*   *(January)*

                                                                                 40

Right Honorable.

17/ of of: *dittography*   19/ past: *inserted in left margin at the start of a line*

My affection and desire to se your Lordship had drawne me into the cuntry
this Cristmass, if my Doctors aduice, and the importunitie of my Lady, had
not hinder'd my resolution till such time as with more strength, and health
I may be able to serue you.

Here is no news stirring now but of the reuells at Court in all which mr   5
Villars is a principall actor. the last night at the play, there wer three vnknowne
sisters, appareled in seuerall but strange, and curious attires, which with the
rareness of there beutie caught the eies, and admiration of all the courtiers, ye
Kings Maiestie not excepted. All the married Ladies goe very ciuill in black
and the maids very gallant, amongst these my Lady of North[⟨.⟩]humberlands   10
daughters, and Isabella Rich carries the vaunt de plus belles. Thus with
the remembrance of my seruice I rest. Your Lordshipes humble brother:
Peregrine Bartie
I besech your Lordship to remember my humblest and affectionate seruice
to my Lady   ·   15

1629–35
Robert Bertie's List of Costs for Services to the Crown   LA: 10 ANC/341/1
f [1]

                                                                                         20

A briefe Recitall of the services aswell in forreigne parts as otherwise
whereunto the late king Iames and his Maiesty now reigning haue heretofore
commanded me./
…

ffor tenne yeres together I haue been commanded to attend the Court   25
sometime to assist in Barriers & Maskes, sometime to be present at
entertainment of Ambassadours sometime upon other occurrents as they
happened, which hath giuen me occasion of spending
…

                                                                                         30

CONY OF BASSINGTHORPE

1572
Thomas Cony's Household Book   LA: M.C.D. 864
f 65v col 1   *(20 December)* *(Inventory of the dining parlour)*   35
…
Item a paire of double virginalles with a frame of wainescott
…

14–15/: I besech … Lady: *written vertically in left margin of the letter*

1577
Thomas Cony's Household Book LA: M.C.D. 864
f 69v col 1 *(7 September) (Inventory of the dining parlour)*

...

Item a paire of double verginall*es* with a frame of wainescot 5

...

HATCHER OF CAREBY

1583 10
Inventory of Thomas Hatcher LA: HOLYWELL H.2/2
mb 2* *(11 December) (In the parlour)*

...

...one payre of virgynals...

... 15

HOLLES OF GRIMSBY

A *c* 1608–36
History of the Holles Family Longleat House: Portland Papers volume XXIV 20
f 98* *(Description of Elizabeth Kingston, mother of Gervase Holles)*

...

...Not long after that (for a misfortune seldome walkes unaccompanied)
followed his most heavy and pressing affliction of all the rest, ye death of
my mother his only and most entirely beloued childe, who died (as hath 25
beene said before) ye last day of October. 1608. in childebed.

He had been carefull to giue hir ye best and choysest Education, wh*ich*
renderd hir, who had judgem*ent* beyond most of hir Sex, æqually accomplisht
with the best of them. I haue heard many say y*at* shee playd Excellently
well vpon a lute (according to ye way of Musique in those times) and sung 30
as Excellently. Shee wrote an hand far better then most weomen vsually
write, and (wh*ich* in y*at* sex is strange) exact Ortography, as will appeare by
seuerall of hir lett*re*s to my Grandfather Holles, wh*ich* I yet haue; hir stile
was better than hir hand, weighty and vnaffected. And to proue that a great
fancy may sometimes accompany great virtues, shee compiled in verse the 35
passages of hir whole life, wh*ich* my vncle Holles (after hir death) borrowed
from my father w*ith* Importunity, and lost as negligently....

f 100v* *(Description of Gervase Holles, of Grimsby)*

...

40
Whilst yet an Infant I lost my mother; After whose death my grandfather
Kingston desired me from my father, and w*ith* all ye tendernes y*at* might

be tooke care of my Education whilst he liued. Vntill I went to ye Gramar Schole (which I did about six yeares of age) I had no other Tutor but my good Grandmother, who had taught me to read English perfectly. At the Gramar Schole (which was ye Free Schole of Grimesby) I was first vnder ye care of Mr William Dalby, who likewise taught me Musique; Then of Mr Herbert Hindmarsh, a good scholler and a worthy and reuerend deuine, who together with literature, endeavored to Instruct his Schollers in piety and religion....

...

f 104v*   *(Christmas 1635–February 1635/6)*

...

The next Michaelmasse Terme I returned to ye Midle Temple, where I was the following Christmas chosen Comptroller of ye house; and about fiue dayes after we resolved to make it a grand Christmas, and haue a Masque. Whereupon we elected Mr Richard Viuian (a Cornish gentleman, whose father was lately dead, and had left him a good estate both in landes and mony) to be Prince d'Amour. This solemnity (or mocke-show of Royalty) lasted from ye beginning of Christmas vntill towardes ye end of February when for three Nightes together we had a Masque, ye second Night being honoured with ye presence of ye Queene, Prince Electour, Prince Rupert, with many of Nobility and Gentry, and most of ye great Ladies and prime beauties in or neare the Towne. The Society carried out ye whole designe equall to Expectation, in which they expended neare 20000. li. Sterling. Of which it cost ye Prince d'Amour about. 6000. li. and myselfe for my share aboue two hundred and fifty. The Masque ended, Viuian layd downe his Title of Prince, and in lieu of it receaued ye next day from the King ye honour of Knighthood.

Besides ye expence of this gay foolery, it cost me a quarrell with one Thomas Ogle, a Northumberland gentleman, who pressing rudely one day into ye Temple Hall when ye English Nobility were treated by ye Prince d'Amour, necessitated me to lay my Comptrollers staffe foure or fiue times soundly ouer his Shoulders. This happened about a fortnight before ye Masque

HUSSEY OF SLEAFORD

1533–4
John Hussey's Household Accounts   TNA: PRO E 36/95
p 62   *(November–November)*

...

To William herper of petreborow   viij d.

...

1534–5
John Hussey's Household Accounts   TNA: PRO E 36/95
p 103   *(November–November)*

5

Lyuerys.
Item paid to Alexander Tailour for vj yardes of brode blew
for two lyuereyes one for Appulby and the other for
wylliam harper   xiij s.
...

Regardes   10

...
Item to the men of welbye the xvij^th daye of November   iij s. iiij d.
...
Item to wylliam harper and Thomas Appulby   ij s.
...   15

p 105*   *(Rewards)*
...
Item to iiij players the xxx^t daye of december   ij s.
...   20
Item to iiij players of my lord of Northumberland the
same daye   vj s. viij d.
...
Item to the players of Lyndsey   xij d.
...   25

p 106   *(Rewards)*
...
Item paid to the players of Kyrkton   xx d.
...   30
Item to the players of Swinshedd   ij s.
...
Item to the players of Kyrtton in Lyndsey the iij^d daye
of Ianuary   xx d.
...   35
Item to the players of tattersall   xx d.
Item to the players of Bedforde   vj s. viij d.
Item to wylliam harper of peterborowgh   ij s.
Item to wylliam harper of Newark   ij s.
...   40
Item to the players of Burne   xx d.

Item paid to wylliam harper of peterborowgh per
mandatum domine   iij s. iiij d.
...

p 109   *(January) (Foreign expenses)*   5
...
Item paid to Robert Buller for players gere that is
to saye for iiij qwaire of white pauper x d. for iiij
qwaire of Grawne pauper ij d. a yard of Canvas
iiij d. x Shetes of pauper gold x d. threde ob. ij   10
Strawe hattes ij d.   ij s. [viij d.] ⌐iiij d.⌐ ob.

p 110

Item paid to Iohn ⟨.⟩trusse for making of iiij Cotes   15
of pauper iij s. for making of a Cote to desyrd x d.
for making of a kyrtell of Satten iiij d. ffor flowers
setting on ij d. for vj Claspys of golde pauper xx d.
for v hery berdes xx d. for the paynter iiij d. in toto   viij s.
Item paid to Buller for terre for the Shepard of   20
old Sleford   ij d.
Item paid to Alexander tailor for dj. yard of Cotton
for Cappys for the players ij d. ob. for viij yardes
lynynge iij s. iiij d. for dj. yard of the same lynyng
⌐ij d. ob.⌐ in toto   iij s. ix d.   25
...

County of Lincolnshire

1622
Lord Chamberlain's Warrant   LA: SP/S/460/5/40
single sheet*   *(20 November)*

The Coppy of a warrant signed by the Right Honorable, the Earle of   5
Penbrooke, Lord Chamberlaine to his Maiestie:

To all Maiors, Shriffes, Iustices of the Peace, Bayliffes, Constables, and other
his Maiesties Officers, True Leige men, and Subiects, whom it may concerne,
and to euery of them. Whereas I am credibly informed, That there are many   10
and verie great disorders, and abuses, daily committed by diuers and sundry
companies of Stage Players, Tumblers, Vaulters, Dauncers on the ropes. And
also by such as goe about with Motions, and Shewes, and orher the like kind
of persous by reason of certaine Graunts, Commissions, and Licences, which
they haue by secret meanes procured, both from the Kings Maiestie, and   15
also from diuers Noble men, by vertue wherof they doe abusiuely claime
vnto them selues a kind of licentious freedome to trauell, aswell to shew
play & exercise in eminent Cities and Corporations within this Kingdome,
as also from place to place without the knowledge and approbation of his
Maiesties Office of the Reuels, and by that meanes doe take vpon them (at   20
their owne pleasure) to act and set forth in many places of this Kingdome
diuers and sundry Playes, and Shewes, which for the most part are full of
scandall and offence, both against the Church and State, and doe likewise
greatly abuse their authority, in lending, letting, and selling, their said
Commissions, and Licenses, to others. By reason whereof diuers lawlesse,   25
and wandering persons are suffered to haue free passage, vnto whom such
graunts, and Licenses were neuer intended; contrary to his Maiesties pleasure,
the Lawes of this Land, his Maiesties graunt, and Commission to the Master
of the Reuels, and the first institution of the said Office. These are therefore

---

13/ orher: *for* other   14/ persous: *for* persons

in his Maiesties name straightly to charge and command you, and euery of
you, That whosoeuer shall repaire to any of your Cities, Burroughs, Townes
corporate, Villages, Hamlets or Parishes, and shall there, by vertue of any
Commission, warrant, or License whatsoeuer: Act, set foorth, shew, or present,
any Play, Shew, Motion, feates of actiuitie, and sightes, whatsoeuer, not   5
hauing a licence now in force vnder the hand and seale of Office of Sir
Iohn Ashley Knight, now Master of his Maiesties Office of the Reuels, or
vnder the hand of his Deputie, and sealed likewise with the said Seale of
Office. That you and euerie of you at all times for euer hereafter, doe Seaze,
and take away, all and euery such Graunt, Patent, Commission or Licence   10
whatsoeuer, from the bringer or bearer thereof, and that you forthwith cause
the said Graunt, or Licence, to be conueyed and sent vnto his Maiesties
Office of the Reuels, there to remaine at the disposition of the afore said
Master of the said Office, and that to the vttermost of your power, you
doe from hence forth forbid and suppresse all such Playes, Shews, Motions,   15
Feates of actiuitie, Sights and euery of them, vntill they shall be approued,
licenced, and authorized, by the said Sir Iohn Ashley or his said Deputie in
manner aforesaid. Who are appoynted by his Maiestie vnder the great Seale
of England to that end and purpose. Herein fayle you not, as you will
answer the contrary at your perills. And for your more certaintie I aduise   20
you to take an exact Coppy of this my Mandat. Giuen vnder my hand at
Whitehall the 20 day of Nouember. Anno Domini 1622.